Asia-Pacific and Literature in English

Series Editors
Shun-liang Chao
National Chengchi University
Taipei, Taiwan

Steve Clark
University of Tokyo
Bunkyo-ku, Tokyo, Japan

Tristanne Connolly
St. Jerome's University
Waterloo, ON, Canada

Alex Watson
Meiji University
Tokyo, Aichi, Japan

Laurence Williams
Department of English Studies
Sophia University
Tokyo, Japan

The Palgrave Asia-Pacific and Literature in English series presents exciting and innovative academic research on Asia-Pacific interactions with Anglophone literary tradition. Focusing on works from the voyages of Captain Cook to the early twentieth century, it also considers previous encounters in the early modern period, as well as reception history continuing to the present day. Encompassing China, Japan, Southeast Asia, India, and Australasia, monographs and essay collections in this series display the complexity, richness and global influence of Asia-Pacific responses to English literature, focusing on works in English but also considering those from other linguistic traditions. The series addresses the imperial and colonial origins of English language and literature in the region, and highlights other forms of reciprocal encounter, circulation, and mutual transformation, as part of an interdependent global history.

More information about this series at
http://www.palgrave.com/gp/series/16211

Bernard Wilson · Sharmani Patricia Gabriel
Editors

Asian Children's Literature and Film in a Global Age

Local, National, and Transnational Trajectories

Editors
Bernard Wilson
Tokyo, Japan

Sharmani Patricia Gabriel
Kuala Lumpur, Malaysia

ISSN 2524-7638   ISSN 2524-7646   (electronic)
Asia-Pacific and Literature in English
ISBN 978-981-15-2630-5   ISBN 978-981-15-2631-2   (eBook)
https://doi.org/10.1007/978-981-15-2631-2

Cover credit: Photographer is my life

This Palgrave Macmillan imprint is published by the registered company Springer Nature Singapore Pte Ltd.
The registered company address is: 152 Beach Road, #21-01/04 Gateway East, Singapore 189721, Singapore

To children and the tales they inspire—
but most especially to Sam, Ellie, Sophie, Evie, Eric and Eshward

SERIES EDITOR'S PREFACE

Bernard Wilson and Sharmani Patricia Gabriel's collection offers an impressive contribution to the new and dynamic field of children's literary studies, and a welcome addition to Palgrave's *Asia-Pacific and Literature in English* series. As the editors stress, this discipline is necessarily global in perspective, due not only to factors of commercial distribution, but also to its inherently translatable nature. The genre moves not only between diverse languages but between multiple media (the essays span film, digital media and graphic novels as well as written texts) yet, as in so many other facets of literary study, Asian scholarship in this area has been comparatively neglected, with a complacent lack of familiarity with children's works in other languages by members of the Anglophone academy (myself included before reading this volume). However, there is also the temptation and threat of opting for a reverse Orientalism, in which Asia as any kind of unified entity itself becomes an ideological construct imposed by the West. Instead, the editors have sought to combine rootedness in specific social and cultural contexts with a broader regional consciousness. The essays range from those cultures most commonly represented in discussions of Asia (China, India and Japan) to numerous other cultural traditions (Indonesia, Iran, South Korea, Malaysia, the Philippines, Sri Lanka and Taiwan) equally worthy of respect and attention.

Emphasis is justifiably placed on the complexity and resonance of children's literature produced in Asia, rather than focusing on the importation and reception history of English-language works. The latter will inevitably have had wide dissemination, if only for their crucial function in second language acquisition. Therefore, Asian children's literature is necessarily in dialogue with the classics of the Western tradition, whether as homage or subversion. One might even see a return of original inventions such as the beast-fable, originating in India, diffused through Europe by Aesop's fables, being re-exported to Asia by Disney, Pixar and Dreamworks in the guise of films such as *Madagascar* and *Zootopia*. The process of re-appropriation might be seen as epitomised by the huge popularity in China of *Kung Fu Panda's* fusion of warrior narrative (wuxia) with the kitsch formulas of 1970s martial arts movies.

As recent scholarship has emphasised, childhood envisaged as an autonomous state developing through distinct phases is anything but a universal given. Indeed, high rates of child mortality may obviously have deterred such an affective investment for, as Ben Jonson's elegy, "On my First Son", laments, "As what he loves may never like too much". The distinctive traditions of child-rearing in Asian cultures must also be acknowledged, but modern concepts of childhood have been largely derived from Western works, particularly in the English language. The environmental determinism of eighteenth-century empiricist psychology supported by increased literacy resulted in the emergence of a children's book publishing industry overlaid by the Romantic idealisation of the child by writers such as Blake and Coleridge, then the nineteenth-century subgenres of adventure, school and domestic fiction, followed by the "golden age" of late Victorian and Edwardian fantasy. Many aspects of the ideology of Englishness thereby promoted might seem an obstacle to broader dissemination, but this clearly has not been the case in, for example, the boarding-school conventions of snobbery in *Harry Potter*. Indeed, perhaps when post-Brexit traumas are finally resolved, Britain's only remaining capital asset might be J. K. Rowling's royalties. (The franchise, currently estimated at 25 billion, is still growing).

One must be cautious, however, before positing a clear divide between individualism and collectivism in Western and Asian children's literature. The works of the Anglophone canon have clearly served disciplinary and regulatory functions, and the Asian texts treated in these essays collectively represent a cumulative dramatisation of ideals of personal fulfilment and freedom. However, in both traditions, childhood may be seen as preserving residual alterity. So I would give the last word to John Locke, often mistakenly identified as a proponent of the child's mind as *tabula rasa*:

"As children's enquiries are not to be slighted, so also great care is to be given, that they never receive deceitful and illuding answers. They easily perceive when they are slighted or deceived, and quickly learn the trick of neglect, dissimulation, and falsehood, which they observe others to make use of. We are not to intrench upon truth in any conversation, but least of all with children; since, if we play false with them, we not only deceive their expectation, and hinder their knowledge, but corrupt their innocence, and teach them the worst of vices. They are travelers newly arrived in a strange country, of which they know nothing; we should therefore make conscience not to mislead them" (*Some Thoughts on Education* 120.3).

If as Wordsworth's "Intimations of Immortality from Recollections of Early Childhood" claims, "Our birth is but a sleep and a forgetting", the emergent discipline, to which the essays in this collection make a notable contribution, might perhaps bring us an awakening to and remembrance of the significance of studies of children's literature.

Steve Clark

FOREWORD

Asian Children's Literature and Film in a Global Age is both welcome and timely, and I am delighted to have been invited to introduce this collection, which has a significant role to play in furthering knowledge about international children's literature and an understanding of the place of diversity in children's literature and film. The impact of major cultural movements in the West during the 1960s and 1970s, especially the rise of multicultural ideologies and the challenge to entrenched gender hierarchies, produced a continuing demand for greater diversity in children's literature. This demand has been primarily focused on representation and intersections of culture, race, ethnicity, gender and class. However, it has not, over the past six or seven decades, nurtured an openness to international literature. In their Introduction, Sharmani Patricia Gabriel and Bernard Wilson make the important point that neither the creative works which are the focus of the following chapters nor the critical exploration of them is to be read within the frameworks of Western multicultural theories. To do so would be to (re-)situate them within self-other binaries premised on essentialist attitudes to cultural otherness which pervasively undermine multicultural literatures. Children's literature and its associated scholarship are apt to be local—even parochial—in their reach, and what is generally accepted as "multicultural literature" (as distinct from international literature, which receives less attention) is apt to be vaguely conceived. This vagueness exists because there is no international consensus as to what the concept *multicultural* embraces, so that it has distinct meanings in those countries which recognise multiculturalism as a matter of social policy or social practice and therefore has distinct meanings in the children's literature of those countries.

In the USA, multiculturalism signifies across a wide spectrum from a narrow sense that it aspires to erase the inequality experienced by people of colour, such as African Americans, Asian Americans and Latino/a communities, to a wide sense whereby it embraces "all minority groups, regardless of the particular demographic characteristics that define them" (Agosto, Hughes-Hassell and Gilmore-Clough 2003, 260). According to this position, to define multiculturalism only in terms of racial identity disregards other marginalised groups, but there is a risk of over-simplification in that within the broad context "the *official* recognition of minority cultures is far from a settled national objective" (Citrin et al. 2001, 250) and may be regarded as a phase preceding cultural integration. What constitutes multiculturalism is always in part determined by social forces in motion during the period of its emergence. In the case of the USA, this is the Civil Rights Movement with its strong concerns with race and equality. In Britain, in contrast, the process began to appear following World War 2, when "the remaking of the British nation and state during decolonisation both gave rise to and conditioned British multiculturalism" (Ashcroft and Bevir 2018, 2). Contemporary debates about multiculturalism involve modes of dress, language policy, race relations, religious freedom, education policy, court procedure and immigration, a heady mix. At the end of the twentieth century, British multiculturalism was undergoing a period of re-evaluation and official support for multicultural policy seemed to be waning. Ashcroft and Bevir speculate that what they identify as a "rhetorical shift in the discourse of multiculturalism" may well "translate into a full-scale retreat at the level of policy and law" (2018, 2). A further contrast is afforded by Australia, where multiculturalism was a product of massive migration from Europe after World War 2 and became official government policy in 1972. Ethnicity is here the key defining factor, but people of colour are not central since at that time ethnic minorities were made up mostly of migrants from Europe, especially Italians and Greeks. Thus when multicultural children's literature developed through the 1970s it mostly dealt with Italians and Greeks, and it was not until the early 1990s that writers began locating perspective within the point of view of minority characters rather than positioning them as secondary and subordinate. Within a few years of the twenty-first century, however,

Australia had entered a "post-multicultural" phase, and multicultural children's literature was no longer produced (Stephens and McCallum 2009, 133–134).

Multicultural literature and cross-cultural reading should be recognised as distinct literary processes, even though both may be implicated in an often uncritical celebration of empathy with otherness. As Heather Snell contends, cosmopolitanism which is the implied value of represented cross-cultural experiences "can become yet another thinly veiled instantiation of global imperialism" (2014, 255). For Western readers, access to cross-cultural reading is generally limited, and hence access to other cultures may be mediated by what is written about them by Western writers. As Susan Stewart argues, if young readers are to develop responsiveness to transnational processes they need to bring to bear their moral, ethical, and political beliefs upon their familial, local, regional, and national understandings (2008, 95–96). Stewart offers four reasons why this outcome is difficult to achieve: international children's literature is not readily available; Western texts that depict other cultures are grounded in Western ideologies; young readers tend to prefer familiar texts and resist those that are culturally different (2008, 96); and texts are too often edited (and homogenised) to render them more accessible to target readers (2008, 97–98).

The task is difficult, but a collection like *Asian Children's Literature and Film in a Global Age* can facilitate it by demonstrating what I have elsewhere described as "ethnopoetics" (Stephens et al. 2018, 2), which argues that uniquely local conjunctions of creative literature and literary criticism are there to be discerned. Such a conjunction is not premised on uniquely local critical or scholarly practices, as global scholarship promotes the movement of concepts and methodologies across the world, but on the potential of the content and theme of a creative work to inform and transform methodologies. As Sharmani Patricia Gabriel and Bernard Wilson observe, mainstream European and North American scholarship on children's literature is either ignorant of or tends to lack interest in what concerns Asian scholars or the intellectual traditions that underpin them. Western scholars will nevertheless encounter some familiar approaches in these chapters: critical content analysis, thick description, historical contextualisation, critical stylistics, conceptual metaphor theory, postcolonial theory, gender theory, performativity, intersectionality, among others. How are such practices impacted upon the local texts they seek to engage? My attention was particularly caught by Andrea Mei-Ying Wu's discussion of *tongxin*, or "child heart", in the first of the contributors' chapters. I have often encountered this concept during visits to China where, at this time of writing, it is much discussed and debated. I am grateful for the exposition of the term here. I suspected it was not a "local inventiveness", as Professor Wu expresses it, but a residue of the Western cultural idea of the Romantic child adapted into Chinese theory about a century ago. Of course it has not been a static concept, but, according to Professor Wu, "a sign of social conviction (or shared ideology) replete with (trans)national and (trans)cultural dynamics and negotiations of childhood imaginations". Such an explanation constitutes a significant contribution to East–West dialogue by showing how things that seem to look the same are not the same.

A different issue suggested by this example reflects on the historical depth preserved in Chinese scholarship, in contrast to the West. One of the most cited scholars in Chinese criticism is Zhou Zuoren, who is often credited with "the discovery of 'children'" and *tongxin* (Zhu 2014, 68). From a Western perspective, where scholarship is restless and constantly shifting to "new" concepts and theories, to base arguments on scholarship published in the 1920s seems unimaginable. Today, in 2019, scholarly work published before 1990 has disappeared and scholars who cite works of the early 1990s are apt to do so to score cheap points ("We don't think like that now").

A third point is the interplay between social assumptions and text analysis, and I will explore this in a brief discussion of a little-known gem from India, a collection of four documentary films made by Indian children released under the title *Delhi at Eleven* (2012). The films were produced as part of a five-year project supported by the Australian National University and funded by an Australian Research Council grant. The outcome of this project, conducted by anthropologist and filmmaker David MacDougall in several places in India, was nineteen films made by children. The project was situated within the discipline of Anthropology, and this situatedness defined its objectives and the subsequent history of the material, which has been archived at the Australian National University as a resource for anthropological reference and only the four films of *Delhi at Eleven* entered the public domain. These films can all be understood as explorations into qualities of well-being, a global term with local nuances. In an informative account of eastern notions of well-being, Mohsen Joshanloo argues that in Asian traditions, "the individual self is de-emphasised in one way or another", in contrast to the western understanding of the self, in which "enhancing autonomy, independence, self-esteem, and a strong ego is considered to be a vital ingredient of a good life" (2014, 482). Joshanloo further contends that western models of well-being (eudaimonia) do not apply in eastern contexts because eastern conceptions emphasise selflessness, adjustment to the environment, and relational virtues, whereas western models emphasise virtues like autonomy and environmental mastery (484). This contrast is important for the analysis of *Delhi at Eleven*, especially because of the kind of conclusions many western viewers might reach in response to the socio-economic level of the environment—for example, the fact that houses depend upon an unreliable water supply from a communal tap in the street might be interpreted as a deficit in well-being.

The anthropological interest in these films lies in the data the children reveal from their insider positioning—perspectives on urban livelihoods, marginality, class, gender, kinship, household economy, poverty, and modernity, in particular. These topics are also central to what we think about in our work on children's literature and film, and I would seek to expound them using several approaches to text I have observed in *Asian Children's Literature and Film in a Global Age*: critical content analysis, thick description, critical stylistics, conceptual metaphor theory, gender theory, performativity, for a start. For example, in *Why Not a Girl?* Anshu Singh cleverly intercuts a collection of interviews which address deficits in female subjective well-being: the girls complain about the amount of domestic work they do, although the complaint isn't that the work exists but that it is inequitably distributed and they are deprived of time for play and study. Urban Western children, in contrast, contribute little, if anything, to domestic work, and Western practice should not be the yardstick for assessing subjective well-being. What these girls want is to be treated equally, to inhabit intersubjective relationships, to have scope for agentic subjectivity, to do a fair share of the family's work, to be free of gender discrimination and violence inflicted by boys and parents, and, finally, to feel loved.

Critical practice that nurtures analysis of locally grounded texts and contexts is always in a state of becoming and, as Sharmani Patricia Gabriel and Bernard Wilson argue, its optimum form is glocalised practice, where local practices absorb and adapt global discourses. Anshu Singh's *Why Not a Girl?* seems to cry out for a feminist reading, but such a reading would need to adapt to the simple fact that the maker of the film is an irate *eleven-year-old Indian* feminist who expresses a paradox of agency by finally interviewing herself in the seclusion of the roof of her house as darkness falls. An unselfconscious feminist reading might reduce the film's subjects and its maker to a simulacrum of theory and deplete its delicate representation of the different ways children inhabit the world. A glocalised practice could avoid this flattening, and it is my hope that readers of *Asian Children's Literature and Film in a Global Age* will find in its pages many pathways to such glocalisation and many opportunities to engage in a dynamic conversation about evolving practice.

John Stephens
Emeritus Professor
Macquarie University
Sydney, Australia

Works Cited

Agosto, Denise E., Sandra Hughes-Hassell, and Catherine Gilmore-Clough. 2003. The All-White World of Middle-School Genre Fiction: Surveying the Field for Multicultural Protagonists, *Children's Literature in Education*, 34 (4), pp. 257–275.

Ashcroft, Richard T., and Mark Bevir. 2018. Multiculturalism in Contemporary Britain: Policy, Law and Theory, *Critical Review of International Social and Political Philosophy*, 21 (1), pp. 1–21.

Citrin, Jack, David O. Sears, Christopher Muste, and Cara Wong. 2001. Multiculturalism in American Public Opinion, *British Journal of Political Science*, 31 (2), pp. 247–275.

Joshanloo, Mohsen. 2014. Eastern Conceptualizations of Happiness: Fundamental Differences with Western Views, *Journal of Happiness Studies*, 15 (2), pp. 475–493.

Snell, Heather. 2014. Global Citizenship in North American Young Adult Literatures, *Children's Literature Association Quarterly*, 39 (2), pp. 252–274.

Stephens, John, with Celia Belmiro, Alice Curry, Li Lifang, and Yasmine Motawy (eds.). 2018. *The Routledge Companion to International Children's Literature*. Abingdon: Routledge.

Stephens, John, and Robyn McCallum. 2009. Positioning Otherness: (Post-) Multiculturalism and Point of View in Australian Young Adult Fiction. In Garde, Ulrike, and Anne-Rose Meyer (eds.), *Belonging and Exclusion: Case Studies in Recent Australian and German Literature, Film and Theatre*. Newcastle: Cambridge Scholars Publishing, pp. 133–146.

Stewart, Susan Louise. 2008. Beyond Borders: Reading 'Other' Places in Children's Literature, *Children's Literature in Education*, 39 (2), pp. 95–105.

Zhu, Ziqiang. 2014. The Discovery of Children: The Origins of Zhou Zuoren's Thoughts on 'Humane Literature'. In Nelson, Claudia, and Rebecca Morris (eds.), *Representing Children in Chinese and U.S. Children's Literature*. Farnham: Ashgate, pp. 63–74.

ACKNOWLEDGEMENTS

As we approach the third decade of our twenty-first century, we felt a book was in order that addressed the asymmetries of power and culture operating on a global level in the area of Asian children's literature and film criticism, one that would also articulate the need to reorient the locus of debate and discussion "eastwards". The entwined goals of redressing the marginal position on the global stage of Asian children's literature and film studies and of establishing Asian traditions and output as a vital point of scholarly reference constitute an important means, we believe, of working our way to a more inclusive and ethical poetics of globalisation. We hope this book in some small way meets those hopes and objectives.

As with all collective endeavours, this book would not have been possible without the support of its constituent contributors. The questions our authors ask, the range of the texts they explore and the diversity of their skills, experience and insights all richly reflect the dynamism of the field. To each and every one of them, we extend our sincere thanks and gratitude for responding so warmly and enthusiastically to our invitation to be a part of this project, and for the eventual form that this book has taken.

We also wish to acknowledge the following:

The chapter by Amir Ali Nojoumian and Amir Hadi Nojoumian is an extended and revised version of the article originally published as "Towards a Poetics of Childhood Ethics in Abbas Kiarostami's Cinema" in *Persian Literary Studies Journal*, 6: 10 (2017): 15–32.

Sharifah Aishah Osman's chapter is an extended version of the article that appeared as "Agency, Adaptation, and Audience: Re-visioning the Legend of *Mahsuri* in Selected Contemporary Malaysian Young Adult Fiction" in *SARE: Southeast Asian Review of English* (Special Issue on Asian Children's Literature, Film and Animation), 55: 2 (2018): 7–25.

The editors and publisher also wish to thank Bhuana Ilmu Populer, Kiddo and Litara Foundation for permission to reprint the images used in Chapter 12.

We would like to express our appreciation to our team at Palgrave Macmillan, specifically to Sara Crowley-Vigneau and Connie Li for their able assistance and prompt responses to our inquiries as we worked to meet our manuscript delivery deadline. To Steve Clark, Series Editor and Professor of English Literature at the University of Tokyo, we extend our warm thanks for his support of the project, his advice in its initial stages and his Series Editor's Preface to this collection. We also thank Ellie Wilson for her close reading of sections of the manuscript and her helpful suggestions. Our unreserved thanks also go to Universiti Malaya and its support staff, particularly to Faridah Salleh of the inter-library loan and services division of Universiti Malaya's Library. Rare is the library officer who understands not only the value of the work scholars do but also the constraints under which they work.

To Professor John Stephens, we offer our profound and particular thanks for writing the book's Foreword. We could not be more honoured and privileged.

In closing, we would like to thank our families, particularly Karen Wilson and Terence Gomez, and our children to whom this book is dedicated, for their love, inspiration and unending support—in all things.

September 2019   Bernard Wilson
                                            University of the Sacred Heart
                                                            Tokyo, Japan

                                            Sharmani Patricia Gabriel
                                                        Universiti Malaya
                                                Kuala Lumpur, Malaysia

Contents

NOTES ON CONTRIBUTORS

Susan Ang is Assistant Professor with the Department of English Language and Literature at the National University of Singapore. She was educated in Singapore and the University of Cambridge [B.A. (Hons), M.A., Ph.D.]. Among her teaching interests are Romanticism, modern poetry, the modern novel, science fiction and its related sub-specialities. She is the author of *The Widening World of Children's Literature*, and has also published work on Diana Wynne Jones, Louis Macniece, Geoffrey Hill, Peter Ackroyd and China Miéville, among others.

Suchismita Banerjee holds an M.Phil. degree from Jawaharlal Nehru University (JNU), New Delhi, India. She is now an independent researcher. The focus of her research is the representation of the child in contemporary Indian English children's fiction. She is the author of "Contemporary Children's Literature in India: New Trajectories" (*Journal of Children's Literature*), "Strategic Empowerment: A Study of Subjectivity in Contemporary Indian English Children's Fiction" [in *Subjectivity in Asian Children's Literature and Film: Global Theories and Implications* (Routledge, 2013)] and "The Crucible: Forging a Hybrid Identity in a Multicultural World" [in *The Routledge Companion to International Children's Literature* (Routledge, 2018)]. She also presented a paper titled "Models of cultural hybridity in contemporary Indian English fiction for children" at the 19th Biennial Congress of IRSCL (Frankfurt, 2009).

Lijun Bi lectures at the School of Languages, Literatures, Cultures and Linguistics at Monash University, Australia. She completed a doctorate at the University of Melbourne in which she identified and documented the role played by moral-political education in China. Her research publications are mainly on Chinese children's literature.

Yasuko Doi is Director and Senior Researcher at the International Institute for Children's Literature, Osaka, Japan. She is also a regular reviewer of children's books for newspapers and magazines. Her research areas are the promotion of reading and the history of Japanese children's literature. She was selected by the IBBY Executive Committee as a member of the 2020 Hans Christian Andersen Award Jury. She is an associate editor of *100 Questions and Answers About Children's Books* (Osaka: Sogensha, 2013) and of a booklist called *Children's Books on War and Peace* (Tokyo: Iwasakishoten, 2016).

Xiangshu Fang is Senior Lecturer in the School of Humanities and Social Sciences at Deakin University, Australia. His research interests cover socialist realism in Chinese literature, Confucianism, and Chinese intellectual history.

Sharmani Patricia Gabriel is Professor of English at the Department of English of the Faculty of Arts and Social Sciences, Universiti Malaya, Kuala Lumpur, Malaysia. Her recent book publications include *Cosmopolitan Asia: Littoral Epistemologies of the Global South* (co-edited, Routledge, 2016), *Literature, Memory, Hegemony: East/West Crossings* (co-edited, Palgrave Macmillan, 2018), and *Making Heritage in Malaysia: Sites, Histories, Identities* (edited, Palgrave Macmillan, forthcoming). She is currently working on several projects, one of which is a book-length study on diaspora and the novel in English of Malaysia.

Sonia Ghalian teaches film studies at the School of Business Studies and Social Sciences, Christ University, Bangalore, India. She holds a Ph.D. in English from the Manipal Centre for the Humanities, India. Her doctoral dissertation focuses on the role played by children in contemporary Indian cinema and contributes to the emergent academic discipline of Indian children's film. She is the recipient of the Charles Wallace India Trust research fellowship (2017) and has published articles and book chapters and presented conference papers on various aspects of both children's film and film in general.

Herdiana Hakim is a published author and a doctoral candidate in Children's Literature and Literacies at the University of Glasgow, Scotland where she also gained her M.Ed. Prior to this, she read for her undergraduate degree in English Literature and Developmental Psychology at Universitas Indonesia. Her research focuses on Indonesian children's literature and covers notions of childhood and agency, as well as discourses of tolerance and diversity.

Gabriela Lee currently teaches creative writing and literature at the University of the Philippines, Diliman. Her fiction has been published in the Philippines, the United States, Australia, Canada, and Norway. Her short story collection, *Instructions on How to Disappear* (2016) is available through Visprint, Inc. Her research interests include children's and young adult literature, speculative fiction, and Philippine literature in English. Her personal website is www.sundialgirl.com.

Sung-Ae Lee is Lecturer in Asian Studies in the Department of International Studies at Macquarie University, Australia. Her major research focus is on relationships between cultural ideologies and representational strategies in fiction, film and television drama of East Asia, with particular attention to Korea. She has numerous publications dealing with these media, especially from the perspectives of cognitive approaches to adaptation and trauma studies.

Amir Ali Nojoumian is Associate Professor of English Literature and Critical Theory at Shahid Beheshti University, Tehran, Iran. He completed his M.A. and Ph.D. studies at the University of Leicester, UK. His doctorate focused on the philosophy of literature through readings of Jacques Derrida. His recent publications (in Persian) include *Signs at the Threshold: Essays in Semiotics* (2016) and *Semiotics: A Reader* (2017). His research interests are interdisciplinary studies, semiotics and narratives of cinema, children's film and literature, philosophy of literature, and comparative criticism. A recent publication is the book chapter "Constructing Childhood in Modern Iranian Children's Cinema: A Cultural History" for *The Palgrave Handbook of Children's Film and Television* (2019).

Amir Hadi Nojoumian is a cardiologist in clinical practice and Senior Lecturer in Medicine at the University of New England, Australia. He has an interest in the medical humanities, medical ethics, the philosophy of medicine and narrative medicine. He uses literature, film and other art forms in medical education to encourage empathy and a deeper understanding of patients' lived experience. He lives in Sydney, Australia and co-hosts a monthly literature and arts society to encourage public debate and discussion on the Iranian diaspora and the role played by literature and cinema in the lives of immigrants.

Sharifah Aishah Osman is Senior Lecturer at the Department of English, Faculty of Arts and Social Sciences, Universiti Malaya. Her research focuses on the intersection between feminism and literature for children and young adults in Malaysia. She is co-editor of *The Principal Girl: Feminist Tales from Asia* (2019), and is currently working on a monograph on *Malaysian Folktales and Folk Tale Adaptations as Literary and Cultural Heritage*.

Neluka Silva is Professor of English at the University of Colombo, Sri Lanka. She is also a novelist and short story writer, and has published in national and international journals. Her research interests include children's literature in Sri Lanka, bilingualism, Sri Lankan fiction and theatre, and South Asian cultural production. She is the author of *The Gendered Nation: Contemporary Writing in South Asia* (2004), *Our Neighbours and Other Stories* (2009) and *The Iron Fence* (2012). She is currently working on a manuscript of short stories for children.

Fengxia Tan is Professor of Literature in the School of Chinese Language and Literature at Nanjing Normal University, China. She has been a visiting scholar at Cambridge University (UK), Macquarie University (Australia) and Illinois State University (USA). Her research areas include children's literature and films, modern Chinese literature and comparative literature. She has published several monographs and papers on children's literature and general fiction and has also translated into Chinese works of children's literature published in English.

Bernard Wilson teaches at the University of the Sacred Heart, Tokyo, Gakushuin University and Tsuda University. He has spent the past three decades teaching at universities in Australia, Singapore, Hong Kong and Japan and specialises in postcolonial literature, children's literature, media, and cinema. He holds a Ph.D. from the Flinders University of South Australia and postgraduate qualifications in teaching from Oxford University and is widely published in Southeast Asian literature in English, Indian and Chinese diaspora literatures, and East/West theory. He co-edited Lee Kok Liang's *London Does Not Belong to Me* (2003) and co-authored *Cultural Connection: The English Language in Literature and Translation* (2011).

Andrea Mei-Ying Wu is Professor of children's literature and Taiwanese literature at National Cheng Kung University in Taiwan. She is currently President of the Taiwan Children's Literature Research Association (TCLRA) and has served on the Executive Board of the International Research Society for Children's Literature (IRSCL, 2013–2017). She was awarded a Fulbright Senior Research Scholar fellowship (2014–2015) and is now working on a research project on archive study and children's literature in 1960s Taiwan.

Lalaine F. Yanilla Aquino is Professor at the Department of English and Comparative Literature, University of the Philippines, where she teaches, among other courses, children's literature, stylistics, language and gender, language and cognition, and Philippine literature in English translation. She is the recipient of the UP Centennial Professorial Chair Award, the UP International Publication Award, and the ONE UP Professorial Chair Award.

LIST OF FIGURES

LIST OF TABLES

CHAPTER 1

Introduction

Convergences, Crossings, Contestations: Children's Literature and Film in Asia

Sharmani Patricia Gabriel and Bernard Wilson

BACKGROUND

Academic interest in Asian literature and other forms of cultural production for and about children has been embraced by Asian researchers, both those located in Asia and other locations, as well as scholars of Asian literature working in various parts of the world to the extent that Asian children's literature and culture is today a global field of research and academic inquiry. Indeed, on the whole, the analysis of children's literature and other cultural forms, including film, information books, picturebooks, graphic novels, animation, computer games, digital texts and multimedia, has enjoyed greater primacy in recent decades.

S. P. Gabriel (✉)
Universiti Malaya, Kuala Lumpur, Malaysia
e-mail: spgabriel@um.edu.my

B. Wilson
University of the Sacred Heart, Tokyo, Japan

1

This resurgence of academic interest can be seen, for example, in the new or increased focus given to the study of children's literature not only at undergraduate levels, but also in M.A. and M.Phil. programmes, both in Western and Asian universities. Furthermore, such a resurgence is symbiotic for, while the children's literature texts used in courses run by university departments of Education provide material mainly for second language acquisition, they also, like the literature of any other genre, function as important points of reference in the Literature classroom for the discussion of questions of form, theme, influence, style, historical period and the social context from which the writings emerge, and the broader cultural issues of nation, class, gender, ethnicity, location, and so on that surround the production of this body of literature.

The Bachelor of Arts in English (Literature) programme at Universiti Malaya, for example, where one of us is based, offered for a number of years an elective course on children's literature. The course was closed in 2010 when the sole staff member who taught the course (having migrated from another field of research late in her career) retired that year. The course will be re-opened as the "Children's and Young Adult Literature" elective in the 2020/2021 academic session and taught by another member of staff (Sharifah Aishah Osman, who has herself moved from another area of research expertise—and who thus will draw from a synergy that can be productive—and who also writes for us here) with a growing specialisation in young adult literature with rootedness in the nation's Malay(sian) folkloric traditions. The new course's focus on local sites of production, including primary texts and reference material published locally, marks a welcome development in the field, and in the Malaysian classroom, and ranges from a consideration of the older generic form of the folktale to its adaptations in the contemporary sub-genres of the novel and short story, which cater principally to young adult readers. The generalist approach to the course as it was taught previously (with canonical Western texts and Western culture used as the main, if not sole, reference point) is to be superseded by local contexts, concepts and circumstances, both in the selection of texts and subject matter.

While children's writings and culture as a field of analysis is a dynamic and evolving terrain, children's literature itself has entered a new and complex territory, what has been termed "a 'post-Harry Potter' phase of development in which no single genre or style can truly claim dominance" (Butler 2014, 1). One emergent trend that we also wish to foreground in this context is the relationship between the written and visual narrative in children's stories, one that has in many ways become inseparable given the increasing number of children's texts that have been adapted and translated and then disseminated from text to screen. The nexus of transmission between written and visual media is one that is growing ever stronger. This has mainly been due to the rapid advances in communicative technologies, diversifying market forces, the audience's changing tastes and the relatively cheap and easy access to cultural products. Although this has helped the international circulation of a number of Asian children's texts, owing to the economic dominance and cultural hegemony of the West, specifically of Anglophone nations, it is images from franchises such as the Disney and Pixar films and the Harry Potter books, for example, that have received a far greater popularity and appeal, and these have come to represent a universal symbol of childhood and adolescence.

Equally noteworthy and relevant in this regard is Western sourcing of non-Western cultural lores and histories for commercial gain and to further serve a predominant neocolonial discourse—the most notable recent instance of which is Disney's *Moana* (2016). Such cultural appropriations and misrepresentations may be politically charged, as in the negative Muslim/Arab portrayals which followed closely upon the First Gulf War in *Aladdin* (1992), historically revisionist reimaginings of the birth myth of modern multicultural America, as in *Pocahontas* (1995), or economically opportunistic attempts by US conglomerates to penetrate foreign markets through the appropriation of non-Western folklore under the authoritative guise of "cultural authenticity", as evidenced by Disney's 1998 animated feature, *Mulan*. These films involve multiple revisions and reinterpretations of source materials, invariably resulting in Western genre expectations and imperialist assumptions being imprinted on a final narrative far removed from its original cultural import. *Mulan*, for example, deploys as its main source text Robert San Souci's *Fa Mulan: The Story of a Woman Warrior*, but both texts (film and children's book) are themselves adaptations of the "Ballad of Mulan", an ancient Chinese poem that traces back to the Southern and Northern Dynasties. The series of transformations engendered by these "translations" of Mulan (as self-interested fairytale "princess", warrior woman, filial daughter) through these successive mediums (animated film, children's literature, poetry) as they are adapted, transmitted and received across cultures raises interesting questions about the translation of children's texts as an ethical project in the cultural agenda of a hegemonic and hegemonising West.

More interestingly, Disney's project of cultural (mis)appropriation in *Mulan* has been interpreted as being exploitative and neo-imperialist in nature (Giunta 2018, 156). Contrary to the original "Ballad of Mulan", which reflects the Chinese ethos of relationalism, filial piety, and loyalty and embraces an alternative form of feminism that is based on the Chinese preference for the collective, the theme of individualism in the Disney version reverts to delimiting racial and gender stereotypes and in doing so reinforces them while simultaneously othering as well as devaluing the culture of the original source text.

This of course reminds us that the position of children, who are the main implied readership and audience of this genre of literature and film and/or who are represented so prominently in it, continues to be the focus of parents, educators, scholars, children's writers, policy-makers as well as children themselves. This is a focus that is justified given the importance of this body of literature and film not only in enhancing their emotional and intellectual development but also in assisting children to conceptualise the diverse societal, cultural, national, and increasingly transnational, contexts and formations in which they exist, to understand at a rudimentary level, and also to contest, the power dynamics and moral codes that underpin all social structures.

Yet the perception of childhood as a crucial series of developmental stages is—certainly in Western history and philosophical thought—a relatively recent phenomenon, as French historian Philippe Aries noted in his seminal work *L'enfant et la vie familiale sous l'ancien régime* (1960). Previously, one may speculate, harsh social conditions for the majority of the populace, such as the use of child labour and high infant mortality rates, may have necessitated an emotional detachment such that children were not seen as anything other than adults in miniature, protected within the nuclear unit only in terms of their immediate and perceived future usefulness to the needs of the biological family and to the larger society beyond that family nucleus.

It has long been asserted that the construct of childhood itself was a product of the Enlightenment. It was also Western culture through Locke and Rousseau that produced the idealisation of childhood and ideal of self-realisation in the eighteenth century, an aesthetic which continues to drive cultural suppositions about children across time and space. Despite these problematic aspects, Locke's seventeenth-century view of early childhood as a period of neutral morality upon which the influence of surrounding adults and the education and literature to which the child is exposed would produce a lasting effect on the development of character, evidences a significant departure from the previous beliefs.[1] Similarly, Rousseau's thoughts on childhood education (*Émile, ou De l'éducation* 1762) and the implicit contract between society and the individual—philosophies which, ironically and rather tragically, were at significant odds with his treatment of his own children in abandoning them to an orphanage—further challenged long-held beliefs on childhood development.

It is also, perhaps, no coincidence that changes in the perception of children in Europe during this period correlated with the rise of the nation-state and an increase in nationalist ideals. In the introduction to a 2013 collection of essays on children's literature and its relationship to national tropes, Christopher Kelen and Bjorn Sundmark observe:

> Nation and childhood are intimately connected through children's literature. It is perhaps for this reason children's literature tends to stay at home, securely rooted in a national context and in culturally specific perceptions of childhood. Indeed, even the exceptions (international children's classics and the products of the global media industry) relate in complex and manifold ways to the idea of nation. [It is] a key instrument of culture connecting child and nation, and defining their relationship. The manner in which children and childhood are represented in a dedicated literature will affect a nation's self-understanding; conversely, the way a nation wishes to see itself will have a bearing on the possible ways in which children and childhood can and may be presented. (2013, 4)

And at the centre of so many children's stories, this adherence to collective ideals and interests, whether biological, social, political, ideological, or a complex mixture thereof, is self-evident. Children's literature and film have indeed invariably been viewed through the prism of *nation* because in the first instance, though they may be born of locality, they are bound to larger collective ideals and imperatives. Theme and narrative in children's texts emerge from a combination of immediate context and broader concerns, and the evidence that nation plays a central role in the analysis of the literature and film discussed in this collection is supported by the framework, and aspirations, of the book itself: broadly regional, specifically national.

Yet clearly there is also something transnational—one may even posit metanational—that is evident in the chapters that follow. This is not to suggest that "the enthusiastic internationalism of the post-war period, which set out from the idea of a supra-national world republic of childhood" (O'Sullivan 2005, 2) has been realised, though globalisation has increased cross-pollination to a certain extent.

But even as we speak of globalisation and its pollinating flows, it is worth keeping in mind that to live critically under globalisation is to be aware of how the story of Asian children's literature and culture has continued to be marked by marginalisation and erasure. For all of globalisation's touted "two-way" dialogue and exchange of ideas and transactions between cultures, the balance of geopolitical power and knowledge still remains asymmetrically weighted towards the West and the North. Indeed, European and Anglo-American discourses on children's literary culture and their regimes of literary and visual representation continue to dominate the global stage, eclipsing, overlooking or excluding voices, perspectives and discourses from Asia. To paraphrase Stuart Hall, "Where [Asia] was a case of the unspoken, Europe was a case of that which is endlessly speaking" (1997, 232).

Implicit in this critique is that, as in other areas of humanities scholarship, mainstream European and North American scholarship on children's literature is either ignorant of or tends to pay very little attention to the academic deliberations of Asian scholars and intellectual traditions that have emerged outside of Europe and the United States. The move, then, to foreground scholarly perspectives and intellectual concepts, along with cultural productions from outside of Europe is, we believe, a necessary undertaking.

It would also be useful in this regard to keep in mind that even positive and inclusive Western tropes and concepts such as cultural diversity, hybridity and tolerance, vaunted in the name of multiculturalism, are premised on uncritical liberal humanist ideals and on stable and secure self-other oppositions that do very little to eradicate unequal power relations and essentialist attitudes to cultural otherness, which continue to shape and inform policy constructions of national identity and multicultural education in schools. Thus, in spite of what has been called "the ongoing multiculturalization of children's literature" (Bader 2003, Quoted in de Manuel and Davis 2006, iv), multiculturalism "can still look discouragingly monocultural" (de Manuel and Davis 2006, iv).

A few words ought to be said at this point about the genesis of this book, which emerged from the publication in December 2018 of a Special Issue for the Universiti Malaya journal, *SARE: Southeast Asian Review of English,* on the subject of Asian Children's Literature, Film, and Animation, the call for papers garnering such a response and overall interest from scholars both in Asia and elsewhere that the idea for a book collection was immediately conceived. This collection of new essays, then, grew in part out of that desire to address the under-representation of children's literature within literary studies as a whole. It is also intended to correct in some small way the imbalance, as mentioned earlier, between the proliferation of studies of Western children's literature and film and the more limited number of studies on Asian children's literature and film, and to give further voice and visibility to Asian writers and academics in this field.

Furthermore, as the production and analysis of children's literature have traditionally centred upon Occidental hegemonic perspectives, shaped and influenced by a canonical Märchen that reflects Eurocentric power discourses and values, it may be inevitable that the Asian texts studied are invariably assessed, and objectified, by the Western gaze and its unequal rhetoric and assumptions, when such literature must be allowed to stand on its own terms. And while some areas of Asian children's literature and media have received considerable attention—the Japanese twin counterculture genres of anime and manga being two such prominent examples—and have been strongly influential on global narratives, and the global market, other regions of Asia have had far less representation and have been overlooked both in terms of the explorations of its scholars and the experiences of its children. This then is to argue that Asian contributions to children's literature and culture warrant far greater consideration than they have hitherto received both from within Asia and more broadly.

The book thus seeks to provide some sense of Asian agency in an area of literary production and children's book criticism that, as we have noted, has been dominated by Eurocentric and American-centric perspectives and to provide representations that go well beyond the exotic "tableau vivant" that the Western gaze has traditionally inscribed upon the East. In addition, we hope our chapter contributors will instigate dialogue not just in response to these more widely known Western positions but within Asia itself, and to provide international perspectives that are simultaneously inflected by local concerns, analyses, and emphases on the complex power relationships between children and their peers, children and adults, children and families, and children and society—and the local, national and transnational elements, as the title implies, that also define these relationships.

In eastern Asia in particular, many of the abiding debates within children's literature studies are centred on the ideological and didactic ends of the systems and structures that surround childhood, child-rearing, and family, and their close adherence to hierarchical formations, an ethos that stems mainly from the teachings of Confucianism and its emphasis on filial piety and the family unit as synonymous with social structure. In many Asian communities, as will be seen in a number of the essays that follow, collectivism is unquestioningly prioritised over individualism and selfhood, yet these essays also suggest that these codes are now being re-evaluated. Contemporary changes to traditional attitudes are evidenced explicitly in Xiangshu Fang's and Lijun Bi's chapter on family values in modern Chinese society, while Yasuko Doi discusses the re-evaluation of the family story within Japanese society and its representation in children's books as a sign of the changing historical and cultural contexts of Japanese society and its family structures. Sung-Ae Lee's essay on those who exist on the margins of family/society in South Korea acknowledges the entrenched notion of the family unit as a metaphor for society itself, but also the way in which it negatively affects those who are seen to fall outside its parameters.

Similarly, and in close connection to the revaluation of family structures in Asia, many of the essays in this collection discuss the changing perceptions of gender roles and sexual identity. The textual engagements with children's and young adult literature emerging from a number of nations within the region—India, the Philippines and Japan being three such examples—show an increasing awareness of gendering, transgendering and queer subjectivities and offer new and innovative interpretations of what were once peripheral identities in traditionally conservative societies, but are now emblematic of another aspect of the region's diversity and of the realities and choices facing Asia's youth.

UNPACKING "ASIA"

The attempt to canvass locally grounded and inspired contexts of critical analyses and reflections so as to retrieve from global obscurity the intellectual pursuits and preoccupations of Asian scholars of children's film and literature is not the same thing as to say, "We want to do children's studies from an Asian perspective". That gesture is both counter-intuitive and counter-productive in a globalised world. It not only endorses but also practises Euro-teleology by reversal.

The question then as to what is "Asian" about Asian children's literature in a global age inevitably requires us to understand the processes of change and connectivity engendered by cultural globalisation. Indeed, when local practices respond to global discourses, and as global influences become absorbed and adapted in local settings, the outcome is "glocalisation"—a practice or perspective that is at once global and local. This means that though we should be mindful of globalisation's totalising tendencies and homogenising effects, we should also be open to the possibility of global processes providing conditions for the local "to come into representation" (Hall 1997, 27).

Thus, characterised by the glocal exchange of cultural influences central to the construction of identity and the exercise of social power, globalisation can facilitate new forms of agency. This suggests that, like other social subjects, scholars are not passive participants in top-down regimes of globalisation, but can utilise "strategies of representation, organization and social change through access to global systems" to empower themselves and transform their conditions (Ashcroft 2009, 93). It is well worth speculating if glocalisation of knowledges could be the outcome of reflecting actively on what the West might mean *to* and *in* Asia, and vice versa.

This resonates somewhat with Gayatri Spivak's assertion that "What globalization requires is a change in ourselves as instruments of knowing" (2016, xix). The cultural and political agenda within Spivak's proposed deconstructive epistemic framework allows for a critique of both Eurocentric globalisms and entrenched localisms from the grounded specificities of the scholar's critical positioning in the post-colony of Asia. The ideological, political, as well as cultural, contours of this locatedness can empower scholars to interrogate the universalist and essentialist tendencies present in First World academic productions on Asian children's literature but also to be critical of the hegemonic inclinations that exist within local contexts of knowledge and cultural production.

Thus, one way of decentring or dismantling the hegemony of Western scholarship and perspectives on children's literature and culture is for scholars to do so from their "insider" locations, that is, from the insights gained from their embeddedness in their cultural and political locations, and from the specificities and complexities of such locations. Every location comes with its attendant priorities. It is our hope that a collection like this, which foregrounds the critical perspectives of Asian children's literature and film scholars and the experiences of Asian children, will help to move the privileged sites of scholarly production away from their current positions in the Anglo-European West.

But we must also remember the related task to subject the idea of "Asia" itself, along with the diverse forms of literary and non-literary culture associated with it, and the cultural assumptions made about it, to careful scrutiny. Asia is neither homogeneous nor monolithic. This means we are also aware, for example, that not only "Asia" but also the constituent national imaginaries and geopolitical locations encompassed by it are categories of incredible internal diversity. Such issues are lent further credence by Asia's many changing faces due to globalisation and with it the metamorphosis of its traditional family units, social structures, and gender associations, and the various and complex issues now confronting its children and young adults at both national and international levels. Thus, children's literature and its associated scholarship need to respond to these local and national complexities and heterogeneities.

In terms of narrative conventions, a key characteristic of the field of contemporary Asian children's literature and film is the merging of genres, mediums and techniques in storytelling. Partly because of this, its boundaries continue to be blurred rather than fixed. The use of written text, illustration, film and animation has to a large extent become interchangeable, given the ready dissemination and exchange of these narratives between multiple textual styles (picture books, novels, graphic novels, comics, manga) and screen and digitalisation (film, animation, online forums, interactive role-playing and gaming), and a number of the essays in this collection engage with this symbiosis. Such fluidity offers tremendous scope through which to inform and influence, yet its very capaciousness makes definitions of the field problematic. And, just as the concept of "Asia" is open and unbounded, there are also no absolute definitions of Asian children's literature and film—most particularly amidst political shifts within the region and across the globe, and amidst transformations in the way social and cultural politics are viewed and enacted. Given the regional framework of this collection it is inevitable that its readership will rightly debate what constitutes the (so often inadequate) idea of "Asia"—that nebulous geographical space and its manifest cultures and influences, the diverse art forms associated with it, and the cultural assumptions made about it. A volume of essays such as this, then, grouped under the heading of "Asian Children's Literature and Film", immediately faces deconstruction by virtue of the very heterogeneities it seeks to somewhat conveniently bring together into some form of coherence, a diversity further complicated by the positioning of Asia within debates on transnationalism and globalisation.

Such debates, as we have mentioned, are lent further complexity by the rapid socioeconomic changes within Asian nations and the resultant reorganisation and reinterpretation of traditional family and social units.

The aim, then, is not to consolidate "Asia", but to conceive of it as a space of many centres and many peripheries, with its own flows of influence and networks of connections, always shifting and moving. While we invoke the limits and oversight of a Eurocentric globalism that emphasises the stable sovereign nation and the individual but fails to provide due recognition to the interrelationships and mutual dependence that propel social identities in motion across time and space, we also need to be vigilant of the narrow insiderisms and parochialisms of the local that might be informing its institutions, structures and cultural productions.

Asia, as this collection shows, is at once disparate and connected, eclectic and unified, and within these chapters such paradoxical connections become clear. In geographical terms, the contributions for this book embrace a broad scope. Children's literature and film from the following countries/regions are represented: the Asian-American diaspora, China, India, Indonesia, Iran, Japan, Malaysia, the Philippines, South Korea, Sri Lanka and Taiwan. As the title suggests, discussions of specific cultures and related issues are foregrounded but in connection to broader transnational dialogues. Its principal purpose is to promote discussion of Asian children's literature and film but also to create a space in which these cultural productions gain greater attention within and beyond their own geographical and ethnic borders. Collectively, the book presents a multifaceted discussion of how these texts respond to as well as resist sociopolitical movements and exemplify cultural processes. It provides depictions of childhood development as it is perceived in different regions of Asia and the Asian diaspora in relation to local systems, contexts and institutions, and participates in more general conversations of "East" and "West" interaction. It offers particularity and individuality in regional and local identities but also, on occasion, clear points of connection.

Thus, the following concerns, among others, are broached: What elements of Asian children's literature and film make them distinctive, both within their own specific culture and within the broader Asian area? How have they represented and shaped the societies and cultures they inhabit? What moral codes do they address, underpin, or repudiate? What aspects link them to these genres in other parts of the world? Collectively, these scholars unpack not only the influence of Asian children's texts within their own specific regional locations, but also explore the often amorphous ability of such texts to cross borders and influence global children's literature and other art forms, to both shape and reflect political and social movements, and to deconstruct cultural and gender stereotypes.

EAST ASIA

The first section of this collection introduces chapters from Taiwan, China, South Korea and Japan that are particularly concerned with the changing structure of the modern family, its core value in these societies, and the reinterpretation of the roles within it. As previously noted, the majority of children's narratives (particularly in realistic fiction, but across a range of genre and subgenre) locate the child within specific social and/or familial frameworks and involve considerations of what nurtures, threatens or challenges the child. These considerations, which may also include social or political directives, are invariably articulated through the prism of cultural and ideological biases and imperatives. Such texts are sites of articulation, construction and contestation both within and beyond the text: children's narratives are invariably created by adults and attempt to reconnect with or appropriate the experience of childhood, as expressed in Andrea Mei-Ying Wu's essay on the representation of Taiwanese children's literature as *tongxin* (or "child heart"). The establishment of the government-affiliated *Ertong Duwu Bianji Xiazu* (Editorial Task Force for Children's Books) in the 1960s in Taiwan and the work of its leading light, the author Pan Ren-Mu, is one such example of literature which, on the one hand, is underpinned by political and social directives but which, on the other, contests those same dominant ideologies by suggesting that even within a relatively monolithic framework, diversity and imagination remain crucial components of child development. The concept and discourse of *tongxin* is seen as critical to the development of children's literature in postwar Taiwan and beyond in that it recognises not just the core of what it is to be a child, but also the necessity of the adult author to remain in concert with that essence—that is to say, the heart of the child must continue to reside in the adult author and allow her to act in consideration of, and in communion with, the target of her writing.

The philosophy of *tongxin*, which acknowledges the moral responsibility and authority inherent in the creation of children's narratives, essentially positions the author as vicarious parent and in part stems from long-held Confucian ideals regarding the power structures inherent in the concept of "family" in East Asia. Yet such structures have undergone redefinition in recent decades. Xiangshu Fang and Lijun Bi probe some of the many changes that have taken place in the stories of parents and parent–child relationships in contemporary Chinese children's literature from 1978 to 2015 and relate these developments to past ideologies and the influence of political movements. The Confucian tenet of filial piety and unquestioning obedience that traditional Chinese society expected has undergone major changes within recent decades, most specifically following the death of Mao, whose regime had seen the education and influence of children strongly linked to collectivist policies and the national ideal, followed by a shift from the emphasis on class struggle and a reaction against authoritative methods, and finally to a Neo-Confucianist re-emphasis of the role of the parent in child-rearing and education. Parental indulgence, related to the one-child policy, and the insurgency of the late 1980s—of which the repression of the students' pro-democracy movement was emblematic—resulted in the state resuming a more stringent central role in child education, the instilment of moral codes, and guidance concerning relationships within the immediate biological family, the extended family, and in connection to the ideology of a larger national "family". Linked to these multiple readings of "family" amidst an increasingly affluent Chinese society are the pressures of a highly competitive education system in which to fail academically is to fail in responsibility to one's family, both in the immediate present but also in the future, and to risk social and economic ostracism.

Such pressures are also readily apparent in South Korean culture, in which the biological family is absolutely fundamental to the structure of social identity itself—so deeply embedded in national discourse and in the individual and collective psyche as to be a metonym for Korean society. Yet the insistence on prioritising biological relationships over all external influences has led to an inflexibility in family, and in the society it is emblematic of, with the consequence that nonconformity (intentional or otherwise) can lead to heavy emotional and physical trauma. For although family is often subjectively defined as a site of *inclusion*, it is also inherently *exclusive* and ruptures in its support base can see massive destabilisation on personal levels, not only for those who experience it at its centre but particularly for those who exist at its margins. Sung-Ae Lee examines three contemporary South Korean films that offer a critique of social values in South Korea but also shed light on the paradoxical nature of family and what it represents. She finds that in each film, though the focus remains on social inequity and the direct and residual effects of exclusion and abandonment, the narrative trajectory offers some opportunities—to a greater or lesser degree—for change. Just as tellingly though, she observes that there are also strong indications in these stories that such opportunities may prove illusory.

Alternatively, greater flexibility in the perception of family is the focus of Yasuko Doi's panoramic look at contemporary Japanese society and its representative children's literature. Doi provides a methodical survey of a selection of texts which address recent changes in this area and which evidence the increasing diversity in the conception and structure of the family unit. The texts Doi draws from reveal a greater awareness of the issues confronting children and families, redefine the Japanese family and its traditional binary gender roles and heteronormative structures, and pave the way for a closer understanding of the complexity of the power balances and relationships therein. These recent but generally favourable representations, which one may speculate will gain further traction as Japanese society begins to recognise greater female equality in the workplace, further acknowledges non-traditional relationships, alternative lifestyles and gender identities, and continues to wrestle with concerns related to increasing immigration, will present significant challenges but will also redefine its predominantly monocultural and patriarchal structure.

The social (re)construction of gender also informs Bernard Wilson's mapping of cross-cultural and sexual subjectivities in Hans Christian Andersen's *The Little Mermaid* through its American (Disney) and Japanese (Studio Ghibli) reinterpretations. Although each of the two earlier mermaid narratives deals with the pain and potential of metamorphosis, and also the cost of challenging societal norms and patriarchal imperatives, Miyazaki's *Gake no Ue no Ponyo* offers a thesis that moves beyond heteronormative codes and binary gender roles by depicting the environment and the species which have emerged from it as deeply interconnected and mutually reliant, and the social performance elements of gender as largely irrelevant. Miyazaki's narrative is a clear melding of Eastern and Western influences and concerns: deeply Japanese in setting and cultural detail, it is also deeply global in the import of its messages of inclusion and the acceptance of entwined differences.

SOUTH AND WEST ASIA

Though geopolitical borders mark the physical (and often illusory) separation of nations, cultural borders are considerably more porous. Cultural interconnectedness has, theoretically at least, been exacerbated by modern shifts towards transnationalism and globalisation, and such effects may be witnessed in the majority of contributions to this collection. The second section of the book groups nations from South and West Asia, specifically India, Sri Lanka and Iran, and centres on issues that may be regional in their immediate import, but which are deeply connected to broader global concerns: differing approaches to parental and institutional education, preferential or repressive treatment based on gender, the ethical considerations of representing children in film and on the page, and the marginalisation of ethnic and sexual minorities.

The first of these chapters concerns the portrayal of children on screen in India. Given the immense output of mainstream Indian cinema, centred as it is on the production mechanisms of Bollywood, its fiscal imperatives and its mass appeal for adult audiences, it is perhaps unsurprising that local production of children's cinema has been relatively minimal. Sonia Ghalian provides an overview of the history of films in the Indian cinema whose principal focus is childhood and children, and traces depictions of children in Hindi films of the 1950s, through Nehruvian socialist ideals, to portrayals in modern film. Apart from economic and cultural considerations, which inevitably dictate the volume of local production and its style and thematic direction, the residual effects of globalisation on the Indian output of children's cinema is also much evident: the pervasiveness of Western franchises and ideas available to Indian children over the last several decades has left less space for local voices and identities. More recently, however, fundamental changes to Indian society from within its own national borders and from beyond in terms of media use, technological innovation and social attitudes, have seen a rise in narratives related to children and young adults. Though these themes initially emerged predominantly in independent cinema, increased local representation has in turn cumulatively transferred to mainstream Indian cinema and a range of sociocultural issues affecting children and families, both within India itself and as a global concern, are now being presented on screen and prompting broader debate.

One such pressing issue is the representation of queer lifestyles and choices in mainstream Indian culture. Suchismita Banerjee examines the important—but invariably underestimated—role LGBTQIA+ literature for children and young adults plays in gaining discussion and acceptance of alternatives to heteronormative society in India. In light of the 2018 Supreme Court reversal of the repressive morality clauses of Section 377 of the Indian Penal Code, Banerjee introduces the novels of two writers— Himanjali Sankar and Payal Dhar—to assess how their work reflects and responds to modern sociocultural tropes. Her chapter provides an analysis of the aims of this writing, but also looks at the issues surrounding the output and publication of such literature through interviews with the two authors in question. Queer representation in Indian literature, as Banerjee notes, is not a new phenomenon, extending as far back as classical texts and scriptures, though not always in approving terms. Yet, beyond occasional stereotypes and caricatures in mainstream Indian media, often in terms of ridicule, homosexual representation has been minimal and reactions from the public invariably hostile. Exposure to Western cultural mores however, appears to be one significant influence in providing such characters with greater public exposure and in lending depth to— and discussion of—their position in Indian society. The best way forward, Banerjee argues, is for children's and young adult literature and media to acknowledge such characters' differences—and their struggles for acceptance because of those differences—but just as importantly to acknowledge their sameness, their shared existences, and their mutual bonds with the larger community.

A primary strategy of children's stories, and one that has long been evidenced in folklore and fairytales, is this evocation of perceived alterity—of that which exists, for better or worse, outside of societal "norms". It is this *otherness* and how we perceive it and respond to it that often defines who we are, what we are, and what we stand for collectively and individually. Neluka Silva provides examples of demon *otherness* in her examination of two popular children's novels, *Mythil's Secret* (2009) and *Asiri's Quest* (2013), by Sri Lankan author Prashani Rambukwella. Each story is connected to the prolonged period of ethnic conflict in Sri Lanka (1983–2009), in that the former was written during the Civil War and the latter written and published in the postwar reconciliation phase, and each recognises the agency that acknowledging and accepting difference may provide. It is inevitable that the long conflict experienced by Sri Lankans in their recent past will give rise to a questioning of the construction of identity and alterity, and an awareness of the demonisation of difference along ethnic or ideological lines. Rambukwella herself has acknowledged the paucity of children's stories in Sri Lanka, and in her tales of youthful engagements with the *yaka* (demon other) her work serves a crucial function as a metaphor for the processes of conflict and resolution in Sri Lankan society. In guiding children towards an acceptance of difference, but also an early understanding of the ramifications of choice, consequence and contestation, the author trusts her readership to comprehend the complexity and ambiguity of such decisions, and refuses to provide the pat solutions that may sometimes be associated with narratives for younger audiences.

The relationship between choice and consequence is invariably central to narratives about and for children, whether those decisions be made by the children themselves of necessity or as a function of free will or, more fatalistically, by those in a position to guide or control. With this in mind, Amir Ali Nojoumian and Amir Hadi Nojoumian analyse a selection of films by acclaimed Iranian director Abbas Kiarostami that feature child protagonists, or children as documentary subjects. They discuss his approach to the aesthetics of representing children on the screen by deploying the framework of Aristotelian poetics. The authors posit two major choices made by Kiarostami's child characters in response to the rigid social environments and often debilitating circumstances they encounter in these allegorical narratives. These responses, the authors argue, often manifest themselves in binary terms and result in choices that encapsulate either a sense of responsibility to the individual protagonist through a refusal to acknowledge the restrictive social codes of the collective, or through an altruistic commitment to those groups—adults, families, institutions—which may be considered to be (certainly from the child's perspective) the authoritarian "other". The techniques used by Kiarostami invite the audience to participate in the ethical choices faced by the children, but never in terms of moral absolutes: his approach to narratives about children is only didactic in the sense that we, the audience, consider the ethical choices themselves and the causes for them, rather than the outcomes of those decisions.

SOUTHEAST ASIA

Contemporary children's stories owe much to the traditions of communal storytelling as a shared cultural activity. They are inextricably linked to the oral traditions of folklore and fairytales that came before them, and to the moral lessons of the Bildungsroman, and predominantly draw on these universal elements—loyalty, courage, ethical choices, crime and punishment, the importance of individualism weighed against collective ideals—while seeking to adjust their narrative detail and thematic choices to reflect the current concerns, practices, and needs of a local (as well as glocal) readership. As such, children's narratives are constantly reinvented, repositioned and reinvigorated to maintain relevance. The third section of this book comprises essays from Southeast Asia (Malaysia, Indonesia and the Philippines) and draws on seemingly disparate sources and styles, ranging from ancient folklore to contemporary stories, from linguistic analysis to digital existence—yet all of them have global resonance beyond their current relevance to the communities from which they emerge.

The chapter by Sharifah Aishah Osman provides three interpretations of the Langkawi legend of Mahsuri—a famous regional tale with its roots in the venerable folktale that in its traditional form depicts the violent extirpation of an innocent female victimised by sexual desire and jealousy, and draws attention to the plight of the disenfranchised. Osman looks at the retellings of this eighteenth-century tale and their representations of repressed females in three contemporary Malaysian texts that have adopted its central tenets: Lee Su Ann's young adult murder mystery *The Curse* (2005), Preeta Samarasan's short story of interracial love "Mahsuri" (2011), and Shireen Zainudin's short story "Grey" (2019). Each adaptation, in different ways, explores female subjugation but also advances the possibility of feminist agency in overtly patriarchal worlds. The first is a contemporary Bildungsroman that is an affirmation of female strength and individualism in the face of restrictive social structures, the second an interrogation of interracial relationships in Malay-dominant Malaysia, and the third a depiction of a platonic male–female friendship, a narrative detail which has strong relevance in modern Malaysian society and which, unlike the original tale, foregrounds intellectual over sexual attraction but retains elements of betrayal. Osman's essay links these three contemporary tales through an emphasis on the importance these narratives can hold for young Malaysians (especially Malaysian females) seeking a sense of self-worth amidst social, gender and ethnic oppression, and the ways in which they perceive themselves individually and collectively.

If the celebration of the diversity of cultures and historical experiences is a thread that runs through this collection, then Indonesia is an Asian microcosm of that diversity in that it is home to approximately seven hundred regional languages and three hundred ethnic groups. Yet

Indonesia's diversity has also been its challenge and has resulted in repressive government-instigated policies—particularly under the authoritarian regime of the former president Suharto—designed to facilitate the outward perception of unity. Herdiana Hakim introduces new children's texts from Indonesia, most specifically books related to Eastern Indonesia and the representation of indigenous groups and Chinese Indonesians. These ethnicities have faced significant prejudice and exclusion, both though societal misconceptions and specific political edicts, and while previous children's texts have invariably reflected the perspective and concerns of the Muslim majority in terms of religion, and the Javanese majority in terms of ethnicity, a number of new inclusive texts which provide implicit rather than explicit instruction are, Hakim argues, providing an instrument for social change and paving a path towards greater understanding and inclusion.

An area that deserves greater attention in the role of children's literature as an indicator of social inclusion and exclusion is the specific vocabulary used within the narrative to convey detail and theme. The language used in children's stories can tell us much about the concerns of the immediate society to which it relates but also of the inherent biases and prejudices within that same community. Lalaine F. Yanilla Aquino provides a close, statistical analysis of the use of language in children's storybooks from the Philippines through the framework of Critical Stylistics, whose central tenet is that all language and its use carries with it contextual baggage and implications. As such, it is of crucial importance to understand the significance of the vocabulary used for young learners not only in terms of the overt influence it has on the readers themselves but also in terms of the covert sociocultural information it provides about the contexts from which such literature arises. The results of Aquino's survey are enlightening, and show the imbalance in voice between adult and child (despite the often adult-like responsibilities entrusted to the child) as a reflection of the imbalance in society and the problematic positioning of the Filipino child within cultural and family structures. While the more obvious surface communication in a realist narrative may provide a positive message to the child, close analysis of the language used and the dialogic interactions therein may also show a coded message at variance with the seemingly positive central theme.

The language of the internet is also a pervasive influence on youth narratives. Digital stories, interactive video and online gaming and role-playing form just part of a relatively recent but increasingly dominant range of storytelling sites for children and young adults. These protean narratives are a central component of, and strong influence on, social interaction across the globe, particularly among children, teenagers and young adults, and are now arguably as relevant as textual or cinematic mediums—perhaps more so. Gabriela Lee's essay explores how a more traditional narrative format—the novel—embraces a newer form of youth narrative, that of digital existence and role-playing. She analyses the depiction of virtual gaming and digital reality in Philippine society as represented in two twenty-first-century young adult speculative novels, *Jumper Cable Chronicles* (2018) by E. K. Gonzales, and the *Janus Silang* series (2014–2017) by Edgar Calabia Samar (each of which forms one component of respective ongoing series). Lee assesses the possibilities which speculative fiction provides in terms of the transfer of virtual action and consequence to the actual choices that teenagers and young adults make, and argues that participation in liminal spheres and digital experiences may form a crucial part of resisting imposed identity, accepting plurality, and shaping imagination.

ASIA AND ITS DIASPORAS

In the same sense that intertextuality is central to shaping children's narratives within and across communities so too is transnationalism, in that it spawns interactive dialogues not only across texts but also across cultures and ethnicities. These crossings and continuities in turn subvert the notion of monolithic social structures and that of discrete national cultures or literatures by providing a framework for studying children's literature and culture in a context that moves beyond and also explicitly questions older Eurocentric models of "comparative" analysis. Such continuities and connections have productively complicated the nationalist paradigm long dominant in these and other fields of academic interest, transformed the nature of the locations we study, and re-oriented our attention to the liminal sites of production between real and imagined borders.

The "transnational" that emerges from this perspective should be seen as a form of writing and a way of thinking that moves us away from the insularities and tidy geopolitical boundaries of post-Enlightenment European nation-states and unsettles its binarisms. There is a "Malaysia" and a "Japan" and an "India" and a "Taiwan" and so on beyond the nationalist framework, beyond the dominant imaginaries of "race" and insular place and geography. Eschewing the unities and boundedness of old paradigms, the transnational enables us to remap literary location in terms of a multiplicity of centres, as a network of flows and connections that is multilingual and multicultural. In short, the transnational is an unbounded poetics of thinking and writing, a paradigm with no fixed point or essence.

The final section gestures to the idea of the transnational invoked above and in the book's title by looking beyond the continent of Asia to Asian configurations in America, and comprises two essays which discuss bicultural and diasporic contributions to the field of Asian-American children's literature. Cultural memory as a shared experience, but also as one which may transcend the rigidity of national boundaries and ethnographies, forms the thesis of Fengxia Tan's chapter, which examines the picturebooks of the Chinese-American author Ed Young. Young's particularly visual literary medium, and his cross-cultural background, provide the conditions for opening a space for the amalgamation of Asian and Western art forms and for an important melding of differing perspectives, rendering a model of "symbiotic aesthetics" through which both tradition and modernity share relevance in an era of globalisation and transnationalism. Such a paradigm acknowledges and makes use of national cultural heritage but also of the heterogeneity of much of modern society, forging a symbiosis between the old and new, the presumed monocultural and the multicultural. In Young's work, Tan argues, this cultural blend does not dilute the quality of the narrative but, rather, enhances it by drawing on each nation's disparate strengths.

In the concluding chapter, Susan Ang examines the Chinese-American children's author Laurence Yep's allegories of Asian-American relations, emerging as these do from antagonism to acceptance to (in some cases) welcomed hybridity, connections that occur and are problematised through her use of Homi Bhabha's meta-epistemological Third space, through the inconstant nature of boundaries, and the construction and reconstruction of place, home, and identity—the paradox of the heterotopian mirror in which one is and one is not. Children's literature, Ang argues, is the real Third space because it is in this space that the child may engage with that which exists and that which does not, that which is seemingly Other but that which is also self. Rather than obliterate the bifurcation of Americanness and ancestral heritage, what Ang terms "the fragile boundary/bridge" is nurtured and infused with even greater relevance and dynamism through this space, embracing rather than rejecting duality, and acknowledging flux and dissemination—not the stasis or fixity of origin—as an integral part of such identities. It is significant that it is Yep's work that Ang mobilises to advance her argument that Asian-American children's literature is a seminal site of dialogic encounter between old and new, past and present. Critics consider Yep's early work, specifically his children's historical novel, *Dragonwings* (1975), as the first text to present a nuanced portrayal of the Asian presence in the American cultural landscape (see, for instance, de Manuel and Davis 2006, vi).

The implications of Ang's articulation of new identities that cannot be fixed in time in Asian-American literary representations also compel a reevaluation of the antithetical race thinking that has shaped and continues to shape Asian-American studies as a field and the place of Asian-American writers for children in American culture. The clearly demarcated and regulated lines between the categories of "Asian" and "American" in the master narrative of American culture and history, so important both for canon formation and hegemonic identity formations, construct Asianness not as a constitutive aspect of the American experience but as separate from and peripheral to it. By seeking continuities between "Asian" and "American" experiences and cultural productions, the Third space identities that Ang calls up interrogate the hegemony of the East–West, black–white binary in academic and public discourse, enabling marginalised interstitial histories and identities to emerge. Such transnational issues and predilections are applicable across other national contexts and boundaries.

Convergences, Crossings, Contestations

In 2002, the American political scientist Joseph Nye observed that, "Globalization – worldwide networks of interdependence – does not imply universality [...]. Globalization has made national boundaries more porous but not irrelevant. Nor does globalization mean the creation of a universal community" (2002, 81–82). In a sense, the same may be said of children's literature and film in its positioning amidst globalisation, and in its relationship to local, national and transnational configurations. Dialogue between diverse ethnic and cultural identities, national ideologies and local sensibilities does not necessarily imply an irrefutable connection between disparate communities, particularly given the recent rise in isolationist policies and the hardening of some geopolitical boundaries—in both the East and West. Globalisation does not imply a utopian fusion of ideas and values nor does it suggest a flattening out of differences. In Asia, local, national and regional considerations—and the intranational and regional voices expressed through children's stories and the analysis of those stories—remain crucial to the discussion of the changing issues affecting children and to their psychological, emotional and social development.

But what is also undeniable is that Asian children's literature and film are now increasingly in dialogue with larger, more amorphous, global movements that further shape modern concepts of the child and the family and their places in society(ies). Children's stories look both backwards and forwards, closely tied to their roots of immediate community, to moral instruction, and to the reinforcement of (at times problematic) social and familial imperatives, but also towards reimagining those communities, moralities and imperatives. They adapt to global movements and to changing landscapes not necessarily by shedding national or regional identity, but by strengthening these parameters through transnational and cross-cultural discourses which may reflect local concerns, but also consider difference, dialogue and otherness.

To accept the transnational, then, as also pointed out by several of our contributors, is to say we are each other's *other* but that we are also intimately connected and inseparable from each other. This is the premise from which to dismantle the essentialist, Orientalist construction of Asian societies as predominantly mystical and despotic, or as irrational and unconcerned with secular domains. This recalls for us Edward Said's reminder of forty years ago in *Orientalism: Western Conceptions of the Orient* (1978) that East and West, and specifically the binary oppositions between them, are products of the Eurocentric Orientalist imagination and its naturalising, hierarchic and dominating bias.

Thus, to think with, through and against globalisation is to uncover a narrative that obscures the discursive hegemony of the Anglophone West under the guise of an endlessly crisscrossing and mutually constitutive influence of capital and ideas across borders. But this also means that we should not other the West. The concept of the transnational offers us a means to move beyond provincialism, disengagement and exclusion. Indeed, thinking transnationally requires focus, flexibility and the ability to see things from the perspective of the other.

As scholars of Asian studies, then, the idea and concept of the transnational warrants that we not only look inwards but keep ourselves open to the circulation and dissemination of ideas within and across Asian societies. It also means that we must keep abreast of research being done outside our national contexts, keeping up with developments in the field outside Asia, in other parts of the globe. Just as importantly, Asian scholars should build alliances and solidarities and "inter-reference" one another (Chen 2010), listening actively and attentively to each other, forming regional frameworks where we can interact and learn from our Asian interconnectedness, intersections, interrelationships and mutual dependence. This is one way to exceed or go beyond the bounded, parochial, and divisive modes of hegemonic knowledge production.

Asian Children's Literature and Film in a Global Age: Local, National and Transnational Trajectories makes it clear that a hallmark of contemporary Asian children's literature and film criticism is its commitment to promoting Asian-centred discussions of social and cultural practice but it does so by foregrounding the embeddedness of this literature in global as well as local and national processes. The literary and cultural productions that are written about in this book are sites of social augmentation but also of social change, transformation and reformation. Across Asia, debates on changes in social and family structures, on the redefinition of gender roles and identities, on the repositioning of the child in local and global contexts, are now taking place. It is intended and hoped that the themes, methodological positions, concepts and paradigms foregrounded by the community of Asian children's literature and film scholars assembled in this book will offer us insightful views of the current state of the field and also move the conversation forward.

Notes

1. In general, Locke's volume *Some Thoughts Concerning Education* (1693) emphasises moral education over all other forms and the crucial part that parents play as role models for this behaviour, while broadly arguing against the merits of academic learning and the rigidity of educational systems.
2. For a deeper discussion of contemporary children's texts, their reflection of social change, and their role in global politics, see Clare Bradford et al. *New World Orders in Contemporary Children's Literature: Utopian Transformations.*

References

Aries, Philippe. 1962. *Centuries of Childhood: A Social History of Family Life* (*L'enfant et la vie familiale sous l'ancien régime*: 1960). New York: Vintage Books.

Ashcroft, Bill. 2009. "Alternative Modernities: Globalization and the Post-Colonial", *ARIEL*, Vol. 40, No. 1, pp. 81–105.

Bradford, Clare, Kerry Mallan, John Stephens, and Robyn McCallum. 2008. *New World Orders in Contemporary Children's Literature: Utopian Transformations*. Basingstoke, Hampshire: Palgrave Macmillan.

Butler, Catherine and Kimberley Reynolds (eds). 2014. *Modern Children's Literature: An Introduction* (Second Edition). London, UK: Macmillan Education.

Chen, Kuan-hsing. 2010. *Asia as Method: Toward Deimperialization*. Durham: Duke University Press.

de Manuel, Dolores and Rocío G. Davis (eds). 2006. "Editors' Introduction: Critical Perspectives on Asian American Children's Literature", *The Lion and the Unicorn*, Vol. 30, No. 2, pp. v–xv.

Giunta, Joseph V. 2018. "'A Girl Worth Fighting for': Transculturation, Remediation, and Cultural Authenticity in Adaptations of the 'Ballad of Mulan'", *SARE: Southeast Asian Review of English* (Special Issue on Asian Children's Literature, Film, and Animation: Guest Edited by Bernard Wilson), Vol. 55, No. 2, pp. 154–172.

Hall, Stuart. 1997. "The Local and the Global: Globalization and Ethnicity". In: King, A. D. (ed) *Culture, Globalization and the World-System: Contemporary Conditions for the Representation of Identity*. Minneapolis: University of Minnesota Press, pp. 19–40.

Kelen, Christopher (Kit) and Bjorn Sundmark. 2013. *The Nation in Children's Literature: Nations of Childhood*. New York and London: Routledge.

Nye, Joseph S., Jr. 2002. *The Paradox of American Power: Why the World's Only Superpower Can't Go It Alone*. Oxford: Oxford University Press.

O'Sullivan, Emer. 2005. *Comparative Children's Literature*. London and New York: Routledge.

Spivak, Gayatri Chakravorty. 2016. "Cosmopolitanisms and the Cosmopolitical". In: Gabriel, Sharmani Patricia and Fernando Rosa (eds), *Cosmopolitan Asia: Littoral Epistemologies of the Global South*. London and New York: Routledge, pp. xiv–xxi.

PART I

East

Children's Literature and Childhood Imagination in 1960s Taiwan: Jen-Mu Pan and the Discourse of "Child Heart"

Andrea Mei-Ying Wu

INTRODUCTION

The mid-1960s, almost two decades after the end of World War II, marked a significant and transformative stage for children's book publishing and childhood reading and education in Taiwan. One crucial factor,

Part of the paper was presented under the title "Children's Literature and Childhood Imagination in 1960s Taiwan: Jen-Mu Pan and the Editorial Task Force for Children's Books" in Roundtable: "East Asia in the 1940s to 60s: Ideas That Crossed Borders and Their Envoys", Children and Youth in a Global Age International Conference (Hong Kong University, Hong Kong, May 25–26, 2018). This study is supported by grants (MOST 103-2410-H-006-068-MY2 and MOST 106-2410-H-006-094) from Taiwan's Ministry of Science and Technology.

A. M.-Y. Wu (✉)
National Cheng Kung University, Tainan, Taiwan
e-mail: meiyingw@mail.ncku.edu.tw

© The Author(s) 2020
B. Wilson and S. P. Gabriel (eds.), *Asian Children's Literature and Film in a Global Age*, Asia-Pacific and Literature in English, https://doi.org/10.1007/978-981-15-2631-2_2

among others, is the establishment of *ertong duwu bianji xiazu* (the Editorial Task Force for Children's Books; which hereafter will be referred to as the Editorial Task Force).[1] Specifically, in 1964, the Editorial Task Force, sponsored by The United Nations Children's Fund,[2] was established under the auspices of Taiwan's Ministry of Education[3] to publish children's books and other reading materials for young readers aged from seven to twelve. The mission undertaken by the Editorial Task Force was immense in content and scope and the vision was revolutionary, given that juvenile publication was then barely a common practice and children's access to books appropriate to their age and in the service of their interests remained few and limited.

As I have elsewhere discussed, the Editorial Task Force in its operation for nearly four decades (1964–2002) has published approximately one thousand children's books, including children's encyclopaedias and a children's periodical.[4] With an aim to offer extracurricular readings for elementary school students, children's books published by the Editorial Task Force were categorised into three main subject areas—literature, science, and health, and later developed into five, by the addition of social sciences and arts. These books were created with considerations of age and grade appropriateness. As such, rhymes, picture books, fairy tales, and children's stories, for instance, were designated mainly for lower and middle graders, while fiction and nonfiction were the major readings for upper graders. The copious publications of the Editorial Task Force in the latter half of the twentieth century have become invaluable cultural assets for child readers across time and space. Published in the previous century, quite a number have been reprinted today and some even reissued, for example, in simplified Chinese to meet the demand of a new group of young readers in China. Created for children in 1960s Taiwan, a selection of the juvenile publications was also translated and circulated in several Asian countries and beyond.[5]

While the juvenile publications of the Editorial Task Force were indispensable in support of childhood reading and learning, they were also pivotal to the formation and development of modern Taiwanese children's literature.[6] Arguably, the undertakings of the Editorial Task Force would not have been effective and productive in their initial stages, were it not for the contributions and dedication of a few female authors prominent in the field of adult literature who stepped in as pioneers of children's literature writers and took up roles as chief editors for the publication of children's books. Among those pioneering authors, Jen-Mu Pan was considered one of the most influential and unparalleled in terms of the quantity and variety of books she wrote, edited, translated, and published for children and young adults. A renowned author best known for her award-winning novel *Lian-Yi biaomei* (Cousin Lian-Yi), Pan was invited to join the editorial team of the Editorial Task Force upon its setup. In her 17-year-long career (1965–1982) as the editor and later editor-in-chief of the Editorial Task Force, she used more than thirty pen names to write stories for children. In her career as a professional author of children's literature, she has written hundreds of books for children and the number of books she edited, translated, and published for children and young adults "reached a total of over five hundred".[7] She is in this regard one of the leading figures and "meaning-makers" of children's literature and one of the few ground-breakers and advocates for "a new narrative" for children and young adult readers in early postwar Taiwan.[8]

Significantly, the "new narrative" practised and upheld by Jen-Mu Pan, as well as her contemporaries in the field of children's literature, is typically governed by a discourse of *tongxin* (child heart or childness). The discourse of "child heart" in its signification and accentuation of the pureness and natural conditions and experiences of the child, albeit registered with individual conceptions, is not so much a "local inventiveness" as a sign of social conviction (or shared ideology) replete with (trans)national and (trans)cultural dynamics and negotiations of childhood imaginations. On the one hand, it can be regarded as resonant—and hence symptomatically a "belated residual"—of the Western cultural idea of the Romantic child.[9] On the other hand, it is evocative of the intellectual endorsement of "child-centredness" in the high tide of the New Culture Movement in the 1920s in the era of Republican China. What characterises such a cultural movement is an emphasis on the discovery of "the child" and a valorisation of childhood that speaks to an urge for social reform and an imperative for building up a (new) nation and its future generations.[10] Such a cultural phenomenon in valorising and epitomising the child figure as the hope for the future, whether in its nostalgic longing for a return to the pre-colonial past or a radical anticipation of social advancement, emerged as well in Korea in the early twentieth century, in part due to the struggles and oppressions under Japanese colonial rule.[11] The discourse of "child heart" and the advocacy of "child-centredness" are in this light viewed as more complex and inexorably charged with political implications than as self-evident and transparent gateways of literary creation for the young.

If the discourse of *tongxin* is indicative of historical contingences, then how might we account for the emergence and later predominance of such a cultural idea associated with the discourse of "child heart" in the production of juvenile texts, particularly in the early decades of postwar Taiwan? It is fitting to say that *tongxin* has since became the crux, the guiding principle, or the golden rule—the consensus and the qualification for the creation of children's texts. Curiously, given the significance and prevalence of heightening "child heart" in the making of children's literature, specifically in 1960s Taiwan, what pivotal events might there be to generate such a social norm and direct public attention to the child and childhood? What individuals were there to encourage and credit such a recognition of "child heart", in particular, those "pioneers" from the field of children's literature and childhood education? If the discourse of *tongxin* conceptualised and highlighted in early postwar Taiwan can(not) be randomly referred to as a "revival" or "residual" of its predecessors from either the West or the East, then what (re)significations of the concept of "child heart" can be identified or singled out in the practice of the juvenile publications in 1960s Taiwan, for instance, by the Editorial Task Force and particularly by Jen-Mu Pan, one of the chief editors and pioneers in creating and defining children's literature in early postwar Taiwan? This chapter will thus interrogate the issues concerning the discourse of "child heart" (*tongxin*), with special focus on Jen-Mu Pan's three children's stories published by the Editorial Task Force in the 1960s. *Ahui de qiyu* (the adventures of Ahei, 1967; which hereafter will be referred to as *The Adventures of Ahei*), *Xiayutian* (a rainy day, 1967; hereafter, *A Rainy Day*), and *Maoqi de yuanbao* (the steaming ingots, 1968; hereafter, *The Steaming Ingots*) will be employed as the three focal texts to examine the discourse of "child heart" and to see how a discourse as such may work to shape and (re)negotiate childhood imaginations in literary creations for the young.

THE DISCOURSE OF "CHILD HEART" IN 1960S TAIWAN

In 1965, approximately a year after the setup of the Editorial Task Force, the "Declaration of the Rights of the Child" (1959), formally issued by the United Nations, was published in the opening pages of a special volume dedicated to the studies of children's literature. This volume, under the title *Ertong duwu yanjiu diyiji* (Studies on Children's Reading Materials Vol. I), was published in celebration of the establishment of a children's magazine, *Xiaoxuesheng zazhi* (Elementary Student Magazine), for a span of fourteen years.[12] What is important about this magazine, according to a senior children's literature critic of the time, Ching-Hsien Ma, is that it was one of the most widely circulated children's periodicals and, in Ma's phrasing, "the most significant spiritual food for children in the early decades" of postwar Taiwan.[13] The chief editors of this children's magazine, Tseng-Yuan Hsu, Shang-Yao Su, Keng Li, and Liang Lin, were then pioneers and later prominent figures in promoting and augmenting children's literature and children's book publishing. The above mentioned special volume dedicated to the studies of children's literature was edited by the four and has now turned into a monumental document, because it was the first and foremost publication, as such, in the early postwar period to encompass professionals and individuals from diverse fields in relation to children's literature and to assemble a wide array of articles addressing various topics and issues concerning juvenile publications, childhood reading and education, the criteria of children's literature, as well as the techniques and principles of writing, editing, and illustrating for children. Unprecedented and wide-ranging, the book is a rare collection and a clear manifestation of the very idea of "child-centredness", given its assortment of discourses about children, childhood, children's education, children's reading materials, and the effects of reading on children's emotional and intellectual growth.

That the "Declaration of the Rights of the Child" appeared in the opening pages of the special volume published by *Xiaoxuesheng zazhishe* (Elementary Student Magazine Publisher) is not incidental but a deliberate reminder and can be rightly regarded as a direct proclamation of the epoch of the child. Specifically, in 1960, the Chinese version of the Declaration was delivered to Taiwan and what ensued was the open announcement of such a declaration by the Ministry of Education to the public in the same year. The UN Declaration (1959) originating from "the Geneva Declaration of the Rights of the Child" (1924) contains ten principles stating the equal rights and welfare for all children, regardless of class, race, gender, language, religion, nationality, ethnicity, and cultural backgrounds. Of the ten principles listed in the special volume, several statements were particularly highlighted in bold typeface. The physical wellbeing of the child, for instance, is underscored in Principle 4: "He [the child] shall be entitled to grow and develop in health", whereas in Principle 6, an emphasis on the child's inner security and the need to be nurtured and fully cultivated is foregrounded: "The child, for the full and harmonious development of his personality, needs love and understanding".[14]

What is more, children's rights to education and recreation are underlined in Principle 7: "The best interests of the child shall be the guiding principle of those responsible for his education and guidance" and "[t]he child shall have full opportunity for play and recreation, which should be directed to the same purposes as education".[15] It remained unclear whether those highlights were originally marked by the United Nations, or by the Taiwan government, or simply out of the book editors' collective visions. What can be perceived however is the centrality of the child, in which "the best interests of the child" is pinpointed as the utmost "guiding principle" for adult caretakers, educators, and those who work for children to bear in mind and take special notice. In those highlights, children's need for "play and recreation" and the opportunities thus granted are precisely articulated and deemed as equally important as their rights to education. That the Editorial Task Force was set up in the mid-1960s to target children as primary readers and to publish books for the edification and entertainment of the child may have a close link with the Declaration to function as the guiding principle.

Such a demand to cater to children's needs is further affirmed by Liang Lin, one of the chief editors of the special volume. At the end of the preface to this book, he writes,

> We print the entire contents of the official Chinese version of the Declaration of the Rights of the Child from the United Nations in the opening pages of the book, because the principles of the Declaration of the Rights of the Child are the **spiritual guiding principles** for the workers of children's reading material.[16]

Lin identifies those who work in the field of children's literature as "workers of children's reading material" (*ertong duwu gongzuozhe*) and his remarks clearly demonstrate the ethos of the time and the upsurge of concern for the child, which was compelled more by a global initiative than a local one. The publication of the ten principles of the Declaration of the Rights of the Child in the special edition is thus not just a common tribute to the vision of the United Nations, but a symbolic and significant gesture of ratification—not only of the rights (and "the right") of children, but also of a consent to and consolidation of the "guiding principle" for children's literature professionals and other associates to abide by.

As can be expected, it is Kung-Fu Chang, the head of *Xiaoxuesheng zazhishe* (Elementary Student Magazine Publisher), who specifies *tongxin* (child heart) as the very essence of the undertaking of children's literature business. In the dedication to *Ertong duwu yanjiu diyiji* (Studies on Children's Reading Materials Vol. I), he passionately asserts that "all who work in the field of children's literature possess a pure and kind child-heart".[17] *Tongxin* or child heart, in Chang's remark, is ideologically deemed a prerequisite for any individual dedicated to working for children. Although Chang does not give a full account of what comprises *tongxin*, he specifically points out that "there is eternal childhood" in the mind of those who work for children. Such a discourse of "eternal childhood" is reminiscent of the Romantic idealisation of the child.[18] To Chang, the "eternal childhood" is "the true *deliufu* (the 6th blessing) in the human world".[19] It is generally understood that *tongxin* is often referred to as a token of "the good of human nature" in contrast to the darkness and coldness of social realities.[20] It is thus often considered "therapeutic and comforting"[21] and a quality, if not a mandate, best suiting those who crave to work for young people.

Notably, such a child-based notion was concomitantly supported and elaborated upon by childhood education specialists. Hsueh-Men Chang, a senior and highly respected forerunner of early childhood education, for instance, maintains that it is important for adults to learn from children and he especially endorses the idea of "collecting materials from children's actions (*cong ertong xingdong zhong qucai*)".[22] What is emphasised in such a child-based concept is children's living experiences and the way to help children learn from natural observation and hands-on practice. In the endorsement of child-centredness, Chang aims to challenge and alter the conventional child–adult binary relationship in which children are frequently positioned as passive and submissive while adults are the authoritative figures. With a new and special focus on the child subject, Chang proposes an alternative approach to childhood education in valuing children's autonomy and subjectivity. He believes that with careful guidance to allow children space and freedom in self-expression, the child can be an active participant in learning and writing and thus become a creative meaning-maker instead of an inert information-recipient.[23] In terms of writing for children, he argues in an article published in the special volume that "the utmost principle for adults to create or rewrite stories for children" is to see to it that what is written "fits with children's experiences and the bottom line is to match with their imaginations".[24]

Chang is not alone in prioritising the child and foregrounding children's imagination. Among those children's literature workers who endorse the idea of "child heart", Sou Tung is the most straightforward in articulation, as he compellingly argues:

> A normal child is kind by nature, guileless and pure, without any habits of envy, hatred, and arrogance, and without any bias of occupation, class, and race. It is most fitting to say that the child is like a piece of white paper.[25]

Interestingly, Sou Tung's remarks, on the one hand, resonate with the Declaration of the Rights of the Child in elaborating the idea of egalitarianism and regarding it as a child's innate character. On the other hand, the analogy between the child and "a piece of white paper" is evocative of the famous diction "*tabula rasa*" ("blank slate") proposed by the British philosopher and Enlightenment thinker, John Locke (1632–1704), in his theory to describe the natural condition of the human mind at birth. The discourse of "child heart" as such is registered with foreign or global influences, an indication of the idea that travels across time and space and takes root in the new ground in postwar Taiwan. Tung's accentuation of the child as pure and kind by nature is not an unpremeditated comment but a resolute articulation to signify "child heart" as the mandatory qualification for children's literature workers to fit in and emulate. A children's (picture) book author, he contends, "must be lively in character and intelligent in mind to possess a child heart and remain sincere".[26] His "random comment" (*xianhua* in his own wording) on *tongxin* (child heart) recorded in the special volume is thus not so much a sign of individual idiosyncrasy, but rather a manifestation of the collective unconscious, or the shared vision, of those involved in the children's literature enterprise of the early postwar era.

The most influential advocacy of *tongxin* nevertheless can be attributed to Liang Lin, one of the chief editors of the special volume, in particular, in his conviction of the employment of *qianyu* (plain or simple language).[27] To Lin, the use of plain language is the best strategy and vital to the writing of children's literature. What Lin means by plain language is not merely simple words for children but the aesthetic expressions of children's language. The primary goal of children's literature writers is therefore to foster a narrative style in ways that "use and capture the language and words that children can savour and comprehend".[28] Liang Lin, in the preface to the special volume, affirmatively argues that the fundamental requirement for being a children's literature worker is "to be aware of both 'the world of children's consciousness' (*ertong de yishi shijie*) and 'the world of children's language' (*ertong de yuyan shijie*)".[29] He further concludes that "without these two basic trainings, there is little hope for a children's literature worker to try a hand on either the design or the writing of children's reading material".[30] *Tongxin*, as well as its related discourses in its valorisation of the child and resort to an understanding of children's experiences, has since become a prevailing concept and functions as the guiding principle to mould, direct, confine, and define what counts for children's literature. The decade of the 1960s witnessed the emergence and predominance of the discourse of *tongxin* in Taiwan, in particular in the field of children's literature. Such a concept continued to be compelling in later decades and remains influential up to the present.[31]

Jen-Mu Pan and the Textual Performative of "Child Heart"

As previously mentioned, Jen-Mu Pan is one of the pioneering children's literature authors and the editor-in-chief (1969–1982) of the Editorial Task Force. Like the female pioneers who paved the way for the development of children's literature in North America, she worked with dignity and earnestness as the chief editor of the Editorial Task Force to maintain a high standard for juvenile publications and help build the canons of children's literature in postwar Taiwan.[32] In a recollection of her life as an editor of juvenile literature, she ponders on the reasons for her venturing into such a career and, retrospectively, conjures up a childhood scenario where she set out at a very young age with her father on a snowy day to borrow a children's magazine from a neighbour. What she clearly remembers is not the pain of trudging in heavy snow, but the delight of holding a book in her hand and the joy of reading to her satisfaction.

In recounting this childhood experience, Pan identifies *tongxin* as the very essence that empowers and facilitates her in doing her work as a children's literature author, translator, and editor. She discloses,

> At the same time, I realised that if one would like to devote oneself to the task of writing for children, what one needs most, in addition to the

required basic writing skills, is to possess a *tongxin* (child heart). Otherwise, what one does will be totally in vain.[33]

"Child heart" (*tongxin*) in her recollection becomes the entry point, and the only solution, to the work of children's literature. In agreement with the other professionals in childhood education and children's literature discussed earlier, Pan sees *tongxin* as the bottom line, a prerequisite for those who aim to write for children. She once compellingly stated that the utmost goal for the Editorial to write and publish books for children was to give young people "outstanding children's reading material" and to offer them "remarkable things in refined and proper language in accord with their thoughts and imaginations".[34] Pan's statements resonate with what Hsueh-Men Chang, the harbinger of early childhood education, advocates in that writing for children needs to suit their imaginations. Her remarks regarding the employment of proper language can also be referred to as a (re)signification of what Liang Lin maintains for the practice of "plain language". To her, writing and publishing for children is not a trivial task, but a noble business in need of special attention and a thorough understanding of the young mind.

THE ADVENTURES OF AHEI

Although the discourse of *tongxin* is evident and may serve as the "guiding principle" for the creation of children's books, the ways Jen-Mu Pan conceptualises "child heart" in literary creations for the young are not monotonous and unsophisticated but, rather, explicitly or implicitly embedded in subversive and radical meanings. The story of *The Adventures of Ahei* published by the Editorial Task Force in 1967, for instance, is a narrative about the uncommon relationship between a little mouse and a "big cat" whom the little mouse deems not as a dreadful enemy but a special friend. Ahei, the personified child protagonist, is said to be an innocent little mouse who wishes to do a good thing in celebration of Children's Day. On his way to find a good thing to do, he sees a "big cat" lying in a tree, looking weak and vulnerable. Compassionate and kind-hearted, Ahei takes the cat home only to find that all his family and friends reject the newcomer. Though discouraged, Ahei continues to care for the cat and make friends with him and the latter gradually gains weight and size as the days go by. The rest of the mice, however, feel threatened and terrified, and so decide to drive the "big cat" out of their community.

As a group of mice get together one day to work out a plan, it happens that their habitation is suddenly destroyed by heavy rain as water rushes in and many are about to drown. At this critical moment, Ahei and the "big cat" come to their rescue. Yet, it emerges that there is no cat at all but a big balloon bearing its appearance. The narration does not ultimately reveal the true identity of the cat but leaves it as a question for young readers to figure out. What is interesting about this story is the way that the young protagonist is positioned as a non-conformist who dares to pit himself against the restrictions of social confinement and question the status quo. Courageous as he is, the title character is also compassionate and willing to render help to whoever is in need, whether they be perceived as friends or foes. Innocent as he is, the little mouse, in his actions of going against the tide of social opinion and treating the cat as a close friend rather than as the other, sufficiently communicates subversive, if not revolutionary, ideas to (young) readers. Clearly, in this narrative the "child heart" is represented as such to signify the need for both kindness and boldness in challenging social norms. The narrative in conveying its radical message may speak much to the dynamics of child subjectivity and the multifold references associated with the discourse of *tongxin*.

A Rainy Day

The concept of "child heart", not as a unitary process but as multifarious in its textual representation for the young, can also be discerned in *A Rainy Day* (1967). The story, narrated in verse form, delineates the creative power and wild imaginations of its female child protagonist, when she is left alone at home on a rainy day. Analogous to the story of Ahei, the "child heart" illustrated in this story is imbued with multiple significations. Hsiao-Lan, the protagonist, is depicted as an obedient and self-contented child at the outset of the story. When she sees that her mother does not carry an umbrella on a rainy day, she starts worrying about her; yet confined to a limited domestic space, she has little alternative but to resort to the power of her imagination in the hope to seek solutions. The story thus continues page after page with descriptions of the different "inventions" in the child's mind. In her make-believe world, substitutes for umbrellas are created and conjured one after another, including a big writing pad to cover her mother's head, a huge pair of clam shells to protect her from the rain, and an enormous umbrella to cover and keep everything dry and clean. "Child heart" as it is thus described in this text is performative, and childhood thus considered is more productive and engaging in terms of its invention and social responsibility than the mere state of a carefree time which may be viewed as tantamount to a "holiday from demands of adult life".[35]

What is most striking about the female child protagonist's active imagination is the way in which she employs a variety of modern technology. As one such example, Hsiao-Lan imagines herself to be a pilot who flies up to the sky, so that she can write "rain" (yu) in enormous letters to give a warning sign to the public. Female inventiveness, intelligence, and, most particularly, female agency are significantly emphasised at this juncture, given that the aircraft is an advanced example of modern technology, particularly in the early postwar era. The control of aeroplanes at that juncture, remained almost entirely a masculine domain; as such, piloting a plane was hardly a common vision and practice for females. The very idea of a female child characterised not only as creative, but interested in science and in new technologies, speaks much to Pan's advocacy of female autonomy and the imperative to represent an alternative female image and self-identity. The story concludes happily, as the girl's mother comes home safe and sound with a new umbrella, and the young protagonist is ultimately free from the confinement of the domestic space (a space in which, ironically, so many adult women also find themselves), and finds delight in playing with the water in the little puddles outdoors. *Tongxin*, in association with the child's capacity for imagination and a free spirit, is clearly articulated in the child protagonist's playful willpower and her redefinition of female subjectivity.

THE STEAMING INGOTS

A variation in the discourse of *tongxin* and an alternative textual representation of childhood imagination are evinced in *The Steaming Ingots* (1969), Jen-Mu Pan's first award-winning children's book. The story itself is innovative in that it is a narrative invented by the author to explain the origin of dumplings (or *yuanbau*), as well as an example to encourage young readers to write narratives from their own imagination about the origin of their favourite food. Providing a rare combination of piety and creativity, the story centres on three brothers from a poor family and how each of them tries hard, but in vain, to please their mother. Eventually, the three join together to figure out what they can do and, after several try-outs, finally succeed in making "steaming dumplings" as the duplicates of *"yuanbau"* (ingots), something their heartstricken mother longs for and which finally satisfies her. The steaming dumplings created by the three brothers, and their pious acts towards their mother, ultimately win the favour of the emperor and they are rewarded with good fortune.

Although imbued with didactic messages, Pan's story invites and encourages its young audience to use their imagination and to dare to be creative and innovative through experiments. The story helps (young) readers understand that a pious child is not necessarily submissive, but can be creative and even daring when circumstances require; as such, twinned character traits are often seen in the child characters in Pan's storybooks. On the one hand, they are docile beings who are obedient, cooperative, and possess moral goodness; on the other hand, they are creative and resourceful, and even transgress social boundaries. Above all, Pan seems to emphasise that one significant way in which a child may play the role of an active and productive member at home and in society is to utilise his or her imagination—a capacity that every child is endowed with. *Tongxin* in this regard, it is clear, is not necessarily for the conformist alone, but also invokes the spirit of experimentation.

CONCLUSION

Children's books have long been considered significant sites for the dissemination and construction, as well as the contestation, of social and cultural ideas of childhood. Children's literature scholars and critics, such as Peter Hollindale (1988), Perry Nodelman (1992), and John Stephens (1992), have pointed out that the ideological function of children's books is to shape the common understanding and development of children and childhood, and to aid in the formation of a child's self-image and identity. It is also understood that childhood images represented in literary production for young readers are often historically contested and contingent, rather than solid, stable and self-referential.[36] Given that children's books are the material sites where cultural ideas of childhood are explicitly articulated or implicitly embodied, a close examination of the pioneering works for children in this regard, in particular, Jen-Mu Pan's literary creation for the young, offers us a way of seeing how the shared and socially constructed notions of children and childhood were carried, transmitted, communicated, and performed in the narratives for young readers in the early decades of postwar Taiwan.

Although replete with discourses of conventional cultural ideas of a docile childhood in which good behaviour and piety to one's parents are valued, Pan's literary creations for young people also provide a vigorous affirmation of children's capacity for imagination and creativity, as well as their propensity for change and the possibilities that it brings. The *tongxin* (child heart) imagined in the three selected texts that Jen-Mu Pan wrote for young readers in the 1960s and which have been examined in this chapter, is not static but dynamic. In each instance, it may be seen that *tongxin* (child heart) as a textual performative can be employed as a positive and radical way to counter social regulations and to accept and embrace the other. In terms of their association with child subjectivity, the texts are not restrictive nor are they overly didactic but, rather, encourage resourcefulness, independence, and creativity.

Kimberley Reynolds, in her study of radical publishing for children in Britain in the first half of the twentieth century, has noted that a number of children's literature professionals have "sought to use writing for children and young people to create activists, visionaries, and leaders among the rising generations".[37] Likewise, Jen-Mu Pan and other pioneering children's literature workers from the era of early postwar Taiwan have consistently aimed to enlighten and entertain young minds through children's books and to promote flexibility and inventiveness. The child characters depicted in Pan's literary narratives, which are created to influence and shape her young readers, are not static and rigid but flexible and open to change. Pan's dedication to childhood imagination in the early decades of postwar Taiwan, especially in the 1960s, showed that subservience to dominant ideologies, which seek to mould children into "perfect" submissive social subjects, must be tempered by more dynamic negotiations of childhood development and potentiality in literary creations for the young.

GLOSSARY OF SELECTED CHINESE TERMS

Ahui de qiyu	阿灰的奇遇
Ching-Hsien Ma	馬景賢
deliufu	第六福
ertong duwu bianji xiazu	兒童讀物編輯小組
ertong duwu yanjiu diyiji	兒童讀物研究第一輯

Hsueh-Men Chang	張雪門
Jen-Mu Pan	潘人木
Keng Li	李畊
Kung-Fu Chang	張光甫
Liang Lin	林良
Lian-Yi biaomei	蓮漪表妹
maoqi de yuanbao	冒氣的元寶
qianyu	淺語
Shang-Yao Su	蘇尚耀
Sou Tung	童叟
tongxin	童心
Tseng-Yuan Hsu	徐曾淵
xiaoxuesheng zazhishe	小學生雜誌社
xiayutian	下雨天

NOTES

1. Another important factor is the change in the length of the compulsory education system from six to nine years, which started in 1968. With the implementation of nine-year compulsory education, children in the elementary schools are now exempt from the pressure of the Joint Entrance Examination and may thus enjoy more free time for extracurricular activities, including reading. The English translation of *ertong duwu bianji xiazu* into "the Editorial Task Force for Children's Books" should be credited to John Stephens (based on an informal interview on August 17, 2019). The rest of the translation from Chinese to English is mine, unless otherwise indicated.

2. According to Mei-Sheng Chen, a section chief in the Educational Department and also the key person in initiating the setup of the Editorial Task Force, the sum granted by the United Nations Children's Fund for its first five-year project in which the Editorial Task Force took a part reached a total of more than $US240,000. See Mei-Sheng Chen et al. *Chen Mei-Sheng xiansheng fangtan lu* (Interview with Mr. Mei-Sheng Chen) (Taipei: Academia Historica, 2000), 241.

3. Formerly it was named *Taiwan Shengzhengfu Jiaoyuting* (Department of Education of Taiwan Provincial Government).

4. For discussions of the Editorial Task Force and its implementations, see Andrea Mei-Ying Wu, "Model Children, Little Rebels, and Moral Transgressors: Virtuous Childhood Images in Taiwanese Juvenile Fiction in the 1960s", in *Ethics and Children's Literature*, ed. Claudia Mills (Surrey,

UK: Ashgate, 2014), 127; Andrea Mei-Ying Wu, "Postcoloniality, Globalization, and Transcultural Production of Children's Literature in Postwar Taiwan", in *Routledge Companion to International Children's Literature*, ed. John Stephens et al. (New York: Routledge, 2017), 125–126; and Andrea Mei-Ying Wu, "Access to Books Matters: Cultural Ambassadors and the Editorial Task Force", *The Reading Teacher* 72, no. 6 (2019): 683–684.

5. For instance, Wu-Hsien Lin, a senior Taiwanese children's literature critic, reported that the United Nations Children's Fund in Bangkok issued a letter of request in 1967, asking the Editorial Task Force to grant the copyright for permission of publication. A collection of children's books published by the Editorial Task Force were accordingly translated and distributed in Thailand, Malaysia, and the United States. See Wu-Hsien Lin, *"Zongheng yu xiaoshuo chuangzuo yu ertong wenxue zhijian: Pan Jen-mu yanjiu ziliao zongshu"* (From Fiction Writing to Children's Literature: A Survey of the Research Materials About Jen-Mu Pan), in *Taiwan xiandangdai zuojia yanjiu ziliao huibian 17: Pan Jen-Mu* (A Compilation of the Research Materials of Taiwanese Contemporary Writer 17: Jen-Mu Pan), ed. Wu-Hsien Lin and Feng-Huang Ying (Tainan: National Museum of Taiwan Literature, 2012), 100–101.

6. Wen-Chiung Hung, *Taiwan ertong wenxueshi* (A History of Taiwanese Children's Literature) (Taipei: Chuan-Wen Publisher, 1994), 26.

7. Wu-Hsien Lin, *"Zongheng yu xiaoshuo chuangzuo yu ertong wenxue zhijian"* (From Fiction Writing to Children's Literature), 100.

8. In a parallel sense, Anne Lundin deems the female professionals and pioneers who work in the field of children's literature in North America "missionaries and managers of a new narrative" and they are thus "meaning-makers in children's books", see *Constructing the Canon of Children's Literature: Beyond Library Walls and Ivory Towers* (New York: Routledge, 2004), xiv and xvii.

9. In the West, the long line of the conceptualisation of the Romantic child, according to Hugh Cunningham, was "framed by the writings of John Locke at its beginning and of the Romantic poets at its end, and with … Rousseau at centre stage" and thus in the eighteenth century it seemed to generate "a degree of sensitivity to childhood" and "some people began to see childhood … as a stage of life to be valued in its own right". See Hugh Cunningham, *Children and Childhood in Western Society Since 1500* (London: Longman, 2005), 58.

10. For a critical discussion of the cultural imagination of "the child" and its close association with the developmental idea of modernity in Republican China, see Andrew F. Jones, "The Child as History in Republican China:

A Discourse on Development", in *Developmental Fairy Tales: Evolutionary Thinking and Modern Chinese Literature* (Cambridge, MA: Harvard University Press, 2011), 103–117.

11. For a detailed discussion of the cultural imagination of the child figure in Korean (children's) literature, see for instance Dafna Zur, "Introduction: The Child and Modern Korea", in *Figuring Korean Futures: Children's Literature in Modern Korea* (Stanford: Stanford University Press, 2017), 1–24.

12. The children's periodical, *Xiaoxuesheng zazhi* (Elementary Student Magazine) established in 1951 and ceased in 1966, ran for a total of fifteen years. The special edition carried a subtitle *"jinian teji"* which means "a special edition for memory", indicating a celebration of the publication of children's reading material, while it also predicts the termination of the old form and the beginning of a new phase of children's book publication.

13. Ching-Hsien Ma, *"Sishinianlai guonei ertong kanwu fazhang gaikuang"* (The Domestic Development of Children's Periodicals in Recent Forty Years), in *Renshi ertong qikan* (Understanding Children's Periodicals), ed. Ming-Chin Chen (Taipei: The Society of Children's Literature, R. O. C., 1989), 9.

14. *"Ertong quanli xuanyan"* (Declaration of the Rights of the Child), in *Ertong duwu yanjiu diyiji* (Studies on Children's Reading Materials Vol. I), ed. Tseng-Yuan Hsu et al. (Taipei: *Xiaoxuesheng zazhishe*, 1965), no page number. English texts of "The Declaration of the Rights of the Child" (1959) are from the web source: http://www.cirp.org/library/ethics/UN-declaration/ (retrieved on July 9, 2019).

15. Ibid.

16. Liang Lin, *"'Ertong duwu yanjiu' xu—tantan zhebenshu de dansheng he xingzhi"* (Preface to 'Studies on Children's Reading Materials'—On the Birth and Nature of This Book), in *Ertong duwu yanjiu diyiji* (Studies on Children's Reading Materials Vol. I), ed. Tseng-Yuan Hsu et al. (Taipei: *Xiaoxuesheng zazhishe*, 1965), 10. The emphasis in bold typeface is mine.

17. Kung-Fu Chang, *"Xianci"* (Dedication), in *Ertong duwu yanjiu diyiji* (Studies on Children's Reading Materials Vol. I), ed. Tseng-Yuan Hsu et al. (Taipei: *Xiaoxuesheng zazhishe*, 1965), 1.

18. David Rudd, *Reading the Child in Children's Literature: An Heretical Approach* (New York: Palgrave Macmillan, 2013), 8.

19. Kung-Fu Chang, *"Xianci"* (Dedication), 1.

20. Quangen Wang, *Xiandai Zhongguo Ertong Wenxue Zhuchao* (The Mainstream of Modern Chinese Children's Literature) (Chongqing: Chongqing Publisher, 2004), 314.

21. Ibid.

22. Hsueh-Men Chang, *"Wei ertong duwu kailu"* (Make Ways for Children's Reading Materials), in *Ertong duwu yanjiu diyiji* (Studies on Children's

Reading Materials Vol. I), ed. Tseng-Yuan Hsu et al. (Taipei: *Xiaoxuesheng zazhishe*, 1965), 65–66.

23. Ibid., 68.
24. Ibid., 71.
25. Sou Tung, "*Tan ertong tuhua gushi—wo dui zhege zhuanye gongzuo de renshi*" (On Children's Picture Stories—My Understandings About This Professional Job), in *Ertong duwu yanjiu diyiji* (Studies on Children's Reading Materials Vol. I), ed. Tseng-Yuan Hsu et al. (Taipei: *Xiaoxuesheng zazhishe*, 1965), 255.
26. Ibid., 253.
27. Liang Lin, *Qianyu de yishu* (The Art of Plain Language) (Taipei: Mandarin Daily News, [1976] 2011), 40.
28. Liang Lin, "*Lun ertong wenxue de yishu jiazhi* (On the Aesthetic Values of Children's Literature)", in *Ertong duwu yanjiu diyiji* (Studies on Children's Reading Materials Vol. I), ed. Tseng-Yuan Hsu et al. (Taipei: *Xiaoxuesheng zazhishe*, 1965), 102. See also, Andrea Mei-Ying Wu, "Postcoloniality", 128.
29. Liang Lin, "'*Ertong duwu yanjiu*' *xu—tantan zhebenshu de dansheng he xingzhi*" (Preface to 'Studies on Children's Reading Materials'—On the Birth and Nature of This Book), 6.
30. Ibid.
31. For instance, a conference held by The Society of Children's Literature (R. O. C.) on a group of senior Taiwanese children's literature authors took place in 2013 and the conference theme was specifically coined as "*tongxin shijie*" (the world of child heart).
32. For a comprehensive discussion, see Andrea Mei-Ying Wu, "Transculturality, Canonization, and the Production of Children's Literature in Postwar Taiwan—Jen-mu Pan, Hai-yin Lin, and the Editorial Task Force for Children's Books", *Journal of Taiwan Literary Studies* 28 (2019): 116–128.
33. Jen-Mu Pan, "*xiaxue de shiqi nian*" (The Seventeen Years of Snowy Days) (Taipei: *Minsheng* Newspaper, [1989] 1999), 258.
34. Jen-Mu Pan, "*Women yaoyou haode ertong wenxue duwu*" (We Need to Have Good Children's Literature Reading Material), in *Ertong duwu yanjiu diyiji* (Studies on Children's Reading Materials Vol. I), ed. Tseng-Yuan Hsu et al. (Taipei: *Xiaoxuesheng zazhishe*, 1965), 130.
35. Marah Gubar. "Innocence", *Keywords for Children's Literature*, ed. Philip Nel and Lissa Paul (New York: New York University Press), 123.
36. Steven Mints, *Huck's Raft: A History of American Childhood* (Cambridge, MA: Harvard University Press, 2004), viii.
37. Kimberley Reynolds, *Left Out: The Forgotten Tradition of Radical Publishing for Children in Britain 1910–1949* (Oxford, UK: Oxford University Press, 2016), 1.

REFERENCES

"*Ertong quanli xuanyan*" (Declaration of the Rights of the Child). 1965. In *Ertong duwu yanjiu diyiji* (Studies on Children's Reading Materials Vol. I), edited by Tseng-Yuan Hsu et al., n.p. Taipei: *Xiaoxuesheng zazhishe* (Elementary School Student Magazine Publisher) (in Chinese).

Chang, Hsueh-Men. 1965. "*Wei ertong duwu kailu*" (Make Ways for Children's Reading Materials). In *Ertong duwu yanjiu diyiji* (Studies on Children's Reading Materials Vol. I), edited by Tseng-Yuan Hsu et al., 65–80. Taipei: *Xiaoxuesheng zazhishe* (Elementary School Student Magazine Publisher) (in Chinese).

Chang, Kung-Fu. 1965. "*Xianci*" (Dedication). In *Ertong duwu yanjiu diyiji* (Studies on Children's Reading Materials Vol. I), edited by Tseng-Yuan Hsu et al., 1–2. Taipei: *Xiaoxuesheng zazhishe* (Elementary School Student Magazine Publisher) (in Chinese).

Chen, Mei-Sheng, et al. 2000. *Chen Mei-Sheng xiansheng fangtan lu* (Interview with Mr. Mei-Sheng Chen). Taipei: Academia Historica (in Chinese).

Cunningham, Hugh. 2005. *Children and Childhood in Western Society Since 1500*. 2nd ed. London: Longman.

Gubar, Marah. 2011. "Innocence." In *Keywords for Children's Literature*, edited by Philip Nel and Lissa Paul, 121–127. New York: New York University Press.

Hollindale, Peter. 1988. *Ideology and the Children's Book*. South Woodchester, UK: Thimble.

Hung, Wen-Chiung. 1994. *Taiwan ertong wenxueshi* (A History of Taiwanese Children's Literature). Taipei: Chuan-Wen Publisher (in Chinese).

Jones, Andrew F. 2011. *Developmental Fairy Tales: Evolutionary Thinking and Modern Chinese Literature*. Cambridge, MA: Harvard University Press.

Lin, Liang. 1965. "'*Ertong duwu yanjiu*' *xu—tantan zhebenshu de dansheng he xingzhi*" (Preface to 'Studies on Children's Reading Materials'—On the Birth and Nature of This Book). In *Ertong duwu yanjiu diyiji* (Studies on Children's Reading Materials Vol. I), edited by Tseng-Yuan Hsu et al., 3–10. Taipei: *Xiaoxuesheng zazhishe* (Elementary School Student Magazine Publisher) (in Chinese).

Lin, Liang. 1965. "*Lun ertong wenxue de yishu jiazhi*" (On the Aesthetic Values of Children's Literature). In *Ertong duwu yanjiu diyiji* (Studies on Children's Reading Materials Vol. I), edited by Tseng-Yuan Hsu et al., 99–109. Taipei: *Xiaoxuesheng zazhishe* (Elementary School Student Magazine Publisher) (in Chinese).

Lin, Liang. [1976] 2011. *Qianyu de yishu* (The Art of Plain Language). Taipei: Mandarin Daily News (in Chinese).

Lin, Wu-Hsien. 2012. "*Zongheng yu xiaoshuo chuangzuo yu ertong wenxue zhi-jian: Pan Jen-mu yanjiu ziliao zongshu*" (From Fiction Writing to Children's Literature: A Survey of the Research Materials About Jen-Mu Pan). In *Taiwan xiandangdai zuojia yanjiu ziliao huibian 17: Pan Jen-Mu* (A Compilation of the Research Materials of Taiwanese Contemporary Writer 17: Jen-Mu Pan), edited by Wu-Hsien Lin and Feng-Huang Ying, 91–106. Tainan: National Museum of Taiwan Literature (in Chinese).

Lundin, Anne. 2004. *Constructing the Canon of Children's Literature: Beyond Library Walls and Ivory Towers*. New York: Routledge.

Ma, Ching-Hsien. 1989. "*Sishinianlai guonei ertong kanwu fazhang gaikuang*" (The Domestic Development of Children's Periodicals in Recent Forty Years). In *Renshi ertong qikan* (Understanding Children's Periodicals), edited by Ming-Chin Chen, 8–13. Taipei: The Society of Children's Literature, R. O. C. (in Chinese).

Mints, Steven. 2004. *Huck's Raft: A History of American Childhood*. Cambridge, MA: Harvard University Press.

Nodelman, Perry. 1992. *The Pleasures of Children's Literature*. New York: Longman.

Pan, Jen-Mu. 1967. *Ahui de qiyu* (The Adventures of Ahei). Taichung, Taiwan: Department of Education of Taiwan Provincial Government (in Chinese).

Pan, Jen-Mu. [1952] 2001. *Lian-Yi biaomei* (Cousin Lian-Yi). Taipei: *Erya* Publisher (in Chinese).

Pan, Jen-Mu. 1968. *Maoqi de yuanbao* (The Steaming Ingots). Taichung, Taiwan: Department of Education of Taiwan Provincial Government (in Chinese).

Pan, Jen-Mu. 1965. "*Women yaoyou haode ertong wenxue duwu*" (We Need to Have Good Children's Literature Reading Material). In *Ertong duwu yanjiu diyiji* (Studies on Children's Reading Materials Vol. I), edited by Tseng-Yuan Hsu et al., 127–130. Taipei: *Xiaoxuesheng zazhishe* (Elementary School Student Magazine Publisher) (in Chinese).

Pan, Jen-Mu. [1986] 1999. "*Xiaxue de shiqi nian*" (The Seventeen Years of Snowy Days). In *Shu de qidao* (A Mouse's Prayer), 249–261. Taipei: *Minsheng* Newspaper (in Chinese).

Pan, Jen-Mu. 1967. *Xiayutian* (A Rainy Day). Taichung, Taiwan: Department of Education of Taiwan Provincial Government (in Chinese).

Reynolds, Kimberley. 2016. *Left Out: The Forgotten Tradition of Radical Publishing for Children in Britain 1910–1949*. Oxford, UK: Oxford University Press.

Rudd, David. 2013. *Reading the Child in Children's Literature: An Heretical Approach*. New York: Palgrave Macmillan.

Stephens, John. 1992. *Language and Ideology in Children's Fiction*. New York: Longman.

"The Declaration of the Rights of the Child". 1959. web source: http://www.cirp.org/library/ethics/UN-declaration/ (retrieved on July 9, 2019).

Tung, Sou. 1965. "*Tan ertong tuhua gushi—wo dui zhege zhuanye gongzuo de renshi*" (On Children's Picture Stories—My Understandings About This Professional Job). In *Ertong duwu yanjiu diyiji* (Studies on Children's Reading Materials Vol. I), edited by Tseng-Yuan Hsu et al., 251–260. Taipei: Xiaoxuesheng *zazhishe* (Elementary School Student Magazine Publisher) (in Chinese).

Wang, Quangen. 2004. *Xiandai Zhongguo Ertong Wenxue Zhuchao* (The Mainstream of Modern Chinese Children's Literature). Chongqing: Chongqing Publisher (in Simplified Chinese).

Wu, Andrea Mei-Ying. 2019. "Access to Books Matters: Cultural Ambassadors and the Editorial Task Force." *The Reading Teacher* 72, no. 6: 683–688.

Wu, Andrea Mei-Ying. 2014. "Model Children, Little Rebels, and Moral Transgressors: Virtuous Childhood Images in Taiwanese Juvenile Fiction in the 1960s." In *Ethics and Children's Literature*, edited by Claudia Mills, 125–141. Surrey, UK: Ashgate.

Wu, Andrea Mei-Ying. 2017. "Postcoloniality, Globalization, and Transcultural Production of Children's Literature in Postwar Taiwan." In *Routledge Companion to International Children's Literature*, edited by John Stephens et al., 123–134. New York: Routledge.

Wu, Andrea Mei-Ying. 2019. "Transculturality, Canonization, and the Production of Children's Literature in Postwar Taiwan—Jen-mu Pan, Hai-yin Lin, and the Editorial Task Force for Children's Books." *Journal of Taiwan Literary Studies* 28: 101–138 (in Chinese).

Zur, Dafna. 2017. *Figuring Korean Futures: Children's Literature in Modern Korea*. Stanford: Stanford University Press.

CHAPTER 3

Parents and Parent–Child Relationships in Contemporary Chinese Children's Literature (1978–2014)

Xiangshu Fang and Lijun Bi

INTRODUCTION

In traditional Chinese society, parents were portrayed as having absolute authority over their children. For over 2000 years, China failed to acknowledge the rights a child has as an autonomous being, separate from her or his parents, a perspective stemming from the Confucian point of view, in which stability and happiness within society can only be achieved through *xiao* (filial piety), the principal value of Confucian morality. Such filial piety is also central to the Confucian rationale for organising social order, revolving as it does around conceptions of superior–inferior status in human relationships: children ought to obey parents, wives ought to obey husbands and subjects ought to obey their emperor. The prevalence

X. Fang (✉)
Deakin University, Burwood, VIC, Australia
e-mail: xiangshu.fang@deakin.edu.au

L. Bi
Monash University, Melbourne, VIC, Australia

© The Author(s) 2020
B. Wilson and S. P. Gabriel (eds.), *Asian Children's Literature and Film in a Global Age*, Asia-Pacific and Literature in English, https://doi.org/10.1007/978-981-15-2631-2_3

of such indoctrination in Chinese children's books can be traced to the Confucian belief that children are only able to reach their full potential as benevolent beings by imitating the proper behaviour of their elders and role models in books. Indeed, the political role of moral training in books worked effectively following the adoption of Confucianism as the state doctrine around 100 BCE, and helped to maintain the dynastic reign for about two thousand years, a status quo which lasted until Western warships and guns shattered Chinese confidence in Confucianism in the late nineteenth century (Bi et al. 2015, 34).

In an attempt to modernise China in the early twentieth century, Chinese literati began to advocate Western, child-centred education theories. These theories recognised children as independent human beings and as entitled to their own rights, as opposed to being subjected to the spiritual lethargy derived from the Confucian cult of ritualised subordination. A shift in values accompanied the advent of revolutionary beliefs, shaping modern Chinese children's literature for the first half of the twentieth century (Bi and Fang 2013, 55). The trend which followed was to represent children as deeply concerned for the well-being of their country, and self-righteously vindictive and unmerciful against internal and external opponents of the country. Notably, this reflected an important ethical shift in literary works in which the moral authority of parents gradually eroded as, in this new age, it was now children who lectured their parents on issues of national interest.

In Mao Zedong's China, after the communist victory in 1949, the interests of individuals were embraced as a component of the interests of the community as a whole. As such, the rhetoric of revolution became a dominant trait of the literature of this era, with the focus on communitarian over individual identities being its central concern. The influence of parents and family was often critiqued in terms of social class background, a criticism reflected in many children's stories produced in that period, in which children were no longer viewed as heirs to the family, but rather to the new socialist motherland and the proletarian revolutionary cause. Stories written in those years are often readily seen, in their political context, as propaganda. In the heat of the Cultural Revolution (1966–1976) according to Jung Chang, the author of *Wild Swans* and a former Red Guard, by the end of Mao's rule China had become "a moral wasteland and a land of hatred" and Mao had "left behind not only a brutalized nation, but also an ugly land with little of its past glory remaining or appreciated" (Chang and Halliday 1992, 659). Chang further observed that every child was singing: "Father is close, mother is close, but neither is as close as Chairman Mao" (339). Symbolically, children's biological parents had been replaced by the nation-father Mao Zedong, a vicarious, symbolic familial relationship which demonstrated Chinese children's new destiny as heirs to the nation.

Yet after Mao's death in 1976, a new ideological system of Neo-Confucianism gradually began to take shape, filling the vacuum left by the decline of faith in Marxism in China. Chinese moral educators argued that Confucianism was not an obstacle to China's development, as had been preached by the intellectuals of the early twentieth century and Maoist ideologues, and that it could actually be conducive to modernisation. As a consequence of this ideological shift, the role of parents as moral educators once again became significant in the programme of reform, and this has been reflected in contemporary children's books from the late 1970s onwards.

LATE 1970S AND EARLY 1980S: PARENTS AS MORAL EDUCATORS

Published in 1978, Liu Xinwu's short story "The Teacher" was the first major work of children's literature in the post-Mao era. It exposes the failure of education during Mao's Cultural Revolution as embodied in the dynamics of a secondary school classroom. The story centres around a teacher, Zhang Junshi, who is devoted to educating three fifteen-year-old students in the third year of junior high school[1] in the new era of reform, the students being representations of the generation brought up during the Cultural Revolution. The first student is a male juvenile delinquent, Song Baoqi, who has just been released from detention. The second student is the Youth League branch secretary, Xie Huimin, who is portrayed as a naïve girl: sincere, well-intentioned, but heavily influenced by the writings of the "Gang of Four" (referring to a powerful political group of ultra-leftists, including Mao's wife, who became the scapegoats for all the wrongdoings of Mao and his Cultural Revolution after his death). The third student is the Youth League branch member in charge of propaganda, Shi Hong, who represents the future and hope for China. In order to know more about his students, the teacher pays visits to each of their parents—the author thus closely linking the behaviour of children to parental guidance (or lack thereof) and influence. The juvenile delinquent Song Baoqi's father is depicted as an ordinary worker, who is addicted to playing cards. He finishes work at six, and then spends hours playing cards with his friends until very late at night. "Without any spiritual meaning in life", the author concludes, "it was no wonder that he had not educated and handled his son well" (Liu 1978, 15). Here, the author emphasises the traditional Chinese conviction of the important educational role that a father plays in his children's growth and an indictment of the absence of that guidance. According to a classical Chinese primer, *The Three Character Classic*, compiled by the Song dynasty scholar Wang Yinglin (1223–1296):

> Bringing up a son
> without educating
> is father's fault. (Wu 1991, 10)

The narrative employs words such as "ordinary" and "busy" to describe Song Baoqi's parents, so that they appear to have a "barren inner life" (Liu 1978, 15). Almost accusatorily, the author includes the observation that with "all the pampering that they give to their only child" (Liu 1978, 15), they appear to be responsible for him becoming a juvenile delinquent by spoiling as well as paying little attention to his moral upbringing.

To illustrate the point that the devotion of parents to their children's moral education itself is not enough, the author presents another pair of parents, those of the Youth League branch secretary, Xie Huimin. They are shown to be always urging Huimin "to follow Chairman Mao, listen to the broadcasts, read newspapers, be disciplined, respect teachers and study hard" yet, in mitigation, they are also depicted as simple-minded, ordinary "workers with strong proletarian feelings" and, "when the bourgeoisie and revisionists appeared in a revolutionary disguise, [such] people with simple proletarian feelings were prone to be duped" (Liu 1978, 11–12). Consequently, under this kind of moral education, the narrative clearly indicates that young people such as Xie Huimin undoubtedly become narrow-minded and confused, and that such education invariably leads to self-deception.

To contrast these previous two examples and to demonstrate the positive influential power of parental guidance, the author introduces a third pair of parents: those of the Youth League branch member in charge of propaganda, Shi Hong, who grows up in a well-educated family. Her mother, a school teacher and her father, a public servant in the district committee, each has the habit of reading, as may be witnessed in the description of their study: "The books on their shelves were dog-eared, underlined and marked for future study" (Liu 1978, 22). In this family, suppertime is always followed by sitting down, reading, discussing and debating around the table. Such philosophical and intellectual discussions involve not only the works of Marx, Lenin and Mao, as may be expected in such a society, but also history, and both foreign and Chinese literature. As a result of these more eclectic influences, Shi Hong's "ability to analyse according to the principles of Marxism-Leninism-Mao Zedong Thought pleased Zhang (the teacher) very much" (Liu 1978, 23).

With Mao's death in 1976, the Cultural Revolution came to an end, and China began to "shift the emphasis of the nation's work to socialist modernization and at the same time threw overboard the slogan 'class struggle as the key link'" (Su Wenning 1983, 5). The new leader of China, Deng Xiaoping (1904–1997), in a sharp departure from Mao's policies, was fully aware of the importance of education and the power of knowledge. According to Emer O'Sullivan, in societies in a transitional phase, the educational status of children's literature is particularly high because there are "new values to be conveyed and old ones to be defended" (2005, 62). Indeed, Liu Xinwu's "The Teacher" attempts to restore the reputation of teachers and bring back the traditional conviction of the importance of parents as moral guardians. The following are the opening lines of the prominent Chinese primer *The Three Character Classic*:

> People, at the beginning,
> have good natures.
> Comparable characters become
> altered through learning.
> With no teaching
> a character drifts downwards.
> The teaching method
> values total devotion.
> Mother of Mencius
> selected residential locality. (Wu 1991, 5–8)

Confucians believe that all people are good by nature in the first instance, and it is the environment and education that either helps children maintain and further this good nature and innate moral sense, or leads them astray. For example, the first of many examples in *The Three Character Classic* is that of the mother of a Confucian sage, Mencius, whose family initially lived near a graveyard. For fun, Mencius imitated the crying of the mourning people. His mother, deciding that such an environment was not suitable for his growth, moved them to a busy town whereupon they soon found themselves near a slaughterhouse. As Mencius took a great interest in the slaughtering, his mother decided to relocate again, this time moving to a place close to the temple of Confucius, where government officials often came to pay their respects to the sage by bowing and kowtowing according to rules of propriety. Observing this, Mencius informs his mother that he will follow Confucius's suit, and his mother feels happy to have found such a good place to live. Her ability to provide positive guidance for her son became the role model for virtuous parents in China for centuries to come. Thus, "The Teacher" demonstrates traditional beliefs, in that it primarily emphasises the role of a parent in moral education and character formation through its depiction of model parents who are devoted and well-educated. It affirms the traditional conviction of the importance of knowledge.

According to Qin Wenjun, a well-known Chinese children's story writer, the trend in the 1980s for Chinese children's literature was to include tendentious passages condemning the Gang of Four's overtly didactic lectures on the need to study the "genuine Marxism-Leninism-Mao Zedong Thought", and empty calls for deep devotion to the cause of national revitalisation ("Striving for Better Literature" 2017, n.p.n.). During this period, there was a strong belief among the official apparatus that the child reader was uncritical and open to guidance and, therefore, that such literature would exert a direct influence on his or her beliefs. Thus, "patriotism" became an explicit message within the children's book market at this time and such nationalist discourse received consistent political endorsement. For instance, the poem *Mama de ai* (Mum's love), written by Liu Binjun (1982), describes the devotional relationship between mother and child. But at the end of the poem, this devotion extends itself to love of the motherland:

> In a very hot night,
> I woke up to see
> Mum fanning me,
> and herself sweating all through.
> Mum's love is like the cool breeze.
>
> One very cold rainy day,
> Mum came to pick me up from school.

The only umbrella covered me
and Mum herself was mostly in the rain.
Mum's love is like an umbrella.

Once, I was ill,
Mum took me to hospital.
Feeling my feverish forehead,
Mum's tears began to roll down her cheeks.
Mum's love is like tears.

One day, I broke a thermos,
and told Mum a lie about it.
Mum's criticism made my face blush,
and I lowered my head, daring not to look at her.
Mum's love is like the strict look on her face.

Once for homework, I had to make a sentence with "most".
I wrote, "I love Mum most."
But Mum said, "The most lovable has to be the motherland,
because she is the Mum for all of us." (cited in Fang 2003, 15–16)

Gradually, though, the problems associated with the one-child policy became more and more obvious, and many of the narratives from *Stories for 365 Nights*, first published in 1980, and followed by twenty-one editions with a total print-run of 4.3 million copies in the following eight years, address these problems. These stories are designed to guide children in what is right and what is wrong through the behaviour of the children characters in the stories, but also reveal the problems of parenting. For example, Fengfeng in the story "The First One and the Last One" is depicted as spoiled and rude, unable to perform even the simplest of tasks, yet is always the centre of attention at home. When his parents want him to do anything, they must arrange some form of competition, such as "who can get dressed first" or "who can finish lunch first". Competition does encourage Fengfeng to attempt to complete the task yet whatever he begins to do, his parents and grandparents immediately rush to help him. Sometimes, when Grandma beats him in the game of "who can finish lunch first", he forces Grandma to eat more so that he can have an extension of the time in which he may finish and then claim to be the winner (Lu 1980, 18–20). Some stories even depict lazy, inept and overly demanding children ordering their own parents about.

As such, these narratives provide clear demonstrations of the problems of improper parenting methods within only-child families.

1990S: RADICAL DEPARTURE FROM TRADITION

After the repression of the 1989 students' pro-democracy movement, in which many young people had revealed their contempt for state authority, the state resumed its role as the absolute moral authority in regulating human relationships by publishing the *New Three Character Classic* (*Xin san zi jing*) (1994). Through this text, the values of "filial piety" and "fraternal submission" were restored as the core of children's moral training and as the foundation of a new national ideal:

> A young pupil
> should show respect
> to senior generations,
> and practice etiquette.
> ....
> Filial piety and fraternal submission
> must pass on.
> Family love me
> and I love family.
> Extend this love
> to our China. (cited in Fang 2003, 21–22)

The recent Chinese adaptation of Confucianism recognises the importance of the role of filial piety, and its readoption has been employed as the base for other moral qualities. Promoted in the 1990s, Neo-Confucianism stresses that the notion of loyalty stems from the idea of filial piety, which is demonstrated in the individual's ultimate responsibility and duty to the nation. However, the fundamental difference between traditional Confucianism and Neo-Confucianism is that the former aims at achieving a tranquil and happy world of benevolence and is based on a long-term, value oriented ideology, whereas the latter contemporary form aims at strengthening the subject–sovereign relationship through regulating the child–parent relationship.

It was in this context that a small group of young authors of juvenile fiction, who had taken quite a radical turn after the crackdown on the 1989 students' pro-democracy movement, challenged conventional representations of the parent–child relationship in their works. Widely acclaimed by Chinese critics as one of the best in the genre of avant-garde juvenile fiction in the 1990s, *Zai xiyuzhong huhan* (*Cries in the Drizzle*), Yu Hua's debut novel (1993), depicts family life in rural China under Mao's rule.[2] The narrator, Sun Guanglin, is the second son of the family. Given up for adoption at the age of six, he lives with another family for over five years but at the age of twelve, returns to his biological parents after tragedy befalls his adoptive family. The same night that he returns, the family house burns down to the ground, a coincidence which makes his superstitious parents believe that he is cursed. His status as an outcast places him in a unique position to observe the relations between his family members and the village.

The description of his birth is quite revealing in regard to the relationship between his parents, his mother being shown to deliver the child all by herself, "just like a labouring female animal" (Yu 1993, n.p.n.). Immediately after the birth, she has to take food to her husband, who is toiling in the farming field: "You want to starve me to death, don't you?" he yells at her. "Sorry for being late", she has to apologise, "but I was labouring and giving birth to a child". Only then does he notice that her body looks different. She goes on to explain that, after the delivery, she had to wash the baby but not interested in any of these details, he impatiently interrupts her, asking "Is it a boy or a girl?" "A boy", she replies (Yu 1993, n.p.n.). Such narrative details reinforce Sun Guanglin's belief that the creation of his life has been the result of his father's ugly behaviour towards his mother and his brutal and animalistic sexual treatment of her.

The intricacy of the father–son relationship dominates the undercurrent of the novel, but with no explanation offered as to why the father hates his son so much, and why he is considered a degenerate and an embarrassment by the father, who decides to give him up at six years of age for adoption. Again and again, Sun Guanglin hears his father inform his neighbours that "it would be wonderful if we didn't have that son of a bitch" (Yu 1993, n.p.n.). The novel captures the vulgar and despicable life of Sun Guanglin's father, who has absolutely no qualm in concealing his selfishness, shamelessness, brutality and hypocrisy: one such example of this being his constant upbraiding of Sun Guanglin about the importance of protecting the reputation of the family, while trying to sleep with as many women in the village as possible. He even attempts to rape his daughter-in-law, Sun Guanglin's elder brother's wife. In *Cries in the Drizzle*, at least six other such father–son duos in the village are described through the eyes of the narrator and Yu Hua's novel is only one of many similar works in the early 1990s that bitterly attack the lack of moral guidance of such father figures.

The significance of such attacks has to be understood in the historical and political context of the period. As indicated previously, in 1989 the state launched a brutal crackdown on pro-democracy movements, killing hundreds, if not thousands, of young lives.[3] Almost immediately, it instigated a patriotic education campaign, in which the country of China was constantly referred to as "the motherland", and in which patriotism was described as being as natural as the "love" of a child for his or her mother. Regarded by Chinese critics as representative of the avant-garde works of the 1990s, Yu's novel does not challenge the nationalistic notion that one's country is one's mother, and indeed the image of the abused and humiliated mother in his novel may be interpreted as symbolic of the state of China at this time. Its status as a representative text lies in its loud protest against patriarchal authority—be that of the father or the Party boss—whose moral bankruptcy has become obvious.

1990s to Present: Realistic Trend

Since the 1990s, many stories for children have presented the lives of contemporary Chinese children with greater realism, depicting a life permeated with various pressures, which include the stress of the requirement for high academic achievement. One such example is Huang Beijia's novel, *I Will Be a Good Girl* (1996), a work of realism which is set in the city of Nanjing. It reflects the characteristics of the time in its critique of the heightened social pressure surrounding entrance examinations, specifically the entrance examination for junior middle school. The novel tells the story of sixth-grader Jin Ling, who is depicted as a quick-witted, kind-hearted and upright girl. The narrative centres on the preparation activities in her school for the forthcoming entrance examination, and the implications of the academic and social expectations of this first of many entrance examinations for pupils is made very clear at the beginning of the novel: a good junior middle school means a higher success rate for entering a good senior middle school, which can be the gateway to a successful university entrance, and at a good university, a successful and profitable career is better guaranteed. Before the pupils and their parents, there are four choices representative of the Chinese social and educational strata: Nanjing Foreign Languages School—recognised nation-wide as being top tier; Yucai Middle School; Number Forty-Nine

Middle School; and Xinhuajie Middle School—the least desirable school, with a reputation for teenage pregnancy.

Jin Ling's mother, Zhao Huizi, is described as particularly anxious as she assesses her daughter's academic ability, and she concludes that a place in the Foreign Languages School is unrealistic. Her decision is to target the second one on the list: Yucai, with Forty-Nine as a leeway. In her mind, if her daughter cannot even obtain a place in Forty-Nine, she must admit to being "a failure as a mother" and "unsuitable to bring up a child", and so "Jin Ling's grandparents should take her to their home" (Huang 2014/1996, 17). Zhao Huizi is depicted as shocked and upset when she hears that her old friend's son is guaranteed a place in the Foreign Languages School because his family has donated a large amount of money to the school, which has become common practice in China. Immediately, both in fiction and reality it may be seen, the façade of equality through examination grading and placement collapses. However, it should be noted that this problem is not specific to contemporary society and has been deep-rooted within Chinese society over a far longer period of time, for even in dynastic China, membership in the elite scholar-official class depended on one's educational qualifications. In theory, any poor but intelligent farmer boy could be admitted to the imperial civil service examinations and therefore had a chance to rise to the highest office in the land, but in reality, such cases were rare, because success in the examinations depended on an expensive and lengthy education. While examinations were public, education was private and costly. A clash between the protagonist's parents breaks out:

> Jin Ling's father argues: "Why must Jin Ling, or anyone else, attend the Foreign Languages School? Please have a look around and tell me how many of our top scientists, engineers, economists, statesmen, and other leaders were graduates of the Foreign Languages School."
>
> Zhao Huizi does not agree: "You are a sage, with a vision of the future, but I am just a very short-sighted common folk. You please look around. In today's society, if your child fails to get a place in a good school, parents have no face in the community, and the score of your child is the yardstick of how well you are parenting". (Huang 2014/1996, 19)

Their argument raises a question: what is the purpose of school education? In the context of the revival of Confucianism in the 1990s in China, the incentive for studying is confusing for pupils and parents: is it for the modernisation of the socialist motherland, as repeatedly declared by the state ideological apparatus, or for a place in a renowned university, a future career, or perhaps most importantly, status?

In the 1990s, many reprinted copies of the Confucian primer *The Three-Character Classic* flowed into the market of children's books. This ancient text summarises its key message in these lines:

> Learn when young
> and apply when mature.
> Serve the emperor with total devotion
> and spread kindness among the common people.
> Your fame will be widely known
> and that brings honour to your parents.
> You glorify your ancestors
> and set up of a shining example for the future generations. (Wu 1991, 85)

Here, the purpose of the hard work of study is twofold: first, to gain knowledge to act with perfect virtue (with the goal of using this knowledge later in servicing the imperial court); and second, to obtain *gongming* (scholarly honour and a high-ranking office). This combination of virtue and fame not only sets up the successful candidate as a role model for the later generations of the family, as well as for the general population at large, but also brings glory to his or her parents and ancestors, thus achieving the greatest degree of filial piety—the principal value of Confucian morality. A disciple of Confucius, Zeng Zi, divided filial piety into three levels: "the highest level of filial piety is to make all the people under heaven respect your parents; the next level is not to bring shame to them; and the lowest one is to look after them by providing physical and financial support" (Lai and Huang 1992, 202). In the Chinese language there is no shortage of expressions to describe the glory that a son can bring to the family through his assiduous work, such as *yijin huanxiang* (to return in glory), an expression usually used for high-ranking officials returning to their hometown after achieving fame through their diligent study.

In Huang Beijia's fictional school, a meeting of all sixth-graders' parents marks the commencement of the final preparation for the junior middle school entrance examination. Again, the announcement of the Foreign Languages School's high success rate of 92% of university admission makes a placement in that school an enviable prize for every parent. Meanwhile, for each class (comprising approximately fifty pupils), lists of the ten best and ten worst candidates are also announced. Somehow, quite to Zhao Huizi's relief, her daughter Jin Ling is in neither list, meaning she is somewhere in the middle—and so, there is still hope. Various evening cramming classes are set up, and Jin Ling is allowed to join an intensive training class run by Teacher Xing, who is portrayed as totally devoted to gaining her students successful scores: she uses a store room for working at night, writing mock examination papers and marking the completed ones, and in the room, she has placed a desk next to her bed to save time from travelling between school and home. Meals are brought to her by her husband a few times a week and are warmed in a small microwave.

After the parents' meeting, each class begins with a reminder of the approaching dates of the examinations. For example, the Chinese language teacher begins her class by proclaiming: "Three months and ten days to go!" The math teacher: "96 days, 16 hours and 35 minutes to go!" And the English teacher asks the question in English: "What is the significance of June 28th?" For all sixth graders, life is described as *santian yixiaokao, wutian yidakao* (a small examination every three days and a big one every five days), in addition to which there are a large amount of mock examination papers to take home for the night (Huang 2014/1996, 45–46). Their school is no longer a place to learn and to gain knowledge, but a training centre to prepare students for the entrance examinations.

Amidst all the commotion of the forthcoming examinations, the protagonist, the eleven-year-old sixth-grader Jin Ling, is depicted as reasonably outgoing, always optimistic, and quite relaxed. She is portrayed as having a rebellious personality, and fights for her right to enjoy childhood. She has a talent in literature and essay-writing but is not good at mathematics; yet despite her rebellious tendencies, she tries to be a "good girl" to please her parents. If the topic is appealing to her, she can produce amazing essays that teachers would recommend for district competitions, but she "couldn't care less" about winning prizes. Invariably, she is critical of the essay topics, pointing out how "rigid" and "pale" they are, and noting their lack of incentive to stimulate imagination. During the period leading to the examinations, she remains calm and relaxed until the evening of June 27, the night before the examinations:

> Mum tells Jin Ling it's time to go to sleep and she needs a good rest. Only then, Jin Ling shows some signs of nervousness.
> "What is the problem?" Mum asks.

"I thought I wouldn't be scared, but I now feel quite nervous."

Zhao Huizi sits down beside the bed, holding her daughter's hand, "Mum knows that you have tried your best, and it doesn't matter even if the result is not good. In three years, there is another opportunity for senior middle school entrance examinations."

"Do you think I am a good girl?"

"Yes, I always think you are a good girl."

"Don't go. Stay here, and hold my hand."

"Sure." (Huang 2014/1996, 86)

Quickly, Jin Ling falls asleep. Zhao Huizi holds her hand, thinking: In three years, she will have another round of entrance examinations for senior middle school, and in six years, she will have a university entrance examination. What will it be like then? Will it be easier or harder? Will she still need me? How can children find their position along this rocky path? The novel provides a realistic rendering of the expectations placed on children in this demanding and often rigid educational system, and critiques this system by describing such pressures and their effects on the individual and the family unit.

Another example of the trend towards realism in contemporary Chinese children's literature can be found in Zhang Xini's autobiographical novel *If I Were Helen* (2005), in which the author writes at length about her mother's experiences, intertwined with her own experience of deafness. Central to the text are the twinned themes of loneliness and isolation. The mother's loneliness is exacerbated by her husband's absence through his working long hours to earn enough for their daughter's costly medical treatment and equipment, which include imported hearing aids, computer software and books, all of this on top of their daily living expenses. Zhang Xini's mother lives in isolation in a totally strange city after the family moves to Shenzhen, a city in which no one knows of her past: she was previously a lawyer, an occupation of which she was very proud. However, for the mother all is not lost, as this new isolation is a source of relief in that it saves her from the Chinese notion of "losing face"—the sense of societal shame she endures from having a disabled daughter. Apart from her sense of loneliness, the author's mother is also overwhelmed by the constant worry of her daughter's prospects: "My mum is worried about me every minute: What will her future be like? How about her schooling, her job and her life? Oh, who will love her, like her own parents, tolerant and patient?" (Zhang 2005, 40). She almost breaks down entirely when her daughter's "irreversible deafness" is confirmed, describing it as "a thunderbolt out of a clear blue sky" to her (Zhang 2005, 45).

Yet, Zhang Xini's mother's resilience is highlighted when she takes her daughter's education into her own hands. First, she refuses to allow her daughter to go to the school for the deaf, where a statue of two hands looms over the entrance, symbolising the segregation of deaf people from society through their ability to only communicate in sign language, described by Zhang Xini as being as difficult to master as *tianshu* (illegible like celestial writing) to those not trained in it. Because of this difficulty in communication, the future of deaf people has traditionally been bleak, as they have been reduced to menial jobs requiring low communication skills, such as carpentry, painting, sewing or straw-hat making. Believing that her daughter can do better, Zhang Xini's mother enrols her in a special training centre that promises to teach Zhang Xini how to speak. This turns out to be a nightmare, as deaf children, both boys and girls, are forced to shave their heads (unexplained in the narrative) and to sit in a dimly lit room, listening to the beating of a drum to get a sense of rhythm, chanting words entirely irrelevant to their life. Soon, they discover that these so-called teachers have no teaching qualifications, let alone qualifications for special education and are employed on a temporary basis only.

As a consequence of this mistreatment, Zhang Xini's mother decides to educate Zhang Xini to speak herself, but in order to make her daughter China's Helen Keller, she too must train herself to be like Helen Keller's mentor and teacher, Anne Sullivan. Books about these two figures become her (and her daughter's) spiritual, emotional and educational support, together with volumes of books in the field of deaf education and Chinese phonetics, and these enable her to conduct five hours of lessons a day in an effort to teach her daughter how to speak. Such a task is not easy, as the tonal structure of the Chinese language presents a real challenge, yet her belief in her daughter's abilities, results in her use of every possible means to push Zhang Xini, including occasional corporal punishment. Such are the frustrations of this qualified lawyer that she even resorts to locking her deaf daughter out of the house as a punishment. Despite her sometimes unconventional and harsh methods, Zhang Xini's mother is portrayed as having devotion, determination and wisdom.

The last example of realism is a short essay written by a third-grader, Hou Ruyi, entitled "If I Were Mum" found among the anthology of works that won the 2014 Bing Xin Children's Literature Award for Primary School Composition. The essay expresses a child's genuine hope of having supportive and understanding parents in a stressful environment, as evinced below:

> Friday afternoon, the test paper of the Chinese language has been returned to us. I looked at the marks. Aya! I didn't do well. It was not a huge surprise that Mum completely lost her temper when she saw the paper that night. She ordered me to "introspect." As I was "introspecting," I began to imagine: If I were a mum and saw my child didn't do well in the test, what would I do? I would give him a hug and gently ask him "how come you made so many mistakes?" I would also tell him: "Let's have a look together at your mistakes." I would then say: "Mistakes can teach you a lot, so that in the future you can avoid them." (Hou 2014, 84)

These simple words express a child's genuine hope of having supportive and understanding parents in a stressful environment. In most realistic stories of this period, the Chinese family is typically nuclear, consisting of two parents and one child, with a grandmother occasionally included in the demographic. The traditional hegemony of the patriarchal family in Chinese society ensures that the father is still depicted in these stories as holding the decision-making power of the family, though children are rarely shown as having close paternal relationships. Mothers are invariably portrayed as protective: able to anticipate their children's every need and whim, at times suppressing their child's independent thought processes and actions, and on occasion, pedantic and bad-tempered. Grandmothers are mostly depicted as ignorant, old-fashioned and excessively pampering. A professor specialising in children's literature, Li Lifang, points out that in recent realist writing about social problems in contemporary Chinese society, some authors of children's literature specifically address the causes of Chinese children's anxiety, sorrow and depression, conditions which lead to confrontations with their schools, families and the broader society. Li argues that such literature is both a strong social indicator and a conduit for social change, and calls for authors to join forces to push for further transformation, and to help children enjoy their childhood, because children's literature is read not only by children, but also by teachers and parents (Li 2018, 397).

Contemporary Chinese parents are often motivated by the idea that their children will look after them in their old age and thus the competition to gain entrance to a good university is vigorous and ruthless, especially so for the one-child generation. As such, childhood has become a preparation phase for this future battle. Chinese parents often expect their children to become the family provider in economic terms and as a consequence the expectation to perform is intense. The pressure to memorise and regurgitate facts begins the moment a child enters primary school, although it should be noted that currently there is a call in society to reduce student workloads, expand the curriculum beyond core courses and allow universities to consider factors other than examination scores (Larmer 2014, n.p.n.). However, these calls have met resistance from many middle-class parents who fear that such reforms could open the door to corruptive practices which favour children from wealthy or influential families and jeopardise opportunities for children from families in the lower to middle socioeconomic demographics. Amidst these social currents in modern Chinese society and the crucial influence education plays, it may be seen that Chinese children's literature underscores not only moral education, but also provides some modifying and alleviating roles to a rigid and oppressive school education system, as may be evidenced from the texts analysed above. Yet, though the tension between the rigorous testing of the current system and proposals for more inclusive and considerate future methods of determining university placements remains clearly evident, ultimate solutions remain problematic. What is crucial, it is clear, is that such discussions continue to take place and for these purposes there is no doubt that contemporary Chinese children's literature provides a necessary and fertile ground for this debate.

Notes

1. Chinese secondary education (high school) consists of three years of junior high school (for ages 12–15) and three years of senior high school (for ages 16–18).
2. The analysis of Yu Hua's *Zai xiyuzhong huhan* (*Cries in the Drizzle*) here, including the translation, draws on Bi, Lijun, Xiangshu Fang and Clare Bradford, 2015, "Parent, Child and State in Chinese Children's Books" in *Papers: Explorations into Children's Literature* 23 (1): 34–52.
3. An exact number cannot be produced because of the secrecy of the Chinese government regarding details of the atrocity.

References

Bi, Lijun, and Fang, Xiangshu. 2013. "Childhoods: Childhoods in Chinese Children's Texts: Continuous Reconfiguration for Political Needs." In *(Re)imagining the World: Children's Literature's Response to Changing Times*, edited by Yan Wu, Kerry Mallan, and Roderick McGillis, 55–68. Heidelberg, Germany: Springer.

Bi, Lijun, Fang, Xiangshu, and Bradford, Clare. 2015. "Parent, Child and State in Chinese Children's Books." *Papers: Explorations into Children's Literature* 23 (1): 34–52.

Chang, Jung, and Halliday, Jon. 1992. *Wilde Swan: Three Daughters of China*. London: HarperCollins.

Fang, Xinagshu. 2003. "Neo-Confucianism in Chinese Children's Books." *Papers: Exploration into Children's Literature* 13 (2): 15–26.

Huang, Beijia. 2014/1996. *I Will Be a Good Girl*. Nanjing: Nanjing University Press.

Hou, Ruyi. 2014. "Jiaru woshi mama" (If I Were Mum). In *The Anthology of Works Wining 2014 Bing Xin Children's Literature Award for Primary School Composition*, edited by Wu Yin et al. 67–75. Hangzhou: Zhejiang shaonian ertong chubanshe.

Lai, Yanyuan, and Huang, Junlang. 1992. *Newly Translated Classic of Filial Piety in Vernacular*. Taipei: Sanmin Publishing House.

Larmer, Brook. 2014. "Inside a Chinese Test-Prep Factory." *The New York Times Magazine*, December 31, 2014. Accessed May 20, 2018. https://www.nytimes.com/2015/01/04/magazine/inside-a-chinese-test-prep-factory.html.

Li, Lifang. 2018. "Recent Trends and Themes in Realist Chinese Children's Literature." In *The Routledge Companion to International Children's Literature*, edited by John Stephens, Celia Abicalil Belmiro, Alice Curry, Li Lifang, and Yasmine S. Motawy, 391–398. Abingdon, Oxon, UK: Routledge.

Liu, Xinwu. 1978. "The Teacher." In *Prize-Winning Stories from China*, translated by Yu Fanqin; illustrated by Li Peige, 3–26. Beijing: Foreign Languages Press (Also translated as "The Class Teacher" and "Class Counselor").

Lu, Bing. 1980. *365 ye gushi* (Stories for 365 Nights). Shanghai: Shaonian ertong chubanshe.

O'Sullivan, Emer. 2005. *Comparative Children's Literature*. Translated by Anthea Bell. London and New York: Routledge.

"Striving for Better Literature." 2017, February. *Macau Closer*. Accessed May 4, 2018. http://macaucloser.com/en/magazine/striving-better-literature.

Wenning, Su (ed.). 1983. *Modernization—The Chinese Way: China Today*. Beijing: Publisher of Beijing Review.

Wu, Meng (ed.). 1991. *San zi jing, bai jia xing, qian zi wen* (The Three Character Classic, a Hundred Family Names and an Essay of a Thousand Characters). Shanghai: Guji chubanshe.

Yu, Hua. 1993. *Zai xiyuzhong huhan* (Cries in the Drizzle). Shanghai wenyi chubanshe. Accessed March 21, 2014. http://book.kanunu.org/html/2005/0716/374.html (no page number).

Zhang, Xini. 2005. *Jiaru woshi Hailun* (If I Were Helen). Beijing: Remin wenxuechubanshe.

CHAPTER 4

SOCIETY IS A FAMILY: Social Exclusion and Social Dystopia in South Korean Films

Sung-Ae Lee

The family lies at the heart of Korean ideology and social organisation. Large corporations are family owned and run; a "family first" mentality means that South Korea has the lowest participation rate in voluntary work of any OECD (Organisation for Economic Co-operation and Development) country; the rate of adoption of orphans or abandoned children is likewise extremely low, as Koreans are reluctant to admit a person into the family who is not of the bloodline. Consequently, when families collapse or lose social face the outcome is a catastrophe with deep implications both for individuals immediately affected and for the underlying conceptual metaphor SOCIETY IS A FAMILY: children may be abandoned, left in the care of relatives who do not want them or cannot adequately support them, socially ostracised and bullied, or generally impoverished materially and emotionally. Films which thematise some of these issues not only portray the plight of neglected or outcast children, but also offer these situations as a metonymy of a more extensive

S.-A. Lee (✉)
Department of International Studies, Macquarie University,
Sydney, NSW, Australia
e-mail: sung-ae.lee@mq.edu.au

© The Author(s) 2020
B. Wilson and S. P. Gabriel (eds.), *Asian Children's Literature
and Film in a Global Age*, Asia-Pacific and Literature in English,
https://doi.org/10.1007/978-981-15-2631-2_4

dystopian element in a society structured around processes of inclusion and exclusion. The biological family and the metaphor SOCIETY IS A FAMILY thus function as sites of mutual support and mutual destabilisation whereby family violence affecting the child (physical or emotional) symbolises society's violence affecting some of its citizens.

This chapter examines the significance of the SOCIETY IS A FAMILY metaphor in three films which explore different aspects of the metaphor in different modes of affective discourse. *Wandeugi* (2011, retitled *Punch* for the English-subtitled DVD) thematises exclusion by virtue of minority status: Wandeuk, the eponymous protagonist, is a rebellious and anti-social 17-year-old who has internalised his community's propensity for violence partly as a response to his socially excluded status: among other factors, he is mixed-race and from a "broken" family. He thus has few opportunities and is subjected to school-sanctioned violence. His estranged mother, whom he meets and grows to love in the course of the story, is likewise excluded: she is a Filipina, and therefore alien, married but separated, and works in a menial job even though she is highly educated. As the film unfolds, Wandeuk's development of regard for others slowly transforms him, and invites film viewers to see his new perception of the world as a model. *Wandeugi* is the most positive and hopeful of the three films because of its humorous approach to exclusion and because it is the only one to achieve closure by affirming an image of a new inclusiveness in both story and theme.

A Brand New Life (French title, *Une Vie Toute Neuve*; Korean title *Yeohaengja*, literally 'Traveller/Tourist', 2009), a South Korean-French co-production set in 1975, tells the story of Jin-Hui who at age nine is inexplicably abandoned by her father at an orphanage. No overt explanation for her abandonment is offered: the director of the orphanage expected her arrival, but an interview between the director and Jin-Hui's father takes place off-screen. When at a later time Jin-Hui is asked by a health officer if she knows why she is in the orphanage she suggests it is because she was accused of trying to harm the baby son of her father's new wife. Her father, grandmother and stepmother had all turned on her. As Gregory Mellema notes, the motivations of those who make others scapegoats and the characteristic injustice invite examination, as well as the fact that scapegoating sometimes takes place because people harbour hostile attitudes towards a particular individual. On the basis of Jin-Hui's skeletal story, viewers will infer a larger context and motivation for her abandonment that reflect social assumptions which motivate the scape-goating of Jin-Hui: a traditional family unit of conjugal couple plus their mutual child(ren) is more acceptable than an incomplete or a blended family; boys take precedence over girls in a patrilineal society; a new wife may be reluctant to take responsibility for existing children; and a motherless female child had little or no social place in Korea in 1975. The ease with which Jin-Hui is discarded, despite some hints that her father has been reluctant to implement her abandonment, suggests a casual every-dayness about the action and points to a social malaise wherein some kinds of relationship are impermanent and affection shallow. The high brick wall and steel gates that enclose the orphanage are continually repeated visual images of exclusion. Jin-Hui's exclusion is finalised when she eventually succumbs to the flow of unwanted Korean children "exported" as international adoptees. *A Brand New Life* is more open-ended than *Wandeugi*, ending at the moment Jin-Hui and her French adoptive parents first face each other at Charles de Gaulle Airport, Paris, with expressions that mingle hope with apprehension.

The third film, *A Stray Goat* (Nunbal, 2016), is much bleaker. The male protagonist, Min-Sik has in some way caused his family to lose face and they have moved to his father's hometown, where his father becomes pastor of a local church. In Min-Sik's class in his new school is Ye-Ju, who functions in the folktale role of innocent persecuted girl but more specifically as a scapegoat (in Korean, 희생양 *huisaengyang*). Ye-Ju has done nothing wrong but has been ostracised because she lives in a motherless family and her father has been suspected of the murder of a teenage girl. She is thus subjected to both physical and emotional bullying. Unexpected affection grows between Min-Sik and Ye-Ju, but it cannot overcome the community's disregard for Ye-Ju's defencelessness and vulnerability. That authoritative community members—teachers and church leaders—are guilty of sanctioning persecution points the film's central theme towards a wider social criticism of a social structure over-addicted to processes of inclusion and exclusion. Separately and together, the three films offer a sharp critique of social values in South Korea.

SCAPEGOATING AS A FORM OF EXCLUSION

A few minutes before the ending of *A Stray Goat*, Ye-Ju, traumatised by emotional and physical abuse, by rape and by abandonment by Min-Sik, her only friend, appears to have suffered a mental collapse. Leading the lost goat she has nurtured and loved, she comes to the church where

Min-Sik's father is pastor. After pausing to dirty her shoes in a muddy puddle, she enters the church during a service and walks down the central aisle towards the altar, her feet and the goat's staining the church with a muddy trail, metaphorically disclosing a stain that lies at the heart of patriarchal Christianity. Stopped and ordered to leave by a male member of the congregation, she turns back and exits, pausing only to stare silently at her rapist, the goat's original owner, who sits smugly in a rear pew. By the close of the film this man has emerged in viewer perspective as the only plausible suspect for the unsolved murder, but viewers have previously seen him giving gifts to the town's incompetent and biased police officers and understand he has bought protection. The church setting and the participants—ostracised girl, goat, pastor uttering religious clichés, authoritative male, and unrepentant criminal—highlight that the film is a realisation of a scapegoating script recounted in the Christian Bible. As a narrative form, a *script* is "a knowledge representation in terms of which an expected sequence of events is stored in the memory" (Herman 2002, 10). That is, an audience calls upon stereotypic plot structures to anticipate the unfolding story logic. The retelling of a familiar narrative prototype such as a scapegoating story will involve a choice among possible variants, and the coexistence of multiple possibilities creates a script. The closing sequences of *A Stray Goat* are more isomorphic with the "scapegoat" ritual described in *Leviticus* 8–26 than is usual in modern scapegoating mechanisms. In *Leviticus,* one goat is sacrificed while a second goat is designated the bearer of the transgressions and sins of the people and driven into the wilderness. Modern applications of the scapegoat script usually involve a situation in which power is unequally distributed and the people with the most power use scapegoating as a technique for maintaining their unfair share (Caplan, 73). Scapegoating thus serves the purpose of entrenching the power of dominant groups while denying power to other groups. The widely discussed theories of René Girard argue that scapegoating is a communal response to internal conflict and the threat of social collapse whereby a community finds common cause in laying blame upon an innocent, unprotected, marginal "other", a surrogate victim or scapegoat (Fleming, 61). The small town in which the film is set teeters on social collapse, although this situation is not recognised by the inhabitants. The economy is distressed, young people of both sexes are bored and violent, and the important cattle industry is about to be ravaged by a disease which presents symptoms of BSE (bovine spongiform encephalopathy).

The two goats of the *Leviticus* script—the sacrificial and the surrogate—continue to frame the film's closing scenes. After Ye-Ju leaves the church she sits in a bus shelter with the goat as night falls, but she lets slip the goat's lead and it suddenly runs off into the night. Greatly agitated, as the goat is the embodiment of the remnants of her subjectivity (rather than a surrogate for the community's sins), she follows the sound of its bleating into the dark (see Fig. 4.1), and as she walks away from the camera the screen fades to black. Since she makes no further appearance in the film, viewers will probably infer that the fade signifies her death (perhaps by suicide). The next day Min-Sik exacts a petty revenge on the rapist by releasing all of his goats and soon after encounters the stray. He stumbles and falls while running across the stubble of a harvested field in an attempt to catch it, and the goat disappears into the wilderness beyond

Fig. 4.1 Disappearance of Ye-Ju. *A Stray Goat*, directed by Cho Jae-Min. Myung Films, 2016

the field while Min-Sik lies in the stubble and weeps as snow begins to fall and the film ends. This is not a story of redemption but of the cruelty inflicted upon an innocent subject by a dystopian society.

EXCLUSION AND INTERSECTIONALITY

Scapegoating is a prevalent mechanism of social exclusion but is only one among many. Persons generally experience social exclusion because situations of inequality are invoked when power asymmetries occur at intersections of race, gender, age, class, ability/disability, economic status and sexuality. As Leslie McCall argues, the concept of intersectionality—"the relationships among multiple dimensions and modalities of social relations and subject formations" (1771)—has the capacity to be a central category of analysis beyond the feminist studies in which it originated. In the three films examined in this chapter, identity categories intersect to produce systemic social inequalities which in turn mutually produce states of exclusion.

The intersecting categories that are the basis for social exclusion are articulated clearly in *Wandeugi*, an adaptation of Kim Ryeo-Ryeong's best-selling Young Adult novel of the same name. Although, as Hye Seung Chung (2018, 145) documents, a consequence of adapting the novel to the film genre of family melodrama produces a narrative outcome more utopian than the novel, that doesn't necessarily negate its depiction of social exclusion. As I will argue below, more attention needs to be paid to the film's cinematic techniques than appears in Chung's content-based ideology critique. However, it does seem paradoxical that the film's handling of categories of exclusion does little to erode what Timothy Lim discerns as "the highly racialized, gendered and patriarchal character of Korean identity and society" (53). The conceptual metaphor SOCIETY IS A FAMILY impedes social change by mapping each category upon the other and assuming the form of each is more or less immutable. In his discussion of the South Korean rhetoric on multiculturalism in the early years of the twenty-first century, Lim makes the important point that it was designed to preserve "existing social attitudes and practices that exclude, marginalize, and/or oppress 'non-Koreans'", and Chung supports this view. But Lim further argues that the emergence of a public discourse "marks the beginning of a profound discursive shift within Korean society by signalling the possibility of social change". Discourse, he argues, provides a foundation for social practices and eventually for social transformation (53). A similar position is held by feminist scholars who employ deconstructive criticism as a methodology within an intersectional approach and who thereby aim to contribute to the possibility of positive social change by deconstructing the normative categories of race, class, sexuality and gender (McCall 1777). McCall asserts that, "Whether this research does in fact contribute to social change is irrelevant. The point is that many feminist researchers employ this type of analysis because of their belief in its radical potential to alter social practices—to free individuals and social groups from the normative fix of a hegemonic order and to enable a politics that is at once more complex and inclusive" (1777). Through its often affable representation of categories of exclusion *Wandeugi* seeks to make a more positive contribution to the discourse of inclusivity than is possible in *A Brand New Life* or *A Stray Goat*.

A wide range of normative categories is delineated in these three films, most explicitly in *Wandeugi*. Just after Wandeuk learns that he has a mother and his mother is a Filipina, he reflects upon how he fits a schema for a "runaway kid": he lives in poverty; he has a disabled father who is approaching old age; and he is of mixed race. Other categories of exclusion associated with him are: he is not yet an adult, he comes from a "broken" family, he performs poorly at school even though he is intelligent, he has minimal educational opportunities, and he is subjected to school-sanctioned violence. The social exclusion of Wandeuk's father, Do Jeong-Bok, stems from his disability (presumably Scheuermann's kyphosis) and his consequent employment as a clownish tap dancer in a provincial cabaret. In embodying what society does not wish to be or become, Do Jeong-Bok functions as a scapegoat in a norm-focussed society that seeks to expel disability to the periphery of consciousness. For example, when he unexpectedly visits the little restaurant where his wife works, another waitress remarks, "I didn't know there are still hunchbacks". Throughout the film, his disability thus functions as a metonym for his (and Wandeuk's) larger marginalisation, as indicated in an early scene in which Wandeuk beats up a classmate for making a jibe about it. As Abelmann and Kim observe, "In South Korea, there is considerable social prejudice against those with disabilities that are classified as in any way biological; that disability is a debit in marriage is a South Korean commonsense" (106). The failure of his contract marriage is attributed to concealment of his disability prior to his wife's arrival in South Korea and to cultural tensions over the nature of his employment and his wife's marginalisation by Koreans. Both marriage fraud and cultural tension have been a common cause of failure in foreign bride marriages in South Korea (Abelmann and Kim, 110). Wandeuk's mother is likewise socially excluded because of multiple, intersecting factors: she is a Filipina and thus an alien, a female (and thus of lower status), a "runaway foreign bride", and she performs low-paid work even though she is well educated. Her difference is marked by skin colour and facial characteristics (that is, Malay features), and her own sense of marginality is flagged by her excessive use of honorifics in her spoken Korean. Her adopted Korean name, Lee Suk-Hui, is referred to on two occasions, but her Filipina name is not mentioned, an implicit allusion to an assumption that foreign brides will assimilate to Korean culture and erase their own.

The other films have fewer markers of exclusion, although *A Stray Goat* depicts the strongest example of sustained scapegoating. As remarked earlier, the scapegoating of Jin-Hui in *A Brand New Life* can be interpreted as a means to an end: her transgression is presumably that she picked up the baby to cuddle him, but the patrifocal women of the family use her action to mask the carelessness of an unfastened safety-pin and as an excuse to dispose of an unwanted girl child. Jin-Hui's subsequent period in the orphanage is a consequence of this scapegoating but does not sustain it. Lecomte's depiction of life in the orphanage includes affection from the staff and among the girls, epitomised by a lay carer who vigorously beats rugs whenever one of the girls is adopted overseas and leaves. That her behaviour is an expression of grief and anger is humorously explicated when Jin-Hui has a violent temper tantrum and the carer takes her to beat rugs to alleviate her anxiety and stress (01:10:06). The anonymous carer's grief and rage is never explained, but viewers can infer that it is distress at the failure of both planks of the SOCIETY IS A FAMILY metaphor and hence at the situation whereby these unwanted and excluded children can only find inclusion by acquiring a new subjectivity in a distant country.

In contrast, *Wandeugi* deals with issues of exclusion in a more complex way. In an episode which has attracted scholarly attention, Wandeuk is asked during a school class about classical art to comment on an icon of Western art, Jean-François Millet's *The Gleaners*, and his attribution to its female figures of an attitude of defiance and resentment towards the dominant culture is derived from a new understanding of experiences of exclusion he has developed after meeting with his mother and thinking about her as a marginalised migrant. When asked to comment on the painting, he says:

> The woman on the far right, she's leering and saying, "What are you look-ing at?" ... They look like women sold into marriage from poor countries, so they needed to be strong in order to protect themselves. The woman on the far right, she's about to make a fist to fight the farm owner. The one on the far left pretends to be working, but she is going to throw that hay at her opponent's face. The woman in the middle is a pro, because she has a rock in her fist. It is a dirty trick, but you fight to win. And those women received good educations in their own countries. (41:30–42:49)

By deconstructing and radically shifting the central images of the painting, Wandeuk's surprising and innovative reading, which leaves the teacher astounded, introduces a discursive shift which signals the possibility of social change, as Lim expressed it, and challenges the presuppositions of the SOCIETY IS A FAMILY metaphor. I thus disagree with Hye Seung Chung's reading of Wandeuk's account of the painting as "a male charac-ter's reinterpreting female subjectivity in the masculine terms of pugilism and militancy across gender and racial lines" (149). In part Chung derives this conclusion from her own characterisation of the painting as an "inter-pretation of simple, complacent working-class life" (149) rather than as a work of social critique as it has been understood since first exhibited. The teacher seems not to have contextualised the painting, and viewers would not expect the character Wandeuk to be informed about social realism in art, but his apparent reading against the text resonates with analyses such as Bradley Fratello's: "[Millet's] brutal depiction of three hunched, female paupers *segregated* from the labourers and the abundant crop in the dis-tance demonstrates his attention to, if not necessarily sympathy for, the plight of the poorest members of the community" (686, my emphasis). Fratello's analysis of the structure of the painting highlights its contrast between inclusion and exclusion: the wealth and abundance in the back-ground of the painting is "a backdrop into which the foreground figures cannot physically enter" (687). I suggest that Wandeuk's reading marks a shift in his understanding of the mechanism of social exclusion that is also a step towards his maturation.

The "meaning" of *The Gleaners* has shifted over time in relation to historical contexts. As Fratello has suggested, the painting is capable of accommodating diverse and evolving constructions of cultural and national identity (685). A similar point has been made by John Stephens, who argues that Wandeuk's re-reading of the physical posture of the three figures in *The Gleaners* is enabled because image schemas (that is, reiterated patterns of our common physical and perceptual interactions with the world) can be polysemous: we may have shared image schemas, but there are moments of ambiguity when a gesture may unfold into one schema or another, and this can be shaped by narrative context (150). Stephens's interpretation also reminds us that we extrapolate image schemas to a higher level of complexity and use schemas to organise perceptual cues into a coherent mental whole, as Wandeuk has done in his resentment-and-resistance reading of the painting.

ALLUSIONS TO FOLKTALE SCRIPTS

Although none of the three films is an extended adaptation of a folktale, each incorporates folktale scripts which bear upon the SOCIETY IS A FAMILY metaphor. As I have argued elsewhere (Lee, 284), folktales—often derived from the most familiar tales of the Grimms' collection—are commonly drawn upon in South Korean films. I argue that "a frequent conceptual blending of horror film and folktale has meant that these tales have been chosen for their dark content" (284), but they may also function in a kind of counterpoint to the film's narrative, in that once viewers recognise an evoked tale they remain aware that the traditional outcome has been refused. Early scenes in *A Brand New Life* are reminiscent of "Hansel and Gretel", although only one child—Jin-Hui—has been abandoned. In her discussion of Yim Pil-Seong's film *Hansel and Gretel* (2007), Park So-Jin details several motifs carried over from the Grimms' *Hansel and Gretel*, including poverty, abandonment, escape, unkind stepmothers, child protagonists and cooperation between children (63). These motifs also appear in *A Brand New* Life. Jin-Hui's escape, in a trenchant critique of the SOCIETY IS A FAMILY metaphor, is to consent to adoption into a family with a distant language and culture.

Orphanhood is commonly associated in fairy tales with being motherless, rather than parentless, and although a father figure still exists, as in *Hansel and Gretel*, he is "hopelessly irresponsible, cannot stop his wife from abandoning his children and even cooperates with her to complete the task" (Park, 62). In "Hansel and Gretel" the father and (step-)mother collude to abandon the children, but the father shows some reluctance and it is to the father that the children return. In *A Brand New Life* Jin-Hui's father delivers her without any explanation to a Catholic orphanage, stopping to buy a cake for her to take with her. Like the breadcrumbs in "Hansel and Gretel", the cake is eaten (by the other children) as an early reminder that the way home is lost. It is emphasised that the cake is too small for all of the children to have a slice. Jin-Hui spends her first day crouching in a patch of brambles in the orphanage yard in a recollection of Hansel and Gretel lost in the forest. The restricted and muted palette of the film here, dominated by greys and almost devoid of colour, underpins a sense of loss and hopelessness. As in many scenes in the film, the camera is positioned at Jin-Hui's eye level, so that when two of the nuns come to try to coax her to come out they are only within the frame if they stoop or crouch to her level (see Fig. 4.2). The father remains a shadowy figure. In scenes in which only Jin-Hui and her father participate he is visible as fragments: his back, his hands, part of his profile (An, 19). His full face, expressing sorrow and regret, finally appears briefly when he looks towards Jin-Hui as she is led away. She never meets him again. In conjunction with the ambivalent relationship between family and society, folktale motifs can work in fictive narratives "to debunk the myth of the ideal family by offering paradigmatic tales of cruelty and loss (wicked step-mothers, orphaned or abandoned children), but they also reinforce that myth by suggesting that an ideal, desired family exists, if only the protagonist could find it again" (McDermott, 68). The closing moments of *A Brand New Life* overturn the moment at which Jin-Hui arrived at the orphanage and sought refuge in the brambles: wearing the same clothes, she engages in another shot-reverse-shot sequence which now holds out the possibility that she has found her forever family (Fig. 4.3).

As noted earlier, the folktale script involved in *A Stray Goat* is what W. F. H. Nicolaisen (1993) termed the story of the "Innocent, Persecuted Heroine". Variants of this script, most widely known in the West as the "Cinderella" story, are found across East Asia where they have derived from a ninth-century tale about a heroine named Yexian that originated among the vanished Zhuang people who lived in what is now the border territory between China and Vietnam. Fay Beauchamp, who argues a case for an Eastern origin of the tale, suggests it might be best "to avoid Western ethnocentrism" and refer to the story as "the Yexian/Cinderella story" (449). The version in popular Korean folktale is known as "Kongjwi and Patjwi", but local adaptations of it are apt to be blended with the Western Cinderella script (see Lee, "Fairy Tale Scripts").

Fig. 4.2 Jin-Hee seeks refuge in the brambles. Low camera placement (as high-lighted by shot-reverse shot)

Nicolaisen, whose study dealt with European analogues other than the versions of Perrault or the Grimms, found that the protagonist was usually motherless and at or approaching nubile age and therefore sexually desir-able. She is ill-treated by less beautiful older sisters or stepsisters (65–66). These elements also apply to "Kongjwi and Patjwi". The three basic ques-tions Nicolaisen asks of the tale type—What form does the persecution take? Where does it happen? Who is the persecutor?—support the con-clusion that Ye-Ju's persecution is social rather than familial and thus her story has been subsumed into a scapegoat or *outcast child* script. How-ever, as is often the case with scripts, it is structurally isomorphic with the most familiar versions, in this case the Yexian/Cinderella script: there

Fig. 4.3 Hope and apprehensiveness: Jin-Hui arrives in Paris and meets her adoptive parents

are female peers (school classmates) who act as persecutors and there is a "prince" (Min-Sik), who offers a prospect of rescue. The possibility of social re-inclusion lies in her first visit to the church, on Min-Sik's invitation, rather than to a ball ("Cinderella") or a wife-seeking gathering ("Kongjwi and Patjwi"). The function of these isomorphisms serves not to produce the social inclusion found in the Yexian/Cinderella story, but to affirm Ye-Ju's social exclusion. All persecutors act with impunity, and instead of being welcomed at the church Min-Sik's pastor father moves to exclude her. The outcast child script is normally patterned upon a rite of passage structure which follows the stages of separation, liminality, and reincorporation. It is unusual for it either to leave the protagonist in the liminal stage or to preclude reconciliation, as either would seem like an affront to justice. On the other hand, a sense that in everyday Korean society power asymmetries regularly obstruct justice is a pervasive theme in film and television drama (e.g. the films *Silenced* [dir. Hwang Dong-Hyeok 2011] and *The Attorney* [dir. Yang U-Seok 2013] or the TV drama series *Innocent Defendant* [dir. Jo Yeong-Gwang and Jeong Dong-Yun 2017] and *Secret Forest* [dir. An Gil-Ho and Yu Jae-Won 2017]), so this outcome can be interpreted as confirmation of social practice dependent on exclusion of society's others.

Wandeugi differs from the other films in that the underlying scripts are not derived from folktales but from folk narratives which are variants of a family romance (not in the sense associated with Freud). This narrative is driven by a reunion of family members after a long period of separation. During the time apart, family members have disappeared and may even be presumed to have died but are reunited by chance circumstances to produce the happy ending of romance. The genre has a long history in Europe (see the summary in Bamford, 145–46) where, as Karen Bamford argues, "These romance plots [...] reflect the interests of a patriarchy in which women mattered primarily in relation to men: as daughters, wives, or mothers of males" (145). However, South Korea's history of intercultural adoption has produced a parallel genre, initially as autobiography, which centres on an international adoptee's search for her or his birth mother. One of the best-known examples is Jane Jeong Trenka's memoir *The Language of Blood* (2003), which towards its end embeds "A Fairy Tale" introduced as "completely plausible and also completely false" (204–5). This embedded story gives readers a romantic version of the genre of the transracial adoption narrative, but here narrated in a hyperbolic discourse which discloses it to be a gross distortion of actual experience. The family romance in contrast hinges on a sin committed by a parent, characteristically the sin of abandoning the child, the guilt that accompanies that sin, a reunion with the child, who forgives her/his abandonment, and the parent's eventual sense of redemption. Bamford suggests that there is a sub-genre which she calls maternal romance because "the plot pre-eminently satisfies a mother's desire for reunion with her child" (147–48).

The intersectional scope of exclusion in *Wandeugi* is accentuated by the parent–child separation motif of the family romance since mother and son between them have accumulated a range that covers most grounds employed to exclude others, especially race, gender, age, class, marital status and economic status. Although mother and son have followed different paths because of the different circumstances of their lives, they share an experience of exclusion because of such mechanisms as institutionalised discrimination or legalised marginalisation. As affection develops between them after their reunion, their common experiences underline that social positions are relational and function as a metonym for the multicultural politics that emerge at the close of the film when Wandeuk's teacher and local activist Lee Dong-Ju buys a local church and converts it into a multicultural community centre. In a fantasy, utopian outcome, all of the principal characters are assigned roles at the Centre, which enable them to share their particular knowledge and abilities with a wider community.

The resolution of the family romance and the utopian social outcome illustrate how film can employ embodied visual meaning to convey abstract conceptual thought: specifically, this process positions viewers to embrace the social attitudes towards excluded individuals and groups which are implicitly advocated within the film. As Stephens demonstrates, a particularly expressive example appears when Wandeuk and his mother are shopping together in a market (see Fig. 4.4). As they walk towards the camera (and therefore the audience's viewing position) they simultaneously turn their heads in the same direction, each wearing a half-smile, and a strong right-to-left vector is constructed by their gaze off the

Fig. 4.4 Wandeuk and his mother in the market: visual isomorphism affirms the mother–son dyad

screen. What they are looking at is not shown, but its absence serves to confirm the togetherness of their looking. Their bodies are almost completely isomorphic, a feature emphasised by the contrast with all other figures in the scene, who face other directions, intent upon their business. An audience will readily accept that this is a mother–son dyad, even as it is aware that the actors, Jasmine Lee and Yu A-In, are, respectively, Filipina and Korean. As Stephens concludes, the visual effect takes us conceptually beyond the simple notion that multiracialism renders the category of race indefinable in that it erases that category (148).

CONCLUSION

A broad script underlying the three films I have discussed follows a trajectory from abandonment through emotional struggle to eventual social reintegration, although the third stage is no more than an elusive opportunity in *A Stray Goat*. The trajectory is clearest in *A Brand New Life*, as after Jin-Hui has been abandoned at the orphanage she continually struggles against accepting her situation and cannot believe that her father will never return. She expresses frustration at a fortune-telling card game played by the other girls because she understands that it acknowledges their complete lack of agency, and she herself tries to exercise agency by presenting herself to possible adopters as undesirable. In a highly symbolic scene late in the film Jin-Hui sets out to bury herself. She scratches out a hole among the brambles, lies in it, and pulls the soil over her, including her face, but soon brushes it off and leaves. In the next scene she is considering adoptive parents. The episode is clearly symbolic, but viewers will interpret it in different ways. Is she burying her past life, her childhood, her links to her biological family, or her identity as a Korean as she prepares for international adoption? The Korean title of the film, "The Traveler", alludes to the conceptual metaphor LIFE IS A JOURNEY. Jin-Hui travels from the happy life she thought she had with her father to the orphanage, where she witnesses several fellow orphans embark on physical and symbolic journeys across the world. At the film's close she too has embarked on such a journey, to new parents, in a new land, speaking a new language—an ambiguous price for the social inclusion her motherland has denied her: SOCIETY IS [ANOTHER] FAMILY [IN ANOTHER LAND].

While each of these three films positions its audience to reflect upon the intersections of inequality which constitute socially excluded subjectivities, each is at least cautious about the possibilities of change. *A Brand New Life* is open-ended, concluding at the moment before Jin-Hui has passed the arrivals barrier to meet her new parents. *Wandeugi* offers a euphoric ending based on a multicultural community and a reunited family, which are symbolic of future social possibilities, but it does not rule out the possibility that it is a wish-fulfilling fantasy that will be hard to achieve in South Korean society. In contrast, the most recent film, *A Stray* Goat, is deeply pessimistic and presents in the scapegoating of excluded others an awareness that the entrenched power of social hierarchy and the elites it favours will preserve social inequality and continue to exclude the others it finds undesirable.

References

Abelmann, Nancy, and Hyunhee Kim. 2005. "A Failed Attempt at Transnational Marriage: Maternal Citizenship in a Globalizing South Korea." In *Cross-Border Marriages: Gender and Mobility in Transnational Asia*, edited by Nicole Constable, 101–23. Philadelphia: University of Pennsylvania Press.

An, Gil-Ho, and Jae-Won Yu, dir. *Secret Forest.* tvN, 16 Episodes, 10 June–30 July 2017.

An, Ji-Yoon. 2018. "The Forgotten Childhoods of Korea: Ounie Lecomte's *A Brand New Life* (2009) and So Yong Kim's *Treeless Mountain* (2009)." *Cross-Currents: East Asian History and Culture Review* 29: 15–30. https://cross-currents.berkeley.edu/e-journal/issue-29/an. Accessed 16/05/2019.

Bamford, Karen. 2010. "Romance, Recognition and Revenge in Marie Clements's *The Unnatural and Accidental Women.*" *Theatre Research in Canada* 31.2: 143–63.

Beauchamp, Fay. 2010. "Asian Origins of Cinderella: The Zhuang Storyteller of Guangxi." *Oral Tradition* 25.2: 447–96.

Caplan, Paula J. 1993. *Lifting a Ton of Feathers. A Woman's Guide to Surviving in the Academic World.* Toronto: University of Toronto Press.

Cho, Jae-Min, dir. 2016. *A Stray Goat.* Myung Films.

Chung, Hye Seung. 2018. "Multiculturalism as 'New Enlightenment': The Myth of Hypergamy and Social Integration in *Punch.*" *Journal of Korean Studies* 23.1: 135–52.

Fleming, Chris. 2002. "Mimesis and Violence—An Introduction to the Thought of René Girard." *Australian Religion Studies Review* 15.1: 57–72.

Fratello, Bradley. 2003. "France Embraces Millet: The Intertwined Fates of *The Gleaners* and *The Angelus.*" *Art Bulletin* 85.4: 685–701.

Herman, David. 2002. *Story Logic: Problems and Possibilities of Narrative.* Lincoln, NB: University of Nebraska Press.

Hwang, Dong-Hyeok, dir. 2011. *Silenced*. Seoul: CJ Entertainment.

Jo, Yeong-Gwang, and Dong-Yun Jeong, dir. *Innocent Defendant*. Seoul Broadcasting System, 18 episodes, 23 January–21 March 2017.

Kim, Ryeo-Ryeong. 2008. *Wandeugi*. Seoul: Changbi.

Lecomte, Ounie, dir. 2009. *A Brand New Life*. Now Film and Gloria Films.

Lee, Han, dir. 2011. *Wandeugi* (*Punch*). Ubu Film and Another Pictures.

Lee, Sung-Ae. 2014. "Fairy-Tale Scripts and Intercultural Conceptual Blending in Modern Korean Film and Television Drama." In *Grimm's Tales Around the Globe: The Dynamics of Their International Reception*, edited by Vanessa Joosen and Gillian Lathey, 275–93. Detroit: Wayne State University Press.

Lim, Timothy. 2010. "Rethinking Belongingness in Korea: Transnational Migration, 'Migrant Marriages' and the Politics of Multiculturalism." *Pacific Affairs* 83.1: 51–71.

McCall, Leslie. 2005. "The Complexity of Intersectionality." *Signs: Journal of Women in Culture and Society* 30.3: 1771–800.

McDermott, Sinead. 2006. "Kate Atkinson's Family Romance: Missing Mothers and Hidden Histories in *Behind the Scenes at the Museum*." *Critical Survey* 18.2: 67–78.

Mellema, Gregory. 2000. "Scapegoats." *Criminal Justice Ethics* 19.1: 3–9.

Nicolaisen, W[ilhelm] F. H. 1993. "Why Tell Stories About Innocent, Persecuted Heroines?" *Western Folklore* 52.1: 61–71.

Park, So-Jin. 2015. "Mothers Are Not Obtainable with Magic: The Uncanny and the Construction of Orphan Children's Desires in Yim Pil-Sung's *Hansel and Gretel*." *International Research in Children's Literature* 8.1: 61–74.

Stephens, John. 2016. "Mapping the Minority Child in Some Films from Asia." In *Cultural Minorities in Children's Literature and Verbal Culture*, edited by Xosé A. Neira Cruz and Gro-Tove Sandmark, 147–56. Santiago de Compostela: campUSculturae.

Trenka, Jane Jeong. 2003. *The Language of Blood*. Minnesota: Minnesota Historical Society Press.

Yang, U-Seok, dir. 2013. *The Attorney*. Seoul: Next Entertainment World.

Yim, Pil-Seong, dir. 2007. *Hansel and Gretel*. Seoul: Barunson Inc.

CHAPTER 5

Family Diversity in Recent Japanese Children's Literature

Yasuko Doi

INTRODUCTION

This chapter introduces and analyses representations of family diversity in recent Japanese children's literature and assesses how contemporary Japanese families are portrayed. Issues relating to modern familial structures in Japan are becoming increasingly complex and recent children's literature has both reflected and shaped these changes, as the citation below shows:

> Interpretation of the portrayal of fictional families requires some understanding of social history. It is now widely acknowledged that concepts of family are socially and culturally constructed, influenced by economic, religious and political trends.[1] (Gamble 2001)

Looking back on the history of postwar Japanese children's literature, the theme of "divorce", along with the issues of poverty, death and sex,

Y. Doi (✉)
International Institute for Children's Literature, Osaka, Japan
e-mail: doi@iiclo.or.jp

© The Author(s) 2020
B. Wilson and S. P. Gabriel (eds.), *Asian Children's Literature and Film in a Global Age*, Asia-Pacific and Literature in English,
https://doi.org/10.1007/978-981-15-2631-2_5

started appearing more frequently in the 1980s, all of which came to be called "The challenge of taboo in children's literature".[2] Before 1980, however, poverty and divorce had been written about in children's books such as *A Verse of Children's Play Song* (1960), *Snail's Contest* (1972) and *Momo and Akane* (1974). The former two works depict family collapse and the effects of poverty and conclude by highlighting the necessity of pursuing social issues and the importance of democracy. The latter portrays divorce from a mother's viewpoint. None of the texts, it should be noted, deal with individual children's thoughts and feelings.

After 1980, however, the number of nuclear families—as opposed to the traditional extended family structure—increased, as did the number of children's books featuring families expressing concern over issues of identity. Many of these texts described children's struggles and feelings set among fraught family situations.

In this millennium, though, a new tendency has appeared. Against the backdrop of an increasing number of adults finding themselves struggling to establish a sense of identity among the multiplicity of family structures and lifestyles which have emerged, some of the works published in this period have involved, for example, a child who has to live with parents who do not, or cannot, play a traditional parental role. Other narratives focus on parent/s and their children exploring how to live together, yet as independent humans. More recently, a host of complex and complicated family issues have arisen, and these include divorce and remarriage, poverty in a seemingly economically stable society, child abuse, social withdrawal, elderly care at home, and a lack of communication among family members due to both parents working and/or the spread of smartphone culture. Such issues have now started appearing in contemporary children's literature.

This chapter specifically deals with the representation of family issues in children's books published in the last five years (from 2015 to May 2019) by Japanese authors, with a special focus on the work of Joko Iwase. Iwase remains of particular interest because she has been writing about families since her debut, *Morning Is Gradually Coming to Be Seen* (1977) and continually finds new themes related to these familial and societal issues, and ways of writing about them.

The Present Situation of Families in Japan

From surveys conducted by the Ministry of Health, Labour and Welfare, three distinctive changes regarding families in Japan can be pointed out. First of all, the number of single parents due to rising rates of divorce is increasing.[3] An overlapping theme in relation to this is child poverty,[4] which is also a growing problem, and which resulted in the government's enacting of the "Act on the Promotion of Measures to Fight Child Poverty"[5] in 2013. An exponential increase in child abuse can be found in the surveys[6] that detail the numbers of consultations about child abuse at children's welfare centres in Japan. In addition, research has revealed that half of Japanese junior high/high school students use their smartphones for longer than three hours a day,[7] which, it may be argued, has led to a breakdown in communication among families, with anecdotal evidence of some children unable to take their eyes off the screens of their smartphones even at the dining table, previously unimaginable behaviour in the traditional family structures and codes in Japanese society.

Families in Joko Iwase's Books

Joko Iwase is an author who dramatises currently emerging family issues and often writes about children who manage to survive serious family traumas. Iwase has published six books in five years, four of them concerned with family issues, as indicated by the following chart (Table 5.1).

For the purposes of this chapter, I will firstly discuss the text, *What I Did to My Brother*, in detail because it deals with child abuse in a provocative way and because it exemplifies Iwase's unique writing techniques. I will provide a series of excerpts from the text which clearly illustrate

Table 5.1 Iwase's work between 2015 and 2019

Family	Title	Year	Theme on family
◎	*What I Did to My Brother*	2015	Divorce, Child abuse, Brother
◎	*Maru's Back*	2016	Divorce, Poverty, Mother
	Piggy Back Please	2017	
◎	*The House Where Haru Lives*	2017	Divorce, Grandparents, Cousin
	My Friend, Toki	2017	
◎	*Spreading Out the Map*	2018	Divorce, Mother's death, Brother

this thematic approach. I will then analyse how families are portrayed in Iwase's other three works, as indicated on the previous chart.

What I Did to My Brother

What I Did to My Brother is a story about a twelve-year-old boy, Mario, who treats his brother violently, faces up to his actions and finally achieves a sense of reconciliation with his younger sibling. Mario lives with his mother and brother, his parents having divorced three years previously because of his father's violence towards Mario.

This work presents six new ways of describing family issues in contemporary Japanese society. First, the child (protagonist) is not only a child abuse victim, but also a perpetrator of violence, and the narrative goes on to show how the child breaks this chain of violence. Secondly, the child meets his father and asks for an apology, but his father does not admit to his actions, an all-too-familiar reaction in Japan. Thirdly, the child talks with his mother about the past. Fourthly, the child is able to view his family objectively through exposure to his friend's family. Fifthly, the child becomes aware of how his brother sees him and his father. Lastly, these incidents are seen only through Mario's eyes and the description of his environment mirrors the boy's feelings. As such, Iwase's text depicts a deeply personal series of events through which the protagonist begins to comprehend the processes of cause and effect and learns the value of empathy and responsibility.

THE CHAIN OF VIOLENCE

The first scene of violence in the narrative occurs when Mario comes home to find out that his brother, Morio, is playing with the jigsaw puzzle that Mario was given by his close friend just before they moved three years ago:

> "You touched my stuff," I said to my brother. As I said this, anger arose from the pit of my stomach.
> …
> "Then, why is my Jigsaw puzzle here?"
> "Sorry," my brother said, looking scared.
> "Do you think that saying sorry is enough?"

"I *am* sorry," my brother said with his lips quivering, tears starting to roll down his face. I caught his arm and pushed him down to the ground.

My brother fell on the jigsaw and the pieces scattered.

"You cry easily. Do you think that crying solves the problem?"

I punched his cheek when he tried to get up.

He stumbled and crouched down with his back arched, and held his head with both arms. My brother was crying silently. He did not fight back at all. He was just trying to get through it. His attitude excited me and I felt that I should hurt him more. Unless I hurt him, I felt that I could not find justice.

I hit my brother's hunched-down head and back with all my strength, thinking to myself, "I am not doing wrong, not doing wrong". Twice, three times, four times. The sound was like a heavy rock being struck.

My brother absorbed it like a stone.

Then, my mother came home. (13–17)

Told in first-person, the narration of how Mario begins to strike his brother is described in detail, together with the feelings it provokes, and Mario's inability to stop himself once he has started is honestly described. Though unpleasant to read, it is clearly the author's feeling that neither Mario, nor the readers, should look away if they wish to ultimately understand his father's abuse of him and the chain of violence it engenders.

After this scene, Mario remembers the many times he was on the receiving end of his father's abuse; when he failed in a softball game (33, 34), when he was locked in a closet (45), his failure at a sport festival (59), his father's cruel words towards him for a low mark in exams (75), when his father forced him to go to school (78), and his father's often-made comment, "You really are a piece of garbage" (88). When he remembers these incidents, he always thinks that his father was right and he was wrong, an understandable response given the paternal hierarchy prevalent in Japanese families. Yet although these memories emerge in fragments, in the latter half of the story, one moment of abuse is described in detail, symbolising a growing maturity and recognition in Mario's development as he shows that he *can* confront what happened between his father and himself, even if this is hard to face:

"Don't skive off!" said my father and pulled off my futon cover. "Get up now," he shouted and dragged me from the bed and roughly pulled off my pajamas. He held out my shirt saying, "Put it on" and ordered, "Do up the buttons". When I clung to my bed crying, my father hit me,

bellowing, "What are you doing?" "You have to go to school. Don't be such a pampered brat! Everybody goes to school!"
My father pulled me off the bed and pushed me down to the floor.
My mother tried to stop this, and he kicked her, yelling, "It's because of you, that Mario has become such a spoiled kid. He takes after you".
I was in tears and I was scared that I might be beaten again.
"Hurry up," my father pulled my arm and forced me to pick up my school bag. Then he hit me shouting, "Don't cry!" His face was full of anger.
(108–110)

In this scene, Mario's father beats him, pushes him and makes him cry, his son's tears only increasing his anger and leading to another beating. This extended act of violence, including the kicking of Mario's mother (his wife), is vividly described and it is this description which reminds readers of Mario's own violence towards his brother, while Mario himself in turn makes a causal connection between the events. Such recognition leads to conciliation, as Mario gives his brother, Morio, a jigsaw puzzle, which had been the cue for his own violent act, and they do it together. Mario reflects on the incident:

I beat my brother because he touched this without my permission. I don't think that being beaten up by me is his role in life. I scared my brother. As his older brother, I thought that was my right. My father beat me because he was my father and I did the same thing to my brother. (123)

Such realisation empowers Mario to be different from his father but, just as importantly, to confront him three years later. This recognition and understanding is further symbolised by a sequence in which Morio becomes fascinated by the jigsaw puzzle with its pictures of butterflies, and he takes Mario to a place where he often goes by himself after being beaten by his older brother. It is a place with a tree in which many butter-flies gather—symbols of beauty, but also of transformation and transcendence. Mario asks his brother about his school life. And at last says:

"I feel bad that I beat you up," I said, feeling like I was releasing everything corked up in my body.
"It was because I touched it without permission," Morio said.
"No," I said. I tried to remember my feeling at that time. It was as if a black hole were in my heart. I fell down into it. It had been there in my

heart without my even knowing it. It might still be there. I don't know if
I can break the hole.
"I shouldn't have beaten you up."
I beat him because I was weak. The black hole was proof of my weakness.
"I'm sorry." (157)

Though the story is one of recognition and responsibility, it does not
have a glib conclusion: Mario's feelings of guilt do not simply lead him to
apologise straight away. Rather, he must first comprehend that he needs to
repair the relationship with his brother and then, when he understands the
cause of the darkness in his own mind and is able to verbalise his feelings,
he may at last say sorry to his brother. Both brothers (and vicariously
the readers) feel the weight of words, reinforced as Morio "looked at me
with a dazzled expression, but he did not say anything" (157). Morio's
respect for Mario's growth is clear, yet Mario's previous actions will never
be erased. Rather, as the text shows, they must be acknowledged and
rectified for the relationship to continue and flourish. Thus, in clearly
depicting the chain of violence that affects generations, and the ways in
which this chain may be broken, Iwase places faith in the restorative and
redemptive powers of comprehension and empathy, not only in her child
protagonists, but also in her young readers.

Confronting Paternal Abuse

When Mario receives a phone call from his father, saying that he
wants to see him before he moves, Mario at first refuses, but then
reconsiders because he wants his father to acknowledge his past
actions and to apologise to him. Contrary to Mario's intention,
his father only talks about the past as a series of good memories.
"Is that why you kicked me?" Mario courageously ripostes. "Why
did you beat me up?" he adds, and "Children are not meant to
be punching bags". However, his father does not seem to remem
ber it at all and says, while taking sips from his wine, "It might have happened once or twice, but everyone knows that it is important to educate
children when they are very young. Education is the parents' responsibility". Such exchanges portray not only a lack of acknowledgement, legitimate communication and redress on the part of the paternal figure, but
also a desire to wilfully obfuscate and misremember.

Significantly in this exchange, Iwase does not choose an unrealistic or simplistic solution, such as a sudden capitulation on the part of the father or a tear-stained apology. Rather, she plunges Mario into a very tough reality, as evidenced by his thoughts following the encounter:

> I could see my father from behind as he walked towards the station. He did not look special as he merged with the crowds.
> I said to myself that it was my father, but said it without feeling. ...
> I thought that there was no connection between and my father. My father was moving further and further away. (144)

Thus, Mario achieves not only physical, but emotional, separation from his father, a significant narrative event in a Japanese social context, because it evidences that family members do not always love each other and that it is right to sever ties with a blood relation, particularly if he hides his violence behind false justification. Such texts in children's literature are exceedingly rare in the overwhelmingly hegemonic structure and *senpai-kohai* or seniority-based relationships that have traditionally dominated Japanese society and, as such, this is a unique way of portraying familial relationships in Japan.

THE POSITION OF THE MOTHER IN AN ABUSED FAMILY

When Mario beats his brother, his mother berates him saying, "I don't want anybody to do such a thing" (8). However, when Mario decides to see his father, his mother engages Mario and talks with him about these matters for the first time. Mario asks his mother, "Did we come here to escape from Dad?" to which she replies, "No" but Mario, as narrator, notes that "her smile was forced" (125). She tells Mario that she used to think that when her husband was violent to her it was because she was in the wrong and that she was the only person who could change him, yet she eventually realised, "Even though we were a couple, it was not an easy thing to change a partner's personality" (128). While revealing this to Mario, she also manages to apologise: "I should have stopped your father at any cost. I'm sorry" (129). And it is this apology that provides both catharsis and a behavioural model for Mario, releasing him from a three-year chain of violence as he apologises in turn to his brother. After this conversation, his mother more confidently says that they did not run away but, rather, the three of them started a new life together.

Communication within a family, both in the present and as a means to understand and exorcise the ills of the past, is crucial in moving forward individually and collectively. This scene shows how such a frank discussion between a mother and her son deepens their understanding of themselves and each other, but also suggests that abuse is not merely a problem for the victim and the perpetrator, but for the whole family.

THE RELATIVISATION OF THE FAMILY

Mario's friendship with his classmate, Kuroda, is mainly described in terms of their school life together but he provides an important focal point through which Mario may gain an objective view of his own family. Though Kuroda always answers his teacher with a lazy, "I don't know" and often skips school, Mario realises that the stresses and strains of Kuroda's home life are the cause of this feigned indifference. His father has divorced and remarried, so Kuroda is living with his step-mother and step-sister. As his step-mother expects him to pass an entrance examination for a private junior high school, he has to go to a cram school much against his will, yet Mario learns that Kuroda thinks that these disruptions and expectations are merely, "what children are supposed to live with" (114).

Thus, through Kuroda's family situation, Mario realises there are many things which children cannot change, but there are some things which they can. Mario asks Kuroda to go to the same public junior high school as him, one which doesn't have an entrance examination, and in proactively providing this alternative path, he learns to change the relationships in his family, which begins by giving his jigsaw puzzle to his brother.

THE BROTHER'S VIEWPOINT

When Mario asks his brother, Morio, if he remembers the house they used to live in three years ago, Morio replies, "There was a huge spider upstairs in that house, wasn't there?" Morio says that the spider was as big as a door and lived in the attic above his father's and brother's room, a clear metaphor for the way in which Morio, who is of preschool age, tries to understand his father's violence (whom he now refers to as "that man") towards his brother. Though he was not beaten by his father and they did not have a close relationship, and although the violence he witnesses scares him to the extent that he wets his bed, he nevertheless expresses sympathy for his father whom he believes, in his young mind, is still living in a house with a huge spider.

After Mario meets his father, his brother wants to know if Mario asked his father about the spider and informs him that he always felt the presence of the spider on the ground floor. When Mario responds, "My room was there where the spider was", Morio asks Mario, "So you were coping with that?" The spider, then, serves a dual purpose as a metaphor, representing the actions of the father yet also representing different perspectives—and interpretations—of those actions. As Mario realises that his father's violence had an impact not only on himself, but also on his brother, he muses that Morio was perhaps looking at his father more objectively than him because he was not beaten, and for Morio the hatred which both his father and his older brother shared was embodied in the spider. Each brother is richer for this shared understanding of differing perspectives: Mario learns to see the world through his brother's eyes and Morio recognises Mario's suffering.

THE PROTAGONIST AND THE "PATHETIC FALLACY"

In Iwase's work, the characters' thoughts are described not only through dialogue, inner monologues and actions, but also in relation to descriptions of their surroundings. *What I Did to My Brother* starts with the following descriptive passage:

> The surface of the river was so smooth and flat that the water did not seem to be flowing.
> However, if I kept my eyes on the river, I could see its slow movement.
> The sun was beginning to set. The shadow of a big tree behind me on the bank was reflected in the river. I was in its shadow. (5)

This scene indicates that despite the peaceful appearance of the surface, something, perhaps, stirs beneath it: though Mario no longer lives with his father, he remains uneasy, unable to escape the shadow of the big tree that symbolises his father's connection to, and power, over him.

In the following narrative, Mario sees a man who looks like his father and runs away to the river bank, beginning to remember the past. The world around him is described in the following excerpts:

The surface of the river face remained calm. A white heron was standing on the other side of the river bank. It stayed stock-still staring intently into the water, maybe because it was looking for a fish. (72)

When I started thinking about my father, something started to swirl and spin inside me.
The white heron on the other side of the river was still peering through the surface of the river.
I felt the pain inside me, swelling like an overripe fruit, from which a bitter juice dribbled. (76)

The white heron on the other side of the bank took off. It was flying away slowly with wings spread pointing upriver. I stood up too. (79)

These passages clearly indicate Mario's identification with the white heron, whose flight encourages him to stand up and go home, but also to acknowledge the source of his pain and his actions. Similar evocations of nature may be seen in the passage below, when Mario is taken to see the tall tree in the children's park by his brother:

I can hear a bee buzzing around. A cloud of butterflies is also circling us in the light.
In silence, we watched the butterflies, which were only gathering around the tree at this moment. (159)

The story ends as the brothers look up at the tree, the butterflies mirroring the picture on the jigsaw in the place where Morio often comes by himself to heal his mind after being beaten by Mario. It has been a secret place for Morio until now, and it is here that Mario is moved to apologise. The beauty and subtleness of the buzzing bees and fluttering butterflies represent both brothers' feelings, the butterflies providing the additional metaphor of change and renewal. The setting, in which the two boys gaze around them indicates to the reader the companionship and empathy their future holds. It is a quietly beautiful and serene conclusion to a narrative that has not shied away from the violence of its subject matter.

This work was serialised in The Osaka Edition of the *Mainichi Newspaper* in September, 2014 under the title, "A Tree of Butterflies", a title which emphasises the relationship between the jigsaw (the piecing together of one's past in order to achieve unity) and the beauty of the climax. The title was changed to *What I Did to My Brother* upon publication, and is complemented by the illustrations by Hasegawa Shuhei in both the paper and the book, which deepen our understanding of the characters' feelings and thoughts.

"Family" in Iwase's Works

Maru's Back

This is a story in which the protagonist is nine-year-old Azumi, who lives with her mother in the wake of her parents' divorce. Their poverty causes Azumi's mother to ask, "Azumi, do you think we will die together in the end?" (4), a proposition which makes Azumi feel very uneasy, as does the memory of the brother she is separated from, who is always talking about his imaginary friend, Zozo.

When Azumi is asked to take care of a cat, Maru, who belongs to the owner of a sweet shop near her house while he briefly goes back to his hometown, the time she spends with Maru makes her realise how lonely she has been. Although the story is written from Azumi's viewpoint, the language used in the work may be considered rather difficult for nine-year-old readers due to its discussion not only of poverty, but also of problematic relationships between mothers and daughters juxtaposed against more positive relationships between the child and her neighbours, both of which are very relevant topics in contemporary Japanese children's literature and society.

In this story, Azumi notes that her, "mum is not like other mothers. She's not good at getting along with other people" (65) and although the details are not very clear because the situation is seen through the eyes of a nine-year-old girl, what is clear to the reader is her mother has a number of issues with communication that may involve a level of disability—something relatively new in this genre and under-discussed in Japanese society.

The House Where Haru Lives

This work also deals with divorce, but the family to which ten-year-old Hinata, the protagonist, belongs is more complicated than those in other stories by Iwase. Hinata and her divorced mother move in with her grandparents and are then joined by her cousin Haru-kun, a thirteen-year-old boy, whose father is dead and whose mother is going to remarry.

The narrative commences with people from three different backgrounds in the first stages of living together as a family, their efforts at overt politeness (another point of close relevance to Japanese audiences) straining the atmosphere.

As mentioned previously, events within the narrative are described entirely from Hinata's viewpoint but when she discovers that Haru is riding his bike all around the town after school every day she nevertheless understands his frustration, as he explains to her:

> When I am riding a bike, I feel that my body is getting lighter: my name, the school I belong to, and the question of who is my family gradually fade away and I let the air get inside of me. That's how I feel and it is very refreshing. (46)

Hinata, and the readers, realise that Haru's bike rides provide the necessary space for introspection and self-examination, important components of personal development which must take place away from the complex social and familial dynamics occurring at home and school.

Accordingly, as Hinata follows Haru on her bike by bicycle and loses sight of him, she too begins to analyse what constitutes her own identity:

> "I am Muramoto Hinata," Hinata tells herself. "Oh no, I am Saiki Hinata now. Whatever... nobody in this town knows who I really am. I am a kid who falls down easily if an adult pushes me, as weak as that cat I had a while ago." (56)

It becomes especially clear that, though these two scenes vividly contrast the thought processes of a ten-year-old and a thirteen-year-old at different stages of personal development, Hinata's journey towards self-awareness has started. The relationship and the empathy the two children enjoy is symbolised in the narrative by a stray kitten that is brought home, and it is at this stage that, for the first time, Haru actively involves himself with the family and stands up to his grandfather, the patriarchal figure. Haru's courage ensures the support of Hinata's mother, grandmother, and Hinata herself as the grandfather relents and agrees to keep the kitten, signifying a collective decision within the extended family structure rather than one made through paternal authority, as has been traditional in Japanese society.

Yet this story favours neither gender specifically. Although, Hinata's father does not appear physically in the storyline, he talks to her on the phone and asks if he and Hinata can meet up in the summer, suggesting a balance between male and female perspectives and that a good relationship can be maintained even after one's parents divorce. Similarly, the boy Haru remains in touch with his mother. Thus, the narrative provides intertwined threads of rupture followed by balance, negotiation and conciliation that provide models for children who are separated from their parents, as is occurring more often in Japanese society.

Spreading Out the Map

Spreading Out the Map is written from the viewpoint of a thirteen-year-old girl called Suzu. As the narrative commences, the reader learns that four years ago, her parents were divorced and her mother moved in with her brother, Kei, while Suzu went to live with her father. The story starts with the death of Suzu's mother from illness.

As in *What I Did to My Brother*, this book is narrated in the first-person by Suzu, the protagonist, and relates how Suzu comes to accept the double loss of her mother—firstly through divorce and then through death—and how her family (Suzu, her father and her brother Kei) is united after being separated for four years.

When they first move away from the family home, Kei asks his father to buy a map of the town. In the latter half of the narrative, Suzu realises Kei has been tracing on the map all the places he visited in his childhood and she understands Kei's anxiety and his efforts to adapt to his new family situation while retaining a sense of his past. Kei's travels around the town on his bicycle echo Haru's actions in *The House Where Haru Lives*, as the map reflects how Suzu and Kei chart their existence in their minds.

The character of Makiko, one of their father's former high school friends, helps Suzu's family, and although not exactly a family member, she plays an important role in their lives, and in the thrust of the narrative, because the presence of someone who is neither a blood relative nor lives under the same roof problematises the Japanese readers' traditional concept of what constitutes "family". Other characters of this nature include Suzu's friend, called Tsukita, who plays a similar role to that which Kuroda in *What I Did to My Brother* did for Mario: by getting to know her friend's family Suzu comes to look at her own family more objectively.

Compared to *What I Did to My Brother*, the story of *Spreading Out the Map* is developed more according to Suzu's thoughts and consciousness, so there is no clear linear narrative, a strategy enabling the readers to follow the protagonist's thoughts as they go back and forth. Just as the description of the river plays an important symbolic role in *What I Did to My Brother*, the river in this story also is very important, as it is on the river's bank, which the father calls his hometown and runs through the middle of the town, where the whole family used to visit together. Suzu and Kei often cross the river in the story, which symbolises their psychological attempts to provide unity to their present and future through their past.

Thus, as it may be seen from the foregoing discussion, Iwase's recent works have increasingly tackled contemporary family issues in Japan and the processes whereby a child without a nuclear family may come to terms with his or her situation and adapt to it. Indeed, the author has noted the necessity of understanding the complexities of context and environment by arguing: "I think that it is important for both adults and children to strip away the veils hiding reality, one by one".[8] To recreate these perspectives from the source, as it were, her works are entirely written from a child's point of view and the thought processes are described in detail to show both the depths—and the limitations—of children's ability to comprehend their own position and context. Her narratives also clearly show that, like children, adults are far from perfect. Yet a further common thread found in her literature is that the texts do not contain conveniently happy endings, but do indicate hope in the lives of the characters. Iwase delivers the message that people are at once free and lonely, striving to find their future selves but unable to do so alone. They know that family is a place in which one may belong, but not necessarily a reliable one, and one which can only be created with the input of all its members through self-awareness and the acceptance of others.

FAMILY IN CONTEMPORARY
CHILDREN'S LITERATURE (2015–2019)

The family situations which Iwase describes, which variously include abuse, poverty, divorce, death of parent/s and non-biological families, can also be found in other contemporary Japanese children's literature. Among these are other family issues which cannot be found in Iwase's works, such as the lives of children in children's homes, and the ongoing social, mental and emotional problems caused by the Great East Japan Earthquake of 2011. I will be discussing these works organised around the issues they raise, by introducing the plot structures of a number of contemporary children's texts which reflect this range of relatively new social and familial issues in Japan.

CHILD ABUSE

Abuse takes many forms but invariably leaves a deep wound in the mind of the child. The books in Table 5.2 feature children who suffer from abuse and who overcome their suffering supported by adults who, as in a number of Iwase's works, are from outside the family. The following provides brief descriptions of significant contemporary Japanese children's texts which address this topic.

Natsume, a fifteen-year-old girl, in *The Kid's Crown* is violently abused by her father. She is scared by her own thoughts of killing him and decides to go to a summer school held at a temple in the countryside. Natsume comes to understand herself through meeting other adults such as the priests at the temple, a five-year-old boy Raita, left there by his mother who is escaping from her husband's violence, and Yosuke, a sixteen-year-old boy who takes goats to the temple to help him clear weeds.

Carnation discusses a mother's neglect of her daughter. Thirteen-year-old Hiyori cannot make her mother love her, however hard she tries. Though her mother also has her share of pain from this lack of emotional commitment, it is her father's indifference to this situation which heightens the sense of Hiyori's estrangement from her mother. The idea that a mother naturally loves her child—a universal assumption, but particularly rigid in Japanese society—makes Hiyori and her mother suffer, yet this text demonstrates that the blame for Hiyori's parents' breakup must be shared equally.

Table 5.2 Children's books on child abuse

Title	Author	Publisher	Year
The Kid's Crown	Ichikawa Sakuko	Kodansha	2016
Carnation	Ito Miku	Kumon Shuppan	2016
Do You Think That You Are a Human?	Arishima Kion	Iwasaki Shoten	2018

Do You Think That You Are a Human? deals with a similar subject matter in describing the indifference of a mother towards her children. Azumi, a thirteen-year-old girl, is bullied at junior high school and thinks of committing suicide, but decides against it because of the plight of her classmate Miyu, who is being sexually abused by her father, and because of the help of her dedicated teacher. The book shows that life-affirming relationships can exist beyond the bonds of familial love.

POVERTY

Although contemporary Japan is generally viewed as a relatively affluent nation, increasing instances of poverty among families in the lower socioeconomic bracket is the result of what may be seen as a fragmented society. In such families it is often children who suffer from neglect, both in practical and psychological or emotional terms. The texts in Table 5.3 describe children who suffer from the effects of poverty and who try to survive in severe circumstances, as may be seen by the following plot descriptions.

A Library at the Top of the Hill concerns a mother and Haruna, her eleven-year-old daughter, who must live on benefits and attend a support centre for single-mothers because they can no longer make ends meet. The text reflects a situation which itself is very new in Japan and Haruna's very real and practical worries are described in detail: What if the electricity is stopped? What if they are kicked out of the support centre? Should Haruna ask her mother anything for fear of her losing her temper? Her mother cannot find a job easily, and in moving from job to job in quick succession, her health fails. However, the centre's support enables her mother to take Haruna to visit the children's nursing home where she stayed in her childhood, and to talk about Haruna's father. Haruna finds a library next to the centre, reads stories there and feels at home. She makes friends with Sakuma, a girl from another poor family. Sakuma lives

Table 5.3   Children's books on poverty

Title	Author	Publisher	Year
A Library at the Top of the Hill	Ikeda Miyuru	Saela Shobo	2016
A Shell for a 15-Year-Old Girl	Kurisawa Mari	Kodansha	2017
The Other Side of the Bank	Yasuda Kana	Kodansha	2018

with her grandmother, who runs a snack bar, but has to suddenly change school when her grandmother becomes ill.

A Shell for a 15-Year-Old Girl chronicles the dire straits faced by a single-parent family. Asami's mother is mentally ill and lives on her earnings as a prostitute. The flat they live in is streaked with garbage. Asami, who is fifteen and who would go hungry if it were not for the school meals, does not have any place to stay during the summer holiday, which exposes her to her friends' invitation to go shoplifting with them and to make some money from prostitution. Asami is fed lunch at a cram school for welfare home children during the summer holiday and meets a number of adults, such as the organiser of the school and the volunteer university students, and it is their influence that enables her to start thinking about her own life. She meets a nine-year-old boy called Kazuma, from a poor motherless family at the cram school, and wants to care for him, but Kazuma's family falls apart and he goes to live with his grandmother. These are realistic depictions of the kind of crises in contemporary society which children are powerless to solve.

The protagonists of *The Other Side of the Bank* are Kazuma, a fourteen-year-old boy from a rich family and Itsuki, his classmate who struggles with poverty. Kazuma is suffering from a confidence crisis because he has had to drop out of the high-achieving school his coercive and controlling father, who is a doctor, had made him attend. Itsuki, on the other hand, lost her father in a traffic accident and lives with her mentally ill mother and her younger sister, who is only able to go to nursery school through their being on welfare. The story starts with Kazuma getting drunk by mistakenly drinking plum wine instead of plum juice and ending up leaning somewhat precariously over the parapet of an overpass, which is where Itsuki comes to his aid. Itsuki tells Kazuma that if he helps her friend Abel with his studies, she will keep the incident to herself. Abel's father is from Nigeria, but although he is a giant of a boy, he is timid, suffers from selective mutism, and is not academically good at school. His father, now in Nigeria, used to beat Abel. This work is unique in Japan because of the depiction of the way in which Kazuma comes to see his and his family's prejudices with regard to class and race, and the way in which Itsuki, who is ashamed of living on welfare, realises that in fact it is her natural right as a citizen to receive it. Kazuma learns about the welfare system and gives advice to Itsuki, an event that suggests that even children only in their teens can find some ways to cope with their family problems. The book does not furnish us with a simplistic "happy ending" but, rather, gives us a realistic reflection of contemporary Japanese society. When Abel is insulted by a drunk, Kazuma is not able to help and regrets this deeply, yet when he meets the same man in front of the café at which he is tutoring Abel, his words are pointed and show new maturity: "I don't mind not being cool. Still I am a thousand times better than you. Do you realise how miserable you look? I don't want to be an adult like you. I despise you". Yet despite this moment of mature recognition, the only result is that the cafe is burnt down by the drunk. Life we learn, even for children—and perhaps especially for children—does not guarantee fairytale endings.

Loss of a Family Member

A considerable number of children's books dealing with the loss of a family member have been published in Japan, especially since 1980, when the taboos on such themes in children's literature finally began to erode. Although such topics in contemporary Japanese children's literature are now relatively common, the works named in Table 5.4 are books which describe the loss of a family member in unique ways.

Walking Haru concerns the central character of Yota, who lost his mother at the age of two and now lives with his father. The text relates how he spends the spring holiday just after graduating from primary school. The place they moved to the previous year is his mother's hometown and Yota walks around the town with a stray dog, which a homeless man gave him, asking him to find its original owner. Walking makes him feel the presence of his mother and also helps him to communicate with his father, whom he calls by his first name, which seldom happens in Japan. The book details Yota's complex feelings of both wanting to be protected and to be respected as a man by his father.

Table 5.4 Children's books on loss of a family member

Lost family member	Title	Author	Year
Mother	*Walking Haru*	Nishida Toshiya	2015
Mother	*Looking for That Scenery*	Nakayama Seiko	2018
Great grandmother	*Where Is Dokodoko Mountain?*	Oyanagi Chika	2018
Grandfather	*Tokujiro and I*	Hanagata Mitsuru	2019

Looking for That Scenery also examines a mother's death. Toko is fourteen and has been brought up by a single mother but has to start living with her grandparents when her mother dies. This book is unique in its description because of the way in which her mother's death and the subsequent telephone call from her father allows Toko to gradually come to see her parents' divorce in an objective light. We also see how aware Toko is of the grief suffered by her grandparents and aunt. Moreover, Toko's understanding deepens as she comes to know her mother's past, including learning from her mother's closest friend of her bullying when she was a child. Toko's grief is made more real for the reader by the book's refusal to idealise her.

The next two works are respectively about the death of a great grandmother and a grandfather. *Where Is Dokodoko Mountain?* is a fantasy work about a girl called Madoka and her farewell to her great grandmother, Hii-chan. Madoka, who is nine, and Hii-chan go to Dokodoko Mountain (literally in Japanese, "where? where? mountain") together many times, but only Madoka returns home on their final trip together. On the mountain, Hii-chan transforms into a young child and she and Madoka play with a boy who is Hii-chan's childhood friend. The fantasy hints at the ways in which the elderly sometimes revert to childhood and also visit the border between life and death, between memory and present many times until they die.

Tokujiro and I is a form of memoir by the central character, Ken, about the relationship between himself and Tokujiro, Ken's grandfather, a short-tempered man who had a tendency to lose his temper and lash out verbally at those around him, including Ken when he was between the ages of four and twelve. Ken philosophically thinks about how, in fact, his grandfather is trying to die with dignity while the number of things he cannot do is increasing. These things are not expressed directly but only through a recounting of what Tokujiro does and says. The family around Tokujiro has its own problems, divorce and truancy for example, which are also described from Ken's point of view, allowing the reader to consider ways of becoming independent from the family.

DIVERSE FAMILY MEMBERS

The number of children who are not able to physically live with their birth parents is increasing rapidly in Japan.[9] Reina, in *Reina Came to Our Island!* is one such child who arrives at a small island school. The book is narrated by ten-year-old Yua, one of Reina's classmates. When Reina comes to school for the first time, she introduces herself by saying, "I'm a foster child of Ms. Hayashi so my name is Hayashi Reina. Before that, I was in a home in Kanagawa" (16). Yua is shocked by Reina's frankness and at how quickly Reina becomes friends with a girl who has stopped coming to school. However, over time Reina's weak points start to appear. She angrily shrugs off a younger schoolmate who tries to hug her from behind, worries about Ms. Hayashi sending her back to the children's home because she eats too much, or is ill and so cannot clean the house. The book shows how Reina gradually settles into her new surroundings both at home and school, but its uniqueness lies in its description of the reciprocal and symbiotic influence Reina and the other children have on each other, and their mutual growth, rather than Reina's impoverished circumstances being the sole focus (Table 5.5).

The Master of Helpers tells the story of eleven-year-old Sawa, who rebuilds her family relationships by accepting her stepmother, Rumi-san. Sawa's parents were divorced when she was six years old. Just before the divorce, Sawa let her younger sister go outside and she fell into a ditch. After the divorce, her mother took only her sister with her, leaving Sawa to imagine that she had been abandoned by her mother because of her irresponsible behaviour. This incident makes her anxious to do anything people ask of her, earning her the nickname as the "master of helpers". However, after Sawa and Rumi-san get through the crisis of her father's illness together and Sawa understands that she is living with her father because that's what he wished, she realises that she should decide what she wants to do rather than what other people want her to do. It is rare for a story to portray a new family member who enables the protagonist to learn how to communicate with others. It also signals a new trend for

Table 5.5 Children's literature with diverse family members

	Title	Author	Year
Orphan	*Reina Came to Our Island!*	Nagasaki Natsumi	2017
Step-mother	*The Master of Helpers*	Takamori Miyuki	2017
Father	*Don't Decide for Me*	Kobayashi Miyuki	2018

Japanese children's literature in that Rumi-san, the stepmother, never tries to be Sawa's mother, but is rather a friend, mentor and role model.

The anthology, *Don't Decide for Me* includes the story "A Night before Being Brothers" by Ochiai Yuka, in which the younger of the two brothers refuses to let the older one act like a "nice older brother" when they start living together after their parents marry and "Shikka Puts the Veil on the Mirror only during the Night" by Kurokawa Yuko, which centres on a girl whose father is Brazilian and whose mother teaches samba dancing.

OTHER FAMILY FIGURES IN CHILDREN'S LITERATURE

See Table 5.6

DIVORCE

Though divorce is now quite a common theme in Japanese children's literature, the works in Table 5.6 show some new trends, particularly in the areas of children proactively working together in reclaiming their lives and personal histories. Once such example, *We Get on the Train to*, is about a girl called Riko who goes on a train journey to try to see the brother from whom she is separated. Yuta, Riko's neighbour, is a railway buff who can see that Riko is suffering and he works out a route to allow Riko to get to where her brother lives.

Another text that uses travel as a metaphor of personal discovery, *Three Wayward Friends on a School Trip*, is a story about three boys who, because they could not go on a school trip, take a trip by themselves. The destination is the flat owned by Fuchi's divorced father, whom Fuchi's two friends resent because he is something of an authoritarian and does not seem to understand Fuchi's feelings. The book suggests that finally meeting a separated parent does not always make the child happy, sharing a thematic thread with *What I Did to My Brother*.

Finally, *Tomorrow's Contrail* describes Yu, a fourteen-year-old girl who cannot find her own place at home because her mother is bed-ridden with depression. She comes to accept her situation supported by her friend, her friend's parent and the music she loves. The book explores the idea that children do not have to be responsible for their parent's illnesses and can find psychological forms of escape.

Table 5.6 Diverse family figures in children's literature

	Title	Author	Year
Divorce	We Get on the Train to	Miwa Hiroko	2016
Divorce	Three Wayward Friends on a School Trip	Ichikawa Sakuko	2018
Mother's illness	Tomorrow's Contrail	Yatsuka Sumiko	2017
Distance	I Am Reading a Book	Tanaka Hiko	2019
Distance	Girls in the Full Moon	Ando Mikie	2017
3.11	You Are on the Other Side of This River	Hamano Kyoko	2018
3.11	The Ship of the Sun	Muranaka Rie	2019

THE DISTANCE BETWEEN FAMILY MEMBERS

Family members may sometimes expect too much of each other, misunderstanding or relying on each other too heavily because they take being part of a family for granted. Tanaka Hiko is a writer whose prevailing theme has been communication, miscommunication, and the distances between family members, since the publication of his first children's book, *Moving*, in 1990. In *I Am Reading a Book*, published in 2019, Tanaka tells the story of Ruka, who keeps secrets from his parents. Yet his parents also respect Ruka's privacy, and the narrative describes the necessary development of Ruka's inner life through reading and thinking about books, as well as establishing friendships through reading. It also shows how Ruka discusses books with his parents, which deepens his understanding, underlining the importance of conversations and discussions for the health and well-being of a family.

Finally, in Ando Mikie's *Girls in the Full Moon*, we meet Mayu, whose mother, although dead, still exerts a hold on her life. Shiho, who is thirteen, gets to know Mayu and her friends, Mitsuki and Shokichi, an experience which enables them, collectively and individually, to make conscious adjustments to the emotional distance between them and their mothers.

FAMILY EXPERIENCES OF 3.11

The Great East Japan Earthquake of 2011 (3.11) caused a great deal of devastation, and neither the problem of nuclear power plants nor the problem of reconstruction from the subsequent tsunami has yet been solved. Many families were suddenly forced to face death, separation and poverty but not many children's books have emerged to tackle these issues. There are exceptions, however. Rino, the protagonist of *You Are on the Other Side of This River*, experiences the earthquake in Miyagi prefecture and loses her brother. Kaito, a twelve-year-old boy, in *The Ship of the Sun*, encounters the earthquake-driven tsunami in Kesenuma in Miyagi and has to move to Nemuro in Hokkaido for his father's job. His father is a boatbuilder and the family works hard and stands together, but the ongoing financial, psychological and emotional stress that the family have endured because of the tsunami lead to his mother leaving home.

CONCLUSION

From the texts discussed, it may be seen that contemporary Japanese children's literature draws on increasingly diverse family structures and relationships that reflect the complex social backgrounds from which they emerge, and the children who, through ingenuity and adaptation, somehow survive the problems these situations often entail. These works enable young readers, many of whom may actually be going through similar situations, to gain a sense of perspective on their problems, or for those who know children in similar circumstances to have more empathy for the issues confronting them that have arisen from the changing circumstances of modern Japanese society. And while these texts draw directly from Japanese contexts, landscapes and cultural mores, what is clear is that they also reveal a universality in many of the themes, such as ways of communicating with and gaining independence from one's parents. In the future, it is likely that a greater number of books with diverse family themes will emerge, covering such relevant contemporary problems as family illness, co-dependence, social withdrawal, children raised in children's homes, and same-sex parents, as well as more books on the ongoing and widespread ramifications of the Great East Japan Earthquake. Such literature represents positive and necessary responses to the changing face of Japanese families and of its society, and more diverse methods should be explored in the way that Iwase has championed children's issues, in order not to simply depict what is happening, but to make self-discovery a part of the story, giving these young readers a deeper experience of literature and of themselves.

NOTES

1. Gamble, Nikki (2001) "Introduction: Changing Families" Tucker, Nicolas and Gamble, Nikki. *Family Fictions.* Continuum, London, p. 1.
2. "Special Issue: Collapse of Taboo" (1978) *Japanese Children's Literature* (『日本児童文学』) vol. 24, May 5, 1978.
3. "Trends in the percent distribution of households with persons aged 65 years and over by structure of household", Director-General for Statistics and Information Policy, Ministry of Health, Labour and Welfare (2018). *From Comprehensive Survey of Living Conditions, 2016, Graphical Review of Japanese Households,* p. 6.
4. "Relative frequency distribution of household members by equivalent disposable income". Same as Table 5.3.
5. http://www.shugiin.go.jp/internet/itdb_housei.nsf/html/housei/18320130626064.htm View July 14, 2019.
6. "The numbers of consultations about child abuse at children's welfare centers in 2017" (2018) https://www.mhlw.go.jp/content/11901000/000348313.pdf.
7. National Institute for Youth Education (2018) "Survey on parent-child relationship in the internet age; Japan, the U.S.A., China and Korea" https://www.niye.go.jp/kenkyu_houkoku/contents/detail/i/129/.
8. IWASE, Joko (1978) "The Real Lives of Children Condition and Children's Literature" *Science of Thought* (『思想の科学』) 300, July, 1978, p. 71.
9. Ministry of Health, Labor, and Welfare https://www.mhlw.go.jp/stf/seisakunitsuite/bunya/kodomo/kodomo_kosodate/syakaiteki_yougo/01.html View July, 2019.

REFERENCES

Miyakawa, Takeo. 1996. "Changes in Children's Literature After the 1980s", from *50 Years of Children's Literature After World War II*, edited by The Society of Japanese Children's Literature, Bunkeido, Tokyo, pp. 55–70.

Nogami, Akira. June 1999–November 2002. "The Myth of the Family" 1–8, *Onigashima Journal*, 33–40.

"Special Issue: Contemporary Families". 1984. *Japanese Children's Literature* (『日本児童文学』) vol. 30, December 12, 1984.

"Special Issue: Family in Children's Literature". 1993. *Japanese Children's Literature* (『日本児童文学』) vol. 39, November 11, 1993.

"Special Issue: Child Poverty". 2010. *Japanese Children's Literature* (『日本児童文学』) vol. 56, April 2, 2010.

‹CHILDREN'S BOOKS MENTIONED IN THIS ARTICLE›

Ando, Mikie. 2017. *Girls in the Full Moon.* (『満月の娘たち』 Mangetsu no Musumetachi), Kodansha, Tokyo.

Arishima, Kion. 2018. *Do You Think That You Are a Human?* (『それでも人のつもりかな』 Sore demo Hito no Tsumori kana), Iwasaki Shoten, Tokyo.

Gamble, Nikki. 2001. "Introduction: Changing Families" Tucker, Nicolas and Gamble, Nikki. *Family Fictions.* Continuum, London.

Hamano, Kyoko. 2018. *You Are on the Other Side of This River.* (『この川のむこうに君がいる』 Kono Kawa no Muko ni Kimi ga Iru), Rironsha, Tokyo.

Hanagata, Mitsuru. 2019. *Tokujiro and I.* (『徳次郎とボク』 Tikujiro to Boku), Rironsha, Tokyo.

Ichikawa, Sakuko. 2016. *The Kid's Crown.* (『小やぎのかんむり』 Koyagi no Kanmuri), Kodansha, Tokyo.

Ichikawa, Sakuko. 2018. *Three Wayward Friends on a School Trip.* (『よりみち3人修学旅行』 Yorimichi Sannin Shugakuryoko), Kodansha, Tokyo.

Ikeda, Miyuru. 2016. *A Library at the Top of the Hill.* (『坂の上の図書館』 Saka no Ue no Toshokan), Saela Shobo, Tokyo.

Ito, Miku. 2016. *Carnation.* (『カーネーション』), Kumon-shuppan, Tokyo.

Iwase, Joko. 1977. *Morning Is Gradually Coming to Be Seen.* (『朝はだんだん見えてくる』 Asa wa dandan Mietekuru), Rironsha, Tokyo.

Iwase, Joko. 2015. *What I Did to My Brother.* (『ぼくが弟にしたこと』 Boku ga Otouto ni Shita Koto), Rironsha, Tokyo.

Iwase, Joko. 2016. *Maru's Back.* (『マルの背中』 Maru no Senaka), Kodansha, Tokyo.

Iwase, Joko/ 2017. *The House Where Haru Lives.* (『春くんのいる家』 Haru-kun no Iru Ie), Bunkeido, Tokyo.

Iwase, Joko. 2017. *My Friend, Toki.* (『ともだちのときちゃん』 Tomodachi no Toki-chan), Froebel-kan, Tokyo.

Iwase, Joko. 2017. *Piggy Back Please.* (『ちょっとおんぶ』 Chotto Onbu), Kodansha, Tokyo.

Iwase, Joko. 2018. *Spreading Out the Map.* (『地図を広げて』 Chizu o Hirogete), Kaiseisha, Tokyo.

Kobayashi, Miyuki, et al. 2018. *Don't Decide for Me.* (『わたしを決めつけないで』 Watashi o Kimetsukenaide), Kodansha, Tokyo.

Kurisawa, Mari. 2017. *A Shell for a 15 Year Old Girl.* (『15歳、ぬけがら』 Jugosai, Nukegara), Kodansha, Tokyo.

Matsutani, Miyoko. 1974. *Momo and Akane.* (『モモちゃんとアカネちゃん』 Momo-chan to Akane-chan), Kodansha, Tokyo.

Miwa, Hiroko. 2016. *We Get on the Train to.* (『ぼくらは鉄道に乗って』 Bokura wa Tetsudo ni Notte), Komine-shoten, Tokyo.

Muranaka, Rie. 2019. *The Ship of the Sun.* (『いつか太陽の船』 Itsuka Taiyo no Fune), Shin-nihon-shuppansha, Tokyo.

Nagasaki, Natsumi. 2017. *Reina Came to Our Island!* (『レイナが島にやってきた!』 Reina ga Shima ni Yatte Kita!), Rironsha, Tokyo.

Nakayama, Seiko. 2018. *Looking for That Scenery.* (『その景色をさがして』 Sono Keshiki o Sagashite), PHP Kenkyusho, Kyoto.

Nishida, Toshiya. 2015. *Walking Haru.* (『ハルと歩いた』 Haru to Aruita), Tokuma-shoten, Tokyo.

Oyanagi, Chika. 2018. *Where Is Dokodoko Mountain?* (『どこどこ山はどこにある』 Dokodoko-yama wa Doko ni Aru), Froebel kan, Tokyo.

Takamori, Miyuki. 2017. *The Master of Helpers.* (『助っ人マスター』 Suketto Masuta), Froebel-kan, Tokyo.

Tanaka, Hiko. 1990. *Moving.* (『お引越し』 Ohikkoshi), Fukutake-shoten, Tokyo.

Tanaka, Hiko. 2019. *I Am Reading a Book.* (『ぼくは本を読んでいる』 Boku wa Hon o Yondeiru), Kodansha, Tokyo.

Yamanaka, Hisashi. 1960. *A Verse of Children's Play Song.* (『とべたら本こ』 Tobetara Honko), Rironsha, Tokyo.

Yasuda, Kana. 2018. *The Other Side of the Bank.* (『むこう岸』 Muko-gishi), Kodansha, Tokyo.

Yatsuka, Sumiko. 2017. *Tomorrow's Contrail.* (『明日のひこうき雲』 Ashita no Hikoki-gumo), Popla-sha, Tokyo.

CHAPTER 6

Mutilation, Metamorphosis, Transition, Transcendence: Revisiting Genderism and Transgenderism in *The Little Mermaid* Through *Gake no Ue no Ponyo*

Bernard Wilson

INTRODUCTION

Feminist analysis of the Märchen genre (which includes stories collected and/or written by the Brothers Grimm, Charles Perrault and, to a certain extent, Hans Christian Andersen) has been largely, and justifiably, negative in relation to the limitations of its female characters as suitable contemporary role models, given these stories' overwhelming representations of heteronormative patriarchies, and the passivity of their central characters' vicarious subsistence through male saviours.[1] Also well documented has been the criticism of gender representation in Disney's adaptations of these tales; indeed, a number of commercially successful Disney adaptations from the post-second-wave era of feminism—*The Little Mermaid* (1989), *Aladdin* (1992), and *Pocahontas* (1995) are three such pertinent

B. Wilson (✉)
University of the Sacred Heart, Tokyo, Japan

© The Author(s) 2020
B. Wilson and S. P. Gabriel (eds.), *Asian Children's Literature and Film in a Global Age*, Asia-Pacific and Literature in English,
https://doi.org/10.1007/978-981-15-2631-2_6

117

examples—have received a raft of negative criticism from scholars across a range of theoretical disciplines that moves well beyond reference to limited gender role models, and includes accusations of cultural marginalisation, implicit and explicit racism, historical revisionism, and overt sexualisation and objectification of the female form. In this chapter, I wish to address some of these issues of patriarchal constructs, gendering and, just as importantly, transgendering, through reference to the adaptations of Hans Christian Andersen's original tale by Disney (1989) and Studio Ghibli (2008), and to assess the ways in which these ideas are expressed, firstly from a traditional Judeo-Christian Euro-American perspective and secondly from Hayao Miyazaki's distinctly unique and transformative viewpoint.

Of specific relevance when discussing stories of gender subjugation and transition, particularly with regard to aphasic narratives and the tropes of silence and repression, is the postcolonial theorising of marginalised voices—while always acknowledging that such theorising in itself carries cultural subjectivities and, more often than not, distinctly Eurocentric perspectives. Motifs of muted and marginalised minorities and those who inhabit the hegemonic (and heteronormative) periphery feature repeatedly in what may loosely be termed as postcolonial fictive responses to a canonical European/Western power base, and bear similarities to feminist responses, in multiple forms of literature, to a patriarchal *norm*. Ashcroft et al. have compared feminist theoretical "writing the body" to postcolonial theoretical "writing place"[2]: a proposition which signifies the female body as the exotic but lesser *other*, as a place subject to male invasiveness, to male colonisation and, inevitably in patriarchal power discourses, either complying to male dominance or destruction. Such a proposition may also be linked to traditional Saidian notions of "Europeans or men construct(ing) themselves as civilized, rational, and objective, by distancing and 'exoticising' the non-European other, (just as) American society constructs itself as objective, rational, and civilized by its 'orientalization' of minority women" (Kray, quoted in Lacroix: 353). Thus, under this theoretical gaze, the mermaid is positioned in silence and subjugation, as the desirable but grotesque *other*.

Yet, while these theoretical applications have often provided useful analytical frameworks, it is also important to be cognisant of (and to interrogate) the limitations of discussing alterity in terms that invariably refocus on Eurocentric biases which mark them as inherently privileged. John Stephens, in discussing approaches to subjectivity in children's literature (in this instance, Karen Coats's application of Lacanian theory in her 2004 book, *Looking Glasses and Neverlands: Lacan, Desire and Subjectivity in Children's Literature*) and the overriding tendency of scholars to accept Western theory in these areas as absolute, argues for new approaches more sensitive to the manifest cultures and subjectivities other than Western which are involved in the production of children's texts. This is because, as he notes, Western theoretical approaches do not necessarily relate to such literary production, nor to the impetus and intent behind that production:

> [Such theories] do not simply transfer to the narratives of non-European cultures, so with the rapid development of children's literature and its scholarly discourses in Asia, it is becoming increasingly desirable to seek a basis for dialogue about the crucial concepts of subjectivity. And, after all, the cultural Other "not native to us at all" in Coats's formulation does not encompass an Other that is outside the subject's specific geographically defined culture. (2013: 3–4)

Andersen's *The Little Mermaid* and the subsequent Disney and Studio Ghibli adaptations of this source material present one such fascinating, though certainly not unique, conflation of multiple cultural and ideological subjectivities—none more so than in the distinctly Japanese, but also distinctly intertextual, reimagining of the original story and the attitudes towards social structure and gender it represents.

But though it is clear that gender stereotypes and representations are shaped by, and reflect, the cultures from which they emanate it is also true, as Anne Phillips notes, that: "Cultures have been misdescribed as organized around static defining values; misrepresented as more distinct from one another than they really are; and wrongly conceptualized as 'things' that determine the action and attitudes of their members" (2010: 5). Anna Katrina Gutierrez, in her informative discussion of glocalisation, hybridity, and metamorphosis in children's literature from an Asian perspective, observes that "hegemonic global culture contaminates and is appropriated by local culture, and the transformative transaction results in an integrated glocal product that is significant both globally and locally" (2013: 21). Such interaction relies on the concept of shared universal values but such values can often be dominated by Western ideas and output. In the case of what Gutierrez terms the "Otherworldly Maiden" tale, the symbols across cultures constitute a global story, yet one that may also be shaped and transformed by the local input of respective regional cultures—a hybrid mixture that allows manifold identities and dialogues across cultural spaces because the "neutrality of the global symbol [...] is what allows it to be a shared element that can be charged with local meaning" (23).

Although an obvious consideration, it is important then to reaffirm that from sociological and literary perspectives the constructs of culture *and* gender, their attributions and representations, their stereotypes and clichés, do not exist in stasis nor in exclusivity. Indeed, each is porous, both reliant upon and reflecting local and global movements, yet also at times existing in contradiction to the other. Gender, and the roles assigned to it, as Judith Butler has noted, denotes complex performance within culture and context:

> Gender ought not to be construed as a stable identity or locus of agency from which various acts follow; rather, gender is an identity tenuously constituted in time, instituted in an exterior space through a stylized repetition of acts. The effect of gender is produced through the stylization of the body and, hence, must be understood as the mundane way in which bodily gestures, movements, and styles of various kinds constitute the illusion of an abiding gendered self. This formulation moves the conception of gender off the ground of a substantial model of identity to one that requires a conception of gender as a constituted social temporality. (1990: 179)

This complexity of performance may be seen in Disney's adaptation of Andersen's tale, in which the restrictive male boundaries of patriarchy are challenged and (briefly) disrupted before the status quo is resumed, but more promisingly in Miyazaki's narrative in which gender and culture themselves are secondary to our collective temporal history of the shared human condition.

INCEPTION: *THE LITTLE MERMAID* (1837)

Hans Christian Andersen's tale of a mermaid yearning for knowledge of the human world as well as for the immortal soul which she learns through her grandmother that Christian humans possess, combines folkloric traditions with Christian principles and positions its central character firmly in the realms of alterity, a figure of both desire and rejection. The mermaid in Andersen's narrative undergoes multiple metamorphoses:

mermaid, human, sea foam, air sprite, and though often seemingly passive, she nevertheless actively seeks a number of these mutations through initial inquisitiveness (human transformation) to self-sacrifice (refusal to kill the prince and subsequent transformation into sea foam). Andersen places significant emphasis on the emotional and psychological toll of these transformations: tolls which, it is clear, readily translate to the transitional strains of female pubescent growth but may also be applied in a retrospective interpretation to the emotional cost of transgenderism and/or transsexuality.

The story stems from European and Nordic folkloric and romantic traditions rather than the direct adaptations or retellings of many fairy tales in the Märchen genre, although it retains elements of these stories of loss and gain, and is in its conception and construction much more an adult morality tale which foregrounds the spirituality and suffering of the outsider, than it is a children's tale. Throughout much of its appearance in folklore, as Erica Hateley has noted, "the mermaid is [...] a peculiarly ambiguous figure of the sexualized female body, signifying at once excess and containment, [and who in her combination of fertility, seduction, and prostitution] is arguably a sanitized version of the monstrous feminine" (2006: 4). In Andersen's narrative, the mermaid's willing mutilation and bloody metamorphosis have invariably been interpreted as female sacrifice for the male ideal, as either consent or inevitable submission to an indifferent patriarchal dominance, and the overt religious didacticism in the story, postscripted as it is by somewhat clumsy Victorian moralising, lends further weight to these traditional analyses of a patriarchal trope. Yet while this is a significant and valid theorization in feminist terms, representations of the mermaid and its associated symbolism(s), both in folklore and Andersen's story, are protean and multitudinous. As Easterlin notes, "closer inspection [of the narrative] shows that the mermaid and her kinfolk evoke a shifting constellation of concerns, not a fixed set of meanings" (Easterlin: 256) and, as such, it is worth here referring in some detail to her discussion of the tale:

> Major features of Andersen's story, including the mermaid herself, who descends from a rich genealogy of water deities, as well as the essential form and content of fairytale plots, are tied to central concerns in human nature. These features indeed constitute a substrate of dominant natural preoccupations and orientations which are manifested thematically and formally. The themes of childhood vulnerability, sexual maturation, pair-bonding,

reproduction, and man's relation to nature, for instance, all arise from fundamental adaptive concerns, just as formal tendencies toward narrative and binary construction arise from adapted patterns of mental organization. More importantly, however, all of the main features are linked by their implications about power—its development, acquisition, abuse, or control—and by the characteristic ambivalence borne of the fundamentally conflictive nature of human existence [...] Careful consideration of Andersen's tale reveals, in fact, that environmental conditions—socially and economically, the development of industrialization and the ensuing movement out of rural communities; culturally, the collapse of the enlightenment and the consequent development of literary romanticism—combined with the similar trajectory of Andersen's own "fairytale" life from humble rural origins to cosmopolitan fame crucially affect the meaning of the story, bringing to the fore not sexual power or threat but our characteristic ambivalence regarding others and communal belonging. (254–255)

Consequently, though Andersen's tale has often—quite rightly—been regarded as Christian didacticism, the characters in his narrative do not suggest the overt Judeo-Christian binaries of good and evil that a number of Disney's adaptations offer, including their adaptation of *The Little Mermaid*, for while the sea witch in Andersen's tale exists among the hideous and grotesque, she is true to her own set of principles in her dealings with the mermaid and with her sisters, while the prince, in his treatment of the mermaid and his marriage to the woman he believes has saved him, remains a deeply flawed symbol of patriarchy.

Andersen's original text, though, certainly provides enough scope to speculate on aspects of the author's sexuality and the attitudes towards transgenderism that may in part drive the direction of the narrative. Biographical analyses of Andersen's life,[3] his personal loneliness and thwarted attempts at heterosexual relationships, have suggested the possibility of a homosexual or transgendered crisis, a repression of masculine identity and desire that manifests itself in a strong personal association with the mermaid and the castration metaphors implied in the text.[4] And it is this marginalised female *other*, the mermaid who is at once exotic and erotic in male-dominant discourse but who is also deviant and grotesque and, therefore, a threat to the patriarchal and heteronormative status quo of such societies, that is further explained through the representations of alterity and transgendering in Disney's adaptation of the story.

ADAPTATION: DISNEY'S *THE LITTLE MERMAID* (1989)

Disney's *The Little Mermaid*, released in 1989 to both critical acclaim and commercial success, though certainly not without its detractors in terms of its perceived ignorance of contemporary feminist issues, provides ample evidence of embedded cross-genderism through its two principal female characters, Ariel, the mermaid and Ursula, the sea witch. Combining aspects of Andersen's story with Shakespeare's *The Tempest*, Disney's version provides its audience with overt elements of the traditional heteronormative fairy tale while also covertly critiquing these patriarchal assumptions through a subversive questioning of gender codes and representations. While Andersen's story subjugates the feminine (at least above the water's surface, for beneath the water's surface there are clear indications of a maternal influence within the patriarchal order through the sea king's mother), Disney's adaptation of the story foregrounds a patriarchal and polarising Madonna/whore dichotomy through its binary depictions of female mutilation and marginalisation. In Disney's version, males occupy the space of clear hegemonic privilege in both sea and on land, the sea king's mother being omitted as irrelevant to the narrative arc and to the obligatory Disneyfied heteronormative resolution that does not take place in Andersen's story.

Yet while this reinterpretation of *The Little Mermaid* appears to underpin heterosexual romantic ideals, such seeming validation is simultaneously destabilised through the psychosexual and transgendered motifs in the narrative. The superficial reinforcement of the Märchen trope—Ariel as the passive and desired feminine whose virginity is symbolically at threat from darker masculine and pseudo-masculine forces—is flagged early in the story not only through Ariel's sisters singing their submissive praise to their alpha-male father, Triton, and emerging from clam-shell wombs in the absence of a mother, but through the shark chase trauma, representing the dangers of masculine penetration, that succeeds this event. And while it is reasonable to equate Ariel's loss of voice with the mutilation of Andersen's mermaid through the removal of her tongue, given that the substitution of voice for legs neatly equates to female intelligence and communication subverted for physical sexuality as desired in a male world, it should be noted that although in Andersen's narrative the mermaid possesses "the most beautiful voice both on earth and in the sea" (Andersen: 67) this is secondary to plot function whereas, in Disney's adaptation, that Prince Eric is first attracted to Ariel by the beauty of her singing, and will only accept her under those terms, becomes fundamental to the narratorial direction. Thus, *voice* in Disney is primarily represented as an ornamental instrument of female sexual attraction and, when lost, necessitates the use of the remaining available instruments of physical sexuality (face and body) to seduce the male, a point to which I shall return.

However, the narrative development that principally separates Disney's adaptation from the original tale, and is particularly interesting from Freudian, feminist and postcolonial theoretical perspectives, is the brief dominance and violent demise of the threatening "otherness" of the highly sexualised, transgendered Ursula, the sea witch who seeks to invert the "norm" of patriarchal hegemony through ascension to phallic power. Disney's *The Little Mermaid* ultimately metamorphosizes into as much a reimagining of *The Tempest* as it is an adaptation of Andersen's story and, as has previously been observed, "it is precisely these elements of heteronormative romance, feminine subordination to patriarchal structures, and a sustained affirmation of paternal figures that Disney appropriates from Shakespeare" (Hateley: 13). As Richard Finkelstein has noted, this "use of Shakespearean comic structure [...] allows the film to circumscribe female desire—for independence, possessions, and sexuality—under the guise of celebrating the triumph of young people over old" (186) yet a postcolonial reading would also position Ursula, in her synthesis of Sycorax and her son Caliban, as a subversive and articulate voice not only for the marginalised and doubly colonised female in the patriarchal world, but also for the multiply marginalised transgendered subject who is positioned at the periphery of both male and female social identities.

It is well documented that the inspiration for Ursula's characterisation came in part from the drag performer Divine, just as it is evident that Disney's subsequent queering of characters such as Jafar in *Aladdin* (1992), Scar in *Lion King* (1994), and Ratcliffe in *Pocahontas* (1995), all of whom exhibit (in less overt form than Ursula) qualities which may place them outside heterosexual or cisgender identities, are equally vilified.[5] Ursula, who like Caliban knows the ironic value of using language to curse the predominant status quo, comically but accurately and insightfully interprets the subordinate female position in the patriarchies that exist both under and above the sea through her advice to Ariel, who is about to be silenced in a male world, repeating the fate of the colonised female subject over the centuries. Gyrating her breasts and rear at the camera in faux ecstasy while bargaining for the removal of Ariel's voice, she instructs the younger female in negotiating the desires of heterosexual men:

> You'll have your looks! Your pretty face! / And don't underestimate the importance of body language! / The men up there don't like a lot of blabber, / They think a girl who gossips is a bore! / Yes, on land it's much preferred for ladies not to say a word, / And after all dear, what is idle prattle for? / Come on, they're not all that impressed with conversation, / True gentlemen avoid it when they can. / But they dote and swoon and fawn / On a lady who's withdrawn, / It's she who holds her tongue who gets her man.

Through this advice, Ursula fulfils the ironic role of mother in absentia for Ariel. In her manifestation as an octopus she is, as Laura Sells has noted in her discussion of women's *jouissance*, "an inverted Medusa figure (who) is the female symbolic encoded in patriarchal language as grotesque and monstrous; she represents the monstrosity of feminine power" (184) but also, in her transgenderism, she exists beyond predefined, simplistic gender associations: a figure who carries not only Freudian associations of castrator and emasculator, but also the rejection of maternal sexuality.[6]

As Sells has convincingly argued, Ursula's camp deconstruction of heteronormative mores provides Ariel with a comprehension of "gender, not as a natural category, but as a performed construct [while] her excessive figure provides the site upon which we can construct the image of the mermaid" (186). Such a revelation, in terms of confronting the processes of patriarchy through metanarrative, may be seen as inherently positive. Yet Ursula's voice, articulating the esoterica of the inner workings of gender and society (unlike Ariel's voice), must also be silenced: her access to knowledge across genders denotes an abomination, the annihilation of which allows Ariel to function within the constructs of heterosexuality and patriarchy. In postcolonial theoretical terms, then, Ursula exists outside of the hegemonic order. She is the subaltern voice not only in the sense of subjugation and exile, but because her transgendered space occupies both self and other—an aberration in the heteronormative world, and in the Disney oeuvre which has reinforced that world. From the periphery, she attempts to destabilise the socially accepted norm of the fairy tale world and to establish a transgendered voice but, despite the period commonly recognised as the Disney renaissance (1989–1999) flirting with representations which extend beyond the cisgender boundaries of previous animation, "happily ever after" remains a constricted and constrictive concept available only to those who adhere to existing social and sexual "norms".

In essence then, Ursula is directly punished, in accordance with the fundamental elements of Kristeva's theory of abjection,[7] for her embodiment of the monstrous, smothering maternal and for her transgression of heteronormative boundaries. And it is for the sin not only of coveting patriarchal power, but also of occupying transgendered difference, not for the entrapment of the younger female but for the attempted castration of males (Triton and Eric) and the bastardization of gender in a patricentric hegemony, that she is punished more violently than any other Disney villain. Transformed by the power she gains from King Triton's trident she mutates into a swollen, grotesque phallus; rising from the depths of male fears of usurpation and emasculation, she is then penetrated by Eric to restore the "rightful" patriarchal order. Ursula is symbolically raped to death for daring to invert traditional gender roles, a fate she has prophesied earlier in her advice to Ariel that attempts to change a pre-existing order will invariably carry a heavy personal cost. In this heteronormative patriarchy, as Ursula knowingly advises Ariel as the mermaid contemplates transformation into a human, "If you want to cross a bridge [...] you have to pay a toll". For inhabiting both gender spaces, for attempting to negotiate and subvert the twin patriarchies beneath and above water, it is Ursula who pays that heavy toll.

TRANSCENDENCE: *GAKE NO UE NO PONYO* (2008)

What then of negotiating traditional gender spaces and traversing boundaries in Hayao Miyazaki's *Gake no Ue no Ponyo*[8]? In Miyazaki's story, the principal narratorial premise remains broadly similar to both Andersen's original tale and Disney's adaptation: fish (or mermaid) becomes human through a determined inquisitiveness which rapidly mutates into love of a male, though in Disney's and Miyazaki's interpretations overt female rebellion against an authoritarian patriarchal figure (Triton and Fujimoto, respectively) is also emphasised. The mermaid/fish is in all three versions of the story, at least initially, prepared to break free from a paternal male control that ensures, in classic Freudian terminology, "the suppression of women's aggressiveness which occurs constitutionally and is imposed on them socially (and which) favors the development of powerful masochistic impulses" (Freud cited in Meyers 2001: 152). But one may further argue, and this is depicted most simplistically in Disney's adaptation, that this *constitutional patriarchal oppression* is supplanted from father to potential husband, thus merely repositioning the desire for female acceptance of male dominance. Conversely, in the narrative of *Ponyo* maternal nurture is doubly emphasised, as opposed to the maternal lack and/or grotesque maternal presence of Ursula witnessed in Disney. This is achieved through two distinctly matriarchal figures: the fiercely independent and determined Lisa (Sousuke's mother) and the Goddess of Mercy, Granmamare (Ponyo's mother), each of whom straddles traditional feminine and contemporary feminist spaces and each of whom is contrasted against weaker father figures, respectively, the largely absent Koichi and the comically overprotective Fujimoto. Ponyo and Sousuke provide variations on the absent parent trope of many traditional fairy tales: Ponyo's father is physically present in much of the narrative while her mother, although seemingly absent for much of the narrative is, in the sense that she is the great mother of the sea, *ever-present*. Providing a variation on the nuclear family unit, and on the majority of traditional fairy tale paradigms, Lisa mentors and influences her son, fulfilling a function that emphasises paternal absence. Unlike Andersen's original story or Disney's adaptation, this is neither a tale of patriarchal colonisation of the menstruating female, nor the destruction of the postmenstrual power-seeking female, nor does it recount the traditional Märchen trope of younger female usurping older female.

As noted earlier, while an archetypal reading of mermaid lore from a Eurocentric perspective is invariably filtered through Judeo-Christian ideology and its attendant overriding concepts of duality and heteronormative behaviour, in terms of narrative structure and dynamics Andersen's tale functions both within and beyond these parameters: mermaid lore traces connections to Babylonian, Indian, Chinese and Japanese mythology (Easterlin: 258) and, diverging in some aspects from the traditional fairy tale form, "draws on cultural symbols and forms that derive from innate and universal preoccupations and ways of organizing" (Easterlin: 273). Miyazaki's tale is clearly positioned in the space of what Gutierrez describes as a global metanarrative with glocal subjectivities (22): a conflation of global and local signifiers, symbols and lore. But because, as she notes, global subjectivities tend towards generalisations and "the appropriation of the global sign does not transform the appropriator into its image and likeness; rather, it is the global sign that is transformed by the appropriator's unique qualities" (23), in his appropriation of the broader concepts of the mermaid tale in global lore, Miyazaki transforms and transcends global hegemony. His adaptation subsumes the multiple possibilities of global identity(ies) and borrows from local signifiers, comprising a transcultural, and *trans-ideological*, narrative that is specifically Japanese while traversing Eastern and Western philosophies, literature and mythologies, but also evokes the evolutionary history from which all cultures emerged. The cultural and religious belief systems inherent in Miyazaki's body of work have been well documented, as has his distinctly individual viewpoint in an artform noted for its creativity and inventiveness.[9] As Susan Napier has observed, "Miyazaki takes anime's basic propensity to defamiliarize consensus reality in a direction that allows him to develop his own agenda, one that incorporates an ethical and aesthetic universe that is both exotic and yet at some level familiar" (2005: 152). The Shinto belief system closely associated with Japanese culture combines, in simple terms, elements of Buddhism and animism and places an emphasis on connection with a past rooted in natural mythology, an association which is clearly evident in the environmental concerns in much of Miyazaki's oeuvre, and which may be most prominently witnessed prior to *Ponyo* in *Kaze no Tani no Naushika* (1984), *Tonari no Totoro* (1988), *Mononoke-hime* (1997), and *Sen to Chihiro no Kamikakushi* (2001).[10] Though Miyazaki clearly foregrounds the animistic component of this philosophy in his work over the more religious associations of Shinto, he is nevertheless cognisant of their interconnectedness in his narratives, having stated, "I do not believe in Shinto [...] but I do respect it, and I feel that the animism origin of Shinto is rooted deep within me".[11] However, in tracing the metamorphosis of the character of Ponyo through its broadly Eurocentric origins to its distinctly Japanese reimagining, it should also be noted that the use of the contested term *animism* is in many ways manifestly inadequate, in that it has been viewed similarly to pantheism after its usurpation by monotheism in many Western cultures. Such a term, as Eriko Ogihara-Schuck correctly asserts, is outdated and culturally biased, inherently bound as it is to nineteenth-century Eurocentric hegemonic discourse, and implying "an inferior and uncivilized belief system, enforcing the supposed hierarchy between religions" (3) which eliminates the transitions and philosophical interconnectedness that are cornerstones of Miyazaki's oeuvre.

Yet, even while acknowledging the limitations of the term from a Western-centric perspective, one cannot deny the significance of ecology and mythology in Miyazaki's thematic coda and in his interrogation of the increasing disconnect between humanity and the natural environment. In discussing *Mononoke-hime*, an earlier film whose central tenet is a philosophical discussion of the interdependence between humans and the spirits of nature, Miyazaki argues: "When we think of the relationship between human beings and nature, we must keep in mind that human beings are suffering for sins committed in previous lives [...] People, beasts, trees, and water all are worthy of life" (2008: 34–35).[12] This advocacy of a spiritual interconnectedness—perhaps even *interchangeability*—between the forces of humanity and nature is also strongly apparent in *Ponyo*: the power and unpredictability of the ocean, never far from the consciousness of the Japanese psyche, holds tremendously destructive[13] but also transformative potential, as does human ingenuity and determination. The ocean's traditional associations with mythology and the subconscious connect all three versions of the story, yet Miyazaki takes this one step further by investing not only those who exist within the sea with character and motivation but infusing the sea itself with these same qualities. His goal, in his own words, is to depict:

> [...] the ocean as a living presence. A world where magic and alchemy are accepted as part of the ordinary. The sea below, like our subconscious mind, intersects with the wave-tossed surface above. By distorting normal space and contorting normal shapes, the sea is animated not as a backdrop to the story, but as one of its principal characters. (2009: 11)

Consequently, in *Ponyo* the traversal of boundaries which is at the core of Miyazaki's worldview is readily apparent not only in the metamorphosis of fish to human, but in the sentience of the surrounding environment, suggesting through its portrayal of the sequence of environmental pollution, tsunami and regeneration, a macrocosm of (d)evolution and transformation. The return to a Devonian period which marks the first land-living vertebrates signifies it as the period of transition between land and sea, and thus as a site of inception and transcendence. Ponyo, the product of a union between nature/mythology (Granmamare) and flawed humanity (Fujimoto), is the embodiment of that symbiosis in that she represents a nostalgic amalgam of physical and metaphysical origins while, in her relationship with Sosuke, she also symbolises the potentiality of future hybridity and, I would suggest, the possibility of non-binary or degendered existence, of transcending traditional gender codes and their restrictive associations.

In her discussion of Takahashi Rumiko's popular manga *Inuyasha* (1996–2008), Mio Bryce observes that "Japanese subjectivities manifest themselves as fluid, ambiguous, and precarious. They are penetrated and pushed around by a society which is highly contextual and empathy-orientated and which embraces ambivalence and fleetingness within a homogeneous yet hierarchical structure" (2013: 164). Such an observation reflects not only the underlying contemplation of ephemera in the Japanese artistic sensibility but also the paradox of constant changeability and adaptability in Japanese artistic production within such seemingly rigid social frameworks. Seven years prior to the release of *Gake no Ue no Ponyo*, Susan Napier had already noted that a clear alternative to the American animation industry and its historically limited interpretations of culture and gender was "the Japanese animation industry, whose products [...] embrace a far wider continuum of approaches to culture, history, and national identity in general than most of the products from the contemporary Hollywood film industry" (2005: 470). She goes on to assert that Miyazaki's body of work has been "both popular and subversive, especially in regard to conventional gender coding" (2005: 470–471). Many of Miyazaki's central female characters display this cultural hybridity, combining the *kawaii* traits of the perceived stereotypical "cute innocence" of the archetypal Japanese girl (*shōjo*) with the independence often associated with contemporary Western feminism,[14] reflecting the modern metamorphosis and fluidity of culture and gender associations. In *Ponyo*, as in a number of his animated features, Miyazaki's method is at times didactic, but not necessarily overtly so. Though the focus of the lens, and the characterisations of Ponyo, Lisa and Gran Mamare lean towards a feminist response to the patriarchal assumptions of the Märchen genre and to much of the heteronormative animation of Disney, Miyazaki redresses the balance through gentle adjustments to both male and female gender stereotypes. In most instances his approach shows a "flexible openness to and appreciation of other cultures" (Napier 2005: 475) that is perhaps more in keeping with a culturally heterogeneous society, and runs counter to the tendencies towards monoculturalism that have been evident in much of traditional Japanese society. Such flexibility may be witnessed in a melding of cultural traits but also in the relatively androgynous portrayal of a number of female and, on fewer occasions, male characters in his body of work. The teenage characters, San (female) and Ashitaka (male) in *Mononoke-hime*, for example, evince these ambisexual qualities even while both are also covertly eroticised (unlike the blatant eroticisation of the female form in Disney's *The Little Mermaid*). Each also undertakes tasks historically associated with the other gender, thus questioning traditional tropes of femininity and masculinity.

One of the crucial differences from the Andersen and Disney narratives in *Ponyo* however, is the age of the two protagonists, both of whom—at least in human form—are five-year olds.[15] Though Ponyo's age precludes her from any form of psychosexualisation, her characterisation clearly combines the traditional Japanese traits of *shōjo* with the broader traits of determination and rebellion seen in the Andersen fairy tale and Disney adaptation. Yet critically, by placing both Ponyo and Sōsuke in an earlier stage of psychological and physical development, while retaining the intensity of emotional commitment, Miyazaki has partially disrupted the traditional heteronormative hegemony in pubescent and post-pubescent literary discourse and has eliminated the familiar narrative arc of sexual seduction and sexual colonisation. The central characters of Miyazaki's story reflect what Gutierrez terms a "glocal heterotopia" (2013: 36), having formed agency not only across cultural spaces but across gender itself. In this sense, he has gone some way towards neutralising traditional fairy tale gender constructs and politics, for in its relative asexuality the children's relationship retains a purity and potentiality that could not exist if coloured by the sexual politics of the more mature protagonists in the other versions of the tale, most clearly evidenced in Disney.

It is this *potentiality*, which is at the heart of Ponyo's story, that extends beyond binary male/female relationships and the romance of innocence regained, and speaks directly to a more hopeful future that may be reconnected to our core primality through a greater awareness of the natural environment and its past, but one which is also less restrictive in interpreting contemporary gender roles. In the same way that *animism* may be seen as an inadequate term in its application to Miyazaki's films (and to Japanese belief systems in general) so too outdated understandings of *gender*, loaded as they are with unrealistic performance expectations linked to culture(s) and society(ies), are less applicable in Miyazaki's more protean and interchangeable conceptualisation. Unlike Andersen's mermaid, whose transition is reliant upon problematic negotiation, sacrifice and redemption, and Disney's Ariel, whose physical change is also reliant on compromise, not only through Ursula but ultimately in acquiescence to the continuation of the patriarchies that exist above and beneath the waves (marked by Triton's delivery of Ariel to Eric at the conclusion of the narrative), Ponyo undergoes a metamorphosis that, like the natural environment itself, ebbs and flows in its conception. Though her father, Fujimoto, temporarily reverses her mutation from (semi)human to fish, he is ultimately powerless against far greater cosmic and natural forces and Ponyo continues to transition between human, semi-formed human and fish throughout the story, reminding the viewer not only of our own origins as a species, but the flux in which our social structures (including gender determinants) exist.

Crucially, in Miyazaki's story, the motifs of female aphasia and muteness that are foregrounded in Andersen and Disney are inverted for Ponyo, whose ability to articulate substantially increases after each metamorphosis because such transitions provide connection to other species and other ideologies, emphasise the necessity for dialogue, and mirror the constant evolution of our environment and of society. Just as Ponyo achieves human empathy and a voice by emerging from the sea onto land, so too do humans regain an affinity with nature and their primal origins by entering the world under the sea following the immersion of all but the cliff upon which Lisa and Sousuke live. And while Napier's criticism of the film's seemingly simplistic resolution is that this is "a rather amorphous vision of love conquering all [and one which ensures that] the film ultimately shies away from its darkest implications, allowing its family audience to get remarkably close to apocalyptic trauma but finally providing them with an escape route from that condition" (2012), the conclusion of the film cuts to the heart of Miyazaki's purpose. For it is this hope, naive or otherwise, not only of a reconnection with our physical and mythological origins, but also of negating and transcending false societal "norms"—and in this we may clearly include restrictive binary gender "norms"—that remains central to the narrative. As Cavallaro has argued in regard to Miyazaki's work in general, the director "refuses to impose definitive conclusions—of either the utopian or the cataclysmic varieties—onto the dramatization of those problems, aware that time and history as they are actually experienced never constitute neat bundles of meaning" (2006: 28). As such, though the conclusion of *Ponyo* may be interpreted in one sense as unnecessarily optimistic despite the threat of apocalyptic dystopia that has preceded it, it is a utopian conclusion with a caveat: in Miyazaki's world outcomes are fluid, dependent always upon a continuing awareness of the fragility of our environment and our reliance upon it, but also of an ability to transcend the limitations of so many of our socially constructed biases.

CONCLUSION

Thus, from the mutilation of the female form depicted in Andersen's tale, we have moved through the darkly Freudian symbolism of castration and rape in Disney, to the tentative regaining of voice and the negation of traditional gender "norms" in *Ponyo*. Though each version of the tale contains rebirth motifs associated with the amniotic fluid of the ocean—so crucial to the evolution of humans—metamorphosis in *Ponyo* functions primarily as an oscillation between pre-human and human, between physical and metaphysical. Ponyo, who by virtue of ingesting Sousuke's blood provides an ironic inversion of the painful menstrual symbols of the original tale, fluctuates between fish, semi-human and human at various stages in the story: her transition references Janus, the god of beginnings and transitions, in that it looks both forwards and backwards. This is because in Miyazaki's interpretation wholeness and healing—across species and across genders—may only be achieved by revisiting and comprehending points of origin, from under the sea onto the land, in the Devonian past in which many of the first major transitions between fish and amphibian took place. Miyazaki's focus and underlying message is the interconnectedness not only of all species and our need to acknowledge this, but also the interconnectedness of gender. His focus is on *inclusion* rather than *exclusion*; his emphasis is on *connectivity* because perceived differences ultimately serve to reflect our similarities.

Consequently, though at a superficial level the conclusion of *Ponyo* mirrors the heteronormative resolutions of much of the Märchen fairy tale trope and Disney's adaptations of that trope, in Miyazaki's vision of fluid society the protagonists' essentially *genderless* space ensures that they represent the equality, the interchangeability—and ultimately the irrelevance—of such socially constructed roles. Encapsulated in the final triumphant freeze-frame of an airborne Ponyo kissing Sousuke in asexual pose is not only Miyazaki's ongoing fascination with flight as a metaphor for transcending human limitations, but also of transcending the repressive binaries of gender and the limitations that an adherence to them inflicts. The conclusion of *Ponyo* then, while referencing the questionable metamorphosis achieved by Andersen's daughter of the air, functions in direct opposition to the destruction seen in the Disney oeuvre of those positioned outside of Eurocentric and heteronormative binary "norms". Rather, it offers an alternative: the affirmation of a society not bound by traditional codes and biases but liberated and rising above these prejudices through perpetual transition and transcendence, through an awareness of its primal origins, and through an affinity with its natural environment.

NOTES

1. As is overviewed, for example, in Donald Haase's "Feminist Fairy-Tale Scholarship" in *Fairy Tales and Feminism: New Approaches* (2004).
2. For a brief summary of the links between the two theoretical positions, see Ashcroft, et al. *Key Concepts in Post-colonial Studies* (93–96) in which it is stated: "The texts of feminist theory and those of post-colonialism concur on many aspects of the theory of identity, of difference and of the interpellation of the subject by a dominant discourse, as well as offering to each other various strategies of resistance to such controls. Similarities between 'writing the body' in feminism and 'writing place' in postcolonialism; similarities between the strategies of bisexuality and cultural syncreticity; and similar appeals to nationalism may be detected" (1998: 94).
3. See, as one such example, Alison Prince's 1998 biography *Hans Christian Andersen: The Fan Dancer*, which details personal circumstances and correspondence that hints at the subversion of multiple sexualities and the possibility of its queering influence on Andersen's writing.
4. See also Meyers, Robert W. "The Little Mermaid: Hans Christian Andersen's Feminine Identification" in *Journal of Applied Psychoanalytic Studies* 3.2 (2001): 149–159 for more detail on Andersen's association with the feminine.
5. For further discussion of Disney's association of transgender characteristics with many of its villains, see Amanda Putnam's "Mean Ladies: Transgendered Villains in Disney Films" in *Diversity in Disney Films: Critical Essays on Race, Ethnicity, Gender, Sexuality and Disability*. Putnam argues that this approach is positioned very much within Disney's promotion of heteronormative values.
6. See Freud's posthumously published 1955 article, *Das Medusenhaupt (Medusa's Head)*.
7. See, in particular, Kristeva's *Pouvoirs de l'horreur: Essai sur l'abjection* [*Powers of Horror: An Essay on Abjection*] (1980). In broad terms, Kristeva's use of the term "abjection" embodies a blurring of the distinction between Self and Other and relates to the theorising of Freud and Lacan.
8. Hereafter referred to in the text as *Ponyo*.

9. See for example, as one such overview, Eriko Ogihara-Schuck's *Miyazaki's Animism Abroad: The Reception of Japanese Religious Themes by American and German Audiences*, in which the author views Miyazaki's animistic outlook and work in terms of Foucauldian discourse, in particular focusing on "its discursive nature, that is, its ability to transgress national boundaries and grow through interaction with other cultural discourses into a new form" (4–5).

10. *Nausicaa of the Valley of the Wind, My Neighbor Totoro, Princess Mononoke*, and *Spirited Away*, respectively.

11. As quoted in *The Independent*, 31 January 2010.

12. As a further example of Miyazaki's spiritual beliefs concerning the natural environment and our obligation to it, in 1996 he argued, "We need courtesy toward water, mountains, and air in addition to living things. We should not ask courtesy from these things, but we ourselves should give courtesy toward them instead. I do believe the existence of the period when the power of forests was much stronger than our power. There is something missing within our attitude toward nature" (quoted in *Ecological Economics* 54 [2005]).

13. In "Studio Ghibli's Otherworldly Fish-Girl" (*The Pleasures of Metamorphosis: Japanese and English Fairy Tale Transformation of "The Little Mermaid"* [2017]), Lucy Fraser draws connections, in terms of the tsunami at least, with Ogawa Mimei's *The Red Candles and the Mermaid* (*Akai r Soku to Ningyo* [1921]), a tale in which human venality is punished. A mermaid child is adopted by human parents but later sold, after which the town and its inhabitants are swallowed by a huge wave. Fraser asserts that the "tsunami may be interpreted as a chaotic force of childhood or feminised nature encroaching on a cynical adult world". The 2011 Great Tohoku Earthquake and Tsunami and its aftermath further underline the power of the ocean and its effect on the Japanese psyche.

14. The character of Kiki in *Majo no Takkyubin* (*Kiki's Delivery Service* [1989]) is one such pointed example of this cultural hybridity.

15. The protagonists in a number of Studio Ghibli films, including *Tonari no Totoro, Sen to Chihiro no Kamikakushi* and *Hauru no Ugoku Shiro* (*Howl's Moving Castle* [2004]) are clearly presexual or, in Freudian terms, positioned in the latency period prior to the genital period.

References

Andersen, Hans Christian. 1977. *The Complete Fairy Tales and Stories*. Translated by Erik Haugaard. London: Victor Gollancz.

Ashcroft, Bill, Gareth Griffiths, and Helen Tiffin (eds). 2007 [1998]. *Key Concepts in Post-colonial Studies*. London and New York: Routledge.

Bryce, Mio. 2013. "All Is Relative, Nothing Is Reliable: *Inuyasha* and Japanese Subjectivities." In *Subjectivity in Asian Children's Literature and Film: Global Theories and Implications*, edited by John Stephens, 163–180. London and New York: Routledge.

Butler, J. 1990. *Gender Trouble: Feminism and the Subversion of Identity*. New York and London: Routledge.

Cavallaro, Dan. 2006. *The Anime Art of Hayao Miyazaki*. Jefferson, NC and London: McFarland & Co.

Easterlin, Nancy. 2001. "Hans Christian Andersen's Fish Out of Water." *Philosophy and Literature* 25 (2): 251–277.

Epstein, Robert. 2010. "Spirits, Gods and Pastel Paints: The Weird World of Master Animator Hayao Miyazaki." *The Independent*, 31 January.

Finkelstein, Richard. 1999. "Disney Cites Shakespeare: The Limits of Appropriation." In *Shakespeare and Appropriation*, edited by Christy Desmet and Robert Sawyer, 179–196. London and New York: Routledge.

Fraser, Lucy. 2017. *The Pleasures of Metamorphosis*. Detroit: Wayne State University Press. Kindle Version, Amazon.

Freud, Sigmund. 1955. "Medusa's Head." In *The Standard Edition of the Complete Psychological Works of Sigmund Freud, Volume XVIII (1920–1922): Beyond the Pleasure Principle, Group Psychology and Other Works*, edited and translated by James Strachey, 273–274. London: The Hogarth Press and the Institute of Psychoanalysis.

Gutierrez, Anna Katrina. 2013. "Metamorphosis: The Emergence of Glocal Subjectivities in the Blend of Global, Local, East, and West." In *Subjectivity in Asian Children's Literature and Film: Global Theories and Implications*, edited by John Stephens, 19–42. London and New York: Routledge.

Haase, Donald. 2004. "Feminist Fairy-Tale Scholarship." In *Fairy Tales and Feminism: New Approaches*, edited by Donald Haase, 1–36. Detroit: Wayne State University Press.

Hateley, Erica. 2006. "Of Tails and Tempests: Feminine Sexuality and Shakespearean Children's Texts." *Borrowers and Lenders: The Journal of Shakespeare and Appropriation* 2 (1). www.borrowers.uga.edu/783082/show.

Kray, Susan. 1993. "Orientalization of an 'Almost White' Woman: The Interlocking Effects of Race, Class, Gender, and Ethnicity in American Mass Media." *Critical Studies in Mass Communication* 10 (4): 349–366.

Kristeva, Julia. 1980. trans. 1982. *Pouvoirs de l'horreur: Essai sur l'abjection*. Paris: Le Seuil [*Powers of Horror: An Essay on Abjection*]. Translated by Leon Roudiez. New York: Columbia University Press.

Lacroix, Celeste. 2004. "Images of Animated Others: The Orientalization of Disney's Cartoon Heroines from *The Little Mermaid* to *The Hunchback of Notre Dame*." *Popular Communication* 2 (4): 213–229.

Meyers, Robert W. 2001. "The Little Mermaid: Hans Christian Andersen's Feminine Identification." *Journal of Applied Psychoanalytic Studies* 3 (2): 149–159.

Miyazaki, Hayao. 1996. Quoted in "The Ecological and Consumption Themes of the Films of Hayao Miyazaki" by Kozo Mayumi, Barry D. Solomon, Jason Chang. *Ecological Economics* 54 (1): 1–7.

———. (director). 2008. *Gake no ue no PonyoGake no ue no Ponyo*. Studio Ghibli.

———. 2008. trans. 2014. *Turning Point 1997–2008*. Translated by Beth Cary and Frederik L. Schodt. San Francisco: VIZ Media.

———. 2009. "A Small Seaside Town." In *The Art of Ponyo on the Cliff: A Film by Hayao Miyazaki*, 10–11. San Francisco: Viz Media.

Musker, John, and Ron Clements. (directors). 1989. *The Little Mermaid*. Walt Disney Company.

Napier, Susan. 2005. *Anime from Akira to Howl's Moving Castle: Experiencing Contemporary Japanese Animation*. New York: Palgrave Macmillan.

———. 2012. "The Anime Director, the Fantasy Girl and the Very Real Tsunami." *The Asia-Pacific Journal: Japan Focus* 10 (11): 3. https://apjjf.org/2012/10/11/Susan-J.-Napier/3713/article.html. Accessed 10 December 2018.

Ogihara-Schuck, Eriko. 2014. *Miyazaki's Animism Abroad: The Reception of Japanese Religious Themes by American and German Audiences*. Jefferson, NC: McFarland & Co. Kindle Version, Amazon.

Phillips, Anne. 2010. *Gender and Culture*. Cambridge, UK: Polity Press.

Prince, Alison. 1998. *Hans Christian Andersen: The Fan Dancer*. London: Allison and Busby.

Putnam, Amanda. 2013. "Mean Ladies: Transgendered Villains in Disney Films." In *Diversity in Disney Films: Critical Essays on Race, Ethnicity, Gender, Sexuality and Disability*, edited by Johnson Cheu, 147–162. Jefferson, NC and London: McFarland & Co.

Sells, Laura. 1995. "Where Do the Mermaids Stand?" In *From Mouse to Mermaid: The Politics of Film, Gender, and Culture*, edited by Elizabeth Bell, Lynda Haas, and Laura Sells, 175–198. Bloomington and Indianapolis: Indiana University Press.

Stephens, John. 2013. "The Politics of Identity: A Transcultural Perspective on Subjectivity in Writing for Children." In *Subjectivity in Asian Children's Literature and Film: Global Theories and Implications*, edited by John Stephens, 1–19. London and New York: Routledge.

PART II

South and West

CHAPTER 7

In the Shadows: Tracing Children and Childhood in Indian Cinema

Sonia Ghalian

INTRODUCTION

Indian cinema is a massive cultural enterprise that includes diverse forms of organisational structures with regard to production, distribution, exhibition, film form and film movements. It covers a range of films, from mainstream commercial cinema, the parallel/new wave films, independent films across languages that differ in their production mechanisms, as well as film content and aesthetics. Indian cinema is known to have diffused economic power relations, with production and distribution being heterogeneous (Prasad 1998, 29), which in turn influences the nature of the genres of Indian films. Due to relations of power and dependency that develop between agents of production, distribution and exhibition, the Indian film industry has carved its own niches and has a number of unique regional genres, which include the devotional, historical, horror, social, romantic and masala film (Ganti 2013). Yet, while film genres are

S. Ghalian (✉)
Christ University, Bangalore, Karnataka, India

© The Author(s) 2020
B. Wilson and S. P. Gabriel (eds.), *Asian Children's Literature and Film in a Global Age*, Asia-Pacific and Literature in English, https://doi.org/10.1007/978-981-15-2631-2_7

141

more concretely defined in the West, with distinct categories such as comedy, romance, thriller and fantasy, within Indian cinema these generic distinctions are broader and often overlap. As a result of these broader, intertwined genres, children's cinema in India invariably finds itself positioned amid many vexed categories that are part of the larger, overall production complex of Indian cinema.

The British film scholar, Noel Brown (2015), while examining films from various studios, genres, countries, and periods, gives us a brief history of children's cinema in India. He posits that the most common observation of any study on children's film in India has been that it is fairly unstructured—children's cinema is seen as a loose and marginal segment of Indian cinema (Brown 2015, 187). For much of its history, both critics and audiences alike have regarded the category of children's films in India with little curiosity. The interaction of genre and audience within the larger segment of Indian cinema can be attributed as one of the reasons for the undefined status of children's film in India. Indeed, Shashi Dharan, the former Director of the National Film Archives of India, in an interview to *The Hindu* (2002) said that "it was very difficult to draw a line between films meant for children and others since even well-known children's films appealed to adults and there was no comprehensive definition of children's films".

Indian cinema enjoys the reputation of being one of the world's largest annual producers of films and has one of the biggest markets in the globe. Yet, the number of films that are child-centric, both by the definition of being *for* children or *about* children is fairly limited. In both Bollywood and regional cinema, children's cinema remains at the periphery (Rajagopalan 2013, 10). Despite having the largest population of children in the world,[1] Indian popular culture seems to have paid little interest towards critically interrogating the lives of young people (Pandey 2011, 2).

Perhaps partially because of this, investment in children's entertainment has been given fairly low priority within the industry.[2] According to the *FICCI-KPMG Indian Media and Entertainment Industry Report, 2015*, "Mumbai's film industry produces around 1400 films a year, and around 0.1% of them are children's films". In spite of such a state of financial affairs, eminent filmmaker, Gulzar, feels it cannot just be about commerce. Recalling Satyajit Ray's contributions, especially in the realm of children's literature, Gulzar tells *The Hindu*:

this kind of work requires a certain consciousness, an involvement with children. Are today's filmmakers indulging in this? Film directors claim a lack of funding; producers bemoan poor distribution and exhibition systems; and both lament the indifference of audiences—largely parents—towards children's cinema. (2017)

The general impression is that children's cinema in India is not only underfunded but also underloved and underwatched. In terms of children's cinema, today's millennials are largely exposed to Western productions, such as Disney films, franchises exemplified by the Harry Potter series, and other major Hollywood films, having had access to television at a young age. The marked rise in India's economy has resulted in a rapid proliferation of television sets in Indian homes across social strata, together with exponential growth in channels and content and corresponding exposure to Western children's content. In terms of local production, India continues to be predominantly a nation of family films, yet whether one can call Rohit Shetty's films—for example, the *Golmaal* series (2006, 2008, and 2010)—"children's" films is a matter worthy of further exploration. Today, most children, if exposed to popular Hindi films, would perhaps be watching films such as *Jagga Jasoos* (Anurag Basu 2017) and *Dangal* (Nitesh Tiwari 2016). The sheer volume of Bollywood films has thus popularised the idea of "family entertainment", blurring the boundary between what specifically constitutes child and family entertainment, and whether the two categories are separate entities. As film-watching is one of the most common pastimes among the adult Indian population, most films are passed off as being children-friendly, because children are taken for films along with the adults, turning it into an exercise of "family time" (Banaji 2006, 13). Yet despite this, in commercial cinema, it is mostly the adult appeal that remains desirable as a means of extending a film's potential reach and, thus, its profit (Brown 2015, 187).

With regard to producing content for children, a persistent debate surrounding the production of children's film in India has been on whether to make didactic films for children or those of a purely escapist nature. In other words, should film for children serve morally and psychologically to prepare the child for the demands of adulthood or should it be made only for pleasure? This issue bears some relation to the traditional debate in India regarding high-culture/popular-culture and the purpose of mass media. Such discussions centre on whether the use of media (in this instance, films) should educate the masses and elevate their tastes or whether films should be considered merely as lowbrow entertainment, with profits as the prime motive (Gokulsing and Dissanayake 2004). With more digitised and global productions, many Indian films have also come to be reliant on the idea of the spectacle, mostly aiming their narrative at the youth audience of the country.[3] Given that young people comprise the largest demographic group within the country, Indian cinema centres its narratives around them, as growing consumerism in the country has ensured that it is not merely the adult but also the young adult and, to a lesser extent, the child who have a stake as a consumer, a theme which is explored in the first section of the chapter. Thus, with the increasing size of the film-watching public, content is often determined by the representation of different age groups within this demographic. As entertainment and profit have invariably been the important determining factors in the production of cinema, and since children's films do not yet have a strong share of that lucrative market, films for children and about children have been few and far between. Bearing this in mind, the following section will focus on tracing a brief history of children and childhood representation in Indian cinema and the various roles they have come to occupy in the cinematic imagination.

TRACING THE FIGURE OF THE CHILD IN INDIAN CINEMA

As with the first films ever made globally, in the Indian context too the figure of the child has been part of popular Hindi cinema from as early as the post-independence era. In existing scholarship on the representation of children and childhood in Indian cinema, most attention has been paid to children in popular Hindi films. Nandini Chandra (2009) explores the earliest depictions of children and young people in 1950s Hindi cinema and notes that films such as *Munaa* (K. A. Abbas 1954), *Ferry* (Heman Gupta 1954), *Dosti* (Satyen Bose 1964), *Jagriti* (Sudhir Mukerjee 1954) and *Boot Polish* (Raj Kapoor 1954) foregrounded the figure of the child in order to focus on the heightened vulnerability of the underclass, especially on their suffering in the aftermath of war. These social realist films established archetypal visions of childhood that have dominated Hindi cinema ever since (Chandra 2009, 130). This genre is located within the Nehruvian socialist and Indian people's theatre association framework and is particularly evident in the work of filmmakers like K. A. Bose, Raj Kapoor, Heman Gupta and Satyen Bose, who specialised in narratives of the lost and wandering child (Chandra 2009, 131). Their views on childhood, as captured in the narrative of their films, were based on manipulating audience sympathy through the use of, for example, the orphan who underwent the trauma of homelessness. The figure of the child in these films was invariably invested with heavy pathos and was depicted amidst unbearable and intolerable destitution, the result of which was a narrative that often bordered on melodrama and precarious posturing.

The biographical accounts of the real experiences of child celebrities in this era reveal a dark side to their film careers as child actors, while also revealing a disparity between their depictions in the narratives and their actual lives as the children who starred in them. The documentary film, *Children of the Silver Screen* (Dilip Ghosh 1990), explores the exploitation of child performers by film studios and ambitious and demanding parents. Shakuntala Banaji (2017) in her recent study also provides us with accounts of child celebrities from Indian cinema. Through many interviews and press articles featuring these child stars who have now grown up, she highlights the paradox of children and childhood in the Indian context alongside their tricky representation in films (Banaji 2017, 56). She also depicts the similarity between corporal punishment as experienced by child stars during their film career with larger sociological accounts of children, be it their occupation as child labourers or those facing demanding social regimes and punishments at schools (Banaji 2017, 57).

Similarly, Chandra critiques the Progressive Writers' Association and the Indian Theatre Association whose members, despite the radical content of the reality portrayed in their films, kept children from marginal backgrounds in a continued state of disadvantage (Chandra 2009, 135). In a number of films, such as *Munna* (1954), *Jagriti* (1954) and *Ferry* (1954), the narrative suggests the aspiration of the state's view of children as future citizens. This version of development believed that the state should redeem the destitute but it also conceded its inability to accommodate everyone in this process which, by implication, meant that if the larger message included the poor, it also created a notion of the "deserving poor".[4] This interpretation then framed the notion of education and school as sites for children in films. The overall construction of the figure of the child in this era became a site for questioning the indifference of the state to the plight of the disadvantaged, while reaffirming its paternalistic authority. The physical features of the children represented in these films are stereotypical—the fair, cherubic face seems to symbolise the nostalgia of an innocent past of plenty and purity, juxtaposed against a background of the criminalised, urban milieu of cities, such as Bombay (now Mumbai).[5]

Alongside this nationalist rhetoric of the child, another domain beyond mainstream Hindi cinema includes other filmmakers such as Satyajit Ray, from the Parallel cinema movement, who portrayed more nuanced experiences and emotions of children and childhood. Known as a master of "realist" filmmaking and widely acknowledged as one of the greatest filmmakers of the twentieth century, Ray was also someone who wrote prolifically for children, as well as making children's films. His lesser known trilogy featured the comic duo, Goopy and Bagha, and comprised *Goopy Gyne Bagha Byne* (1969), *Hirok Rajar Deshe* (1980) and *Goopy Bagha Phire Elo* (1991), while his other children's films include *Sonar Kella* (1974), and *Joi Baba Felunath* (1979). Ray's use of fantasy in his children's narratives differed markedly from the realism he portrayed in his films, and he often employed children's literature for adaptations in children's films (Sircar 2016).[6] Alternative or Parallel cinema during the 1970s seemed more invested in depicting child-centric narratives, as may be witnessed in the work of prominent filmmakers such as Shyam Benegal, Mrinal Sen, Sai Paranjpe and M. S. Sathyu, all of whom were part of the Children's Film Society of India. Films such as *Kitaab* (1977), *Jadoo Ka Shankh* (1974) and *Sikandar* (1976) were popular films about children from this era of Indian cinema.

Exploring the representation of the child figure in later decades in mainstream Indian cinema, Corey Creekmur (2004) points us towards the dissolution of the child in popular Hindi films—primarily the male child figure in the era of the 1970s onwards. He argues that childhood problems or experiences in these films were commonly treated as familial rather than social (Creekmur 2004, 351). With the exception of a few earlier films that featured children in leading roles—*Boot Polish* (1954) and *Dosti* (1964) being two such examples—childhood in Hindi cinema is generally staged as a primal scene that projects the adult protagonist's identity, action and fate (Creekmur 2004, 352). Most of the characters in Hindi cinema from the 1970s are depicted as being wounded or traumatised by their childhood pain, accompanied almost always by the drawing of a direct causal and conscious chain between the suffering of childhood and the acts of adulthood that eventually transform boys into men (Creekmur 2004, 352; Joshi 2015, 70).

Once the hero arrives on screen to continue the child's life, the young boy disappears; he will not reappear in the film, except through a rare flashback sequence as a part of memory (Creekmur 2004, 353). Such temporal leaps reveal a casual attitude towards the nuances of childhood and adolescent experiences in shaping both character and narrative. This approach to representing the attainment of masculinity is usually marked by a quick and abrupt transition to adulthood and is best exemplified by the figure of the frustrated and rebellious male of the cinema of the 1970s. Most of the films of this period, especially those featuring Amitabh Bachchan, have become synonymous with the archetype of the "angry young man" in the popular imagination of the country, in that they depict men who find themselves confronting adulthood too early, and seeking revenge on enemies based on their memories of a traumatic childhood.[7]

In the 1980s, the film *Salaam Bombay* (Mira Nair 1988) brought a sharp focus on the thematic issues of marginality, poverty, class, gender and the ways in which children and childhood seem to negotiate these concerns. Typically considered as not "Indian" from the point of view of production and distribution, the film received mixed reactions from film critics and scholars, who criticised it for having an "outsider" (NRI or Non-Resident Indian) perspective on Indian poverty. The example of *Salaam Bombay* provides an important point of reference to discuss these themes, as it depicts the failure of the state to keep to the promises made to its citizens. Moving beyond the ideals of the Nehruvian era, the film attempts to show the plight of the underclass amid poverty and child labour (Virdi 1992, 31). The childhood experiences of growing up in the slums of Bombay become the landscape against which the myth of a developing India is interrogated. Since the release of this film, the imagery of the slum has come to occupy a significant trope in Indian cinema, particularly in relation to issues of urbanisation and the gentrification of spaces in the urban milieu. Ashis Nandy (1999) highlights the metaphor of the "urban slum" in Indian cinema and its consistency in using the allegory of the slum—one which has the capacity to recreate a sense of community which has its own distinctive lifestyle.

Another film from this period involving children is more in line with family-oriented drama. The narrative of *Masoom* (Shekar Kapur 1983) places the child in the middle of a crisis, typical of the problems which occurred due to the explosion of urban modernity among the Indian masses. According to Brown (2015), this film is in many ways reflective of the influence of modernity on traditional Indian social structures and values, in which the central family unit is nuclear rather than joint. One finds this transition of the Indian family from joint to nuclear, and the representation of issues like extramarital affairs, being represented and reflected upon through the figure of the child. In this instance, it is through the character of Rahul, the nine-year-old son of the protagonist, that the narrative is able to highlight the social and cultural changes that are occurring. In the storyline of the film, circumstances lead a family man to bring his son from an extramarital affair into his present home—much to his wife's disapproval. However, by the end of the story, one sees how the motherly instinct in the wife causes her to accept the boy into the family and she forgives her husband. Brown reads such a narrative as one which is reflective of the social conventions of Hindu culture in which the wife is subservient to the husband and upholds a mother's nurturing role (Brown 2015, 191). Though the film is not made for children, it depicts the child's emotions in a way that most family entertainment films which emerged later in the 1990s did not.

During the decade of post liberalisation (the 1990s), the number of child-centric narratives becomes fewer and one sees children appear only intermittently, as dramatic devices, in some commercial Hindi films. Two such examples are the character of Anjali in *Kuch Kuch Hota Hai* (Karan Johar 1998) uniting her father with his lost love, and little Raju as the sidekick who chaperones the adult lovers in *Raja Hindustani* (Dharmesh Darshan 1996), but rather than provide a focus on children, what one sees is the emergence of a hero who never grows up (Creekmur 2004, 354). One of the reasons for this decline in the narratives about children, it may be argued, is the fading out of the parallel film movement in the 1980s. Popular films from this period featuring actors like Shah Rukh Khan and Salman Khan are conspicuously devoid of a narrated childhood (Creekmur 2004, 361), and when one contrasts the characters played by Bachchan and Khan, and the imaginative transformation of the hero that they both represent in their respective films, one realises that:

> Bachchan's characters were unhappy adults forced to grow up too soon; Khan's characters, first encountered as young adults, threaten to never grow up. Their childhood is irrelevant because as adults they appear childish, happy old boys rather than angry young men. (Creekmur 2004, 367).

According to Banaji, this trend of the 1990s of "making the hero behave in juvenile fashion through actions like falling over, stammering, sucking on lollipops, dressing in dungarees and other markers of teenage fashion, reveal a strengthening of the resistance to representing childhood for and in itself" (Banaji 2017, 58). Indeed, most of the films of this era do not include the figure of the child at all, and one mostly witnesses "adults miming a very particular version of childhood, making friends, fighting shyness, learning to dance and rollerblading through their bedrooms piled from floor to ceiling with stuffed toys and train sets" (Banaji 2017, 59; Chattopadhyay 2011). These traits of heroes acting like children, according to Banaji, suggest a rendering of a specific childhood—an urban, Western, middle-class childhood that was by now starting to become more common in the wake of neoliberal conditions in India (Banaji 2017, 61).

Typically, in Indian cinema during this period, children are not cast as central protagonists and they seldom enjoy autonomous agency within cinematic representation. Towards the end of the 1990s, though, one breakthrough film that does focus exclusively on a child's coming of age, experiences and emotions is the film *Rockford* (Nagesh Kukunoor 1999), a film that explores adolescent life at boarding schools, which were then establishing themselves in the popular educational imagination of India. In his film, Kukunoor brings out the nuances of childhood days, while evoking the sensitive and often unspoken issue of sexual awakening among adolescents in India.

Alternative to this solitary example of representing adolescence that one finds in *Rockford*, the period of the early 2000s essays another set of transformations and brings new paradigms of characterisation. Films such as *Dil Chahta Hai* (Farhan Akhtar 2001) and *Bombay Boys* (Kaizad Gustad 2000) focus instead on affirming Indian forms of masculinity through coming-of-age narratives, most of which waste no time on the childhood of the protagonists. Depicted as NRIs or "rich kids", the narrative allows them to spend their early adulthood in finding themselves vis-à-vis "aimless" adventures (Creekmur 2004, 371). Such films capture the homogenisation of representation in popular Hindi films as they serve as harbingers of the arrival of Indian versions of global youth culture. These youth films not only represent an upper middle-class lifestyle in their narrative, but also completely dissolve the marginal presence of young children (boys) and men that existed in the earlier films before liberalisation. These new representational schemas must be read alongside the socio-economic transformations occurring in Indian society, with cinema popularising the multiplex and creating consumer-driven audiences whose lifestyles simultaneously found greater representational space in the cinematic medium. What such films brought about was a fundamental homogenisation of the popular imagination, of particular ideas of aspiration, achievement, love and fantasy that marginalised any other kind of representation, and under these circumstances, reflective of the societal changes taking place in modern middle-class India, one may understand that within the scope of cinematic representation of identity there has been a gradual but steady exclusion of the representation of working-class stories and their realities, and the children emerging from those realities.

A globally successful film which did bring back the depiction of a childhood from the margins was *Slumdog Millionaire* (Danny Boyle 2008). As yet another foreign production, the film was much criticised by media locally on similar grounds to that of *Salaam Bombay*—of providing an outsider's perspective on Indian conditions.[8] This film takes us to the urban slums of Bombay while weaving a popular narrative, that of a happy ending in which a poor child grows up to win a highly rewarding quiz show and unites with his dream girl, thus changing his destiny (Collins 2009). Such representations can sometimes be seen to be a form of cinematic manipulation, where the poor child is often constructed into an exceptional on-screen avatar in an attempt to draw on humane sentiments. Many such narratives represent the drive of the poor towards entrepreneurship and creativity to overcome their metaphorical or very real difficulties, and such fairytale stories of unlikely success appear to be shrewdly crafted to suit mainstream middle-class sensibilities, often failing to address the larger structural issues of caste, class, merit and gender.

Beyond the success and external critical acclaim of films such as *Slumdog Millionaire* (2008), Banaji (2017) reveals to us the coercive power of the rising Indian middle-class children as conspicuous consumers for whom the industry sometimes sensationalises marginal entrants as a deliberate strategy of neoliberalism. Although the viewer may be drawn in by new cinematic techniques and industry ploys, closer analysis reveals that these trends are being manifested against an absence of the representation of working-class childhoods in popular cinema. Analysis of this strategy, supported by existing research, draws attention to the increasing marginalisation of children from working-class backgrounds as performers in Hindi films (Banaji 2017, 54). This dominant trend remains prevalent, partly because it is mostly the children of the rich and famous who become stars and remain stars in cinema, creating a self-perpetuating cycle. As one example of many, in the film *Stanley Ka Dabba* (2011), the protagonist Stanley, is played by Partho Gupte, who is the son of Amol Gupte, the film's director. *Stanley Ka Dabba* (Amol Gupte 2011) depicts an orphan who, through his ingenuity, charm and talent, manages to become popular within the milieu of a middle-class convent school.

CONCLUSION

Through this brief historical account it becomes apparent, when one looks at the representation of children within the larger oeuvre of Indian cinema, that different decades have had different trajectories in representing children and childhood in film narratives. The role of children and childhood in popular Hindi cinema from the early years of independence up to contemporary Bollywood films has changed in line with changing national and social imperatives and ideals. The Nehruvian era drew largely upon an inclusive post-independence communal vision in which citizens from all walks of life were encouraged to sublimate their individual desires to those of the new Indian state and its modernising tendency, a rendering that culminates in the predominance of urban consumerism as is experienced today. Banaji sums up this gradual change in the portrayal of children in the following manner:

> Metaphors for the nation to the powers in family and community in the early films seems to have been replaced with liberalisation for a more celebratory form—relying on precociousness, cuteness, infantilism, consumerist and extended character of adolescence which in turn leaves very little space of depiction of actual children and their childhood world. (Banaji 2017, 55)

With the impetus for making films shifting from a Nehruvian socialistic and public platform to a more private platform, one also finds a marginal role for cinema in terms of nation-building and an increase in cinema representing neoliberal forms of branding the nation (Devasundaram 2016). However, this conceptualisation is now undergoing further changes in the films emerging from contemporary Indian cinema.

More recently, the role of children and child-centric narratives seems to have gone a step further, transforming along the lines of the development and the rising popularity of more independent cinema that is now taking form within the larger body of Indian cinema. Recent scholarship from childhood studies in India points to the diversity of the experiences of children in a country that is undergoing transformation on multiple fronts—globalisation, technological advancements, an increasing emphasis on access to school and the impact of education and urbanisation on changes in family structures (Saraswathi et al. 2017, 2). Alongside these fundamental changes in the spectrum of Indian society, there has been a considerable rise in children's cinema in the last ten years or so, a rise which seems to resonate with the sociopolitical changes affecting the lives of the children.

Today, one finds children stories, and representations of childhood, returning in a new light and context as a thematic subject in the narratives of many films within the larger oeuvre of Indian cinema, from both popular as well as independent films. Vishal Bhardwaj, an Indian director who has made a number of children's films, has observed in one of his media interviews that, "with the advent of digital technology, the future for children's films looks very bright as it can be made with very low budget". In recent years, there has been a growing number of child-centric films, which include: *The Blue Umbrella* (Vishal Bharadwaj 2005), *Taare Zameen Par* (Aamir Khan 2007), *Tahaan* (Batul Muktiyaar 2008), *Thanks Maa* (Irfan Kamal 2009), *Bumm Bumm Bole* (Priyadarshan 2010), *Chillar Party* (Nitesh Tiwari and Vikas Bahl 2011), *Stanley Ka Dabba* (Amol Gupte 2012), *Hawaa Hawaai* (Amol Gupte, 2014), *Dhanak* (Nagesh Kukunoor 2016) and *Sniff* (Amol Gupte 2017), to name but a few. The commercial success, both at national and international levels, of a number of these films, which centre on the theme of childhood, is perhaps the primary reason emerging contemporary filmmakers feel motivated to continue to tell stories through children.

While Hindi cinema is more popular in India and has contributed to various narratives about children, films from regional cinemas are also beginning to centre a number of their narratives on children. Within the last decade or so, one can find quite a few films that are child-centric and depict various nuances of childhood in Marathi children's films (Wani 2015). Films such as *Tingya* (Mangesh Hadawale 2008), *Vihir* (Umesh Kulkarni 2010), *Shala* (Sujay Dahake 2012), *Timepass* (Ravi Jadhav 2014), *Balak Palak* (Ravi Jadhav 2013), *Fandry* (Nagraj Manjule 2013), *Killa* (Avinash Arun 2014), *Elizabeth Ekadashi* (Paresh Mokashi 2014), *Aayna ka Bayna* (Samit Kakkad 2012), *Tapaal* (Laxman Utekar 2014), *Baboo Band Baaja* (Rajesh Pinjani 2012), *Avatarachi Goshta* (Nitin Dixit 2014), *Salaam* (Kiran Yadnyopavit 2014) and *Yellow* (Mahesh Limaye 2014) have led to the resurgence of Marathi cinema and have contributed considerably to the larger component of children's film at a national level.

The thematic and narrative treatment of characters and plot in many of these recent films seem to have been inspired and influenced by cinema from other global locations, particularly the Iranian and French "New Wave" child-centred cinema.[9] Whether in their use of authentic locations, or realist narrative strategies and stories based on the experiences of childhood, many of these emerging Indian filmmakers seem to draw particularly upon the language of Iranian cinema. Thematically, the majority of these films deal with the various nuances of childhood and the circumstances of children's everyday lives, moving into the spaces and places of childhood to explore the vulnerabilities and struggles of young children as they spatially negotiate the physical and mental dynamics of an adult world. They depict sensitised themes that represent identities at the brink, that question belonging, that capture the urban–rural divide, the class and caste consciousness, and provide narratives that would otherwise struggle to gain a foothold in mainstream debates in the popular media at large.

NOTES

1. Government of India, *Provisional Population Totals Paper 1 of 2011 India*, Series 1 (New Delhi: Registrar General & Census Commissioner, India, 2011). India, with 1.21 billion people, constitutes the second most populous country in the world, while children represent 39% of the total population of the country. It has the world's largest child population, at 400 million.
2. Sanjukta Sharma, "Movie Time with My Child," *Livemint*, July 21, 2017, https://www.livemint.com/Leisure/pVeWm0h8BBMfHQT83JwuPJ/Movie-time-with-my-child.html. In this article, Annette Brejner, creative director of the Sweden-based Financing Forum For Kids Content, which collaborates with filmmakers from across the world to develop and produce films for children, says: "There are no political agreements made in India that specifically are aimed at supporting a children's film culture, whereas in my part of the world, it has taken several different initiatives to make it happen over the years. Some countries have ruled that 25% of the governmental yearly film subsidies must be given to children's films".
3. Mihir Sharma, "India's Youth Are the World's Future," Bloomberg, Sept. 8, 2017, https://www.bloomberg.com/view/articles/2017-09-08/india-s-youth-are-the-world-s-future. This article informs us about a recent

Bloomberg News analysis which discovered that India has the largest population of youth, and is likely to have the world's largest workforce by 2027, with a billion people aged between 15 and 64.

4. Chandra studies the child stars of the 1950s and the 1960s and their realities in the industry. What is less known is the actual life narratives of the child artists of these films, who often struggled between these various notions of nationalism and the demands and lifestyle of cinema itself. She has researched not only on the construction of childhood during this period, along the Nehruvian vision of the nation and its citizens, but has also collected the narratives of the child actors who acted in these films, namely Daisy Irani, Master Romi and Jagdeep (of the 1950s) and Master Raju and Mehmood (of the 1960s and 70s). These social realist films, as they were recognised, reserved the most clichéd role for children, where the bourgeois child played the central "cute kid" and the working class played the other lesser side-characters. None of these had ever been to school, and all of them were Muslim. They suffered either due to bourgeoisie parents who exploited them for money and forced them into roles in the films, or due to poverty, having to deal with the harsh city and its lifestyle single-handedly.

5. The majority of these films were shot in the urban landscapes of Bombay, which is where the Hindi cinema industry is located.

6. Ajanta Sircar, *The Category of Children's Cinema in India* (Shimla: Indian Institute of Advanced Study, 2016). Sircar analyses Satyajit Ray's realist films, which are mostly focused on questions of female desire, his children's world being peculiarly masculine. According to her, subtle themes and messages pervasive in these films were more than just a fantasy, but, rather, became a strong socio-political commentary on the notion of war and peace. Ray coedited the Bengali children's magazine "Sandesh" started by his grandfather Upendrakishor Ray.

7. The cinematic avatar of Amitabh Bachchan as 'the Angry Young Man' represented the anger and frustration of the impoverished working class and the helpless middle class of India. His films such as *Zanzeer* (Prakash Mehra 1973), *Roti Kapada Aur Makaan* (Manoj Kumar 1974), *Deewar* (Yash Chopra 1975), *Amar Akbar Anthony* (Manmohan Desai 1977), *Khoon Pasina* (Rakesh Kumar 1977), *Kaala Pathar* (Yash Chopra 1979), *Kaalia* (Tinnu Anand 1981), *Namak Halaal* (Prakash Mehra, 1982), *Andha Kanoon* (Rama Rao 1983), *Coolie* (Manmohan Desai 1983), *Shehanshah* (Tinnu Anand 1988) and others portray both the plight of, as well as the struggle of, the poor against the rich in India.

8. Bryan Alexander, "Bollywood Star: "Slumdog Millionaire" Not an Indian Film," NBCUniversal, Aug. 10, 2010, https://www.nbcdfw.com/blogs/popcornbiz/Bollywood-Star-Aamir-Khan--Slumdog-Millionaire-Is-Not-An-Indian-Film-100317154.html; and Paul MacInnes, "How Slumdog

Millionaire Is Changing Film-Making in India," *Guardian*, June 4, 2009, https://www.theguardian.com/film/2009/jun/04/slumdog-millionaire-india.

9. Umesh Kulkarni, in discussion with the filmmaker, September 6, 2017, (Manipal, India). While in conversation with Umesh Kulkarni, director of the award winning film *Vihir* (2010) and many other compelling films, he agreed that there was a lack of cinema for children or about childhood in the Indian context. He also casually mentioned how, in terms of inspiration for such a subject, one can and does look at Iranian cinema.

References

Alexander, Bryan. 2010. "Bollywood Star: "Slumdog Millionaire" Not an Indian Film." NBCUniversal, Aug. 10, 2010. https://www.nbcdfw.com/blogs/popcornbiz/Bollywood-Star-Aamir-Khan–Slumdog-Millionaire-Is-Not-An-Indian-Film-100317154.html. Accessed on March 10, 2019.

Banaji, Shakuntala. 2017. "Bollywood's Periphery: Child Stars and Representations of Childhood in Hindi Films." In *Childhood and Celebrity*, edited by Jane O'Connor and John Mercer, 53–65. New York: Routledge.

———. 2006. "Young People Viewing Hindi Films: Ideology, Pleasure and Meaning." *Merz: Medien+Erziehung* 3: 12–18.

Brown, Noel. 2015. "A Brief History of Indian Children Cinema." In *Family Films in Global Cinema: The World Beyond Disney (Cinema and Society)*, edited by Noel Brown and Bruce Babington, 186–204. London: I.B. Tauris.

Chandra, Nandini. 2009. "Merit and Opportunity in the Child-Centric Nationalist Films of the 1950s." In *Narratives of Indian Cinema*, edited by Manju Jain, 123–144. New Delhi: Primus Books.

Chattopadhyay, Saayan. 2011. "Boyhood, Ideology, and Popular Hindi Cinema." *Thymos: Journal of Boyhood Studies* 5, no. 2: 138–151.

Collins, Alfred. 2009. "Salaam Slumdog! Personal and Cultural Trauma and Restitution in the Mumbai Slums." *Psychological Studies* 54: 194–201. https://doi.org/10.1007/s12646-009-0026-1. Accessed August 3, 2017.

Creekmur, Corey K. 2004. "Bombay Boys: Dissolving the Male Child in Popular Indian Cinema." In *Where the Boys Are: Cinemas of Masculinity and Youth*, edited by Murray Pomerance and Frances K. Gateward, 350–376. Detroit, MI: Wayne State University Press.

Devasundaram, Ashvin I. 2016. "Bollywood's Soft Power: Branding the Nation, Sustaining a Meta-Hegemony." *New Cinemas: Journal of Contemporary Film* 14, no. 1: 51–70.

Ganti, Tejaswani. 2013. *Bollywood: A Guidebook to Popular Hindi Cinema*. New York: Routledge.

Gokulsing, K. Moti, and Wimal Dissanayake. 2004. *Indian Popular Cinema: A Narrative of Cultural Change*. Trent, UK: Trentham Books.

Joshi, Priya. 2015. *Bollywood's India: A Public Fantasy*. Columbia University Press.

KPMG. *FICCI-KPMG Indian Media and Entertainment Industry Report, 2015*. https://assets.kpmg.com/content/dam/kpmg/pdf/2015/03/FICCI-KPMG_2015.pdf. Accessed on April 12, 2019.

MacInnes, Paul. 2009. "How Slumdog Millionaire Is Changing Film-Making in India." *Guardian*, June 4, 2009. https://www.theguardian.com/film/2009/jun/04/slumdog-millionaire-india. Accessed on April 30, 2019.

Nandy, Ashis. 1999. "Indian Popular Cinema as a Slum's Eye View of Politics." In *The Secret Politics of Our Desires: Innocence, Culpability, and Indian Popular Cinema*, edited by Ashis Nandy, 1–18. New Delhi: Oxford University. Accessed on April 19, 2019.

Pal, Shubhodeep. "No Child's Play." *The Hindu*. May 14, 2017. https://www.thehindu.com/todayspaper/tp-features/tp-sundaymagazine/no-childs-play/article18450324.ece. Accessed on April 25, 2019.

Pandey, Siddarth. 2011. "Interrogating Masculinity Through the Child Figure in Bombay Cinema." In *Networking Knowledge: Journal of Media, Communication and Cultural Studies Association* 4, no. 1: 1–21.

Prasad, M. Madhava. 1998. *Ideology of the Hindi Film: A Historical Construction*. Delhi: Oxford University Press.

Rajagopalan, Jayashree. 2013. "Heal the World, Make It a Better Place: Social and Individual Hope in Indian Children's Cinema." In *Bookbird: A Journal of International Children's Literature* 51, no. 1: 10–19.

Saraswathi, T.S., Shailaja Menon, and Ankur Madan, eds. 2017. *Childhood in India: Traditions, Trends and Transformations*. New Delhi: Routledge.

Sharma, Mihir. 2017. "India's Youth Are the World's Future." Bloomberg, Sept. 8, 2017. https://www.bloomberg.com/view/articles/2017-09-08/india-s-youth-are-the-world-sfuture.

Sharma, Sanjukta. 2017. "Movie Time with My Child." *Livemint*, July 21, 2017. https://www.livemint.com/Leisure/pVeWm0h8BBMfHQT83JwuPJ/Movie-time-withmy-child.html.

Sircar, Ajanta. 2016. *The Category of Children's Cinema in India*. Shimla: Indian Institute of Advanced Study.

The Hindu. "Children's film movement fails to make its mark." Dec. 14, 2002. http://www.thehindu.com/2002/12/15/stories/2002121502720400.htm. Accessed on April 15, 2019.

Virdi, Jyotika. 1992. "Salaam Bombay! (Mis)Representing Child Labor." *Jump Cut: A Review of Contemporary Media* 37: 29–36.

Wani, Aarti. 2015. "'The Child' of New Marathi Cinema." *Studies in South Asian Film & Media* 7, nos. 1–2: 59–70.

CHAPTER 8

Engendering Identities: Gay and Lesbian Characters in Contemporary Indian English Young Adult Fiction

Suchismita Banerjee

INTRODUCTION

Whoever voluntarily has carnal intercourse against the order of nature with any man, woman or animal shall be punished with imprisonment for life, or with imprisonment of either description for a term which may extend to ten years, and shall also be liable to a fine.

The above words comprise the text of Section 377 of the Indian Penal Code (IPC), which has been the subject of much controversy, litigation and activism in recent times in India.

In order to better understand this contentious area of law and the debate which surrounds it in modern India, one should first examine its history. Ironically the UK, upon whose Victorian-era laws India's

S. Banerjee (✉)
Jawaharlal Nehru University (JNU), New Delhi, India

© The Author(s) 2020
B. Wilson and S. P. Gabriel (eds.), *Asian Children's Literature and Film in a Global Age*, Asia-Pacific and Literature in English,
https://doi.org/10.1007/978-981-15-2631-2_8

penal code is based, decriminalised homosexuality in 1967, yet this anachronistic legislation of 1861 has often been misused to harass and exploit members of the LGBTQIA+ community in contemporary India. Section 377 has had a tumultuous history of opposition, repeal, reinstatement and further repeal over the past couple of decades in India. Indeed, a Delhi High Court ruling in 2009, which had repealed this IPC section, leading to widespread jubilation among the public, was reversed in a 2013 Supreme Court judgement which claimed that India's LGBTQIA+ community represented a "minuscule minority", thus once again effectively criminalising this community. In a further about-face, on 6 September 2018, the Supreme Court ruled that Section 377 of the IPC, as applied to consenting adults, violated India's constitutional morality, a landmark judgement which was received with great celebration in civil society, and which turned the spotlight once again on the LGBTQIA+ community.

Though the latest judgement makes it legally possible for the LGBTQIA+ community to live with dignity and in peace in India, the ground realities are still sombre and unlikely to change in the near future. In an interview given to the daily *Deccan Herald*, psychoanalyst Sudhir Kakar commented on the significance of this ruling:

> The judgement is of enormous significance for those still struggling with their sexual identity, a vastly greater number than those who have accepted their homosexuality and constitute the gay movement. The phrase 'coming out' refers to the public acknowledgment of one's homosexuality, but there is an analogous internal 'coming out,' a sort of self-realisation that one is a homosexual.

> My identity does not take place in a vacuum but needs my culture's validation: not only my inner assertion, 'I am this,' but the culture's 'Yes, you are that.' The court judgment makes it possible for our society to begin the process of validating homosexual identity, i.e. 'You are a homosexual, not a criminal.' (Kakar 2009)

The purpose of this chapter is to discuss key trends and attitudes towards queer people in contemporary Indian society, specifically gays and lesbians, through an examination of the power dynamics inherent in their representation in media, and especially in young adult fiction. In order to illustrate the issues involved and the challenges faced by authors in securing visibility and fair representation for the community, the chapter includes an interview I conducted with two authors of young adult novels dealing with, but not restricted to, the issue of homosexuality.

Is Homosexuality a Modern Western Construct?

The Supreme Court ruling has upheld the right of the LGBTQIA+ community to live with dignity and conferred on them the right to choose their partner irrespective of gender. Yet while many perceive this as an acknowledgement of a contemporary reality, the idea of same-sex relationships was not unknown in ancient India.[1] Kakar and mythologist Devdutt Pattanaik have noted that several Hindu scriptures such as the *Dharmashastras* (Hindu law books) contain references to, though not approval of, homosexual acts. As a further example, among the erotic sculptures that adorn the Khajuraho temples in the state of Madhya Pradesh, one depicts a homosexual act. In relation to historical references to homosexuality, Sudhir and Katharina Kakar note:

> In classical India the disparagement for the homosexual was not devoid of compassion. The homosexual belonged to a deficient class of men called *kliba* in Sanskrit... 'Kliba' was a catch-all term to include someone who was sterile, impotent, castrated, a transvestite, a man who had oral sex with other men, who had anal sex as a recipient, a man with mutilated or deficient sexual organs, a man who produced only female children, or, finally, a hermaphrodite. 'Kliba' is not a term that exists any longer but some of its remnants — the perception of a deficiency, and the combination of pity, dismay and a degree of revulsion towards a man who is unable to marry and produce children, continues (sic) to cling to the Indian homosexual. (Kakar and Kakar 2009, 102)

Though the Indian mindset tends to ascribe the practice of homosexuality as a corrupting trend originating from Western society, Sudhir and Katharina Kakar point out that in ancient India, homosexual activity was ignored or considered inferior, but not actively persecuted. The law books prescribed mild punishment for male homoerotic activity. Even after the advent of Islam in India, this attitude did not change materially. Though Islam condemns homosexuality as a serious crime, Islamic culture in India had a Persian cast wherein homoeroticism was celebrated in literature. In Sufi mystical poetry, both in Persian and later in Urdu, the relationship between the divine and human was expressed in homoerotic metaphors (Kakar and Kakar 2009, 103).

In another article on homosexuality in India, Sudhir Kakar comments:

In general, then, India has a tradition of "benign neglect" of alternate sexualities, a tradition that is very much a part of the Indian mind. The laws against homosexual activity, such as the act of 1861, are all examples of a repressive Victorian moral code. It is ironical that reactionaries, both Hindu and Muslim, who reject homosexuality as a decadent Western phenomenon, subscribe to the same foreign code that is so alien to the Indian tradition. (Kakar 2007, 4)

Similarly, Pattanaik argues that homosexuality existed in societies of ancient India, and was not specifically opposed. Based on his examination of erotic temple imagery, sacred narratives and ancient law books, Pattanaik concludes that same-sex intercourse did exist in India. Though the *Dharmashastras* valued heterosexual marriage and sex that resulted in production of sons, they did grudgingly acknowledge that other forms of sex existed (Pattanaik 2016).

Pattanaik draws upon ancient Hindu myths and characters from Hindu mythology to assert that gender fluidity existed in ancient India and that the notion of the third gender is not a "modern" and western construct. There are several figures in Hindu mythology that are of ambiguous gender, the most prominent among them being Shikhandi (a character in the epic *Mahabharata*) and Bahuchara Mata (considered the patron of members of the third gender in India). He notes that:

Shikhandi embodies all queer people – from gays to lesbians to Hijras[2] to transgendered people to hermaphrodites to bisexuals. Like their stories, his story remains invisible. But the great author, Vyasa, located this story between the ninth night and the tenth day, right in the middle of the war.[3] This was surely not accidental. It was a strategic pointer to things that belong neither here nor there. This is how the ancients gave voice to the non-heterosexual discourse. (Pattanaik 2009)

These observations conflict with the prevalent notion in India that homosexuality is a modern-day transgression of "Indian" culture. As I have noted elsewhere, although the Indian demographic comprises significant numbers of Muslims, Christians and followers of other religious denominations, the categories "Hindu" and "Indian" tend to be unproblematically conflated because Hindus are the majority community in India (Banerjee 2018, 195). This trend has gathered momentum in the past four years due to the ruling dispensation, which has relentlessly and publicly pursued a Hindutva[4] agenda and injected a distinctly communal/religious flavour into the nationalist discourse.

CULTURE AND NATIONALISM

The constitution of culture and its intersection with nationalism has been a subject of rigorous research globally. In India, there is a tendency to conceive of "Indian culture" as a monolithic entity and ascribe to it certain (hetero)normative ideals against which individuals in society are judged and evaluated. This entity derives its power from its positioning as the upholder of ancient traditions and is fundamentally (I use the word advisedly) opposed to what it perceives as the "polluting" effects of a pervasive modern Western culture, that is similarly constructed as a homogeneous entity. As Tejaswini Niranjana points out:

> The culture question is posed in the Third World – or, more broadly, non-Western societies – as part of a colonial contestation; in India, for example, the term *sanskriti*, which translates as 'culture', is emblematic of a system of representation that calls 'Indian culture' into being. Here, the culture question is an intimate part of the formation of a national(ist) modernity, but culture in modernity tends to be represented as something that remains outside of modernity. (Niranjana 2007, 211)

In her discussion on the relationship between feminism and nationalism, Niranjana observes that criticism of feminism across Asia stems from the notion that it is disconnected/alienated from "our culture". Implicit in this notion is the assumption that feminist demands are modern demands, and that modernisation necessarily entails the erasure of one's native culture and the adoption of Western values and ways of life (Niranjana 2007, 211).

The opposition to same-sex relationships partially stems from a similar deeply entrenched notion that homosexuality is innately alien to "Indian" culture and an import from the west. Although a study of the sociological implications of a lack of acceptance and active resistance to homosexuality is beyond the scope of this chapter, it is important to record a few key observations on the structure and nature of the family and community in India today and the impact they have on the persona of children and young adults as they explore their sexuality and sexual identity.

THE INFLUENCE OF FAMILY AND COMMUNITY

As in most societies, the family is the basis of community living in India. While it is inadvisable to unproblematically pose a clear dichotomy between Indian and Western, especially in today's globalised world, there is ample evidence and research that indicates that the Indian way of life is strongly influenced by community values while Western society encourages the spirit of individualism. As noted psychiatrist B. K. Ramanujam has observed:

> The social structure does not permit the emergence of a cogent adult role as perceived in Western societies. Subordinating one's individual need to the interests of the group [...] is upheld as a virtue. Thus, self-assertion becomes selfishness, independent decision-making is perceived as disobedience. The response from the in-group is tacit disapproval if not outright condemnation. Under such circumstances, it is easier to play safe. (Ramanujam 1979, 54)

In this scenario of conformity, what does it mean to be different in India today? How does society perceive people who are viewed as different? Although Indian society does not consist of a homogeneous community and differences between rural and urban society, as well as socio-economic factors such as caste and class, need to be taken into consideration, there is a no gainsaying the fact that there is a common thread of tacit or explicit disapproval of same-sex relationships. The acceptance is more among the upper classes, where the privilege of power and class insulates members from persecution or discrimination. In rural India or among the economically weaker sections of society, same-sex relationships tend to be pursued clandestinely for fear of social ostracism: they often come to light only when they result in a criminal act, such as the murder of a partner or a public fracas that is reported in the media.

REPRESENTATION IN MEDIA

This brings us to the question of how homosexuality and the LGBTQIA+ community are represented in the media in India and the influence of the media on attitudes towards members of this community. In her discussion on representation and mainstream cinema, Rajeswari Sunder Rajan comments that representation involves what she terms as "power, regulation and the policing of discursive boundaries":

> Mainstream cinema both draws from and significantly shapes larger social realities (as well as fantasies). This is particularly true in a country like India which has the second largest film industry in the world, and where viewership cuts across class, age, region and language. (Rajan 2008, 69–70)

Until recently, representation of homosexuals in the Hindi film industry (known as Bollywood) has largely consisted of caricatures, and these characters have conventionally been the object of scorn and parody. However, globalisation and the influence of western culture has been instrumental in enabling a recognition and an acceptance of alternate sexualities, as well as a more matter-of-fact attitude towards the LGBTQIA+ community. In the past few decades, films such as *Fire* (1996), *My Brother Nikhil* (2005), *I Am* (2010), *Aligarh* (2016) and *Kapoor and Sons* (2016) have portrayed homosexual characters with sensitivity and empathy and, despite protests by certain sections of the populace, they have succeeded to some extent in altering the public perception of homosexuals.

Representation in Young Adult Fiction

How has this newfound acceptance been represented in young adult fiction? The focus of this paper is the representation of LGBTQIA+, specifically gay, characters in contemporary young adult fiction by Indian writers in English. It is a telling comment on the state of the publishing industry that there are very few young adult works of fiction in English by Indian writers that feature gay characters. My study of two of these novels will explore how gay characters are represented in contemporary young adult fiction and assess the influence of these novels on the shaping or reinforcing of societal and cultural tropes. It aims to deconstruct gender stereotypes and depictions of cultural or gender expectations within modern Indian society. How do gay characters in these novels deal with their sexuality and the awareness of their difference from heteronormative societal codes? How does society perceive these individuals? What is the influence of peers in the process of identity formation? This chapter will also examine the intersection of gender and class in these novels and the defining role of family and community in constructing and upholding gay identity. The two novels under discussion are *Talking of Muskaan* (2014) by Himanjali Sankar and *Slightly Burnt* (2014) by Payal Dhar. A brief summary of each of these novels follows.

Talking of Muskaan portrays the lives of a group of teenagers in a school and how they come to terms with the fact that their classmate Muskaan is a lesbian. The book opens with Muskaan in hospital after an attempted suicide, and the rest of the narrative consists of her friends' recollections of the circumstances leading up to this event. *Slightly Burnt* traces the changing dynamics between two friends after Komal discovers that her best friend Sahil is gay, and is attracted to her own brother.

Both stories feature teenaged characters negotiating relationships in school, at home and in the world around them. While *Talking of Muskaan* is told in alternating voices and with multiple perspectives, *Slightly Burnt* is narrated from the point of view of Komal, a seventeen-year-old girl. Both use suicide (or the fear of it) as a trope that forces the characters to acknowledge the protagonists' struggle for identity and acceptance. It is not mere coincidence that both books were published in 2014, the year after the Supreme Court reversed the earlier judgement and recriminalised homosexuality. Both novels include scenes in which the characters discuss the judgement, and the impact of this judgement and the debate around it is evident in the growth curve of the main characters. In my interview with the authors (see below), both mentioned that they had reviewed each other's manuscripts. Evidently, the books were written in response to a felt need to tell the stories of these characters and draw attention to a reality that has been hitherto ignored or treated with awkwardness in contemporary society, particularly among adolescents.

Talking of Muskaan opens with Muskaan's friends being summoned to the school principal's office. They are told that Muskaan had attempted suicide early that morning and is fighting for her life in hospital. This news triggers a flood of reminiscences for each of the characters whose memories, tinged with remorse, guilt and self-righteousness, form the narrative. They trace Muskaan's journey from discovering that she is lesbian, coming to terms with this fact, sharing the truth with her best friend Aaliya and being bullied at school when her classmates realise she is gay, to the climax when she is publicly humiliated and Aaliya rejects her appeal for support, declaring that she is a criminal because of her sexual identity.

Slightly Burnt depicts the relationship between Komal, her best friend Sahil and her brother Vikram. The blurb features a defining extract from the story, in which Komal tries to prepare herself to gently reject Sahil's confession of love for her. The narrative, however, reveals that Sahil has confessed to his best friend that he is gay. Komal later discovers that Sahil is in love with her own brother Vikram, and is plunged into a maelstrom of emotions. The story then traces Komal's journey from disbelief, confusion and awkwardness to gradual acceptance and the discovery that "Everything's just the same" (Dhar 2014, 174).

Dealing with Stereotypes

In both novels, the gay characters are delineated with authenticity and empathy, and without resorting to gender stereotyping. Sahil in *Slightly Burnt* is depicted as a "regular" guy, who enjoys vigorous sports, such as swimming and tennis. His friend and partner Vikram hates cricket and swimming but is passionate about photography. In *Talking of Muskaan*, the male characters find Muskaan physically attractive, but she does not reciprocate their interest in her. The author, however, draws attention to Muskaan's difference from the others: she does not enjoy the "girlie" things that her gang insists on doing, such as waxing, shopping for dresses at malls and discussing dating and fashion. She prefers dressing in jeans and shirts and wears "white converse shoes, with neon coloured laces on one and blue laces on the other" (Sankar 2014, 11).

Neither novel attempts to pigeonhole the teenaged characters into categories but, rather, focuses on the exploration of their identities, of which sexuality is just one aspect. Moreover, this exploration of sexuality and experimentation is not restricted to the gay characters: some of their friends also admit to being confused about their preferences. In *Talking of Muskaan*, Aaliya is first made aware of her best friend Muskaan's sexual preferences when Muskaan kisses her. Rather than being outraged, she enjoys it and kisses her back. Yet, later, Aaliya rejects this realisation and tries to reassure herself that she is "normal" like other girls:

> I was glad I'd kissed a boy at last. I didn't want to be lesbian or even bisexual. Everyone made fun of gays. Besides, I really did enjoy kissing that Rishi. (66)

She recalls the feeling of kissing Muskaan and compares it to her experience of kissing a boy:

> If I had to be very honest I would admit that that had blown my mind and made the rest of the world disappear [...] On the other hand, I'd just kissed a guy I didn't know at all and quite enjoyed it. I am so not gay. (66)

The implication is that unless there is an overwhelming preference for same-sex partners, it is "safer" to ignore or actively reject one's leanings towards same-sex relationships and opt for conventional pairings:

> I've been paying close attention to the way the laws of attraction work
> for me. And I've realised something significant. It was, like, gender didn't
> matter to me – it was the person. I could equally well be attracted to a boy
> or a girl. But I plan to condition my mind to be attracted to boys only
> […] I could let the boy attractions grow and the girl ones I could ignore.
> It would make life that much easier if I could just do that. (100)

This itself is a telling comment on a society in which conservative attitudes
compel adolescents to deny their instinctive leanings and to attempt to
fit into heteronormative or socially accepted modes of behaviour, often
leading to tragic consequences when the conflict is unresolved.

Perception Versus the Inner World

It is significant that both books focus more on external perception of the
gay characters (that of peers and society) rather than tracing the internal
conflicts and journey towards resolution of the protagonists themselves.
This underscores my argument that in India, the primary focus is always
on conformity and consonance with community mores, so individual conflicts and struggles for self-realisation are always framed within the larger
context of the community. On the one hand, this focus on the community's response to and attitude towards the gay characters serves to build
awareness of the need for change. On the other, it does the characters a
disservice by drawing attention away from the primacy of their struggle
for identity and relevance.

As one such example of this external, superficial perception, in *Talking
of Muskaan*, Muskaan's friends are aware that she is different from them
in many ways, but they strive to erase this difference and make her "normal". When Muskaan resists their efforts to get her to wax her body hair,
her friend Divya says, "We're the best friends she has. And she's so silly
about so many things. We can't just, you know, give in every time. We're
thinking of what's right for her, aren't we?" (18–19).

To which, Muskaan replies, "What's right for me? […] Waxing?
Removing body hair? Of all that's wrong with the world, that's what you
think needs fixing?" (19).

Muskaan's response is an indicator of her confusion over her identity
and apprehension of societal disapproval of her sexual preference. While
her friends acknowledge she is going through a stressful phase, they do
not probe deeper into the cause for this emotional upheaval.

Similarly, in *Slightly Burnt*, Komal voices many of the stereotypical reactions to the discovery of a person's preference for same-sex relationships.

> How could it have happened? Sahil has always been such a normal boy. He wasn't girly or anything, it's not like he used to play with dolls or wanted to wear dresses. I know that much. He's good at sports too. He lives in a normal home and all. So [...] how could something like this happen? (63)

The implication here is that homosexuality is a finite event that happens as a result of specific habits and within a specific environment that is conducive to the development of a certain kind of sexual preference.

GENDER AND CLASS ISSUES

The intersection of gender and class plays out prominently in *Talking of Muskaan*. One of Muskaan's newfound friends in the novel is Subhojoy, who comes from an economically disadvantaged background and is ill at ease among his more privileged classmates. The two bond over the feeling of being outsiders within their peer group and discuss the struggle to resist being overpowered and judged by their peers. Prateek reacts to Muskaan's confession of being attracted to girls with mild curiosity. He is more preoccupied with the class divide between them and cannot understand her angst at being bullied and teased about her sexual choice. To him, dealing with financial hardship is far more difficult. On her part, when Muskaan learns that Prateek is uncomfortable attending the birthday parties of their more well-to-do classmates because of the economic disparity between them, Muskaan is surprised because she had never considered this to be as big an issue as her sexual preference:

> You should appreciate the fact that you're straight, that you like girls, the way 'normal people' do! That's one luxury of thought I don't get to have. (80)

INFLUENCE OF AUTHORITY FIGURES

The influence of adults on shaping adolescents' attitudes is evident in the reaction of the teen characters when they discover that their friend is gay. In *Talking of Muskaan*, the discussion between Muskaan's classmate

Prateek and his father about Muskaan is emblematic of the privileged, patriarchal and homophobic mindset typical of a large swathe of Indian society:

> "That's not a nice thing," he said. "You should not really be friends with such people. These homosexuals are just trying to get attention. Best to avoid them."

> "But, Papa, it's cool these days really." Papa can be old-fashioned. "And it's not like she talks about it – this girl, but people just know."

> "Of course people will know if you are not a normal person. People are not fools," Papa said. (68)

Thus, it may be seen that Prateek considers homosexuality to be an aberrant form of behaviour that is "cool" as long as a safe distance is maintained from homosexuals. He proceeds to warn his girlfriend Rashika against mixing too freely with Muskaan, citing his father's words.

On the other hand, Aaliya's mother reacts with indignation when it is announced on television that the verdict decriminalising homosexuality has been overturned. Despite this, Aaliya is not entirely convinced about the genuineness of her mother's sentiment:

> But had she ever done anything that was deviant and weird? [...] Ma belonged. So did Dad. And it is elegant and nice to ask interesting questions when you belonged. But if you didn't? Then did you rave and rant at society? Or did you just wish you belonged? (135)

In *Slightly Burnt*, when Komal discovers Sahil is gay, she seeks the help of her school counsellor Usha McDowell to come to terms with this realisation. Usha helps her understand that "at some point it has to stop being about you" (76) and that she should focus on being able to support her friend who has trusted her with his deepest secret:

> Komal, you realise that our society doesn't make it easy for people who don't conform, who don't live traditional lives, get married, have children and so on? [...] You were trusted because someone felt safe talking to you. Felt safe in a world that is hostile and narrow-minded. If it wasn't, being gay wouldn't be a big deal, would it? (79)

The manner in which both novels conclude is in some ways a comment on the magnitude of the problem the LGBTQIA+ community faces when it comes to acceptance and understanding. Komal, Sahil and Vikram tacitly agree to keep the secret between them, mainly because they are unsure and afraid of the consequences of a public acknowledgement of this truth. Muskaan's parents are relieved that she has survived the suicide attempt, but there is no mention of their knowing the truth behind it.

THE POLITICS OF PUBLISHING

The issues faced by writers and publishers in articulating the concerns of the LGBTQIA+ community through young adult fiction are manifold. To illustrate these concerns, below are extended excerpts from an interview I conducted with the authors of the two novels discussed in this chapter.[5] They articulate some of these issues and give an insight into the current state of publishing in India with special reference to young adult fiction.

1. How did the idea of the book come about? Was it specially commissioned or did you need to do the rounds of publishers to convince them to publish it?

   Himanjali: I remember I was discussing book ideas with my publishers, Duckbill. At that time Article 377 was in the news and we were talking about the paucity in representation when it came to homosexuality in Indian young adult fiction. It wasn't specially commissioned but the idea for the book came from that conversation.

   Payal: Sexuality isn't a subject that Indian books have ever talked about, except maybe in terms of sexuality education. I've always felt that we need more books with more diverse themes and settings, inhabited by Indian characters. That is, stories that readers can identify with and feel they can own. I had long wanted to write this book, about two friends, one of them being gay, and the repercussions of that on their lives. I had sounded out Himanjali Sankar about it. When Himanjali joined Bloomsbury, she got in touch and asked me to submit the manuscript. She herself was working on *Talking of Muskaan* at that time.

2. Did you have a formal launch of the book? Did you or the publisher anticipate or face any adverse reaction to its publication?

Himanjali: We didn't have any formal launch and I don't think we anticipated any reaction on publication.

Payal: No, there was no formal launch. My publisher did raise a concern that marketing the book as young adult fiction might attract protests and wanted to position it as adult fiction, but I held my ground. I don't think the book has been read widely enough to provoke a reaction.

3. What was the general reception like? How have the sales of the book been since its publication?

Himanjali: Generally we got decent reviews—the book continues to sell I think, and attract new readers. Some schools were hesitant about inviting me as an author because the book dealt with homosexuality—that continues to be the case.

Payal: I've done just the one school session and one other session at a children's festival around the book. Schools have been extremely wary of touching it; bookshops don't seem to be stocking it. There appears to be a problem at the publisher's end itself. One marketing manager at Bloomsbury was openly homophobic, saying that he "wouldn't like" his 14-year-old son to read "books like these". I've been told many times how it was a mistake to pitch this as a YA book and that it would have worked much better as a new-adult one. I believe overall sales are under 500 copies, which has to mean that the publishers haven't made a concerted effort to distribute it.

4. Do young readers reach out to you to talk about their identification with the characters/their own experiences of homosexuality and/or the conflicts arising from the perception of being different?

Himanjali: Yes, I've had young readers thanking me for writing this book since they feel it's a subject that is hardly represented in children's fiction. At a panel discussion recently, a teenager came to me and said she had read this book a few years back and it had helped her to understand her own sexual orientation. It's gratifying as an author when young readers reach out with positive feedback.

Payal: Yes, I do get occasional messages from people who identify with one of the characters.

5. What is your assessment of the current publishing scene in India after the recent verdict on Section 377? Do you believe more publishers will come forward to publish books with gay/queer characters? Books that do not reduce them to caricatures and explore their experiences and conflicts with empathy?

Himanjali: When it comes to adult fiction I don't think this has been a problem—children's publishers are more cautious about these subjects because parents and teachers, even those who haven't been against Section 377, often feel there is no need to expose kids to such ideas. The verdict of course helps, but it might take a little longer to change mindsets. And yes the caricaturing which was offensive and annoying is hopefully on the wane now!

Payal: Yes, I am more hopeful that there will be more books written on this subject after the verdict. Generally speaking, I don't think there are enough young adult writers in India today. We need to have more people writing, and more books on the subject of same-sex relationships.

6. Do you feel your book is reaching the intended audience? If not, what do you think can be done to increase readership?

Himanjali: The book has been around for five or six years now so I guess it's doing well enough. I don't think I have an intended audience in mind for this book—anyone who wants to read it is welcome.

Payal: No, the problem is that bookstores don't really want to market Indian writers. I feel that Indian writing should not be slotted or marketed as a separate category or geographical entity. These books should be placed along with books of the same genre without consciously segregating them. They would probably gain more visibility if the focus is not on the country of origin.

7. Generally speaking, writers do not have to "be" their characters in order to write compelling stories. However, do you feel that books featuring the struggle for gay identity and acceptance are more authentic if written by gay authors? Is there an apprehension of appropriation or inauthentic representation if such books are written by "straight" writers?

Himanjali: Well, appropriation and authenticity are hot topics now and it is easier perhaps to write about one's own experiences but then again, if a writer chooses a certain story it means that he or she feels strongly about the need to tell that story. I wouldn't choose a topic that I am not personally invested in, for whatever reason, so the authenticity and identification will come if I feel passionately about what I am writing.

Payal: There's always a danger of appropriation when writing about a marginalised segment of society, especially if a writer doesn't do their homework properly, or when a straight author assumes that they are the authentic voice of a queer character. While I feel it is extremely important to have own-voices books, I also believe it is possible to write an authentic, empathetic story about queer children by straight authors. Perhaps the biggest challenge that faces children's publishing in India today is how to break out of the middle-class, upper-caste, cis-het-ableist lens that all stories are told from. I have recently written about disability and neuro-divergence in children's literature, and the same arguments apply to gender and sexuality-themed works, as well as to making ALL fiction more inclusive.

8. *Talking of Muskaan* is told from the point of view of Muskaan's friends. There is a deliberate omission of Muskaan's point of view and there are just a few glimpses of her internal struggle and her inner world. You have mentioned in an interview that the editors at Duckbill suggested this approach to telling the story. Do you feel that the character of Muskaan has been given a raw deal in the process? That her voice is not adequately heard? Would you have approached the book differently if you were to write it today?

Himanjali: I think it works the way it is. Since Muskaan's story is told through her friends it allows greater narrative tension and also the multiple points of view, sometimes clashing, sometimes complementary, lead to a fuller, more complete story.

9. *Slightly Burnt* is told from Komal's point of view. Do you feel this does a disservice to Sahil's character by not focusing enough on his internal struggle and need for acceptance?

Payal: In retrospect, I feel the book should have been told from Sahil's point of view—he does not get enough of a voice in the book. My next book will probably do this.

CONCLUSION

Following the Supreme Court's latest verdict on Section 377, there have been encouraging trends in Indian media that point to a gradual acceptance of the rights of the LGBTQIA+ community. Some radio stations have talk shows hosted by gays that feature gay people discussing their struggles to come out to their family and society. There are blogs, websites and newsletters that specifically cater to the LGBTQIA+ community. The *Times of India*, one of India's national newspapers, recently launched a campaign titled "Out and Proud" that features classified advertisements by members of the LGBTQIA+ community seeking partners.

In the genre of young adult fiction, however, there will always be the question of whose voice should be considered authentic and the danger of appropriating the experiences of homosexuals and claiming to represent them. Can books on homosexuality only be written by gay writers? Do heteronormative writers lack the empathy to write about homosexuals? How authentic is their representation of their life and experiences? A reviewer of *Talking of Muskaan* argued that the book was not by any means an authentic portrayal of homosexual characters. While many others questioned his argument, the more important point to be noted is that the book ignited a debate about inauthentic and authentic representation and caused people to discuss these issues in a public forum. This is just the kind of visibility young adult fiction needs, because it will encourage debate and dissension, but hopefully ultimately generate the acceptance that the community seeks.

What is the way forward? It must be underscored that promoting young adult fiction featuring homosexual characters should not be done in the spirit of awarding a concession to a marginalised section of society or as a cursory nod to inclusiveness. Neither should it be done with an eye to exploiting a new mine of content for commercial gain. There is an urgent need to write and publish books about homosexual characters that focus on their angst and their struggles for identity and acceptance, but equally on the sameness and routine of their lives without othering them. This will enable them to claim their rightful place in society by making them visible, giving them a voice and offering them a platform for authentic representation rather than mere caricature. The process of engendering identities is necessarily multilayered and complex, but it is important to initiate and sustain this process. Bearing in mind India's past legislations and prejudices in this area, the role of children's and young adult fiction in ensuring that the process is ongoing and that it continues to interrogate received assumptions and prejudices cannot be overemphasised.

Notes

1. Since ancient India did not exist historically as a nation-state, I use the term here to mean the various regional societies that existed during that time in the Indian subcontinent.
2. This is a term traditionally used for members of the transgender community in South Asia.
3. This refers to the great war, described in the ancient Sanskrit epic poem *Mahabharata*, between two groups of cousins, the Pandavas and Kauravas, who fought for the right to rule the kingdom of Hastinapura.
4. Literally, "Hinduness", this term has been appropriated in recent times by various political parties in India who seek to use it as a metaphor for Hindu nationalism and the propagation of "Hindu" values among the community.
5. Interview with Himanjali Sankar, May 21, 2019; Interview with Payal Dhar, July 14, 2019.

References

Banerjee, Suchismita. 2018. "The Crucible: Forging a Hybrid Identity in a Multicultural World" in *The Routledge Companion to International Children's Literature*. Abingdon, Oxon and New York: Routledge.

Dhar, Payal. 2014. *Slightly Burnt*. New Delhi: Bloomsbury Publishing India Pvt Ltd.

Kakar, Sudhir. 2007. "Homosexuality and the Indian" in Little India, Issue dated August 17, 2007. Accessed September 14, 2019. http://web.archive.org/web/20070815111253/, http://www.littleindia.com/news/145/ARTICLE/1835/2007-08-17.html.

Kakar, Sudhir. 2009. "The Judgement Helps Validation of Homosexual Identity". https://www.deccanherald.com/content/15272/judgment-helps-validation-homosexual-identity.html, July 22, 2009.

Kakar, Sudhir and Katharina. 2009. *The Indians: Portrait of a People*. New Delhi: Penguin Books India.

Niranjana, Tejaswini. 2007. "Feminism and Cultural Studies in Asia," *Interventions: International Journal of Postcolonial Studies*, 9(2), 209–218. https://doi.org/10.1080/13698010701409152.

Pattanaik, Devdutt. 2009. "On Krishna's Chariot Stands Shikhandi" in *Sunday Midday*, Mumbai, July 12, 2009.

Pattanaik, Devdutt. 2016. "What Do Manusmriti and Dharmashastra Have to Say About Homosexuality?" in www.dailyo.in, December 30, 2016.

Rajan, Rajeswari Sunder. 2008. "English Literary Studies, Women's Studies and Feminism in India" in *Economic and Political Weekly*, 43, 66–71. https://doi.org/10.2307/40278104.

Ramanujam, B.K. 1979. "Toward Maturity: Problems of Identity Seen in the Indian Clinical Setting" in *Identity and Adulthood*, edited by Sudhir Kakar, 2nd ed. Delhi: Oxford University Press.

Sankar, Himanjali. 2014. *Talking of Muskaan*. Chennai: Duckbill Books.

CHAPTER 9

The Demon as "Other" in Sri Lankan Children's Literature: Rambukwella's *Mythil's Secret* and *Asiri's Quest*

Neluka Silva

In his book, *Inventing the Child: Culture, Ideology and the Story of the Child* (2001), Joseph Zornado argues that "the stories we tell our children – and that we tell ourselves about the child [...] are no innocent things; rather their innocence is an ideological projection" (Zornado 2001: 3). Taking this observation as a point of departure, this chapter explores two popular Sri Lankan children's novels, *Mythil's Secret* (2009) and *Asiri's Quest* (2013)[1] by Prashani Rambukwella as "a special site for ideological effect, with a potentially powerful capacity for shaping audience attitudes [...] with its intention being to foster in the child reader a positive apperception of some sociocultural values which, it is assumed, are shared by author and audience" (Stephens 1992: 3). The "sociocultural values" explored in this chapter concern the continuing stereotyping or "othering" of ethnicities in Sri Lanka, and Rambukwella's attempt to challenge them within the genre of children's writing.[2]

N. Silva (✉)
University of Colombo, Colombo, Sri Lanka

© The Author(s) 2020
B. Wilson and S. P. Gabriel (eds.), *Asian Children's Literature and Film in a Global Age*, Asia-Pacific and Literature in English,
https://doi.org/10.1007/978-981-15-2631-2_9

Historically, in Sri Lanka, notions of ethno-racial, cultural and religious exclusivity have been fossilised and in periods of exacerbated sociopolitical tension, ethnic identities have become crucial in defining the self/other binary. Nation-states strive towards "homogenising the nation" so that its peoples will unite in times of crisis against the threats from without (Graham 2001: 105). The anxiety to promote and safeguard images of ethnic purity has been manifest in public discourses and the popular imagination. Contending nationalist forces seek solace in representations of an anachronistic or mythical utopia, in which monolithic formations of ethnic identities are divested of any transforming potential. While nationalist discourses may emphasise ethnic purity and while the nation itself often employs the condition of denial to prevail against the challenges and trauma of revolutionary change, some literary works have not been complicit in reinforcing such myths, but are a potentially empowering site for change. A historical trajectory of nationalist discourses in Sri Lanka reveals the stereotyping of ethnicity, while emphasising ethnic purity. During the ethnic conflict in Sri Lanka, these stereotypes were blatant and relayed through popular culture (Silva 2004).[3] For instance, overarching ethnic stereotypes—of the Tamils as cunning and stingy, or the Muslims as business-minded, or the Burghers as frivolous and promiscuous—have been historically reinforced (Silva 2004). Throughout the conflict, the binary of self/other was deployed by contending parties to instil fear and mobilise support for each side.

MS was written during the prolonged ethnic conflict in Sri Lanka, and published immediately after the conflict ended in 2009. *AQ* was written and published during the post-war reconciliation phase. The two novels correspond to Michelle Superle's view that "positive outcomes are the overarching norm in children's novels, which comprise an aspirational literature with a transformative agenda" (2011: 4). Rambukwella won the Gratiaen award in 2009 for *MS*.[4] Both novels inscribe a "transformative agenda"—that of unveiling the fear of the "other" which is overcome by the child hero.

Deploying the paradigm of the "rite of passage", where the child protagonist comes to terms with "the strangeness and magic of life" (Bagchi 2009: 172) situated within a sociopolitical landscape of conflict and post-conflict reconciliation, Rambukwella interrogates how the configuration of "difference" becomes enabling, and results in the acceptance of the "other" (in this case a demon, who is bestowed with positive qualities).

Children's Literature
and the Construction of Identity

"It's only a children's book", is a simplistic statement often applied to children's texts, yet it is a collective area which Peter Hunt asserts is a "highly complex" literature (2004: 2). Incorporating an array of genres, including mystery, adventure, the realms of magic and fantasy, children's books are pervasive in their dissemination of societal values and thus "[are] a perfect vehicle for disseminating information about diverse experiences, adding depth and understanding to what otherwise tends toward generalisation, homogeneity and stereotyping" (Rutter 2006: 5). The stories told to children and the books they read contribute to the development of values and norms, and to personal, cultural or national identity. The attitudes of the narrators of the stories, their inclusion and exclusion of various peoples, even their settings, convey messages about what and who are fit subjects to write about, and whose stories are worth telling (Desai 2006: 164). Indeed, a fundamental function of much of regional children's literature is that it "is able to create a vital link with the child reader through developing an indigenous form of literature that portrays the distinctive identities that are constructed within that particular community or nation" (Niles 2012: 2). Rambukwelle's work fulfils this and may be considered "a landmark work of Sri Lankan English fiction for another reason: it is the first work of Sri Lankan literature in English for children that is recognisably 'Sri Lankan'. [...] Her popularity among her target audience of children attesting to her success in the genre" (Wickremagamage 2014).

Identity is a "socio-cultural process" which is "constantly under construction. [...] The self is always constituted in relation to difference because a thing can only be known in relation to what it is not" (Singer and Singer 2001: 310). The "distinctive identities" recreated in the two novels evoke a vocabulary that centres around the continuing preoccupation with identity in the Sri Lankan public consciousness.

Research has demonstrated that children's literature is deeply embedded in their culture, and that the binary of self/other in relation to race, gender and class underpins the themes and motifs of stories (Meek 2001; Kelen and Sundmark 2013). The notion that childhood is innocent and children's stories are devoid of stereotyping, has been challenged and "because children do use their literature for sites of identification, both authors and critics often focus on identity with a qualifying adjective—gender identity, national identity, racial identity, ethnic identity, class identity" (Coats 2011). As such, it is clear that children's literature becomes a site to subvert the hegemony of political discourses for, as Judith Butler argues "Although the political discourses that mobilise identity categories tend to cultivate the identifications in the service of a political goal, it may be that the persistence of disidentification is equally crucial to the rearticulation of democratic contestation" (1990: 4).

Bearing these considerations in mind, one may argue that children's texts are useful fictions that embody the social construction of a particular historical context; they can be intended to redress reality as much as to reflect it (Myers 1989: 52). The significance of texts written for children need to be regarded as "[…] not aids to sensitivity nor adjuncts to the cultivated life. They are theories with which to think forwards […] and understand backwards" (Inglis 1993: 214). Thus, how one group of people represents another is "particularly significant […] in books for children and adolescents, where the beliefs, constructs and attitudes of the readers are still in the making" (Ja´szo´ 2001: 33).

In general terms, ideological interpellation through which children identify with dominant models and ideals, but also through which they become cognisant of the processes of reinforcing or challenging existing identities can be achieved through the consumption of literature, an identification which is particularly relevant in relation to regional literatures and the ways in which they influence or reinforce cultural and national identity. Christopher Kelen and Bjorn Sundmark (2013) have also reaffirmed the compelling ways in which children's literatures have constructed and represented historically different national experiences.

Just as nationalist discourses foist gendered roles on both men and women, and women are acutely "burdened" with these subject positions, the nation and childhood are also intimately interconnected. If women's positions have typically been circumscribed, according to nationalist discourses that elide biological with cultural reproduction, then this precept also produces particular positions for children as the future products and expressions of these cultural or national identity projects (Burman 2007: 16). In addition to their influence on personal and cultural identity, children's books influence readers' sense of national identity by presenting some groups as "us" and some as "them", some "like us" and some "strange" (Desai 2006: 166). However, these positions can also be challenged, and stories which grapple with difference can be read as allegories for debunking the existing stereotypes in the sociopolitical contexts they inhabit.

The construction of identity vis-à-vis the presence of a demon character, is a literal enactment of the way in which identity construction is reliant upon "demonising" the other. The dominant characteristics associated with "demons" are deployed in humans and rendered fearful in ethnic stereotyping, stereotypes which Homi Bhabha (1994) describes as "an arrested, fixated form of representation", and one which can never capture the complexity of a human being (1994: 75). The construction of a viable identity through the demon "other" represents a reality—the proof of the possibility of living together with the "Other"—which has to be suppressed by the nationalist forces. Given that it is acknowledged that stories are very important in the formation of national/cultural identity, it is this construction of identity that I wish to examine because, as Charles Sarland has argued, children's fiction represents some groups at the expense of others, and some groups are negatively represented in stereotypical terms (quoted in Hunt 2004: 41).

CONFLICT AND POST-CONFLICT SRI LANKA: DEBUNKING THE DEMONS IN *MYTHIL'S SECRET*

Children's author Rambukwella shared, "I wanted to write a book for Sri Lankan children because when I was growing up there seemed to be a sad dearth of books written in English for Sri Lankan kids".[5] Sabreena Niles has pointed out that there was a vacuum in children's writing in English in Sri Lanka particularly for pre- and early teenagers. Most of the published stories show nostalgia for the simplicity and camaraderie of village life and appreciation for its values, but in the process they often characterise village life as a thing of the past. Many of the stories that take place in the village are folk tales in which magic is common.

Some recent books for children which have been published locally have been included in libraries and used as prescriptive texts in the syllabi of schools, thereby indicating that while a culture of reading Sri Lankan books in English is promoted within these schools, educationalists are convinced that these texts are of a high standard (Niles 2012). Some literary texts have not been complicit in reinforcing such myths, but have provided a critical illumination and potentially empowering site for change. Recognising that children's texts have an ideological purchase, *MS* and

AQ self-consciously eschew simplistic formulations, such as the binary of good self/evil other.

The author's intentions are asserted in the following excerpt:

> *MS* was written while the conflict was still raging though it was published a few months after it ended. But I did think, while writing it, that themes such as 'the other' would be relevant in an era of conflict or post-conflict. While I don't presume to present any easy solutions to conflict, Mythil's story revolves around understanding the other. When he is frightened of the yakas his power to force them into taking their own shape is raw and uncontrolled. It puts him in danger. But after he befriends Asiri his power is more controlled. He ceases to see the yakas as monsters.[6]

In this sense, *MS* can be viewed as a coming of age story: a young boy's discovery of the meaning of family and friendship, as he embarks on a journey into a world of *yakas* (demons), becomes their target and overpowers them. The intertwining of Sri Lankan myth and folklore with the travails of an Anglicised middle-class family, as the child protagonist Mythil stumbles upon a "feeble demon" Asiri during his stay with his grandmother, is an effective plot construction. Mythil, an angst-ridden boy, preoccupied by his parents' incessant altercations relating to their financial struggles, becomes a hero when he rescues Asiri from the evil demon, Bhishani. Starting out as an introverted boy, Mythil develops in stature through confronting the evil that resides in his ambit—be it in the forest or the domestic realm. Narrative space within the context of the story is devoted for Mythil to mature as a character.

Albeit situated within the realm of the exotic, transporting the reader into an unknown world involving deep, magical powers, *MS* establishes a backdrop of "realism" that is then traversed by the protagonist. While trying to make sense of the exigencies of his home life, Mythil's engagement with the supernatural challenges while aiding Asiri to escape the clutches of malevolent demons, becomes a tale of tension and adventure as well as friendship.

The representation of the demons and humans in both *MS* and *AQ* is crucial in terms of debunking binaries of self/other and the symbolic, traditional rendition of good vs evil, in that neither the humans nor the demons are cast as either entirely "good" or "evil", thereby negating simplistic configurations of characters that are associated with children's literature. Often, the ideology of authors through the creation of stereotypical characters is either inherent or overtly thrust upon the child reader, such literature for children being marked by "high contrast dualities". For instance, characters are invariably either good or evil; there is little ambiguity in their personalities, and the good characters are always victorious (Shepard 2012: 25). In *MS* and *AQ* the reader is compelled to consider characters' *individual actions*, instead of merely viewing the characters as "good" or "evil" where, as Iris Shepard argues: "good" characters do destructive things while "bad" characters do constructive things (2012: 87).

Using the mode of fantasy, Rambukwelle employs a facet prevalent in children's stories that interweave fantasy whereby "the protagonists appear to have more agency than customarily bestowed on characters in children texts" (Shepard 2012: 61), but the genre of fantasy ultimately precludes the reader from accepting this agency, as the resolution is often situated within the domain of "realism", where the child returns to the setting of the "normal", as is evident in *MS* and *AQ*. Shepard also argues that the dramatic and absolute triumph of good over evil at the culmination of the main conflicts in many fantasy texts marginalises the protagonist's personal struggles. No matter how subversive certain elements of the plot may appear, fantasy texts tend towards contained endings that reinscribe the status quo, thus reinforcing the dominant ideology (2012). Yet the erasure of the child hero's personal angst is absent in Rambukwelle's work, representing a rupture in the conventional modus operandi that underscores the sensitivity with which she frames the plot.

A possible site for subversive readings is the blurred distinction between good and evil characters (Shepard 2012: 87) which can be construed in both texts. Neither the humans nor the yakas are constructed as entirely good or evil. Each group is constituted of nuanced characters. For instance, even the "evil" character Bhishani, according to the author "... is simply protecting her own kind from discovery - although she goes to reckless ends to do so". Likewise, the adults are not conferred with purely "good" or "evil" traits, although the adults, for instance, Mythil's parents, his grandmother and aunty Nilmini do not appreciate the power and insights of children. They are cast as unsupportive in their refusal to accept Mythil's ability to see yakas.

However, Rambukwella counterbalances these negative portrayals by introducing the *bahirawaya* (a wise spirit), who treats Mythil with respect by showing a willingness to listen to him. The bahirawaya's triumph against the "evil" yakas at the culmination of the story is made possible by enlisting the assistance of the children who enable him to restore his powers. When Mythil tries to describe the countenance of the Old Woman in the shop (her "long fangs"), his father's reaction can be construed as "typical" of adults: "There are no such things as monsters or aliens or whatever you thought you saw" (*MS*: 39) and Aunty Nilmini's knowledge of child psychology precludes her from accepting an alternative to Mythil's explanation of the existence of the supernatural. She rationalises it as a form of escape from the anxiety of his home situation, with the consequence that he seeks refuge in the realm of fantasy.

Though depicted as a sympathetic and loving figure, when Mythil tries to explain to his grandmother about the encounter with the "tree spirit", she merely indulges him by listening to the story. Although he tries to impress upon him that what he saw is "real", his insistence provokes the following response:

> 'Then shall I tell you what you saw?' Archchi said with a comforting chuckle. 'I'm sure you saw one of the village boys playing in the jungle. He would have seen you and thought of frightening you a little for fun'. (*MS*: 19)

Mythil's frustration at the rejection he experiences from adults posits the dilemma of the child hero, in which "adults are depicted as flawed and limited human beings. The heroes are ordinary children who struggle to do the best they can in a difficult world" (Hourihan 1997: 217). Although it has been recognised that adult figures in many children's books are considerably negligible in terms of the overall narrative, when they play an active role, they are often portrayed in a negative light or censorious tone. In *MS*, it is the latter, as Mythil's relationship with Asiri is undermined by the adults, who consistently cast doubt on his own mental security, falsely transposing the anxieties he experiences within his domestic realm with his ability to see yakas.

When he discovers his "superpower", Mythil is deeply troubled. The narrative is replete with images of his discomfiture, unveiling its "burden": "Well, he was upset because Ammi and Thathi were fighting. If they stopped fighting, perhaps the yakas would go away. [...] His head hurt. [...] He worried about the yakas" (*MS*: 39). Such a state of unease, apprehension coupled with fear, precludes a facile and instant bond to be forged between the child and "other". Rather, the author allows narrative space for the "burden" to develop into an understanding by the child protagonist of it as a "gift" which leads to a deep friendship with the yaka.

Cognisant of the perils of stereotyping, Rambuwella's modus operandi in the narrative is to grant Mythil the ancestral gift of being able to "see" yakas, thereby enabling him to forge a relationship with the yaka Asiri, and accept Asiri as an ally. Asiri, enfeebled by the powers of the evil yaka is conferred with attributes, such as loyalty, which facilitate the human/yaka nexus. By avoiding a simplistic rendition of the relationship between Asiri and Mythil, Rambukwella sensitively captures the trajectory of acknowledging and then accepting difference. The mutual suspicion foregrounds an empowering reality that the relationship between Self and Other is not a permanent configuration but is liable to change (Gibbins 2012: 60).

Such an inability to accept alternative ways of seeing, of acknowledging "difference" typifies the compulsions within narratives of conflict at national and sociocultural levels. In post-conflict Sri Lanka, juxtaposed against the state's insistence on reconciliation runs a parallel discourse which is overlaid by Sinhala Buddhist formulations of ethnic supremacy. Since the novel enables a reading which allows for allaying fears regarding what is perceived as divergent, the adult reactions to Mythil's ability to "see" yakas can be read as symbolic enactments of the monolithic underpinnings of identities that overdetermine nationalist discourses, an interpretation supported by John Fiske, who argues: "Finding discourse in a text that makes sense of one's experience of social powerlessness in a positive way is the vital first step towards being able to do something to change that powerlessness" (1987: 70).

MS empowers the reader to recognise and accept the "other" amidst—and despite—oppositional forces, thus opening up a space for altering the "powerlessness" that the "other" confronts. The sequel to *MS*, *AQ*, which is written in a post-conflict milieu, inscribes a progression in confronting and negotiating alterity through the framework of reconciliation, and reveals the exigencies faced when retrieving memory and contextualising the history of a marginalisation that has been foisted upon this "other".

ASIRI'S QUEST: MEMORY, HISTORY AND RECONCILIATION

Post-war discourses in Sri Lanka have stressed that reconciliation is paramount to achieve lasting peace. However, since 2009, reconciliation has been fraught with the challenge of an escalating Sinhala nationalism which reinscribes the hegemony of the dominant culture as an important component of "national identity". A significant number of literary works and popular culture in the post-war scenario has exhibited what Karunanayake and Waradas term "A shift in focus", an identity reliant upon ethnicity and religion of the victor, which "dwells much on history and memory, and are highly arbitrary and nebulous artefacts" (2013: 4).

Although Rambukwella is not invested in overtly interrogating the ramifications of conflict in a post-conflict landscape, *AQ* underpins the significance of history and memory in engaging with the "other" and demonstrates their links with present-day events. Reconciliation or healing is enabled by exploring an alternate history and necessitates an engagement with the vicissitudes of history. In this case, this is achieved by juxtaposing the narrative of Asiri's previous engagement with Sena with his present behaviour. As Karunanayake and Waradas comment, "Remembering is always present-situated, as memories bring the past into the present, and thus, it is a meaning-making process that occurs in the present in response to the past" (2013: 5).

The "meaning-making process" is imperative in the early stages of the story. Asiri's tantrum, in the first chapter, reveals the antithesis of the sweet and lonely character evident in *MS*. Asiri's insistence on finding Sena is followed in the text by:

Asiri's features changed from sunny to thundery in an instant.

"I don't know, but you have to!" he yelled fiercely at Mythil. "You have to!" Mythil was taken aback. He had never seen Asiri angry before. (*AS*: 18)

Asiri's destruction of Mythil's house—"The room was a complete mess!" (*AS*: 20)—follows his tantrum. As Mythil gets over the shock of engaging with a different dimension of Asiri's personality, he strives to view the situation from the yaka's perspective, arriving at the realisation that, "Maybe feeling powerless made you mean – he thought. Maybe that's what turns you into a bully" (*AS*: 21). This pattern of behaviour is rationalised by the author: "This is because he's getting his memory back. Memories of being bullied, feeling helpless and betrayed. These feelings are pulling him towards anger - a very natural response of course, once the hurt and disbelief die down".[7]

What is the urgency for Asiri to unearth his history? When Asiri accidentally comes across a picture in a newspaper of Ṣena, his "human" friend from the past, the narrative exposes Sena's importance to Asiri to regain his memory. It is this preoccupation that determines his subsequent violent behaviour. He feels that Sena can provide him with the answers to what has been suppressed/erased from his memory. Asiri's physical response enacts what Viet Thanh Nguyen has demonstrated: "that memory is a bodily experience that cannot be escaped, with post-traumatic stress disorder, dreams and nightmares, guilt and both moral and physical wounds all acting as constant reminders of their past" (Lacroix and Fiddian-Qasmiyeh 2013: 689). The partial memories that Asiri recovers produce a deep sense of disquiet, both at the physical and metaphoric levels. The historical narrative that Asiri strives to reclaim can be understood by pursuing a trajectory of physically seeking Sena and piecing together a documented historical narrative. The author affirms the need for this repossession of memory:

> Of course, painful memories of injustice can turn anyone into a monster and you can even say that they're perfectly within their rights to behave monstrously. But then where does it end? You become a monster because you were treated unjustly and as a monster you behave unjustly towards others who in turn become monsters themselves. Someone has to acknowledge the pain of the monster and empathise even if they can never fully comprehend what went into making the other a monster.[8]

Thus, the act of remembering is crucial for Asiri, and his inability to "remember" renders him powerless. The narrative energy devoted to the retrieval of memory, corresponds to the way in which memory is "a search for silenced voices, marginalized and traumatized" (Mallot 2012: 3–4) and "keeps alive minority voices" (Mallot 2012: 19). Asiri is clearly cast as the minority, and cogently captures how "Memory can provide an antidote to the lies and omissions of history, can finally reveal the truth about what happened in the past, can offer the occasion for justice in verbalizing the truth of past oppression, and in doing so, can begin the process of healing" (Mallot 2012: 20). Going back to history is an endeavour to seek the truth of the oppression that Asiri has endured and his conviction that Sena will "fill in the blanks" provides a legitimate and compelling narrative.

It is also an expedient plot mechanism that enables Mythil to enlist Harith's assistance in an "adventure" and facilitates a seamless nexus between foregrounding the "bullying" that occurs in the past with the trauma that Mythil is subject to in the present. The intertwining of information pertaining to Ceylon in the 1940s with Mythil's story is empowering in providing narrative space for the transformation of the relationship between Mythil and the bullies. The quest for Sena also fulfils the necessity for the positive resolution that is presumed within the genre of the children's story.

Mythil is transformed when he empathises with Asiri. The ambivalence displayed at the beginning of the story by Mythil is dispelled when the child hero identifies that the position of being divested of power can manifest in bullying. A substantial part of the narrative energy of *AS* pivots around bullying, which is only a marginal issue in *MS*, since the narrative pivots around establishing the relationship between the child protagonist and the yaka, and its implications on the challenges faced by Mythil on the domestic front. Bullying, as a thematic discourse, gains purchase in its contemporary relevance for the child reader and provides a nexus for facilitating the allegorical reading of Rambukwella's work.

The novel opens by underscoring the effects of bullying: "He looked around for support and Mythil's heart sank. This was what he had been afraid of – that Jehan would get the others involved in the bullying" (*AS*: 7). There is no respite for Asiri, as he is forced to also endure the bullying tactics of his neighbour, Harith: "Harith suddenly pushed Mythil against a parapet wall. [...] He grabbed Mythil by the back of his collar and swung him around to face him" (*AS*: 23). Notwithstanding rationalising their need to assert power over him, Mythil still endures fear when trying to escape from Jehan and Harith. Hence, Mythil is invested with the capacity to gain appreciation of the behaviour of the "other", and to recognise that Harith, who considers himself a "strong man", can be exploited to participate in what he perceives to be "dangerous". Although Harith denigrates Mythil for his weakness, soliciting Harith's help serves a dual purpose—it confers power on Harith, enabling Mythil to carry out his mission. Unfortunately, when they eventually locate Sena, the old man only briefly remembers Asiri, which is wholly disappointing. It can be inferred that Sena is aware of his loss but rejects the chance to rekindle the bond with Asiri, to avoid jeopardising the life he has secured. Though Asiri experiences a sense of abandonment, he diverts his energies to strengthening his relationship with Mythil, affirming the bonds of friendship and loyalty. The process of demonisation and exclusion experienced by Asiri is reinscribed in Mythil's experiences with Jehan and Harith, and he is compelled to manoeuvre these tensions for, as the author notes: "The emphasis is on how you're likely to be singled out if you're different - again, if you're the other".[9]

Ultimately, the possibility of forging a constructive relationship between human and "other" relays a powerful message for reconciliation. The world of yakas coexists with that of the humans; even a handful of adults such as the Veda Mahattaya and Gurunnanse, that is, the *yakae-duras* or *kattadiyas*, can call the yakas at will to do their bidding.

As such, this depiction of a necessary coexistence between alterities carries in it a larger message to the reader of coexistence between seeming opposites in nationalist discourse in Sri Lanka, between the "other" that has been demonised in dialogues within a Sri Lanka involved in conflict, and through this provides a blueprint for a post-conflict society. What is narrativised is not a simplistic mapping of this process, but the complexity of navigating the existence of the "other" by historically contextualising the emotions that are brought to the forefront, which prefaces the need to understand how to deal with the "other".

An essentialist identity, in which a core set of characteristics can be apparently plotted, underpins acceptance and exclusion. Going back into history becomes an exposition of the existence and fossilisation of discrimination. *AQ* is predicated on exposing the forms and levels of marginalisation that are transmuted as bullying, a phenomenon that gets played out throughout history.

CONCLUSION

MS and *AS*, situated within a conflict and post-conflict landscape, interrogate the ambiguities and ambivalences in the construction of self and other, through the child protagonist and his relationship with the yaka. Rambukwella disavows the conventional homogenisation and classifications that are replete in identity formation. Although the construction of identity is forged out of difference, loyalty and friendship are a testimony to commonality, which is as much a potent force as dissimilarity, as is argued by Justin Gibbins: "Difference need not degenerate into antagonism and that we-feeling, although too often the contrary, can be forged by friends and not via the seemingly eternal pursuit of enemies" (2012: 317).

The present-day narrative interfused with the historical chronicle validates the dominant discourses of post-conflict Sri Lanka and reinvests Rambukwella's plea for a pluralistic vision of diversity. These two novels can be read as encapsulating a response to Stuart Hall's crucial question: "Can a dominant regime of representation be challenged, contested or changed?" (1997: 269). Discursive techniques, be they employed to reveal presuppositions or subject positioning, reveal the restrictions in the development of identity and sustain discourses of difference, privilege and power (Howarth 2004). Rambukwella's work is testimony that the "dominant regime of representation" can be challenged through providing us with the template to view our perceived enemy or opposite as self by disavowing simplistic solutions that are commonplace in children's literature because there are no simple solutions to social differences or unrest in Sri Lanka.

Children's books are often discounted as producers of ideology, but the purported "innocence" is illusory. As Shepard accurately observes:

> Books and films are commodities. Many of them, deliberately or otherwise, promote the dominant ideology of any given historical moment and since writers and directors are developing their texts from within the dominant, historically determined narrative, their stories are laced with mainstream ideology. (2012: 91)

Within this context, *Mythil's Secret* and *Asiri's Quest* are courageous attempts. Dominant narrative platforms, which co-opt configurations of monolithic identities complicit in naturalising ethnic exclusivity and effacing its ramifications, are ruptured by the deliberately ambiguous endings the author provides in both novels: "I purposely engineered it like that because there's no neat bow-tied ending when it comes to reconciliation. But with commitment to this ideal we may get somewhere".[10]

NOTES

1. Hereafter referred to as *MS* and *AQ*, respectively.
2. My sincere thanks to Sabreena Niles for giving me access to her material for the writing of this chapter.
3. The separatist conflict between the majority Sinhalese state and the Tamil Tigers (LTTE) spanned over 26 years. 1983 is considered the watershed in modern Sri Lankan consciousness when the ethnic question gained magnitude in the public imagination, after intense ethnic riots, followed by increasing armed conflict.
4. The Gratiaen Trust was founded in 1993 by Michael Ondaatje, the internationally renowned novelist, poet and essayist of Sri Lankan origin. It was funded with the prize money Ondaatje obtained when his novel *The English Patient* co-won the prestigious Booker Prize in 1992. Named after Ondaatje's maternal family, the mandate of the Gratiaen Trust is to promote and recognise creative writing in English by Sri Lankan authors who are resident in Sri Lanka, promote and recognise translations into English of Sinhala and Tamil language creative writing by Sri Lankan authors resident in Sri Lanka, publish translations between Sinhala and Tamil language writing to foster cross-ethnic relations within Sri Lanka, and advance the international recognition of Sri Lankan creative writing. http://gratiaen.com/.
5. Personal communication with author, October 2018.
6. Personal communication with author, October 2018.
7. Personal communication with author, October 2018.
8. Personal communication with author, October 2018.
9. Personal communication with author, October 2018.
10. Personal communication with author, October 2018.

REFERENCES

Bagchi, B. 2009. Cheery Children, Growing Girls and Developing Young Adults: On Reading, Growing and Hopscotching Across Categories. In R. Chatterjee and N. Gupta (eds.), *Reading Children: Essays on Children's Literature*. New Delhi: Orient Black Swan, pp. 163–181.

Bhabha, H. 1994. *The Location of Culture*. London: Routledge. Print.

Burman, E. 2007. *Child, Image, Nation*. London and New York: Routledge. Print.

Butler, J. 1990. *Gender Trouble*. New York: Routledge. Print.

Coats, K. 2011. *Keywords for Children's Literature*. https://keywords.nyupress.org/childrens-literature/essay/identity/. Accessed 5 March 2019.

Desai, C. M. 2006. National Identity in a Multicultural Society: Malaysian Children's Literature in English. *Child Literature in Education*, 37, pp. 163–184. https://doi.org/10.1007/s10583-006-9002-8.

Fiske, J. 1987. *Television Culture*. London: Methuen and Co. Print.

Gibbins, J. 2012. *British Discourses on Europe: Self/Other and National Identities*. Unpublished Thesis, University of Birmingham. http://etheses.bham.ac.uk/3830/1/Gibbins12PhD.pdf. Accessed 25 January 2019.

Graham, J. 2001. The Same or Different: Children's Books Show Us the Way. In M. Meek (ed.), *Children's Literature and National Identity*. Stoke on Trent, UK: Trentham Books, pp. 103–110. Print.

Hall, S. 1997. *Representation: Cultural Representations and Signifying Practices*. London: Sage.

Hourihan, M. 1997. *Deconstructing the Hero: Literary Theory and Children's Literature*. London and New York: Routledge. Print.

Howarth, C. 2004. Representation and Resistance in the Context of School Exclusion: Reasons to Be Critical. *Journal of Community and Applied Social Psychology*, 14, pp. 356–377.

Hunt, P. 2004. *International Companion Encyclopedia of Children's Literature*. London: Routledge. https://doi.org/10.4324/9780203325667.

Inglis, F. 1993. *Cultural Studies*. Oxford: Blackwell. Print.

Ja´szo´, A. A. 2001. Friend or Foe: Images of the Germans in Hungarian Literature for Young Readers. In M. Meek (ed.), *Children's Literature and National Identity*. Stoke on Trent, UK: Trentham Books, pp. 33–42. Print.

Karunanayake, D. and Waradas, T. 2013. *What Lessons Are We Talking About? Reconciliation and Memory in Post Civil War Sri Lankan Cinema*. Colombo: Karunaratne & Sons (Pvt.) Ltd., pp. 1–18. Print.

Kelen, C. and Sundmark, B. (eds.). 2013. *The Nation in Children's Literature: Nations of Childhood*. London and New York: Routledge.

Lacroix, T. and Fiddian-Qasmiyeh, E. 2013. Refugee and Diaspora Memories: The Politics of Remembering and Forgetting. *Journal of Intercultural Studies*, 34 (6), pp. 684–696. https://doi.org/10.1080/07256868.2013.846893.

Mallot, E. J. 2012. *Memory, Nationalism, and Narrative in Contemporary South Asia*. New York: Palgrave Macmillan. Print.

Meek, M. (ed.). 2001. *Children's Literature and National Identity*. Stoke on Trent: Trentham Books.

Myers, M. 1989. Socializing Rosamond: Educational Ideology and Fictional Form. *Children's Literature Association Quarterly*, 14 (2), pp. 52–58.

Niles, J. S. 2012. The (De) Construction of Gender Identity in Children's Literature Written in English by Sri Lankan Authors. *Journal of the Faculty of Graduate Studies*, University of Kelaniya, 1, 98–108.

Rambukwella, P. 2009. *Mythil's Secret*. Colombo, Sri Lanka: Popsicle Books.

———. 2013. *Asiri's Quest*. Colombo, Sri Lanka: Popsicle Books.

Rutter, J. 2006. *Refugee Children in the UK*. Maidenhead: Open University Press.

Shepard, I. G. 2012. *Ideology in Popular Late Twentieth and Twenty-First Century Children's and Young Adult Literature and Film*. Theses and Dissertations, 557. http://scholarworks.uark.edu/etd/557.

Silva, N. 2004. *The Gendered Nation: Contemporary Writing from South Asia*. New Delhi: Sage. Print.

Singer, D. and Singer, J. 2001. *Handbook of Children and the Media*. Los Angeles, USA: Sage.

Stephens, J. 1992. *Ideology and Language in Children's Fiction*. London: Longman.

Superle, M. 2011. *Contemporary English-Language Children's Literature: Representations of Nation, Culture, and the New Indian Girl*. London: Routledge.

Wickremagamage, C. 2014. In the Wonderland of the Young. Review of *Asiri's Quest*. http://www.sundaytimes.lk/140406/plus/in-the-wonderland-of-the-young-91349.html.

Zornado, J. L. 2001. *Inventing the Child: Culture, Ideology, and the Story of Childhood*. New York: Garland Pub.

CHAPTER 10

Towards a Poetics of Childhood Ethics in Abbas Kiarostami's Children's Films

Amir Ali Nojoumian and Amir Hadi Nojoumian

Introduction

Abbas Kiarostami's cinematic oeuvre has been the subject of various studies and analyses. His Koker Trilogy—*Where Is the Friend's Home?* (*Khaneh Doost Kojast*, 1987), *And Life Goes On* (*Zendegi va Digar Heech*, 1992), and *Through the Olive Trees* (*Zeer Derakhtan Zeytoun*, 1994)— depict human beings' never-ending faith in the sacredness of life despite

An earlier version of this article appeared as "Towards a Poetics of Childhood in Abbas Kiarostami's Cinema", in *Persian Literary Studies Journal*, 2017, 6 (10): 15–32. We thank the editor of the journal for her kind permission to reproduce a revised version of the article.

A. A. Nojoumian (✉)
Shahid Beheshti University, Tehran, Iran

A. H. Nojoumian
University of New England, Armidale, NSW, Australia

B. Wilson and S. P. Gabriel (eds.), *Asian Children's Literature and Film in a Global Age*, Asia-Pacific and Literature in English, https://doi.org/10.1007/978-981-15-2631-2_10

their suffering. In the middle of this project, Kiarostami embarked upon making another series of films, starting with *Close-Up* (*Namaye Nazkeek*, 1990), *Taste of Cherry* (*Tam-e Gilas*, 1997), and *The Wind Will Carry Us* (*Bad Ma Ra Ba Khod Khahad Bord*, 1999), which dealt with more philosophical notions of reality versus appearance, fiction versus non-fiction, and life versus death. Kiarostami continued his artistic projects in the form of various genres into the twenty-first century, until his sudden death in 2016.

Of his entire body of artistic works, Kiarostami's early films made at the "Institute for the Intellectual Development of Children and Young Adults" aptly focused on the world of children in line with the Institute's targets and objectives of establishing an organisation for nurturing creativity and educating children. *Two Solutions for One Problem* (*Do Rah-e Hal Baraye Yek Masaleh*, 1975), *Colors* (*Rang-ha*, 1976), *Toothache* (*Dandan-Dard*, 1980), and *Orderly or Disorderly* (*Be Tarteeb ya Bedoun Tarteeb*, 1981) are among the films made during this early phase. However, as one could notice from these very early works, Kiarostami was not going to make simple didactic films for mere educational purposes. From his first film, *The Bread and Alley* (*Naan-o Koucheh*, 1970), through his later works for or about children, such as *Breaktime* (*Zang Tafrih*, 1972), *The Experience* (*Tajrobeh*, 1973), *The Traveler* (*Mosafer*, 1974), *A Wedding Suit* (*Lebasee Baraye Arousi*, 1976), *First Case, Second Case* (*Ghazieh, Shekl Aval, Shekl Dovom*, 1979), *The Chorus* (*Hamsorayan*, 1982), *First Graders* (*Avaliha*, 1984), *Where Is the Friend's Home?* (1987), and *Homework* (*Mashgh Shab*, 1989), Kiarostami started to develop a form of aesthetics in which children's mental and physical worlds are depicted with subtle sensitivity. Although Kiarostami's child characters are invariably neglected by their parents, their employers, the educational system, and society in general, they continuously attempt to find ways to liberate themselves from oppression. Children in these films are confronted with the unsympathetic world of adults, to say the least, and make unconventional ethical choices in order to sustain the vitality that is being taken away from them.

The purpose of this chapter is to define an ethical configuration and map out a "poetics" of ethical relations in Kiarostami's children's films. In his deeply significant treatise *Poetics*, Aristotle aspires towards a structure for tragedy. Accordingly, what *Poetics* in general does is to designate representational systems in art, follow their transformational evolution, and investigate how to categorise them. The present article turns to such an understanding of the term "poetics" to interpret the grammar and structure of the ethics of childhood in Kiarostami's children's films and identifies two major ethical choices made by Kiarostami's child characters: an ethics of altruistic care and responsibility to the other and an ethics of resistance and refusal in order to sustain a responsibility to oneself.

KIAROSTAMI'S ETHICAL METHOD

Ethics has long been regarded as a value-oriented, rule-governed, essentialist, universal, and internal system defining right and wrong, and prescribing moral manners. Terry Eagleton in his book, *Trouble with Strangers: A Study of Ethics* (2009), discusses how this aspect of morality is a "decaying apparatus":

> Morality as we know it is 'herd' morality, suitable enough for the timorous, spiritually mediocre masses but fatally stymying for noble, exceptional souls. [...] Morality is a conspiracy against life on the part of those who are fearful of joy, risk, cheerfulness, hardness, solitude, suffering and self-overcoming. It is as chimerical as alchemy. This whole decaying apparatus must now collapse, given that its metaphysical buttresses have been increasingly weakened. (170)

Kiarostami's cinema is a crusade against this "herd" morality and a departure from "moral statements" and an arrival at "ethical questions". He reconsiders absolute presuppositions and situates them in a relativist and self-assessing evaluation system. Kiarostami's understanding of ethics, therefore, is not universal and does not offer an arrangement of moral principles, but a contextual and dialogical system in permanent endeavour to redefine itself. Emanuel Levinas, the twentieth-century philosopher of ethics, believes that the concept of ethics only makes sense when it is consistently viewed in its relation to the other. He maintains that ignoring the overwhelming presence of the other will undermine what ethics is supposed to mean and question the validity of our ethical conclusions. Consequently, the ethical responsibility, as Levinas observes, is not understandable without accepting the other.

Although Levinas deals with a vast range of philosophical and non-philosophical matters and is influenced by several sources, his work is "dominated by one big idea" (Bernasconi and Critchley 2004, 6), the movement of which is compared by Jacques Derrida to the crashing of a wave on a beach, always the same wave returning and repeating its movement with deeper insistence (Derrida 1978, 312). Levinas's recurring thesis is that ethics is "first philosophy" and should be understood as a relation of "infinite responsibility" to the other person. Such an understanding of ethics does not count on erecting an objective and universal moral monument on rational foundations and does not function through some already-written and prescribed codes that we could *know* prior to the immediate encounter with the other. Ethical thinking is thinking "otherwise than being". In ethical thinking, it is not expected that comprehension of the other will be achieved in terms of passive and constant identities; instead, it prioritises "signification" over "significance", "saying" over "said" or, better to say, "relating to the other" over "being oneself".

It is interesting to study children's relationships with each other and their encounters with adults in light of this understanding of ethics. Childhood is not a unified, biological, and natural concept, but a construction made up of discursive and narrative signs construed and defined through implicative relations. As Jack Zipes observes, children and childhood are social constructions formed by social and economic conditions and signify differently in different cultures (Zipes 2001, 39). Accordingly, a series of varying and contradictory implications of the term "childhood" can be found in words and expressions such as wild, natural, innocent, sublime, insightful, wicked, guilty, lacked, righteous, responsible, sexless, sexualised, little adult, the object under investigation (the miniature man), the protected/supported creature, and the abandoned. Each of these implications, in relation to the dominant discourse of a historical period, could define the term "childhood".

In Kiarostami's films, children are depicted with great diversity, and their individuality is portrayed in schoolyards, classrooms, and other social occasions and situations. In these contexts, the child is a solitary figure left on his/her own, is dominated by adults, has traumatic experiences, and speaks in a self-contradicting discourse. In *First Graders*, this inconsistency is manifestly depicted through the humorous language of the film, in which the child blends the childish content of his sentence with the more formal features of adult language, such as in this example: "This gentleman kicked me". Even though children in Kiarostami's films are lost and confused in the oppressing discourse of adults, they manage, ironically, in some ways, to reclaim that language in their own childlike voices.

Roderick McGillis in "Postcolonialism, Originating Difference" (2004), argues that,

> children are both objects of desire, figures of that which we wish we could be, and objects of transformation into what we think we are. In other words, we both idealise and abject children. We want to be them and we want them to be us. Is this not the colonial state? The colonizer controls and distances the colonised, while at the same time he feels drawn to those he controls. (899)

In Kiarostami's cinema, children are disciplined by opinionated adults who do their best to speed up the process of their children's growing up by teaching and preaching moral lessons. However, Kiarostami's young heroes are "stubborn and determined" (Elena 2005, 60) and insist on following their childlike goals, regardless of the outcome. Nevertheless, Kiarostami avoids idealising this candid endeavour and is determined to show a realistic representation of these struggles within a much wider ironic setting. Peter Matthews in "A Little Learning" (2002), an essay on *Homework*, believes that the child, in order to survive, has to select between what he/she wants and what is publicly assumed as appropriate:

> So it appears that a good part of the tuition consists in learning to stifle their natural instincts and master the meek deportment officially demanded of them. These children don't lack all individuality; it only seems so. For a primary socialisation has already taught them that survival depends on gauging the distance between private desire and acceptable public face. (31)

Similarly, Kiarostami's narrative shows how the child could eventually reveal his desires amidst the multitude of social norms imposed by the adult world. To draw out an "ethical method" from Kiarostami's cinema, we need to regard his films as aesthetic representations of modern self-assessing ethics which turn away from prescriptive morality. He makes an effort to avoid passing judgment and suggesting absolute ethical statements, and contents himself with posing ethical questions. Accordingly, he explores the possibility of an ethical form of narrative in which performance and selection are not reduced to statement, or, to use Levinas's words, the "Saying" is not contained by the "Said" (Levinas 1981, 35).

Levinas, in his magnum opus, *Totality and Infinity* (1979), discusses two philosophical and ethical approaches. To him, "totality" reflects the conventional Greek and European philosophy in which a sense of total completeness of the autonomous self is proclaimed. He believes that Western philosophy has long been involved with asserting the ego as the self-conscious knowing subject, which he calls "the Same" (35–40). In Kiarostami's children's films, the Same could be translated into the way adults approach the world as the all-knowing, egocentric subjects attempting to reduce and assimilate the other (children) into their own selfhood realm.

This is in contrast to an alternative ethics and philosophy, an "ethics [that] occurs as the putting into question of the ego, the knowing subject, self-consciousness, or what Levinas, following Plato, calls the Same" (Critchley 1992, 4). This is the realm of "infinity" which is characterised by the "other". In this ethical approach, one is on a face-to-face relationship with the other, with "infinite responsibility" (Levinas 1979, 244). Instead of declaring absolute and abstract universalising statements, in this ethical approach, the self encounters the other. The way Kiarostami's child characters behave and relate to one another has close affinity with this alternative form of ethics, which Levinas calls "infinity". Instead of pronouncing moral values, Kiarostami's child heroes "face" the other and react according to the circumstances without any preconceived or finalised judgements. Therefore, children take the place of "infinity" in Kiarostami's films, in which they refuse to be contained or possessed by adults. They do not act out of a reciprocal sense of responsibility, but feel responsible towards the other in the way that the other's needs become the self's obligations.

In *Two Solutions for One Problem*, Kiarostami narrates a short and simple story about two schoolmates. Nader and Dara are friends. Nader lends his book to Dara. On returning the book, Dara realises that the cover of the book is torn. The film gives two versions of the story. In the first version, Dara returns the book and Nader, realising that the cover is torn, tears Dara's book. The retaliation continues in a tit for tat manner ending in broken stationery and a broken head and a bruised eye. In the second narrative, Dara fixes the cover of the book with glue and they remain friends. The film only narrates the two alternative stories and leaves the ethical decisions to the child spectators.

In *First Case, Second Case*, a student bangs on his desk with his pen in the classroom when the teacher is writing on the blackboard. The teacher, who cannot find the wrongdoer, tells the last two rows of the classroom to either expose the wrongdoer or leave the classroom and receive temporary suspensions for one week. The students face an ethical dilemma, ultimately deciding to get suspended and not expose their classmate. While the spectator faces the same ethical question, the second part of the film has a surprising twist. The film's narrator asks a few politicians, statesmen, artists, and thinkers to imagine that they are parents to one of these suspended students. Do these adults endorse such an act of solidarity and refusal, or do they ask their child to deliver the wrongdoer and return to class? Interestingly, the adults translate the ethical dilemma to the political discourse of the early years of the 1979 Islamic Revolution and examine the duality of solidarity versus betrayal in the political paradigm of those years. However, the closing credits reveal the director's response to the dilemma, as the credits are accompanied by the constant rhythmic sound of a pen banging on the desk.

Alberto Elena, in his book, *The Cinema of Abbas Kiarostami* (2005), believes that Kiarostami's view of ethics resembles that of mathematical theorems: he proposes two different premises and asks the audience to choose. Elena maintains that Kiarostami keeps distancing himself from the ethical questions he asks and avoids identifying with any of the ethical choices proposed in the context of the film (30–31). In *Homework*, a film that consists almost entirely of interviews with a number of students and two fathers, the filmmaker employs a Brechtian "alienation effect" (Brecht 1961, 130) through cinematic "punctuations" which expose the camera and the cinematographer, lest we situate ourselves in the context of the film, and are drowned in a form of sentimental partiality through identifying too closely with the interviewees.

Ethics of Care: Infinite Responsibility to the Other

As indicated earlier, according to Levinas, the concept of ethics is always understandable in relation to the other. More precisely, for Levinas, ethics is the occurrence of this relation. Similarly, Kiarostami's children's films orchestrate the relation between children and adults on one hand and between children and children on the other. The indifferent and domineering adults in these films are unable, or unwilling, to make what Levinas calls "the movement outward" which is "the ethical impulse towards or openness to the other that effects a release from the confines of the self". In other words, the oblivious grown-ups in Kiarostami's films do not respond to "the spontaneous and immediate desire to escape the limits of the self, a desire generated as those limits are experienced in their narrowness, even their sheer absurdity" (Gibson 1999, 37).

In response to the lack of care or understanding of grown-ups, children, in an altruistic fashion, attempt to care for one another. The first of Kiarostami's Koker Trilogy, *Where Is the Friend's Home?* is perhaps the best example of this "ethics of care": "In Levinasian terms, we look to theories of justice for insight into how to convey care for the other in our actions, and a good theory will be one that, among other things sharpens our capacity to recognize the other, that sharpens our ability to hear her call" (Shaw 2008, 123). *Where Is the Friend's Home?* is a paragon of this "care for the other".

In the narrative, Ahmad struggles to hand his friend's exercise book back to him in order to stop their teacher punishing his classmate for not writing his homework. On his arduous and epic journey, he confronts many obstacles. At the start, Ahmad's grandfather, sitting in the village square and talking to his friends, tells him to get back home and bring his pack of cigarettes. When Ahmad is away, the grandfather gives a lengthy lecture on how children need to be disciplined and punished regularly even when there are no grounds for such punishment: "You may stop giving them pocket money, but cannot stop beating them!" On his way back home, he encounters a man negotiating a trade with another person, a sequence which situates Ahmad as an innocent child against the opportunistic, deceptive, pretentious, and indifferent discourse of an adult. The man needs a piece of paper to record some figures for the deal (as a metonymy for the deceptive and business-minded world of adults) and asks Ahmad to remove a sheet from the notebook (as a metonymy for childhood friendship). This is the notebook Ahmad wants to hand to his friend intact yet, despite his initial resistance, the notebook is taken away by force and a sheet of it is literally and symbolically torn. In *Where Is the Friend's Home?*, the notebook functions as a plural and fluid sign on which almost all the ethical implications of the film are loaded. The notebook which, at the beginning of the film, signifies commitment to the educational principles of the adult world, becomes the symbol of dealings in the corrupt world of trade before it eventually reclaims its meaning as the sign of children's friendship, loyalty, and responsibility to each other.

Although there is a close focus on ignorant and neglectful adults in Kiarostami's films, it should be noted that even those adults who care for children do not have an organically appropriate relationship with them, invariably exhorting the children to conform to the adults' habitual discourses. As an example, the old carpenter in *Where Is the Friend's Home?*, though very kind, symbolically fails to "keep pace" with the walking boy. As the night falls and Ahmad continues to search for his friend's house in an alien village, the old man says that he cannot walk fast when he talks, to which the boy replies, "So, please don't talk". The discrepancy between the walking speed of the child and the old man represents a deep gap between their worlds. Furthermore, this is the wise and kind old man who, lost in his own past, eventually leads Ahmad to the wrong house, the result of which leads to time-wasting and the return to his own village empty-handed. Even among supposedly "caring" adults, the child cannot experience that "moment of pure touching, pure contact" (Levinas 1997, 41).

In *The Chorus* (1982), the grandfather's deafness, which makes him unable to hear the doorbell and open the door for his grandchildren, similarly reveals problematic connections between the two worlds. At the end of the film, although the children beyond the window on the street chant together, "Grandpa, open the door", the grandfather hears nothing since he has removed his hearing aids. This crucial sequence of the film is an extraordinary representation of how the adult does not hear the child's cry of "invitation" to open a door of mutual understanding and friendship. Within these narratives, then, even the caring adults are literally and symbolically unable to hear the children's call to face the other.

In Kiarostami's films, the family is solely concerned with and "attached to [...] its own being" (Bernasconi and Wood 1988, 172), and constantly imposes its value systems upon children and assigns disproportionately large tasks and duties to them without noticing its responsibility to them. In *Where Is the Friend's Home?*, in a sequence set in the classroom, we see a boy spending most of his time not *at* his desk but *under* it. Later in the film, through Ahmad's odyssey, when we see the boy again in the village carrying two large milk containers, and realise that this is his regular daily task, it emerges that he suffers from chronic backache. In the same film, Ahmad—the protagonist of the story—has difficulty communicating with his own mother and, after a fruitless conversation during one sequence of the film, the two are drawn into a quarrel. Such depictions may be directly contrasted with John Wall's views in *Ethics in Light of Childhood* (2010), in which he argues for a "generative" view of family:

> To call families 'generative,' therefore, is to say that the fundamental ethical purpose of family life is to create shared worlds with others. Being human involves not just living alongside others but also making new narratives with them and responding singularly to them. Family generativity arises out of a variety of biological, psychological, social, cultural, traditional, historical, and spiritual constructions. It does not spring from nothing. But its underlying ethical purpose is neither to impose nor to overcome such conditions, but rather to reconstruct them in new ways responsive to each new person. Such is the generativity of love. It is neither self-centered nor self-sacrificial but self-decentering. (148)

This "generative family" is simply nonexistent in Kiarostami's films. Rather, Kiarostami employs bitter and dark humour to depict the complications of the relationships between families and children. In *Homework*, for example, Kiarostami asks the child, "Who checks your homework at home?". Surprisingly, the child replies that it is *he* who checks his mother's homework. These inversions of the traditional parent/child hegemony make consistent appearances in Kiarostami's work. In *The Traveler*, Ghasem's mother takes him to school and asks the principal to beat him in front of her for stealing a few coins. In *Homework*, in spite of the fact that the filmmaker does not intrude into the privacy of children's domestic lives, the audience gradually learns about the hidden dismay of the families' worlds through the students' responses to the interviewer's questions. These interviews reveal the abject circumstances in which the vulnerable children are being raised by ignorant, illiterate, jobless parents and violent, polygamous families in which they are constantly tormented.

Kiarostami refers to his personal "memories of school" as "still traumatic" (quoted in Elena 2005, 63), a trauma which reveals itself in his films, in which the educational system is characterised through its constant "othering" of children, and through subjecting them to normalising and discriminating discourses, the immediate effect of which is to demolish the child's creativity by way of surveillance and vigilance. Cathy Caruth defines such "trauma" in the following terms: "In its general definition, trauma is described as the response to an unexpected or overwhelming violent event or events that are not fully grasped as they occur, but return later in repeated flashbacks, nightmares, and other repetitive phenomena" (Caruth 1996, 91). In *First Graders*, the school principal, despite the wise, fair, and responsible impression he gives, is the epitome of absolute authority and power, the reflection of which can be seen in the eyes of the traumatised children whom he encounters. He summons each one after another and, after a trial-like procedure of interrogation, pronounces his final "wise" verdict:

> [T]he interrogations in the headmaster's office form the backbone of the film and impose a single meaning on the various events filmed by the director: this first contact with school is also the first contact with a world made up of rules, which must necessarily be learned and obeyed as quickly as possible. (Elena 2005, 61)

In this way, *First Graders* becomes one of the most outspoken films made by Kiarostami because it critiques not only the educational system itself but also takes as its central subject the open, harsh encounter between the disparate discourses of children and adults within that system.

Ethics of Refusal and Resistance: Moving Towards Freedom

It is in this dire condition of "child exploitation" (Saeed-Vafa and Rosenbaum 2003, 73) that Kiarostami's child characters choose to *resist* the domineering sources of power and *refuse* the confining moral standards of the family and society in the hope of a higher form of ethics, namely freedom. And it is these twinned themes of resistance and refusal in Kiarostami's children's films that are fundamentally related to his ethical concerns.

Disobedience may be a common theme in many cinematic works, but what makes Kiarostami's films particularly remarkable is the different approach he takes from mainstream Iranian cinema. While the theme of disobedience in conventional narratives is commonly represented by a hero or heroine breaking through authoritarian obstacles through courage, intelligence, and/or adherence to moral principles, Kiarostami's characters do not shy away from doing what may be considered the morally "wrong" thing—from telling lies, for example—to protect themselves against domestic violence and restrictions, and the resulting confrontations become important sources of tension and struggle in the filmmaker's storylines. This form of "relativist ethics" does not distinguish between "the moral" and "the immoral" in absolute terms. In *The Traveler*, for example, Ghasem has to cheat and lie to make his dream of watching a live soccer match come true—a dream that is not acknowledged and supported but constantly suppressed and mocked. In the breath-taking sequence in which his mother reports his theft to the headmaster, home and school join together in punishing him, instead of trying to understand him. Subjugation and domination are prioritised over acceptance and comprehension in these domestic and educational environments, and function as broader references to social problems. Living in a poor urban setting, Ghasem represents the prototype of millions of children all over the world, many economically or socially disadvantaged, who see their love of sports as the main source of self-actualisation and identity. Though the drab portrayal of Ghasem's conditions at home and at school, and the shocking conclusion to the film in which the exhausted Ghasem, after all his endeavours to attend the game, falls asleep and misses it, might seem like a pessimistic ending which negates the efforts of a child to move beyond the conformity of a provincial life, the film nevertheless exhorts the ingenuity of the child, his courage and strength of will, and his determination to reach his goal. The conclusion, as befits the child's environment, is realistic rather than sentimental (Fig. 10.1).

Similarly, in *Where Is the Friend's Home?*, the protagonist Ahmad lies to his mother, takes significantly risky trips to an unfamiliar environment, and finally writes his friend's homework in an act of "infinite responsibility", to save him from punishment. While his socio-economic conditions may seem better than Ghasem's, and his family does not appear

Fig. 10.1   Abbas Kiarostami, *The Traveler*

particularly poor, the prospects of familial and societal communication, understanding and support are equally dismal. The rural setting of the film, which could have perhaps raised the possibility of closer interpersonal relationships and understanding, does not, in fact, benefit Ahmad any more than Ghasem's poor urban background. Each remains as isolated and unsupported as the other, and both films seem to argue that the problems of misunderstanding, ignorance of others' needs, and the use of violence to discourage disobedience exist regardless of social class and neighbourhood. School is again no better than home in helping children achieve their goals, but the conclusion of each film positions children's enterprise and strategy on a much higher level than any social shortcomings. Ahmad and Ghasem, each in their own distinctive way, overcome the limitations of their circumstances, and if Ahmad's self-sacrifice is a sign of "infinite responsibility" towards the other, Ghasem's epic journey is an act of self-discovery and individuation.

Neglected children in Kiarostami's cinema gradually construct a subculture far from the reach of adults, in which they resort to telling lies as a "self-defense mechanism" (Elena 2005, 64) against aggression and violence. Kiarostami's child heroes are talented, inquisitive, daring, and sharp rather than innocent and otherworldly, and intentionally and wilfully subvert the rules by which the adults' worlds are governed. In *Breaktime*, a student is called to account for and then punished for playing ball games. Through the superimposition of a medium shot of a broken window on to the scene of the ordeal of punishment, the filmmaker creates effective interconnected images that reveal the depth of the child's agony. After being beaten by the principal, the boy leaves the school while holding a ball in one hand and a notebook in the other and does so throughout the remainder of the film. This representation forms a dichotomy between the duty imposed by the world of grown-ups on the one hand, and the freedom and play of the world of children on the other, forming what Terry Eagleton calls, "the deathly cat-and-mouse game between law and desire" (2009, 143). At the end of this short film, the boy, entangled in this dichotomy, walks in the opposite direction to the grown-ups' cars, and disappears over the horizon, waving at the indifferent cars which pass by and throw dust into the air, a conclusion that may signify one of the most controversial aspects of ethics—what is termed the "ethics of freedom". For the noted writer and academic, J. M. Coetzee, "freedom [is] irresponsibility, or better, [...] responsibility toward something that has not yet emerged, that lies somewhere at the end of the road"

(Coetzee 1992, 246), and it is this configuration of freedom which aptly fits with the Levinasian concept of "infinity" as explained earlier.

Gender and the disciplinary formation of sexuality in children also form the focus of some of Kiarostami's works, most notably in *The Experience* and *A Wedding Suit*. In these works, puberty is represented as the bitter central experience of a child's entry into the strange world of adulthood, and in each narrative the boys' efforts to relate with the other—here, the opposite sex—are doomed to failure because of the gap between social classes. Despite these failures, both films reflect how the adolescent heroes are nevertheless ready to take great risks to cultivate their individuation.

One may observe the same attempt at individuation in one of the last works by the director. In 2010, Kiarostami made a short film entitled, *No*, in the form of an interview with a little girl who loves acting in movies. The interviewer (Kiarostami) agrees to cast her in the main role as long as she fulfils one task, the sole condition being that in the course of the plot, the girl's hair should be cut off. Surprisingly, the girl refuses to acquiesce and decides not to act in the movie. In other words, she decides to maintain and cherish what seems to her to be her identity, namely her hair. While Kiarostami tells the story and passes no obvious moral judgment, there are signs to indicate that he is not a completely impartial bystander and that his child characters must be ready to break society's traditional codes of conduct and accepted moral norms in order to achieve a higher ethical goal, that of individual freedom. Entrapped in an unjust mesh of social relationships, they are forced to make difficult ethical choices amidst less than ideal circumstances. They implement this refusal to accept their current state at times by lying, stealing, deceiving, taking unreasonable risks and ignoring the adults' norms yet, interestingly, this refusal and disobedience is invariably non-confrontational and peaceful, comprising a form of passive resistance to the dictates of family and society. Kiarostami's child characters ignore the rules rather than confront them.

Conclusion

Human beings usually justify their own mistakes and failures by way of the circumstances they have experienced, but attribute others' mistakes and failures to their character flaws. This is considered to be one of the well-described biases of the human cognitive system and is called "fundamental attribution error". Kiarostami masterfully stages his plots in ways through which we may begin to break away from this prejudice and recognise supposedly immoral behaviour in its socio-economic context. Thus, we as viewers (and consequently as vicarious participants in the narratives) begin to ask why Ghasem has to cheat on his classmates to watch a soccer game; why he is unable to talk to his mother; and, more importantly, why his mother is unable to listen to him. We may even ask ourselves why we often prematurely judge others by their presumed character rather than by their true circumstances. We become curious to know how the whole story would have ended if Ahmad was accompanied and supported by his parents. What society considers normal could be more fluid than we think. Kiarostami takes the focus of our cognitive lens from the child's actual behaviour into the context in which this behaviour happens: he redirects and reorients our ethical enquiry and helps us to see the filmic text in its context.

Because of his ethical method, it may be argued that Kiarostami has become the modern-day gadfly, his cinema reminding us of the conversation Socrates had with Euthydemus in which Socrates asks Euthydemus whether being deceitful is counted as being immoral. The answer is positive. He then asks whether stealing a knife from a friend who is suicidal could be considered immoral. Euthydemus is not sure how to respond. Socrates thus shows that being deceitful is not necessarily immoral in all situations (Warburton 2011, 2). Context may thus be crucial when codes of morality are assessed. Similarly, in Kiarostami's films, refusal alone supports and promotes a much more valuable human quality, which is freedom and happiness. We love Kiarostami's characters not because they achieve much but because they either risk their lives so as to care for each other or break societal norms and expectations in order to be free, which encapsulates a more relativist approach to ethics than the traditional universalist view of moral values.

In the final sequence of *Homework*, we see an insecure schoolboy who is so tormented by suppression and the flawed expectations of the adult world that he cannot tolerate school without the continuous presence of his classmate by his side. When Kiarostami asks him to recount a poem he knows by heart, he recites a poem by Ali Mousavi Garmaroudi (1981), which is included in primary school textbooks in Iran. The recitation of the poem acts as the ending credits to the film and emerges as "verbal irony" in the context of what the filmmaker wishes to reveal about the world of the children. This ending not only effectively exposes the hypocrisy of teaching children a poem that is deeply inconsistent with the life they experience at home and school, but also conveys the tormented children's heartfelt yearnings for happiness and joy:

> O' God of beautiful stars,
> O' God of colorful world,
> Who brought Venus,
> And the moon and the sun,
> Mountains, hills and seas,
> These beautiful fruitful trees,
> Butterfly's pretty wings,
> And nests for the birds,
> And joy and game and strength,
> And eyes for us to see,
> And rain and snow, heat and cold.
> O' God! You brought all these,
> You granted what I wished,
> Fill our hearts with happiness and joy. (*Our Translation*, 2)

References

Aristotle. 1996. *Poetics*. Translated by Malcolm Heath. London: Penguin Books.

Bernasconi, Robert, and David Wood, eds. 1988. *The Provocation of Levinas: Re-thinking the Other*. New York and London: Routledge and Kegan Paul.

Bernasconi, Robert, and Simon Critchley, eds. 2004. *The Cambridge Companion to Levinas*. Cambridge: Cambridge University Press.

Brecht, Bertolt. 1961. "On Chinese Acting." Translated by Eric Bentley. *The Tulane Drama Review* 6 (1): 130–136.

Caruth, Cathy. 1996. *Unclaimed Experience: Trauma, Narrative, and History*. Baltimore and London: The Johns Hopkins University Press.

Coetzee, J. M. 1992. "Confession and Double Thoughts: Tolstoy, Rousseau, Dostoevsky." In *Doubling the Point: Essays and Interviews*, edited by David Atwell. Cambridge, MA: Harvard University Press.

Critchley, Simon. 1992. *The Ethics of Deconstruction: Derrida and Levinas*. Oxford: Blackwell.

Derrida, Jacques. 1978. *Writing and Difference*. Translated by Alan Bass. London and Henley: Routledge and Kegan Paul.

Eagleton, Terry. 2009. *Trouble with Strangers: A Study of Ethics*. Oxford: Blackwell.

Elena, Alberto. 2005. *The Cinema of Abbas Kiarostami*. London: Saqi Books.

Gibson, Andrew. 1999. *Postmodernity, Ethics, and the Novel*. London: Routledge.

Levinas, Emmanuel. 1979. *Totality and Infinity: An Essay on Exteriority.* Translated by Alphonso Lingis. The Hague: Martinus Nijhoff.

———. 1981. *Otherwise Than Being or Beyond Essence.* Translated by Alphonso Lingis. The Hague: Martinus Nijhoff.

———. 1997. *Proper Names.* Translated by Michael B. Smith. Stanford: Stanford University Press.

Matthews, Peter. 2002. "A Little Learning." *Sight and Sound* 12 (6): 30–32.

McGillis, Roderick. 2004. "Postcolonialism, Originating Difference." In *International Companion Encyclopedia of Children's Literature,* edited by Peter Hunt. Second Edition. Vol. 1, 891–900. New York: Routledge.

Mousavi Garmaroudi, Ali. 1981. "God of Stars." In *Religious Studies: Textbook for Second Year of Primary Education.* Tehran: Ministry of Education Publishers (Persian).

Saeed-Vafa, Mehrnaz, and Jonathan Rosenbaum. 2003. *Abbas Kiarostami.* Chicago: University of Illinois Press.

Shaw, Joshua James. 2008. *Emmanuel Levinas on the Priority of Ethics: Putting Ethics First.* Amherst, NY: Cambria Press.

Wall, John. 2010. *Ethics in Light of Childhood.* Washington: Georgetown University Press.

Warburton, Nigel. 2011. *A Little History of Philosophy.* New Haven and London: Yale University Press.

Zipes, Jack. 2001. *Sticks and Stones: The Troublesome Success of Children's Literature from Slovenly Peter to Harry Potter.* New York: Routledge.

PART III

Southeast

Folktale Adaptation and Female Agency: Reconfigurations of the *Mahsuri* Legend in Selected Contemporary Malaysian Young Adult Fiction

Sharifah Aishah Osman

Of the many popular folktales and legends from Malaysia, the legend of Mahsuri, the maiden of Langkawi, Kedah, must surely count as one of the most controversial and gruesome in the collection. With its themes of jealousy, polygamy, mob violence, vengeance, and class struggle projected upon the brutalised body of Mahsuri as the victim of slander and injustice, the tale appears as such to be a rather contentious choice for the consumption of young adult readers, even more so impressionable children. Yet such themes were largely prevalent in a genre widely known to present "the stark realities of power politics without disguising the violence and brutality of everyday life", and in which stories dealing with "starvation and abandonment of children, rape, corporeal punishment, and ruthless exploitation" familiar to the lower classes in pre-capitalist societies were

S. A. Osman (✉)
Department of English, Universiti Malaya, Kuala Lumpur, Malaysia
e-mail: saosman@um.edu.my

© The Author(s) 2020
B. Wilson and S. P. Gabriel (eds.), *Asian Children's Literature and Film in a Global Age*, Asia-Pacific and Literature in English, https://doi.org/10.1007/978-981-15-2631-2_11

215

common (Zipes 2012a: 8). As the oldest and most widely known form of literature for children, the folktale, with its central theme of "might makes right", reflected the concerns of a "monarchistic, patriarchal, and feudal society" (Zipes 2012a: 8) and its attendant limitations. Thus, the presence and use of magic and the supernatural in such tales are often linked to the "wish-fulfilment and utopian projections of the people", and "serve to rupture the feudal confines and represent metaphorically the conscious and unconscious desires of the lower classes" (Zipes 2012a: 8). Similarly, as Alison Lurie argues, folktales are among the most subversive texts in children's literature, and often "support the rights of disadvantaged members of the population – children, women, and the poor – against the establishment" (16). Apart from being perceived as a middle- and working-class genre, the folktale was also associated with women, with stories passed down as a form of oral tradition from generation to generation, and that frequently depicted women not only as central characters, but also often endowed with magical or supernatural powers (Lurie 19).

Rooted as they were in oral traditions, folktales, like fairy tales, "had never been explicitly told for children" and "do not belong to children" (Zipes, *Fairy Tales* xi). In examining the fairy tale as a specific type of folk narrative and its origins as a literary genre for children, Zipes notes that "educated writers purposely appropriated the oral folktale and converted it into a type of literary discourse about mores, values, and manners so that children and adults would become civilized according to the social code of that time" (3). In short, as Lurie, Cashdan, Haase, and Jones have all noted,[1] as part of the process of being adapted for the consumption of children, and out of concern over the inherent dangers of "wild" folktales on impressionable and imaginative young minds, many of these tales underwent "sanitisation" in the hands of nineteenth-century European middle-class editors and collectors, and were constructed as "part and parcel of a general civilising process" meant to reinforce "dominant religious and patriarchal attitudes about gender, mating, law, and order" (xi) and to instruct their young audiences on the significance of morality, charity, virtue, and good conduct. Likewise, Maria Tatar observes that once folktales reached print by the eighteenth and nineteenth centuries, they "lost their subversive edge and became assimilated into the official canon of children's literature, which had always been more interested in producing docile minds than playful bodies" (5), and thus "took on a protective didactic colouring that has been virtually impossible to remove" (11).[2] The presence of an "adult agenda" in the production of children's literature in the nineteenth century thus explains the popularity of cautionary tales and exemplary stories as the two main models available for writers who were adapting folktales into stories for children of the time (8). The emphasis on moral lessons and the punishment of villains, particularly for "disobedience" and "deviant conduct" (25), thus accounts for much of the added violence and "remarkably vivid scenes of torture and execution" (7) present in such tales.

Yet the folktale and the fairy tale have also benefitted richly from their evolution into "a conflicted cultural field", in which writers use such stories "to question conformity to the dominant civilizing process of a society" (Zipes xi). In this regard, as Victoria Flanagan points out, the retelling or revision of traditional fairy tales has been one of the most significant tasks undertaken by feminist writers for children and adolescents, perceiving such tales as offering the opportunity "to promote feminine agency and interrogate normative constructs of gender and sexuality" and as the ideal space "within which to contest patriarchal notions of gender and power" (26–27). Such feminist revisions "emanate from a basic impulse for change within society", and play a significant role in "questioning socialisation" by enabling audiences to reflect on how such tales function in the conditioning of women and children (Zipes 1987: 14). In a similar vein, Stephen Benson, citing Sandra Gilbert's "revisionary imperative" in feminist theory to "review, reimagine, rethink, rewrite, revise, and reinterpret" historical and cultural events and documents, notes that feminist adaptations of the traditional fairy tale constitute "a re-energizing of a tradition and subversion of traditional interpretations" (Gilbert, cited in Benson 200).[3]

The traditional Malay folktale, like many of those from the Southeast Asian region, reflects the world view as well as the cosmological order of the Malay world, and to an extent, the ideology of the existing ruling class, with most of the stories relating to the social relationship between the masses and the rulers, and with the inequality in status between the ruler and the ruled often being emphasised (Selat 53). Such tales not only served as entertainment for both young and old among the common village folk, but were also meant to "educate and inculcate good moral values in the people" (53). The instances of gender stereotyping seen in many traditional Malay folktales written for children in Malaysia thus reflect and perpetuate patriarchal and feudalistic values in their heavily didactic underpinnings, often by emphasising female virtue and moral behaviour, a trait that has also been observed in European fairy tales (Zipes 2012a: 39–56, Tatar 94–119). Tales like *Puteri San-tubong* and *Bawang Merah, Bawang Putih*,[4] among others, demonstrate how the definition of "feminine" qualities in such stories is influenced by an inherently patriarchal ideology, where women appear either as dys-functional figures in conflict with each other, or as passive "damsels in distress" awaiting rescue by the hero. Exemplary heroines are often physically attractive, chaste, filial, and rewarded for their submissiveness by marriage to a rich and/or powerful man. Conversely, female villains appear as wicked stepmothers or sisters, obstacles or rivals in the heroine's quest for the love of a worthy man, and consequently punished through death or marginalisation (Osman, Lai, and Kassim 413–414).

The plot, setting, and themes of the legendary tale of *Mahsuri* reflect all of the concerns raised in such folklore scholarship, particularly the class struggle between the peasantry and aristocracy, and the oppression of the marginalised poor, revolving as the story does around the white-blooded maiden from a rural village on the island of Langkawi, who is accused unjustly of adultery and executed publicly in cold blood. Born under mysterious circumstances to a poor paddy farmer, Pandak Maya, and his wife, Mek Andak Alang, the beautiful Mahsuri attracts many suitors, including the wealthy village Chieftain, Datuk Karma Jaya, who already has a wife, Mahura, and several grown children. Humiliated by her husband's intention to marry Mahsuri, Mahura bears a grudge against her. Although Mahsuri marries their son Mat Deris instead, and bears him a son, Mat Arus, Mahura remains jealous of Mahsuri and vows revenge. When Mat Deris is called to war, Mahura spreads rumours about Mahsuri's apparent infidelity, and convinces Datuk Karma Jaya and the entire village of Mahsuri's affair with the itinerant poet and storyteller, Deramang. In the commotion that ensues, Deramang manages to escape but the helpless Mahsuri is arrested and sentenced to death for adultery without trial, despite her protestations of innocence and the appeals of her aggrieved family for justice and sympathy. The executioner makes several attempts to stab Mahsuri but fails; she confesses that she can only be killed with a sacred *keris*.[5] When the executioner finally kills Mahsuri, white blood gushes from her wound and white mist surrounds her, proving her innocence and supernatural powers. Before she dies, Mahsuri curses the villagers with seven generations of bad luck for the senseless accusations and injustice inflicted upon her. Langkawi is invaded by the Siamese and left desolate and barren ("padang jarak, padang tekukur"[6]) for many generations, emphasising the potency of Mahsuri's curse. Aptly glorified as a symbol of righteousness and purity, her story serves as a stark reminder of the power of female agency in the face of societal injustice and patriarchal oppression, warning against envy, rumour-mongering, and cruelty towards the innocent.

The tragic tale of *Mahsuri* is clearly inseparable from the historical and cultural identity of the people of Langkawi, and continues to be appropriated for its commercial tourism potential, an intangible cultural legacy imparted to the millions of visitors to the island annually, all while partaking of the more earthly and modern attractions of its innumerable beach resorts and duty-free malls (Ismail 75, Larsen 86, Hijjas 249). Despite its graphic depiction of mob violence and brutality, and perhaps even because of it, the legend retains its hold on the collective memory of many Malaysians. As a cultural product that forms part of the intangible heritage of the nation, the legend of *Mahsuri* is widely regarded as reflecting the feudalistic social order and patriarchal values of Malay communal life of the eighteenth century in which the story is set, and continues to be taught in national schools and anthologised in local folktale collections as part of the cultivated literature for children and young adults in Malaysia.[7]

In acknowledging the subversive power of the folktale, especially in its ability to examine and challenge the ideological position of the Malay woman as constructed by the nation-state, this essay argues that the legendary story of *Mahsuri*, and its subsequent adaptations, can provide important insights into the contemporary relevance of the folktale to the propagation and contestation of patriarchal, feudalistic, and nationalistic ideology of modern, multicultural Malaysia. This essay thus examines three contemporary textual representations of the legendary tale of *Mahsuri*—Lee Su Ann's young adult murder mystery, *The Curse* (2005), Preeta Samarasan's short story of interracial love, "Mahsuri" (2011), and Shireen Zainudin's allusive retelling, "Grey" (2019)—in order to illustrate how each of these "subversive" literary texts draws attention to the subjugated status of women in contemporary Malay society. Through the exploration of the dynamics of patriarchal oppression, and in the case of Samarasan's text, the additional complexities of racial marginalisation in Malaysia, the stories foreground the struggle for power and possession over the body (and by implication, the mind and the spirit) of the idealised Malay woman, represented by the character of "Mahsuri" in these three stories. In doing so, these adaptations of the legendary tale reflect the critical engagement with, and interrogation of, issues of gender, racial, and religious identity in contemporary multicultural Malaysia through their mutual emphasis on the repercussions of Mahsuri's "curse" on their respective protagonists.

AGENCY IN ADVERSITY: LEE SU ANN'S *THE CURSE*

The selection of *The Curse* as the prescribed text for the literature component of the Form Five English Language paper of the Sijil Pelajaran Malaysia examination affirmed its status as a work of Malaysian young adult (YA) fiction. While it ostensibly revisits the original legend in its treatment of the plot, setting, and major themes, Lee's novel distinguishes itself through its use of the murder mystery genre, and in its depiction of a compelling "feminist protagonist", the university student Azreen, who returns home to her village in Langkawi from her studies in England to unravel the mystery that shrouds her sister Madhuri's sudden death under suspicious circumstances. As Roberta Seelinger Trites states, a defining trait of the feminist children's (and by implication YA) novel is where the protagonist's "agency, individuality, choice, and nonconformity are affirmed and even celebrated", and are used to reverse traditional gender roles in the story (6). John Stephens notes a similar impetus in adolescent fiction, in which the narrative focus on the protagonist's maturation or personal growth is dependent on the ability to "express self-recognition and agency" (5), as does Robyn MacCallum, who asserts that "subjectivity is intrinsic to the major concerns of adolescent fiction" (3). The main character's recognition of her agency and voice thus leads to some sort of "transcendence, usually taking the form of a triumph over whatever stricture or system was repressing her" (Trites 7). The narrative of self-discovery that underlies the novel also enables us to consider the text as an example of what Rita Felski terms the "feminist Bildungsroman" (133), with its "concern with questions of identity and autonomous selfhood" as well as a plot that marks a journey from "alienation and lack, to self-knowledge and a potential for self-determination" (150).

Indeed, *The Curse* reflects all of the progressive qualities of adolescent fiction in the author's development of Azreen's character as she journeys towards independence and self-awareness. As an intelligent young girl who yearns to overcome her life of rural poverty, she relishes her freedom as a student in London, and while grateful to be given the opportunity to leave her tiny village to study abroad through the generous sponsorship of her wealthy adopted parents Datuk Zulkifli and Datin Sharifah, Azreen also works hard to improve her circumstances. In contrast to her beautiful, conservative older sister Madhuri who conforms more traditionally to the role of the submissive wife and daughter, Azreen is perceived by her family and the village community as rebellious, "fiery-tempered", tomboyish, and too outspoken and stubborn for her own good. They regard her as a "trouble maker", criticise her interest in hockey and her inclination to hang out with boys, laughing "like a bunch of hyenas", and her general disinterest in being "socially accepted" by those she doesn't much care for (Lee 38). As she declares to her friend, the Old Lady of the forest, when the latter admonishes her for not behaving "in a more feminine manner", "[If] it meant having to obey everything a man asks of me without a chance of voicing my opinion, I think I'd rather stay *un*feminine my whole life!" (68, emphasis in original). Her defiance of patriarchal rule is epitomised in the strained relationship between Azreen and her stern and disapproving father Saleh, who frequently compares her to the more docile and accommodating Madhuri, a bond which deteriorates even further after the death of both Madhuri and her mother.

However, it is also Azreen's courage, persistence, and nonconformity to societal expectations that enable her to stay true to herself, and to disregard the judgment of others in order to remain strong in the face of personal obstacles: her defence of her good friend Asraf, whom she loyally protects when he is accused of negligence by his employer; her decision to befriend and remain close to the Old Lady of the forest, whom all the villagers treat as a witch and an outcast, but who in fact killed her abusive husband in self-defence; her ability to forgive her emotionally distant and authoritarian father when she realises that it was he who had accidentally killed Madhuri in a fit of anger when he discovers her secret affair with Asraf; and her decision to return to England to continue her studies despite having lost her entire family. The story does portray a range of women mired in stereotypically gendered roles—Normala, the village gossip and rumour-monger; Fatihah, the first wife of Madhuri's husband, Hj. Ghani, who is consumed by jealousy and hatred for Madhuri; Azreen's weak and docile mother whose mental fragility is compounded by her physical disability (she is paralysed after an accident, and also stricken with Alzheimer's disease), and of course the angelic Madhuri herself, whose beauty, piety, and melodious voice enchant all the men in the village, but is powerless to decide who she wishes to marry. All these women, however, serve as foils that only reinforce the strength and agency of a female character like Azreen. As Trites observes of the feminist novel and its revisionary ideology, "[I]t is only against the passive female, the silent female, the objectified female, that the feminist protagonist's achievements can be fully understood" (6).

If the legend of *Mahsuri* illustrates how her curse functions as a form of resistance in the face of limited agency and serves as a potent response to the threat and infliction of male violence or hypermasculinity (what Khoo Gaik Cheng has termed the performance of "authentic masculinity in crisis" 20), then Lee's novel also critiques the destructive impact of such competitive displays of "masculine" power through the depiction of male characters like Madhuri's father Saleh, her secret lover Asraf, and her husband Hj. Ghani. It is after all the selfish actions and machinations of these three men combined, all of whom are guilty of objectifying, victimising, and silencing Madhuri to some extent or the other, that culminate in her eventual death. Saleh for instance, agrees to Hj. Ghani's proposal of taking Madhuri as his second wife without giving his daughter the opportunity to raise any objections, believing that the wealthy village headman will provide her with a better life than the one he can afford as a poor farmer; in a fit of rage he also ends up murdering Madhuri (albeit accidentally) upon discovering her and Asraf together at the rubber plantation, perceiving their affair as a blemish on his honour. Likewise, the cowardly and insecure Asraf watches Madhuri married off to a far older man despite his being in love with her. Unable or unwilling to make his intentions known by officially asking for her hand, he keeps their affair a secret rather than suggesting that Madhuri leave her husband so that they can be together instead. Asraf's display of hypermasculinity, leading the mob on a rampage towards the Old Lady's hut with a torch in hand in the middle of the night ("loss and anguish fuelled his actions") to seek justice for what he believes is the Old Lady's role in his grandmother's death, is also shown to be a clear moment of weakness based on injured pride and the misguided belief in rumour and superstition, one that resolves nothing but only results in the tragic death of the Old Lady, and almost causes Azreen's death as well. Finally, Madhuri's husband, Hj. Ghani, whose wealth and position as the village headman enable him to possess her as a status symbol through the means of a polygamous marriage endorsed implicitly by religious law, reflects the masculine display of feudalistic "might makes right", common in a social order where powerful men can "win women as prizes and social prestige" (Zipes 2012a: 8), and where women function symbolically as "trophies, (or) indicators of the hero's success" (Hourihan 199). Despite his grief in having lost Mad-huri, Hj. Ghani's anxiety over the public revelation of his wife's affair with Asraf, and his insecurity over the prospect of "being laughed at for not being capable of keeping such a pretty young bride happy" causes him to conspire with his men to keep the circumstances of her death a secret, and Madhuri thus forever silenced (217).

Like the thorn alluded to in Madhuri's name,[8] Lee's reincarnation of Mahsuri in the novel suggests that as beautiful and desirable as Madhuri was, it is the fear of her sexuality and the desire to possess or assert con-trol over her (sexualised) body that proves to be the prickly underlying issue that afflicts, and ultimately destroys, all three men as a result of their own fragile egos. The novel thus enacts what Khoo, citing Butler's theo-rising of "gender trouble", describes as "a fantasy construct inscribed on the surface of bodies" (163). Alluding to Butler's concept of gender as performance, Khoo's definition of hypermasculinity as a form of "gender panic" which manifests itself as male violence and is derived from "the discursive authentic male's inability to cope with modern changes to gen-der roles and relationships" can thus be seen in the destructive actions of Madhuri's father, husband, and lover as they each attempt to deal with their own inadequacies in the face of what they perceive as "uncontrolled and uncontrollable feminine desires" (20).

Lee's adaptation of the legend of *Mahsuri* in the novel thus raises inter-esting points of contemplation for its young adult audience through the portrayal of the heroine Azreen as a "feminist protagonist" who manages to transcend the family curse and, by implication, the patriarchal stric-tures that confine her as a young Malay woman. It may seem ironic that despite its prominence in the title of the novel, Mahsuri/Madhuri's curse does not find actual expression in the novel. It is only alluded to briefly in Normala's gossip-fuelled claims as she speculates over the cause and circumstances of Madhuri's death, and yet is shown as capable of causing strife, death, and destruction, bringing natural disasters, and damaging the communal bonds among the villagers. In re-visioning the tale of the wronged maiden of Langkawi, Lee's novel suggests that the wrongful belief in the presence of a curse can be as potent and destructive as the curse itself. By the same token, the refusal to believe in its power can be a means of releasing oneself from its oppressive grip. Although Azreen appears to have been cursed, having endured the deaths of all her loved ones in the span of a year (her sister, her mother, her beloved friend and source of emotional support, the Old Lady, and finally, her father), her refusal to let her past tarnish her future is a mark of her transcendence and agency as a feminist protagonist. Moving the story beyond the traditional morality tale and the thematic emphasis on injustice and vengeance associated with the original legend, Lee's novel foregrounds instead the protagonist's personal growth and maturation, a central tenet of adolescent fiction. Thus, the ending of the novel optimistically depicts Azreen basking in the natural beauty of autumnal London after completing her statistics exam, contemplating her future, and possibly with a new romantic interest in the form of her college friend, Julian Ng. Cleansed of the sins of the past, and with no "baggage" or liabilities to hold her back, she is now free to forge her own path in life, and to seek or create her own happiness.

"HOWLING ABOUT HONOUR AND SHAME": PREETA SAMARASAN'S "MAHSURI"

Samarasan's reimagining of the *Mahsuri* legend in her eponymous short story is presented as a blighted interracial romance between a married Malay woman, Mahsuri, and an Indian man, Dharma (instead of Deramang, the itinerant *penglipur lara*—"the soother of cares"[9]). The story is told from the perspective of Dharma ("a good boy, polite, hardworking, gives his mother five hundred ringgit every month"), the heroic knight in shining armour to Mahsuri's damsel in distress, who soothes her cares by offering her friendship and performing various acts of kindness for her as she tries to adjust to the challenges of city life. As the idealised Malay woman, Mahsuri is described as "a simple kampung girl, like from a P. Ramlee movie, sopan santun, lemah lembut, face also like a 1960s poster" (76). Although Dharma and Mahsuri begin as friends and colleagues, their relationship deepens when she discovers that her husband, who is away working in the Middle East, has been having an affair with another woman. As Mahsuri turns increasingly to Dharma for comfort and companionship, this causes the rivalry between Dharma and her manipulative, bullying brother to intensify: "If her brother had not been so useless I'm sure she would have asked him, but he gave her extra headache only, good for nothing bastard, so who can blame her for turning to me?" (77). Unable to obtain money from Mahsuri to support his drug habit, her brother insults her by attacking Dharma, and accuses them of having committed adultery: "Don't think I don't know that you're fooling around with that keling mabuk todi! Isn't he paying you properly for what you're giving him?" (82). The accusation is unjustified, however.

As Dharma maintains, they were close and in love, but their relationship "did not include the act of adultery," for he was "an honourable man" (a virtue alluded to in his own name) and "she too knew what was right and what was wrong" (81). Their plans to marry are tragically thwarted as the story ends with Dharma describing how Mahsuri's brother, in a drug-induced rage, steals from her and ends up stabbing her with a knife, but defends his actions in the following manner: "In court he looked straight at their faces and said, I did it to protect my family's honour. I did it because my married sister was going with a non-Muslim and I couldn't bear to see it" (83). To Dharma, the punishment that her brother receives for committing this heinous crime does not befit the unforgivable injustice of Mahsuri's senseless murder, and his insurmountable grief in having lost his beloved Mahsuri forever: "...even all their suffering put together will not be enough to satisfy me" (84).

As Samarasan states, her aim in retelling the story of Mahsuri was motivated by the attempt to address the following questions:

> How do you tell a contemporary story about female sexuality and female power (and the patriarchal fear of female sexuality and power) without addressing race and religion? Sexuality in Malaysia cannot be separated from race and religion. Who gets to have sex with whom, who gets to have sex at all, what it means to be a good girl: all these depend on which boxes have been ticked for you on official forms. (85)

Indeed, the intricacies of issues of gender, race, and religion, as they are lived and experienced in multicultural Malaysia, and how they are constructed, linked, as well as contested in the story through the romance between Mahsuri and Dharma, are intimated from the opening lines of the story, in which Mahsuri warns Dharma of the very real risk of being beaten up should her brother find out about their relationship:

> We have to berhati-hati because of my brother. He's the dangerous type. He and his friends. Dadah or what I don't know, but they're a rough crowd. He whacked up a boy at our school once because he thought the boy was fresh with me. *And you, not Malay some more. He'll go crazy if he finds out.* (75, emphasis mine)

Through this dramatic introduction, as well as in other parts of the skillfully developed plot, Samarasan brings her readers straight to the heart of the story, familiar in its rendering of a recognisable theme: the male fear of female sexuality, and the brutal display of male violence as a means to possess, control, or regulate this sexuality through the dubious means of upholding "family honour". Much like the original version of the legend and Lee's novel, *The Curse*, "Mahsuri" reflects the power struggle between two men who attempt to assert their masculinity over the sexualised body of the idealised Malay woman. Compared to Lee's feminist portrayal of Azreen in *The Curse*, Samarasan's Mahsuri appears more stereotypically gendered and less empowered. Yet her economic independence (she works and supports both her aged mother and her jobless older brother), her choice to begin a romance with Dharma, and her decision to remain in the relationship despite the risk of her brother's wrath, demonstrate courage and self-determination. Thus, despite the idealised image that Dharma paints of her, Mahsuri's role in the story as a transgressive modern Malay woman who challenges traditional notions of race and gender cannot be overlooked. Tragically, she pays the ultimate price for her self-assertion in death.

The story is also particularly revisionary in the way it draws attention to the intricate complexities of race and religion as factors that inhibit true integration among Malaysians, one that calls into question the perpetuation of a nationalist state ideology through the image of a diverse, multicultural Malaysia reflected in glossy tourism brochures. Mahsuri's brother is depicted as a belligerent, abusive, manipulative drug addict who has no qualms beating up his own father and sister, and his sense of entitlement over Mahsuri is buttressed not only by his dominant status as her older brother (their father has died, hence he regards himself as the family patriarch and her protector, as endorsed by Islamic law), but also by his superiority complex over Dharma as a man from a marginalised minority race. His use of racial slurs like "keling mabuk todi" (alcoholic Indian) to belittle Dharma and his insistence that the latter is sexually exploiting his sister reflect an inherent racism that in fact belies his fear and insecurity over losing Mahsuri as a convenient source of financial support, one that is masked by his claims of protecting family honour.

Despite the beauty and innocence of the couple's "colour-blind" relationship, the fear and distrust of the racialised Other also appears among Dharma's family members. His cousins tease him over his choice of a Malay girlfriend ("why a Naatukari?"[10]), while his mother, concerned over his blossoming romance with Mahsuri, declares, "Aiyo Dharma, not a Malay girl of all things. Even Chinese would be okay, but not Malay, please!" Embedded in this remark lies her fears over the loss of her son to the Muslim Mahsuri, the subsequent erasure of his ethnic, cultural, and religious identity, and even the dissolution of their family ties:

> My mother was already thinking about conversion, about marriage, about all those terrible stories you hear nowadays: converted sons not wanting to eat what comes out of their own mother's kitchens, not being allowed to attend their non-Muslim parents' funerals, daughters-in-law keeping the grand-children far far away from non-Muslim grandparents. (80)

Through the author's attention to such details, the story gives voice to the realities and challenges of interracial marriages in Malaysia, especially those between majority Malay Muslims and non-Muslims, implying that love and romance alone often cannot sustain such marriages—there needs to be a concerted effort by both families to be inclusive, and to treat and respect each other as equals, as well as a community support system, for true harmony to exist and flourish between the races.

Furthermore, in emphasising that Mahsuri's death is in fact not just the fault of her brother, but also the collective responsibility of the entire community, the story raises the issue of the elusiveness of gender equality in Malaysia, in the face of the lack of morality among its citizens, and the lack of political will to address such imbalances of power between men and women in its administration through the implementation and enforcement of proper policies and legislation. For as long as there are abusive men like Mahsuri's brother "howling about honour and shame" yet getting away with (literal) murder, and neighbours who would judge and gossip about Mahsuri and her misfortunes rather than listen and lend a helping hand, Malaysia's nationalist project of modernity aligned with ideas of gender equality will remain at best, lip service, and at worst, a pipe dream. Reflecting with bitterness on how Mahsuri's murder could have been prevented, Dharma declares:

> You think even one of them [Mahsuri's neighbours] came forward to talk to her, to listen to her side of the story, to find out the truth? Hah. No need to answer also.
> That is why I blame those bastard neighbours just as much as I blame him [her brother] and his friends. That is why I say her blood is on their hands also. At least he had dadah for an excuse. [...] But they, what excuse did they have for sitting and watching the whole thing while eating kuaci like as if it was a TV drama for their own personal entertainment? Later on of course they said they didn't hear anything that night. No, no, nothing. All of them looked at the police like angels. (83)

In attacking Mahsuri's neighbours for their hypocrisy and moral cowardice, and likening their emotional detachment over her death to a form of grotesque amusement, Dharma's comment also alludes to the public spectacle of Mahsuri's execution in the original legend, in which the villagers fall prey to rumour-mongering and, as such, are punished for seven generations for their lack of discretion. Centuries may have passed, but human nature remains disappointingly consistent in its subscription to herd mentality. As Dharma muses, "But of course people started to talk. What else do they know in this country? They cannot fix the politicians or the price of fish in the market so they console themselves by gossiping from morning to night. It is the pastime of the impotent" (77). Furthermore, the narrator's direct engagement with the reader through the discomforting, intermittent questions that pepper his story, "Are you telling me I should not have helped her at all?" (77); "And you, who do you think was right?" (81); "And whose side do you think they were on?" (84), not only heightens the confessional tone of the text but also serves to remind all readers that they too bear a collective guilt in the death of this innocent young woman.

The story also critiques the public shaming of women as a means of punishment, implying that the policing of women's bodies through the exploitation of ideas of "honour and shame" and how these claim to serve "to teach women all those important lessons" (84) is a method both archaic and morally repulsive. The visual spectacle of the public execution is not only a form of double victimisation that strips women (and humans in general) of their dignity and humanity, but also reflects the cruelty and inhumanity of those inflicting and witnessing such judgments. Partaking in the suffering of the innocent, even if vicariously, and especially through the cowardly mask of anonymity, invites the risk of misfortune and calamity, and is a message for the general public worth remembering even in this digital era, regardless of age.

In this regard, Samarasan's retelling of the tale of *Mahsuri* has more than "captured the spirit of the original version," in that it "more effectively conveys to a contemporary audience the moral questions of the original" (85). Updated and reconfigured as a tragic love story of modern multicultural Malaysia, the appeal of "Mahsuri" as a work of young adult fiction lies in its immense potential for debate and discussion on notions of gender, race, and religion, and also in its sensitive exploration of the possibility of fulfilling "the Malaysian dream of a real multicultural society through the overcoming of ethnic barriers" (Khoo 17). As the thwarted interracial romance between Mahsuri and Dharma seems to imply, however, much remains to be done before this beautiful dream can become a reality. For as long as the struggle for economic and political power continues to plague its citizens, and mutual trust, respect, and understanding among the various races are not nurtured and protected, our nation will be at risk of regressing into instability, insularity, and isolation—the curse of modern Malaysia in its reckless pursuit of progress and prosperity.

"The Spectre of Injustices Past": Shireen Zainudin's "Grey"

In Zainudin's retelling of the *Mahsuri* legend in the short story "Grey" (2019), the theme of injustice present in the original tale as well as in the two adaptations previously discussed is updated for the millennial age. In this version, the protagonist is Su, a female college student majoring in photography, who embarks on a field trip to Langkawi with her gay best friend Man, as part of their collaborative final year project, a photo essay documenting the racial riots that had broken out on the island a few months earlier. In choosing to depict the purely platonic relationship between Su and Man, Zainudin negates even the slightest possibility of a romance between the two main characters, unlike the adulterous affair hinted at (but never proven) between Mahsuri and the poet Deraman in the original legend, rumours of which eventually resulted in the former's brutal execution. In a refreshing acknowledgement of the reality and commonality of non-sexual male-female friendships in contemporary Malaysia, Man asserts that his bond with Su as kindred spirits is based on an intellectual and spiritual connection, rather than physical attraction. While Su's loyalty and devotion to her "perfect" boyfriend Wan is unquestioned, her affection for Man, and his for her, is just as clear: "We'd been best friends from the day we met on our first day at college." […] "It was always Su and I sharing a love of food, liking the same movies, exchanging favourite books. Sharing a love of words." […] "We just agreed about most things in life, it would seem" (195, 198).

Readers are drawn into the thematic link to the original legend through the development of Su's character, as emphasised by the observations that Man makes of her as they work together on their project. He notes how as a talented photographer, Su's work is her *raison d'etre*, the most definitive aspect of her identity. She is portrayed as taking great pride in her passion, creativity, and integrity as an artist, as revealed in the time and effort

she had invested in her "masterpiece", her solo final year project that
consisted of "sixty monochrome photographs of sixty historical buildings
in the country" which she spent seven months travelling around Malaysia
to complete (197). Man is witness to such dedication, and admires Su all
the more for it:

> She'd worked tirelessly on this endeavour; sacrificing weekends, surviving
> on precious little sleep for months. She was propelled as always by the
> purity of her vision. A passion that had always struck me as quietly, curi-
> ously noble. This instinctive yearning to chronicle her narrative. It was
> almost a desperation, this eagerness of Su's to always showcase Her Truth
> through her extraordinary photographing of the ordinary. (197–198)

Despite the effort and time spent, however, Su's academic advisor pronounces her final year project "unoriginal", as "it had been done before,
he said" (197). As a young artist in search of agency and self-definition
through creative expression, the pain and anguish that Su suffers over
the "hooded accusation" hurled at her by her mentor and her peers for
committing this transgressive act of "artistic plagiarism" is crushing:

> And so the cacophonous whisperings amongst her course mates reached
> her loudly. Her questioning gaze pleading the honesty of her work to
> her peers was left unmet. There was a complete withdrawal of support
> from a community she'd always thought was hers. All that was left was a
> harsh, unjust accusation of creative theft. All that she felt was dishonesty
> and dishonour. Destroyed, she withdrew into herself. [...] shattered and
> inconsolable for the rest of the semester by what she perceived to be a
> permanent stain on her integrity. (198)

The parallels between the two young women in both stories are clear
in that both Su and Mahsuri are depicted as victims of envy, wrongful
accusation, and injustice. Dismissed, silenced, and denied the opportunity
of clearing her name, Mahsuri is condemned to death by the villagers in
her community, giving rise to the vengeance of her curse and its power,
inflicting as it does a seven-generation long "barrenness" on the island
of Langkawi and its people. Su's psychological and emotional turmoil in
the face of patriarchal authority and societal judgment is compounded
by the betrayal and cruelty of her peers, and while admittedly far less
violent compared to Mahsuri's tragic execution, is nevertheless debilitating to Su's emerging selfhood. It results in feelings of inferiority and

worthlessness, and her intuitive withdrawal from society foregrounds her marginalisation and subordination as a misunderstood and "destroyed" young woman. Even after months have passed, the memory of this betrayal still causes her pain; as she shares her anguish with Man, she struggles to "[shut] her swelling eyelids against the intruding sting" (198). Her friendship with Man is one of the few that she values and comes to depend on in her journey to heal her mind and spirit from this traumatic episode in her life.

The inclusion of "Grey" in *The Principal Girl: Feminist Tales from Asia* (2019), a collection of short fiction aimed at young adults and based on Malaysian folklore, provides important insights on the underlying ideology for Zainudin's portrayal of Su as a young Malay woman in this contemporary adaptation, one that is clearly meant to interrogate traditional views of gender and the patriarchal status quo. The author's representation of Su as a modern reincarnation of Mahsuri reflects the feminist theme that imbues all the stories in the collection, which aims to emphasise "female empowerment" and to "privilege the agency, strength, and wisdom of young girls and women, over conventionally idealised traits of femininity such as beauty, obedience, conformity, and passivity so frequently depicted in traditional male-centric folk tales" (Osman and Dutta 2019: ix). Thus the ideas of selfhood, identity and agency which serve as the central concerns of adolescent fiction that appear in Lee's *The Curse* and Samarasan's "Mahsuri" are also inscribed in Zainudin's "Grey", which examines the construction of female subjectivity through the depiction of Su as a protagonist, and the challenges that she has to overcome in her quest for personal, social, and intellectual growth.

Central to Su's transformative journey into a feminist protagonist is a key scene from the story, which depicts her supernatural encounter with the spirit of Mahsuri in "a sheltered corner of the adjacent Field of Burnt Rice" (Padang Beras Terbakar),[11] a location of historical significance in Langkawi myth and folklore:

> We heard a soft female voice greeting us and looked up to see an exquisitely pretty maiden standing over us. There was no more fitting description, for she was neither "girl" nor "woman" to me. *Mahsuri.* I just knew. She was pale, almost translucent, wearing a simple white baju kurung with tiny white embroidered flowers. (199)

The sudden appearance of the ghostly Mahsuri, while shocking and distressful to Man ("I was sure I screamed, but could hear nothing"), elicits a contrasting response from Su, who is "perfectly calm, openly curious and reassuringly friendly" (199). To Man's disbelief, the two young women, "who connected instantly, like the spiritual kin that they obviously were" (200), proceed to have a deep discussion, the details of which remain a mystery to him: "Su gushing forth like someone releasing pain she had only just realised resided within her. The maiden listened, a soft inward smile playing over her lips. Silently knowing. Sentient to Su's pain" (200). The sight even prompts Man to ask himself incredulously, "Is this what the spectre of injustices past looked like?" (199).

Man's initial response of terror when faced with Mahsuri's spectral form is indicative of conventional societal attitudes towards ghosts and spirits, despite the uneasy acceptance of the presence of supernatural beings in Malay (or for that matter, global) popular culture, and as reflected in the rise of Asian horror in particular, both as a cinematic genre and a subject of academic scrutiny.[12] Yet Zainudin's depiction of the spirit of Mahsuri here does not conform to the conventions of the traditional ghost story featuring a vengeful female spirit, a recognisable and often negatively typecast archetype of Asian folklore and horror films. In fact, as Andrew Ng Hock Soon has observed with regard to the representation of this cinematic archetype, a "more sympathetic rendition of the monstrous feminine" is often adopted by Asian filmmakers, who choose to "substantially downplay" the 'monstrosity' of the female spirit in order "to foreground her victimised status instead" (Ng 171).[13] Indeed in this adaptation, Zainudin revises the figure of the legendary Mahsuri as a vengeful woman who curses the entire island of Langkawi, choosing instead to portray her as a sympathetic and compassionate guiding spirit to Su. As Man notes:

> Once she brushed a white hand over Su's black hair, pushing it off her face. She cradled Su's left hand within both hers […] I cannot recall if words were actually spoken by the maiden throughout this whole encounter, or now that I think of it, how she even greeted us. I was just transfixed by her presence, transported by *her quiet strength* and the peace that washed over us. (200, emphasis in original)

In a recent interview,[14] Zainudin explains that the impetus for her characterisation of both Su and Mahsuri in "Grey" was to distance her own retelling of the story from the destructive violence of the curse linked to the original legend, focusing instead on the moment of constructive healing that arises from the encounter between the two female characters, one that symbolises not only the bridging of past and present, but also the dissolution of the cycle of death and destruction crucial to a reconfiguration of the self. It was thus important to her as an author of YA fiction (and in line with the feminist theme embedded in the story) that Su emerges from the spiritual interaction with Mahsuri with a strong sense of agency, one that Zainudin suggests is linked to her skill and voice as a photographer and storyteller, for therein lies her power to deal with past suffering and injustice as well as the uncertainties of the future, through the firm belief in her own value as an artist. As Su asserts in the concluding paragraphs of the story:

> "You know, Man, everything we do is just part of a journey. Like picking oneself up 'cause *you* are the only person in charge of you. Or working hard to find the right project to work on with your bestie." [...]
>   "The truth, Man. It's about telling the truth. At least trying to. How lucky are we that we have the power to do this? To bear witness to life and tell the stories we choose to tell. So let's give these stories the honour they deserve."
>   "Is that what *she* told you?"
>   "She didn't tell me anything. She just made me think. She made me realize that I should be more receptive to life. A little more...porous. To the joys, the challenges, the possibilities. It's all a journey, innit?" (200–201)

As an empowering tale aimed at young adults, the guises in which both Su and Mahsuri appear in "Grey" suggest the incorporation of familiar figures from the Western fairy tale canon, a blending of both "the innocent persecuted heroine" archetype as well as "magic help" in the form of "a supernatural being" (Zipes 2012b: 81),[15] but adapted to underscore the experiences of both characters as young Malay women tied to the legendary story of the maiden from Langkawi. This revision of Mahsuri's character from a vengeful young woman to a sensitive and inspirational guide who assists Su in her transformative journey towards selfhood is just one such instance of what Anna Katrina Gutierrez describes as a form of "cross-cultural reconfiguration" that has resulted in the "glocalisation" of children's (and by implication YA) literature, defined as "the adaptation of a global outlook to local conditions, and the reciprocal reinvention of global signs and local meanings" (2018: 12). The concept of a "glocal" literary text is of particular relevance to my discussion of "Grey" as a reconfiguration of the legend of Mahsuri, especially in light of Gutierrez's assertion that "glocal literature necessarily involves a movement back to folktales […] and retelling and reconfiguring those tales, practices and elements so that they may be thrown outwards to the postmodern world" and thus imparted with "a new significance" (2009: 160–161). Zainudin's appropriation of glocal blending as an example of "cross-cultural dialogue between Western and non-Western discourses of subjectivity" (Gutierrez 2018: 15) is also seen in her portrayal of Su's developing intellectual and emotional maturity as she explores both Western and non-Western philosophical ideas associated with the construction of the self, ranging from the postmodern notion of the fragmented self ("there was no reason Su could not be many Sus at any one time", 196) to Kantian philosophy and Sufi mysticism (200).

In focusing on the numerous ways with which Su chooses to explore and express her multiple subjectivities as a young Malay(sian) woman, Zainudin's narrative disempowers the traditional story of *Mahsuri* of its oppressive link to the violence and brutality of the legendary curse, emphasising instead how the postmodern anxiety over the unknown can also be a liberating means of freedom and independence, thus creating a new version of the tale in which Su is cast as a glocal subject who selectively combines aspects of the foreign and native culture in order to create an empowered identity. Her acceptance and even embrace of ambiguity in her quest for self-definition is reflected in the conclusion as well as the very title of the story: "Su looked down at the gritty tarmac, at the snaking road which would take us to where we needed to get to. It was shiny with rain and possibility. And it was grey" (201). Indeed, it serves as a fitting metaphor for the limitless potential afforded by folktale adaptations as a medium for exploring the ideas of multiple and shifting subjectivities that pervade young adult literature, whether in Malaysia or beyond.

CONCLUSION

As contemporary reappropriations of the legend of *Mahsuri* and representative works of young adult fiction, Lee Su Ann's *The Curse*, Preeta Samarasan's "Mahsuri", and Shireen Zainudin's "Grey" illustrate the subversive potential of the folktale for the contestation of patriarchal, feudalistic, and nationalistic ideologies in modern, multicultural Malaysia in illuminating ways. Through critical engagement with nationalist constructs of gender, racial, and religious identity, all three texts offer significant insights into the status of the young Malay woman in contemporary Malaysia through the depiction of their female protagonists, as each struggles to resist or overcome the remnants of traditional Malay feudalistic society through acts of agency and self-assertion. While Lee's protagonist Azreen transcends the limitations of her marginalised position as an economically disadvantaged young woman from a rural background through a firm belief in the emancipatory power of education, she is only able to do so at the expense of losing all her family members, and by extricating and distancing herself from her communal past. Additionally, Lee's decision to conclude the story with Azreen contemplating her future in London suggests an implicit indictment of the restrictive gender roles imposed upon the protagonist by Malaysian society, since the broadening of her horizons (both intellectually and psychologically) is only made possible through leaving her provincial home and the ghosts of her past behind. Significantly, Azreen's success is also built on the love and acceptance of two significant women that serve as her mentors and role models, who guide and support her in her journey of personal growth—the wealthy Datin Sharifah, who sponsors her studies in England and regards her as her own daughter, and the Old Lady in the forest, with her impressive knowledge of traditional methods of healing, who offers her advice, comfort, and emotional support (which she lacks at home) in dealing with the tumultuous challenges of young adulthood.

In a similar vein, Zainudin's retelling of the *Mahsuri* legend interrogates issues of gender identity through the portrayal of her protagonist Su, who is only able to overcome her subjugated status as a young college student accused of artistic plagiarism once she attains a firmer understanding of herself, a view that is not dependent on the validation of her peers but which rests on her own faith in her personal integrity. Her refusal to be defined by those who lack insight and awareness of the truth, as well as her belief in her own voice and agency, is what defines her as a feminist protagonist. Nevertheless, this transcendent state is not achievable without the moral and emotional support of her best friend Man, as well as the pivotal encounter with the spirit of Mahsuri (in a symbolic blending of the human and the supernatural worlds) which enables her to discern the significance of embracing the unpredictability and uncertainties of life in the journey to adulthood. Like *The Curse*, "Grey" illustrates Su's journey from "alienation and lack, to self-knowledge and a potential for self-determination" (Felski 150) intrinsic to YA fiction, but just as importantly, reveals the power of folktale adaptations in revising articulations of Malaysian feminine identity. Additionally, Zainudin's depiction of Su as a glocal subject not only facilitates "intercultural dialogue and exchange" (Gutierrez 2013: 20) but also emphasises the value of cross-cultural fertilisations in the construction of multiple subjectivities experienced by the protagonist.

In comparison, Samarasan's Mahsuri is less fortunate. Transplanted from the village to the city, this definitive "good girl", while financially independent, finds herself trapped in a loveless marriage, and copes with loneliness, abandonment, fear, and isolation by seeking refuge in the arms of Dharma, the one man who showers her with kindness and support in a cold and hostile environment. Despite her attempts to chart her own path to "self-recognition and agency", without an adequate support system for surviving the brutal realities of city life, as well as the strength and resilience to resist the destructive forces of gossip and the toxic masculinity of her violently abusive brother, Mahsuri eventually succumbs to the forces of patriarchal oppression and slips through the cracks, dismissed and forgotten by all but Dharma, who remains haunted by grief and the memory of their love.

An appreciation of the subversive qualities of these three textual adaptations of the tale of *Mahsuri*, however, can only be made possible through the acknowledgment of the same aspect present in the original version of the tale. As an example of how folktales, through the use of magic and the supernatural, are often linked to the "wish-fulfilment and utopian projections of the people" (Zipes 2012a: 8), the tale of *Mahsuri* distinguishes itself through its emphasis on the power of the female curse, reminding its readers "of how the unjust murder of an innocent calls down destruction on the state" (Hijjas 249). Like the tales of the *penglipur lara* of Malay literary tradition, skilled raconteurs capable of enthralling their audiences with representations and reinterpretations of popular and well-known tales, the three textual adaptations of the *Mahsuri* legend discussed in this chapter demonstrate the ease with which such folktales lend themselves to contemporary political appropriations, breathing life into the original through strong character development and the amplification of familiar themes, and interweaving the old with the new.

As Tatar reminds us, "fairy tales can still be told and retold so that they challenge and resist, rather than simply reproduce, the constructs of a culture" (237). Indeed, textual adaptations like those by Lee, Samarasan, and Zainudin demonstrate the possibility of transforming canonical texts like the original legend of *Mahsuri* into "tales that empower and entertain children [and by implication, young adults] at the same time that they interrogate and take the measure of their own participation in a project to socialise the child" (237). Likewise, such stories also enable children and adolescents to "satisfy the urge to experiment with gender (and other forms of identity) without the need to destabilise their real-life identities" (Simons 157). While the "reinvention through intervention" approach that Tatar recommends concedes to the coercive nature of the "adult agenda" in these texts, it also acknowledges the young reader's power, and provides opportunities for both parties to engage in a "joint interpretive effort" to "create a new story based on the old" (236).

Such strategies are particularly important in view of the challenges that threaten to erode the reading habit among young Malaysians, especially those posed by internet and social media usage. A recent survey[16] involving 16,182 parents and guardians of Malaysian children aged 5–17 revealed particularly unsettling findings related to the reading habit of teenagers (those in the 13–17 age group): compared to younger children, teenagers were least likely to engage in reading books for pleasure, preferring instead to spend their leisure time on digital devices indulging in video streaming and social media; the internet also served as their main source of information and reading material (as opposed to physical, or even e-books), with 38% of teenagers spending as much as five hours a day on their gadgets, rather than reading physical books or participating in sports. Reading for academic purposes was also perceived as more important than reading for leisure or to cultivate the imagination, raising concerns over the negative implications of internet usage on the culture of reading among young Malaysians in general, both now and in the future.

In light of such concerns and in the face of globalisation, rapid modernisation, and technological advancement, the role of producers of children's literature and young adult fiction in Malaysia is even more crucial in engaging the attention of young readers in order to address their lack of interest in reading books for leisure. As a relatively young nation at the crossroads of tradition and modernity, Malaysia and its literary scene provide fertile ground for exploring the vast potential in catering to a young audience eager to understand its place in the world. The dynamic growth of children's and YA fiction genre, given the volume, diversity, and availability of works currently produced by local writers and publishing houses, are heartening signs of progress. More, however, remains to be done in order to transform the wealth of local canonical materials and classics into tales that both "empower and entertain" their target audience. Just as "each age creates its own folklore through re-readings as well as retellings" (Tatar 230), as this chapter hopes to have shown, adaptations of folktales (whether as literary texts, films, or other forms of media) are essential to their survival, for it is precisely such spirited re-imaginings that will keep the Malaysian folktale alive, dynamic, and relevant for generations to come.

NOTES

1. See Lurie (20–21); Cashdan (7–8); Haase (10–13); and Jones (18).
2. As evidence of how such didacticism continues to pervade children's literature, Melinda Greenblatt notes that in developing countries like Kenya, "books were not purchased for children unless they were thought to be educational". Acknowledging the influence of economic forces on the choice of reading material for children, she states that "if you could find parents who had the funds to purchase children's books, you had to market them as educational materials" (Tomlinson 40). From 1975–1988, Greenblatt was the director of the U.S. Committee for UNICEF's Information Center on Children's Cultures in New York, where she oversaw one of the more extensive collections of international children's books, focusing on books from developing countries.
3. For more on the feminist fairy tale as a literary genre and contemporary feminist fiction for children, see Zipes, *Don't Bet on the Prince* (14); Cosslett (82–84); Trite (1–9); Pinsent (84–87); and Haase (14–21).
4. *Puteri Santubong*, a legend from Sarawak, tells of two sisters, Santubong and Sejinjang, who are sent down to Earth by their father, the King of Kayangan (fairyland), to end the feud between the villagers of Pasir Putih and Pasir Kuning. They are warned not to fight with each other, or to be influenced by human folly. Conflict arises when both fall for Prince Serapi, a mortal. Unable to decide whom to wed, he proposes to both, leading to a bitter quarrel between the sisters. Such selfishness and lack of filial piety incur the wrath of the King, who punishes both daughters by turning them into two mountains, Mount Santubong and Mount Sejinjang, which dominate the landscape of Sarawak until today. Like *Puteri Santubong*, the tale of *Bawang Merah, Bawang Putih* highlights the theme of female rivalry over a man, first between the wicked Mak Kundur and the kindly Mak Labu for their husband Pak Ali, and then between their two

daughters, Bawang Merah and Bawang Putih for the Sultan's hand in marriage. Upon the death of both her parents, the virtuous Bawang Merah, like Cinderella, endures abuse from both her stepmother and stepsister, but is later rewarded for her sufferings through a singular power (her alluring voice) which gains her the notice and affections of the Sultan. Through the distinct oppositional qualities between Bawang Merah and Bawang Putih, the tale reproduces a familiar trope that reinforces the subsidiary role of women in a patriarchal society, by suggesting that female desirability lies in the balance between sacrifice and the stoic display of virtue in the face of injustice and oppression.

5. An asymmetrical dagger, traditionally made of iron, nickel and several alloys, and famous for its distinctive wavy blade. In some versions of the legend, Mahsuri is executed through even more gruesome means, by being impaled from the anus to the stomach ("hukum sula" in Malay). See Hijjas (248).

6. Translated as "a plain where the castor oil plant grows and where the turtle doves dwell; a typically desolate place", in R.J. Wilkinson (1903), *A Malay English Dictionary*, Kelly & Walsh Ltd., Singapore (444) and cited in Hijjas (248).

7. For a more comprehensive and contextual discussion of folktales, myths, and legends in the canon of Malaysian children's literature, see Osman, Lai and Kassim (410–420).

8. From the Malay "duri" which means thorn.

9. Translated as "the soother of cares", "penglipur lara" was a term used to describe the oral story-teller whose trade it was to entertain the village folk with marvelous tales. Md. Taib Osman cites Sir Hugh Clifford, who describes the role of such storytellers in the traditional Malay village: "Such minstrels are greatly loved by the villagers, who hold them in high honour, giving them hearty welcome, and the name by which they are known in the vernacular bears witness to the joy which they bring with them withersoever they go." See Osman (1984: 137–138).

10. Translated as "people of the land," a common term used in the Tamil language to refer to the Malays.

11. Haji Ismail explains the historical significance of Beras Terbakar which is located in Padang Matsirat, Langkawi, and notes that "not long after Mahsuri's death the Siamese invaded Langkawi with a big army. Fearing that the Siamese would capture the rice granary situated at Padang Matsirat, Datuk Karma Jaya ordered the granary to be burnt to the ground. Even today, visitors may be able to pick up a few pieces of the burnt rice at the place where the granary was." The invasion of the Siamese army and the huge loss of lives among the islanders (including Datuk Karma Jaya and Mahura) is frequently recounted as an outcome of "the curse of Mahsuri

that brought the tragedy as a punishment for the unjust treatment against her" (101–102).

12. See for example *Horror to the Extreme: Changing Boundaries in Asian Cinema*, ed. Jinhee Choi and Mitsuyo Wada-Marciano. Hong Kong: Hong Kong University Press, 2009, which discusses the Asian horror film as a form of cultural production and consumption.

13. Ng's discussion of the sympathetic depiction of the figure of the Pontianak ("an Eastern vampire") as a wronged victim of male violence and societal injustice in Malay films and popular culture has been useful to my analysis of Zainudin's portrayal of the ghostly Mahsuri in her story. Ng's assertion that "the Pontianak in local films is often sympathetically portrayed to reflect the plight of women in a social system that clearly privileges men" (171) is of particular relevance to my argument on the marginalization of both Mahsuri and Su as maligned and misunderstood young women in this chapter.

14. This was conducted via email and telephone on 4 July 2019.

15. See Zipes, who discusses this figure in Chapter 5 of *The Irresistible Fairy Tale* (2012: 80–108).

16. Findings of the survey were published by E-Sentral, a Malaysian online bookstore, in April 2018 in conjunction with World Book Day. The article which reports these findings, "Internet beri kesan negatif budaya membaca" was published in *Berita Harian* on 1 May 2018. https://www.pressreader.com/malaysia/berita-harian5831/20180501/283953178195607, accessed 26 October 2018.

References

Benson, Stephen. 2003. *Cycles of Influence: Fiction, Folktale, Theory*. Detroit: Wayne State University Press.

Berita Harian. 2018. Internet beri kesan negatif budaya membaca. https://www.pressreader.com/malaysia/beritaharian5831/20180501/283953178195607. Accessed 26 October 2018.

Butler, Judith. 1990. *Gender Trouble: Feminism and the Subversion of Identity*. London: Routledge.

Cashdan, Sheldon. 1999. *The Witch Must Die: The Hidden Meaning of Fairy Tales*. New York: Basic Books.

Cosslett, Tess. 1996. Fairytales: Revising the Tradition. In *Women, Power and Resistance: An Introduction to Women's Studies*, ed. Tess Cosslett, Alison Easton, and Penny Summerfield, 81–90. Buckingham: Open University Press.

Felski, Rita. 1989. *Beyond Feminist Aesthetics: Feminist Literature and Social Change*. Cambridge, MA: Harvard University Press.

Flanagan, Victoria. 2010. Gender Studies. In *The Routledge Companion to Children's Literature*, ed. David Rudd, 143–158. London: Routledge.

Gutierrez, Anna Katrina. 2009. *Mga Kwento ni Lola Basyang: A Tradition of Reconfiguring the Filipino Child. International Research in Children's Literature* 2.2: 159–176.

———. 2013. Metamorphosis: The Emergence of Glocal Subjectivities in the Blend of Global, Local, East, and West. In *Subjectivity in Asian Children's Literature and Film: Global Theories and Implications*, ed. John Stephens, 19–42. London: Routledge.

———. 2018. Globalization and Glocalization. In *The Routledge Companion to International Children's Literature*, ed. John Stephens, Celia Abicalil Belmiro, Alice Curry, Li Lifang, and Yasmine S. Motawy, 11–21. London: Routledge.

Haase, Donald. 2004. *Fairy Tales and Feminism: New Approaches*. Detroit: Wayne State University Press.

Haji Ismail, Mohamed Zahir. 2000. *The Legends of Langkawi*. Kuala Lumpur: Utusan Publications.

Hijjas, Mulaika. 2010. 'The Legend You Thought You Knew': Text and Screen Representations of Puteri Gunung Ledang. *South East Asia Research* 18.2: 245–270.

Jones, Steven Swann. 1995. *The Fairy Tale: The Magic Mirror of Imagination*. New York: Twayne.

Khoo, Gaik Cheng. 2006. *Reclaiming Adat: Contemporary Malaysian Film and Literature*. Vancouver: UBC Press.

Larsen, Anne Kathrine. 2007. Tradition as Reflexive Project in Norway and Malaysia: Witch, Whore, Madonna and Heroine. In *Cultural Heritages as Reflexive Traditions*, ed. Ullrich Kockeland and Máiréad Nic Craith, 75–88. Basingstoke: Palgrave Macmillan.

Lee, Su Ann. 2007. *The Curse*. Kuala Lumpur: Utusan Publications.

Lurie, Alison. 1990. *Don't Tell the Grownups: The Subversive Power of Children's Literature*. New York: Little Brown.

McCallum, Robyn. 1999. *Ideologies of Identity in Adolescent Fiction*. New York: Garland.

Ng, Andrew Hock Soon. "Death and the Maiden": The Pontianak as Excess in Malay Popular Culture. In *Draculas, Vampires, and Other Undead FORMS: Essays on Gender, Race, and Culture*, ed. John Edgar Browning and Caroline Joan (Kay) Picart, 167–186. Lanham, MD: Scarecrow Press.

Osman, Mohd. Taib. 1984. *Bunga Rampai: Aspects of Malay Culture*. Kuala Lumpur: Dewan Bahasa dan Pustaka.

———. 1999. The Tradition of Storytelling in Malaysia. In *Traditional Storytelling Today: An International Sourcebook*, ed. Margaret Read McDonald, 138–141. London: Fitzroy Dearborn Publishers.

Osman, Sharifah Aishah, Lai Suat Yan and Siti Rohaini Kassim. 2018. Recent Trends and Themes in Malaysian Children's Fiction. In *The Routledge Companion to International Children's Literature*, ed. John Stephens, 410–420. London: Routledge.

Osman, Sharifah Aishah and Tutu Dutta. 2019. Editors' Introduction. In *The Principal Girl: Feminist Tales from Asia*, ed. Sharifah Aishah Osman and Tutu Dutta, vii–x. Petaling Jaya: Gerakbudaya.

Pinsent, Pat. 1997. *Children's Literature and the Politics of Equality*. London: David Fulton.

Samarasan, Preeta. 2011. Mahsuri. In *Malaysian Tales: Retold and Remixed*, ed. Daphne Lee, 75–85. Petaling Jaya: ZI Publications.

Selat, Norazit, Yaacob Harun, and Lynne Khadijah Norazit. 2010. The Folk Literature of Malaysia. In *ASEAN Folk Literature: An Anthology. Vol. 1. General Introduction*, ed. Nicanor G. Tiongson, 52–54. Vientiane: ASEAN Committee on Culture and Information.

Simons, Judy. 2009. Gender Roles in Children's Fiction. In *The Cambridge Companion to Children's Literature*, ed. M.O. Grenby and Andrea Immel, 143–158. Cambridge: Cambridge University Press.

Stephens, John. 1999. Constructions of Female Selves in Adolescent Fiction: Makeovers as Metonym. *Papers: Explorations into Children's Literature* 9.1: 5–13.

———. 2013. The Politics of Identity: A Transcultural Perspective on Subjectivity in Writing for Children. In *Subjectivity in Asian Children's Literature and Film: Global Theories and Implications*, ed. John Stephens, 1–18. London: Routledge.

Stephens, John and Robyn McCallum. 1998. *Retelling Stories, Framing Culture: Traditional Stories and Metanarratives in Children's Literature*. New York: Garland.

Tatar, Maria. 1992. *Off with Their Heads!: Fairy Tales and the Culture of Childhood*. New Jersey: Princeton University Press.

Tomlinson, Carl M. 1989. Children's Literature in the Developing Nations: An Interview with Melinda Greenblatt. *Early Child Development and Care* 48: 39–48.

Trites, Roberta Seelinger. 1997. *Waking Sleeping Beauty: Feminist Voices in Children's Novels*. Iowa City: University of Iowa Press.

———. 2000. *Disturbing the Universe: Power and Repression in Adolescent Literature*. Iowa City: University of Iowa Press.

Zainudin, Shireen. 2019. Grey. In *The Principal Girl: Feminist Tales from Asia*, ed. Sharifah Aishah Osman and Tutu Dutta. Petaling Jaya: Gerakbudaya.

Zipes, Jack. 1987. Introduction. In *Don't Bet on the Prince: Contemporary Feminist Fairy Tales in North America and England*, ed. Jack Zipes, 1–36. New York: Routledge.

———. 2012a. *Fairy Tales and the Art of Subversion: The Classical Genre for Children and the Process of Civilization*. London: Routledge.
———. 2012b. *The Irresistible Fairy Tale: The Cultural and Social History of a Genre*. Princeton: Princeton University Press.

CHAPTER 12

Seeking "Unity in Diversity": Contemporary Children's Books in Indonesia

Herdiana Hakim

The British scholar of children's literature, Peter Hunt, once famously noted that "children's books do not exist in a vacuum" (2005, 1). Just as adult literature has always been a product of society, drawing on and reflecting those environments and issues from which it emerges, so too does children's literature invariably reflect sociocultural regional concerns. Indeed, both the history and trajectory of children's literature in the Western world have been closely related to relevant changes in society, movements which explain how the content and presentation in children's literature over centuries have shifted from "instruction" to "delight".[1] The same case can be seen in Indonesia, which has been enjoying a recent flourish in the publication of children's books. With 80 million children under the age of 18 years old of the total population of 260 million, it has

---

"Unity in Diversity" is the literal translation of the national motto of Indonesia: "Bhinneka Tunggal Ika".

H. Hakim (✉)
University of Glasgow, Glasgow, UK
e-mail: h.herdiana.1@research.gla.ac.uk

© The Author(s) 2020   245
B. Wilson and S. P. Gabriel (eds.), *Asian Children's Literature and Film in a Global Age*, Asia-Pacific and Literature in English, https://doi.org/10.1007/978-981-15-2631-2_12

now become obvious that children's books represent the largest market share in the country (Prinsloo 2019).

As an emergent literature in Indonesia, it has been clear that the dominant theme in children's texts has mirrored similar concerns in early children's literature in the Western world: many narratives combine moral lessons with didactic religious teachings to the young. Religion remains an important component of identity in Indonesia and, as the largest Muslim-populated country in the world, such religious children's books are in abundance. In accordance with books that teach religious values and show samples of pious children, stories with moral purposes are easily found, indicating the common perspective and purpose of children's literature to be its use as a means of socialisation and instruction. In line with changes in the social and political contexts of Indonesian society, the past few years have also seen fascinating shifts in the content and themes found in Indonesian children's books. Consequently, Indonesia is now witnessing the emergence of children's books with previously taboo themes—including death, divorce, family structures, lifestyle choices, and sexual education—that would have been neither welcomed nor permitted in children's content during the authoritarian era of President Suharto, the military general who ruled the archipelago from 1966 to 1998. Themes of social, cultural, and ethnic diversity previously seen as "sensitive" have also found their way into picture books and children's novels.

Historically, Indonesia's diversity has always been its largest capital, but also its weakness and a trigger for societal disintegration. Immediately after independence in 1945, Indonesia adopted a national motto of "Bhinneka Tunggal Ika" (Sanskrit for "unity in diversity") and the ideology of *Pancasila* ("five principles") that aimed to address all Indonesians, regardless of their ethnic and religious principles. However, under Suharto's New Order regime, the world's largest archipelagic state (17,000 islands, 700 regional languages, 300 ethnic groups, and hundreds of local beliefs alongside six state-acknowledged religions) did not have the freedom to express this diversity. Through a rigid focus on unity over diversity, the national motto was implemented under a heavy assimilationist perspective (Kuipers and Yulaelawati 2009).

During the New Order period, all media and publications had to comply with the "SARA" regulation, which forbade them from producing or referencing content related to the following four areas: *suku* (ethnicity), *agama* (religion), *ras* (race), and *antar-golongan* (class), because these issues were deemed too sensitive and precarious for the nation's unity

(Hefner 2013). These restrictions sacrificed the opportunity to acknowledge and respect the different social, cultural, and religious groups in Indonesia (Hoon 2013; Parker 2010) and, as a consequence, most children's content—books, movies, and TV programmes—shied away from portraying the country's diversity. Rather, themes such as nationalism and the values of "ideal citizens" were dominant in children's books published in this era (Partiningsih 2016), and only after the regime collapsed and democracy entered the nation's discourse could content about diversity emerge in popular culture. As a result of these previous restrictions, although Indonesia is a largely diverse country in which children face pluralism in daily life and where multicultural children's books should be the norm, they are currently more an exception, comprising a small proportion of what may be considered larger and safer themes, such as family love, folktales, fables, and stories emphasising morality and societal codes.

Despite the fact that the number of Indonesian children's books depicting the archipelago's cultural diversity is comparatively small, I would argue that these publications encapsulate a strong potentiality for both the younger Indonesian generations and for the larger society. Unfortunately, the majority of these contemporary books fall into the category of blatant propaganda, and despite their often positive themes related to tolerance, they are invariably merely vehicles for conveying the explicit message of valuing difference while often sacrificing literary aspects. Rather than providing strong and layered narratives, the books are overtly didactic and focus on delivering moral lessons. Yet, a few contemporary children's books, encouragingly, attempt to employ literary merit in both content and illustration and it is in these books, in which children from different religious and ethnic backgrounds have meaningful interactions and dialogues and exercise their agency, that a greater integration of social representation and literary aesthetics may be witnessed.

This chapter examines selected contemporary children's books from Indonesia that seek to present these multicultural values. It is divided into four sections. The first part lays out a brief overview of multicultural children's literature and its potential. The second section sets up the social and historical context of Indonesia. The third section starts with the text selection and framework, followed by an analysis of the text, while the fourth and final section summarises my argument on Indonesian multicultural children's books.

WHY MULTICULTURAL CHILDREN'S LITERATURE?

In global terms, ethnic diversity and multiculturalism have recently garnered broad interest in both education and publishing, as evidenced by social media phenomena such as #WeNeedDiverseBooks or #WNDB. Starting as a social media campaign in 2014, #WNDB is now a non-profit organisation that commits itself to promoting multicultural childhood experiences in books, and is a direct response to educators' exasperation when seeking greater diversity in children's books. A further response to this situation may be seen in an important study by the Centre for Literacy in Primary Education in 2018. Published under the name "Reflecting Realities" in the United Kingdom in 2017, the survey looked at more than 9000 books aimed at children aged 3–11 and confirmed what had triggered the #WNDB campaign several years before: books with non-Caucasian characters only comprise 1 percent of all children's books published. A number of scholarly works have also explored these issues of diversity, one such example being *Imagining Sameness and Difference* by Emer O'Sullivan and Andrea Immel (2017), a collection which features essays examining the presentation of tolerance and the portrayal of human similarity and diversity in children's books and magazines. Most recently, *Inclusive Young Adult Fiction* by Melanie Ramdarshan Bold (2019) investigates the under-representation of diverse ethnicities in young adult books in the United Kingdom.

Children's books that address issues of diversity and pluralism fall into a genre called "multicultural children's literature". The rise of this genre, Mingshui Cai (2002) argues, is more a political than literary movement, particularly since the concept is closely linked to multicultural education. James A. Banks (2016) has noted that multicultural education is a "reform movement" aimed to transform educational institutions so "students from all social class, gender, racial, language, and cultural groups will have an equal opportunity to learn" (3). Born from the Civil Rights Movement of the 1960s in the USA, the movement seeks to expunge discrimination towards African Americans in many aspects of life, particularly education. The principal demand is that "schools and other educational institutions reform curricula to reflect their experiences, histories, cultures, and perspectives" (Banks 2016, 4).

Although the genesis of this movement primarily manifested itself in books related to African American concerns, the genre has since become more inclusive as other marginalised groups, particularly those who have felt "victimized, oppressed, or discriminated against in some way by the dominant majority", have gained increasing representation (Bishop 1997, 2). Mingshui Cai and Rudine Sims Bishop (1994) have argued multicultural education is "a reform effort intended not only to combat intolerance and foster a sense of inclusion, but to fundamentally change education and society" (58). Likewise, Donna Gollnick and Philip Chinn (2013, 19) have proposed that multicultural education "acknowledges the important role of diversity in students and builds on it to promote equality and social justice in education". These arguments call attention to the prominent objectives of multicultural education: diversity and equality.

Multicultural children's literature adopts similar goals to these educational strategies. Ambika Gopalakrishnan (2011) has defined it as children's books about "the sociocultural experiences of previously underrepresented groups" (5) while Bishop (1997), a notable thinker on multicultural children's literature, has stated that this genre aims to contribute to students' knowledge cultivation regarding their own multicultural societies, which in turn becomes a fundamental catalyst for social change. This is because multicultural children's literature is "closely tied to ideologies of social justice, educational equity, and critical pedagogy" and is "aimed at helping students learn to function effectively in a pluralistic society and become advocates for social justice" (Bishop 2012, 9).

Junko Yokota (1993) has succinctly defined multicultural children's literature as "literature that represents any distinct cultural group through accurate portrayal and rich detail" (157). Likewise, proponents of multicultural children's literature as a vehicle of social change agree on the importance of cultural specificity and authenticity as critical elements (Bishop 2012; Cai 2002; Gopalakrishnan 2011). Bishop (2012) has argued for culturally conscious literature which is written with the "insider" perspective and reflects both the distinctiveness of the cultural experience and the universality of human experience. Equal emphasis on diversity and similarities allows readers from either outside or inside the culture to relate to the stories, and thus the literature will not only be a "mirror" for the children from the marginalised group, but also a "window" for children from different cultures as they learn about different beliefs and traditions in the world. Drawing on Bishop, Cai (2002) maintains that multicultural literature needs to produce positive effects on its readers; such effects are not to be confused with positive portrayal, which can lead to misrepresentation and deviate from the aim of multicultural literature to portray actual experiences of diverse groups. In addition, multicultural children's literature must not neglect the significance of sound literary elements. Stories that may be considered mediocre in literary form and content, Cai (2002) has posited, will not be effective because such literature "cannot give children an engaging aesthetic experience; neither can it move their hearts or enlighten their heads" (91).

As a site of ideology, all literature merits examination. However, due to the complexity of its themes—prejudice, bias, discrimination, pluralism, and tolerance—multicultural literature calls for more urgency in its observations. Patricia Ramsey (2009) has warned that "even some popular award-winning picture books that have been hailed as 'multicultural' have misappropriated and misrepresented material from marginalized groups" (229). In her analysis of two picture books from Denmark, Nina Christensen (1999) remarked that although both books present the similar theme of tolerance, their different executions of the theme produce different effects on readers. Christensen then advocates for poetic and literary stories that invite readers to ask questions, rather than stories that are more overtly didactic and explicit. Similarly, Claudia Mills's (2016) examination of four children's books that were meant to tackle prejudice revealed that such books might misfire and endorse the negative attitudes they were attempting to redress. She argues that children's literature can be a double-edged sword: intentioned to impart morals but inadvertently encouraging the very attitude it condemns. The danger of stereotypes is also arguably more critical in books for children than for adults, because stereotypes "not only injure dominated cultural groups mentally, but also breed ignorance and prejudice in children of the mainstream culture" (Cai 2002, 71). When a book perpetuates stereotypes rather than challenges them, it becomes a part of the problem and not the solution.

THE ISLANDS OF "UNITY IN DIVERSITY"

Unlike Western multiculturalism, which emerged from increasingly diverse societies due to migration, Indonesia is unique in that it is indigenously diverse. In fact, it seems impossible to discuss Indonesia without acknowledging the vastness of its pluralistic nature. As stated previously, the world's largest archipelagic state hosts hundreds of ethnic groups and regional languages, as well as local beliefs alongside the state-acknowledged religions: Islam, Christianity, Catholicism, Buddhism, Hinduism, and Confucianism. Nevertheless, for three decades (1966–1998) under the authoritarian rule of Suharto, Indonesia's second president after Sukarno, freedom of expression was highly restricted under the "SARA" regulation. In education, the learning of diversity was reduced to presentation and memorisation of the (then) 27 provinces and their symbolic traditional dances, clothes, food, and houses. This approach is what Elsie Begler (1998) dubs the "Five Fs", a reference to the presentations of cultural diversity that focus on tokenism, i.e. food, fashion, fiestas, folklore, and famous people. While this focus is not entirely without merit, such presentations merely offer "a touristic view" of the cultures, and do not engage students in a deeper understanding of the multiple constructs of culture and diversity. In portraying diversity, the New Order education system seemed to apply what James Banks (2009) refers to as the "additive" approach, in which the "Five Fs" from different cultural groups in Indonesia were showcased in classroom posters but not discussed further, exposing the risk of superficiality in learning about diversity (Gopalakrishnan 2011). Such a method is not far removed from the "colour-blind" approach in the USA where explicit discussion of racial issues is not encouraged because it may be considered to cause discomfort among students (Ramsey 2009).

Following Suharto's forced resignation in 1998, the people of Indonesia have awoken to the necessity and significance of acknowledging their diversity, yet the Reformation era that followed Suharto's resignation has been scarred with increasing ethnic and religious tensions. Ben Laksana and Bronwyn Wood (2018) have asserted that the young generation have been affected by escalating cases of religious tolerance. The Indonesian Child Protection Commission reported multiplying cases of prejudiced behaviour among children, particularly in hostility towards peers who come from different religions (Wiwoho 2017), and educators are reported to be facing an enormous challenge fostering tolerance among youth (Aritonang 2017). As Lyn Parker et al. (2014) have noted: "While Indonesia post-1998 is a much more open and democratic society [...] there are still several factors hindering open and tolerant multiculturalism" (467). Against this backdrop of dissent, the discourse of multiculturalism has begun to emerge, with multicultural education being seen by many as a potential solution for these tensions. Several scholars have attempted to assess the fitness of multicultural education in the Indonesian context (see Raihani 2017; Harjatanaya and Hoon 2020; Hoon 2013; Parker 2014), and overall analyses suggest that multicultural education seems appropriate to address Indonesia's challenge, as it concerns not only diversity, but also critical thinking and equality in its aims for all students' academic achievement (Banks 2016; Gollnick and Chin 2013). Close research on multicultural education has been conducted in Indonesia recently, particularly with concern to high school and university students, to explore the state of, and effects of, religious diversity, multiculturalism, tolerance, and religious education in contemporary Indonesian society (Firdaus 2018; Parker 2014; Parker et al. 2014; Laksana and Wood 2018; Sterkens and Yusuf 2015).

Yet, despite growing research on multicultural education, academic studies that investigate multicultural children's books published in the country are still scarce. While there have been a greater number of books that attempt to address issues of diversity and multiculturalism in Indonesia, the majority of publications still present the multiple cultures and ethnicities in the form of superficial travelogues that ask the child readers to "travel around" Indonesia's thirty-four provinces to introduce them to the traditional clothes, house, food, and dance of various regions. Recently, the analysis by Christia Spears Brown et al. (2018) of the use of such stories to reduce young children's prejudice towards Papuans in the region revealed the inefficacy of the intervention. The study seems to heavily focus on the quantitative measure of developmental psychology, yet not enough attention has been given to the quality of the stories used. For one thing, the stories used as interventions were written by the researchers and thus did not necessarily comply with the required complexity of multicultural children's literature.

CHILDREN'S BOOKS ON EASTERN AND CHINESE INDONESIA

The selected books I will examine in this chapter follow the criteria of good multicultural literature as laid out by Cai (2002) and Yokota (1993); namely, that they are texts that portray the marginalised group with both cultural authenticity and sound literary elements. Under these terms, I have chosen to assess six books, published between 2014 and 2018 in Indonesia, that narrate two minority groups in the country: Eastern Indonesians and Indonesians of Chinese descent. Both groups have distinctive cultural and religious identities, have been marginalised, and are heavily under-represented in children's books. The books that portray the Eastern Indonesians are all illustrated chapter books. The first one is *Warna-Warni Cerita Seru dari Raja Ampat* (Colorful and Exciting Stories from Raja Ampat, 2017) and a three-book series of *Lintas Anak*

Nusantara (Children Across the Archipelago), namely *Kisah dari Alor* (Stories from Alor, 2017), *Kisah dari Banggai* (Stories from Banggai, 2017), and *Kisah dari Sumba* (Stories from Sumba, 2018) (Fig. 12.1).

Fig. 12.1 Covers of Indonesian children's books about Eastern Indonesia: *Warna-Warni Cerita Seru dari Raja Ampat* (2017), *Kisah dari Alor* (2017), *Kisah dari Banggai*, and *Kisah dari Sumba* (2018)

Fig. 12.1   (continued)

The texts that represent Chinese Indonesians are *Cap Go Meh* (The Fifteenth Night) and a chapter book titled *Misteri Kota Tua* (The Mystery of the Old Town), both published in 2014 and both of which gained international accolades. *Cap Go Meh* was nominated for the SingTel Asian Picture Book Award 2013, while *Misteri Kota Tua* was mentioned in the IBBY Honour List 2016 (Fig. 12.2).

In examining the selected texts, I will employ the critical multicultural analysis model proposed by Maria José Botelho and Masha Kabakow

Fig. 12.2 Children's books about Chinese Indonesians: *Cap Go Meh* (Jakarta: Litara, 2014) and *Misteri Kota Tua* (Jakarta: Kiddo, 2014)

Rudman (2009). This model "acknowledges that all literature is a historical and cultural product and reveals how the power relations of class, race, and gender work together in text and image, and by extension, in society" (1). Critical multicultural analysis focuses on the reading process and on the readers' capacity to dissect and identify underlying ideologies representing a specific cultural group. In their model, Botelho and Rudman (2009) referenced guiding questions by Nathalie Wooldridge (2001) who, in a critical literacy workshop for teachers in a lower socioeconomic area in South Australia, applied a set of questions that enabled readers to critically deconstruct texts and observe the sociopolitical aspects of discourse. The questions I will apply to my reading of these Indonesian texts are: "What assumptions does the text make about age, gender, and culture (including the age, gender, and culture of its readers)?" and "Who is silenced/heard here?" (Wooldridge 2001, 261).

In her investigation of 150 children's narratives published between 1965 and 1979 that featured characters of Black ethnicities, Bishop (2012) observed what stories are being told and how they are told. She employed three main queries to help deconstruct the text's underlying cultural agenda:

> Who is the primary audience? To what extent is the distinctive cultural experience reflected? What is the author's implicit cultural perspective?

Another method of investigation in reading multicultural texts is proposed by Janelle Mathis (2015), who adapted Liu's queries in an examination of identities in Asian-American literature. The questions focus on agency in personal, social, and cultural dimensions:

> How do the characters define and position themselves in the dominant social group?
> Are they insiders or outsiders?
> How do characters position themselves in their own ethnic group?
> Do they reveal agency to support their own language, culture, and traditions?
> Do they encounter conflicts within their own group?
> (209–210)

Gopalakrishnan (2011) proposes that readers situate the text against its social and political context: "Multicultural children's literature needs to be viewed and analysed from a sociohistorical point of view, as arising from the social, historical, and cultural contexts of the 20th century and all the controversies and struggles of that time" (24). Moreover, critical multi-cultural analysis expects readers to not only critically investigate text, but to also "interrupt" the status quo in society, particularly in relation to cultural hegemony. It endorses readers' awareness that "meanings found in children's books are not from language alone but from institutional practices, power relations and social position" (Botelho and Rudman 2009, 101). Bishop's (1990) powerful metaphor of "mirrors, windows, and sliding glass doors" in children's books also strongly informs my reading of the selected texts and becomes my framework in assessing the texts' cultural position: whether they reflect the experiences of the marginalised, offer the possibility to see differences and welcome inclusion, and invite readers to take action to eliminate discrimination and achieve equality.

TREASURING THE FORGOTTEN

Warna-warni Cerita Seru dari Raja Ampat can be regarded as the first publication by a major publishing house that attempts to portray Indonesia's diversity with the complexity and depth of a literary narrative. Consisting of eight independent stories—collections of stories are a popular form in Indonesian children's books—the book is adorned with colourful illustrations and "fact-sheet" pages. All the stories are set in Raja Ampat, West Papua, the easternmost region of the archipelago and a coveted tourist destination due to its unspoilt nature. Perhaps because the 1500 islands in the area are home to the world's largest diversity of coral reefs as well as some endemic animals, half of the stories in the book feature non-humans as main characters. From eagle, manta ray, nuri bird, to the bird-of-paradise, and cenderawasih, the animal characters provide examples of the range of wildlife diversity in Indonesia that are facing extinction. Indeed, many contemporary Indonesian children's books present endemic and often endangered animals to raise children's awareness of their environment and their responsibilities towards it, though this approach can rob the narrative of the Papuans' human voice.

Moreover, a close reading of the stories reveals that visitors to the region have more voice than the local Papuans. As recurring characters in seven out of eight stories, tourists are often pictured as people who bring happiness (and material things) to the area. Illustrated as light-skinned and straight haired, the tourists are juxtaposed against the visibly "different" Papuans, who are dark-skinned and curly haired. The visitors seem to resemble the Javanese, the largest ethnic group in Indonesia, and their presence in the stories indicates the underlying hegemonic perspective of the dominant ethnic group in Indonesia that has enjoyed significant economic development and privilege. As Clare Bradford (2010) points out, children's books can sometimes "disclose conceptions of and attitudes to race, ethnicity, colonialism and postcolonialism, responding to the discourses and practices of the societies where they are produced" (39) and in these texts, it is readily apparent that an underlying preconception about an ethnic minority is revealed.

In the first story, *Surga itu Bernama Pulau Wayag* (The Paradise is Called Wayag Island), four male tourists (instead of the locals) become the saviours of a wounded eagle while they are visiting the region. In another story, *Bertamasya ke Desa Arborek* (Vacation in Arborek Village), a young female tourist who comes to Arborek acts as the source of happiness for the local children as she gives them books and coloured pencils (see Fig. 12.3). Similarly, in *Cap Tangan Misterius di Teluk Kabui* (Mysterious Handprint in Kabui Bay), an injured tourist gives a local girl her pre-paid spot on a boat tour to Kabui Bay. This brings joy to the local girl because she has been dreaming of seeing the prehistoric handprint in Kabui, but the boat ride—albeit close to her home—is too expensive for her (see Fig. 12.4).

The predominance of tourists and animals as main characters in the narratives leaves only a small platform for the Papuans to tell their own stories, a space which could have provided a more complex exploration of the reasons for regional poverty and underdevelopment despite the attraction of its natural beauty for global visitors, or ways in which locals may improve their lives. While the local children have taken centre stage in nearly half of the stories (three out of eight), they are still portrayed as passive bystanders in their own life stories and unable to contribute to social or economic change.

The national motto of "Unity in Diversity" also finds its way into the stories through the national anthem sung by the tourists on Wayag Island and by the children in Arborek Village. While some might argue that this narrative construct is not too far-fetched, it is nevertheless difficult not to see the act of belting out patriotic hymns in the far east of the archipelago as a promotion of national pride. The Indonesian outsiders to this specific local culture will invariably view these people as fellow citizens, while the Papuans are provided with an ideal nationalistic sample to follow: amidst the inequality and underdevelopment they suffer, they

Kulihat Adel sedang berjingkrak-jingkrak memegang sebuah buku. Dia dikerumuni empat teman lain yang juga berseru kegirangan. Di hadapan mereka, seorang wanita juga tertawa riang. Karena penasaran, aku pun mendekat.

"Sheila, lihat!" teriak Adel.

Aku terkejut. Ada buku yang sampulnya bergambar ikan warna-warni. Wanita asing itu membagikan bukunya satu per satu kepada kami.

Fig. 12.3 Illustration for *Bertamasya ke Desa Arborek* in *Warna-Warni Cerita Seru dari Raja Ampat* (2017) shows a young domestic tourist bringing presents to Papuan children

Turis yang berbaju biru tersenyum.

"Kaki teman kami keseleo."

Marina tersenyum lebar. "Wah! Mamaku bisa mengobati terkilir. Mari mampir ke rumahku," ajak Marina.

Ketiga turis itu setuju. Mereka lalu pergi ke rumah Marina. Setibanya di rumah Marina, Mama segera merawat kaki turis yang terkilir itu. Turis itu bernama Luna. Dua turis lainnya bernama Ratna dan Dewi. Mama mengolesi kaki Kak Luna dengan minyak rempah.

98

Fig. 12.4 Illustration for *Cap Tangan Misterius di Teluk Kabui*, one of the stories in *Warna-Warni Cerita Seru dari Raja Ampat* (2017). An injured tourist allows a Papuan girl to take her place on a costly boat trip to the historical Kabui

must yet see themselves as part of the Indonesian whole. Thus, under the guise of inclusivity within the hegemonic order within the texts, a nationalist agenda may also be seen to be at play, given that the West Papuans have had a long history of dispute with the Indonesian state and have been staging separatist movements for many years. The main factors behind the push for separation stem not only from inequality and the exploitation of natural resources (Mashuri and van Leeuwen 2017), but also from the distinctive cultural characteristics that make the West Papuans identify as very different from the rest of Indonesia: "Papuans see themselves as racially and ethnically distinct from all other regions in Indonesia and identify more with other Melanesian populations, than with Asians" (Kanem and Norris 2018, 3).

One of the few instances of veracity in the stories is the representation of the poverty of the locals in this "hidden paradise" though, as mentioned earlier, no context for the causes of this are provided. In one story, a six-year-old girl is upset because her sister must leave their village to attend school in Sorong, a two-hour boat ride away. The arrival of a tourist with simple presents—books and colouring pencils—excites the girl and her friends who lack basic facilities on the remote island. The theme of modesty in life as an attribute is more visible in *Bertualang di Teluk Mayalibit* (Adventure in Mayalibit Bay), in which a little boy demands a present for his birthday. Though the present is eventually simple—his father, a humble fisherman, takes him to fish together for the first time—the dazzling evening sea and the magical school of fish following the oil lamp manage to make the little boy happy and no expenses are needed (see Fig. 12.5). The reference to local people being unable to enjoy their own natural locations in the Kabui Bay story also reveals how tourism is often promoted at the expense of local lifestyles.

Poverty is an unfortunate fact in West Papua. Raja Ampat, the costly tourist destination, is one of the least developed and disadvantaged regions in Indonesia, yet the portrayal of poverty in the stories from Raja Ampat does not account for the root causes of the problem, specifically economic inequalities and injustices in society. Instead, the book endorses the message often found in Indonesian children's stories: accept your fate and be happy. Given the significance of agency in multicultural stories, it is necessary for the child characters from this deprived area to be depicted in active roles according to their capacity which could contribute to bringing about change. The stories can then be a strong advocate for multicultural education: stories that empower children, either from inside or outside

Michael dan Papa pun naik perahu. Papa meletakkan lampu petromaks di ujung depan perahu. Perahu mulai bergerak di atas air, dan hanya ada kegelapan di sekeliling mereka.

"Kenapa semuanya gelap? Kenapa cuma perahu-perahu saja yang terang?" desis Michael.

"Coba intip di sisi perahu, Michael," kata Papa sambil terkekeh.

86

Fig. 12.5 Illustration for *Bertualang di Teluk Mayalibit* in *Warna-Warni Cerita Seru dari Raja Ampat* (2017) reveals the modest life of a Papuan family

the culture. If books for children are to contribute to the nation's integration while also respecting minority groups, text creators must ensure that the portrayal of these same minority groups depicts social reality and is positive, while also highlighting the roles they play in contributing to larger Indonesian society.

Next, I will analyse the books in Lintas Anak Nusantara, a series developed to "bring Indonesian children closer to each other through exchanging of stories of culture, daily life, places, homes, languages, local heroes" as expressed in the Foreword of the three books published so far: *Kisah dari Alor*, *Kisah dari Banggai*, and *Kisah dari Sumba*. The stated intention is to "build bridges and fill the information gap about [the children's] culture and region, so that [the children] can be closer to each other, and avoid the misunderstandings and fanaticism that often arise through differences in cultures, ethnicities, religions, and others" (Wihardja 2018, 5).

The first in the instalment, *Kisah dari Alor*, is authored by Hanny Kusumawati (2017) and comprises five stories describing children in Alor, the biggest island in an archipelago of ninety in south-eastern Indonesia. Several stories put forward the theme of pride in local culture, such as can be seen in *Aloysius Si Pemetik Kediding* (Aloysius the Kediding Player), in which a boy learns individual bravery by performing on a traditional instrument while his friends are playing modern instruments. A similar theme is found in *Lusia Si Pemalu* (Shy Lusia), in which Lusia is encouraged to realise that her ability to perform the traditional dance of *lego-lego* strengthens her cultural identity. This is a "moral message" which is favoured in modern Indonesia, as globalisation brings with it the fear that the nation's youth will become "Westernised" and neglect their own local culture. The book is not exclusively about cultural diversity, however, as the theme of environment also has a prominent focus. The stories *Pahlawan Pulau* (Hero of the Island) and *Anak Baru dari Jakarta* (The New Kid from Jakarta) are didactic narratives which instruct readers that taking care of nature is their responsibility. What Amalia, the new kid from Jakarta, tells the children in Alor in one story seems to mirror more adult concerns, as she advises locals on the benefits of their clean environment over the polluted capital city. Such an approach represents a recurring message of quasi-nostalgia in children's texts which address issues of poverty and inequality in rural Indonesia: rather than question and challenge, one must accept the status quo and be grateful for what one has.

The next book in the series, however, explores diversity more boldly and with more sophistication. *Kisah dari Banggai* (2017) is written by the young volunteers who joined the initiative, *Indonesia Mengajar*, and were posted in Banggai for one year. Comprising ten stories, the book is more explicit in addressing diversity, both in ethnicity and religion, and directly models religious tolerance, which is understood as "respect for one another through differences" as repeatedly found in the book. Explicit descriptions of ethnic diversity can be found in several of the stories, such as in this description of the diverse makeup of Ondo-Ondolu village:

> In addition to the Javanese, the Balinese, and the Lomboknese, our school friends also come from the ethnic groups of Saluan, Bugis, and Sunda. Our school becomes more colourful. We live harmoniously and are good friends here. Bhinneka Tunggal Ika, isn't it? (22)

Interestingly, this description of diversity is adorned by positive words and phrases such as "colourful", "harmoniously", "good friends", and "Bhinneka Tunggal Ika".

In *Kedatangan Guru Baru* (The Arrival of the New Teacher), a Christian teacher in a predominantly Muslim school offers the opportunity for students to learn about religious diversity. Some curious questions ("Does [being Christian] mean you don't pray in a mosque?" "Can you recite the Quran?", 15) trigger open dialogue that fosters positive inter-religious friendships rarely found in Indonesian children's stories. After learning about their new teacher's religion, the Muslim students adjust their swimming time to their teacher's worship time on Sunday. Another open dialogue occurs in *Kartu Ucapan Hari Raya* (Holiday Greeting Cards). In another primary school, tension rises as first-graders are separated for their religious lessons.[2] Tian, a Christian pupil, argues with Wahyu, a Hindu pupil, about their differences. Here, the paradox of teaching acceptance through differences is shown in the school's policy for "developing religious tolerance in all students" such as special holidays and celebrations at school and "allowing students to pray according to their own religions and faiths before and after the lessons" (59). The teacher, illustrated as a Muslim, attempts to apply the value of tolerance (again, understood as "respect for differences") by asking the students to create greeting cards for different religious holidays (see Fig. 12.6) and to give them to one another: "The children exchange cards with smiles.

"Oke. Selanjutnya, kita akan menuliskan selamat hari raya yang sudah ditentukan tadi. Jika akan diberikan ke teman beragama Islam, maka Selamat Idul Fitri. Jika kepada teman beragama Hindu, tulis Selamat Hari Nyepi. Kepada teman beragama Kristen, tulis Selamat Hari Natal. Setelah itu, kalian bisa kasih hiasan gambar supaya kartunya menjadi lebih indah. Paham?" Ibu Guru memberi tahu tahapan kedua.

"Paham Bu..." murid-murid kembali menjawab. Mereka pun langsung sibuk dengan kartu yang dibuatnya.

Lima belas menit berlalu, anak-anak sudah sibuk bertukar kartu ucapan hari raya. Mereka saling bertukar dengan senyuman. Semoga dengan bertukar kartu ucapan, bisa menumbuhkan kesadaran di antara mereka bahwa perbedaan bukan hal yang perlu diperdebatkan, melainkan hal yang mempersatukan. Sebab, perbedaan itu indah.

Fig. 12.6 Illustration for *Kartu Ucapan Hari Raya* in *Kisah dari Banggai* (2017) shows a Muslim teacher encouraging her students to create holiday greeting cards for the state-acknowledged religions in Indonesia as a way of teaching tolerance

Hopefully by exchanging greeting cards, an awareness can grow in them that differences are not something to debate, but rather something that unites. Because differences are beautiful" (66).

A further example of the promotion of tolerance is found in *Aku Saluan, Cinta Indonesia* (I am Saluan, Love Indonesia). This story's setting is in a Christian classroom, where the teacher opens the lesson with The Lord's Prayer followed immediately by the teaching of religious tolerance, which he does by writing on the board: "MUST LOVE ONE ANOTHER" (89). Unity is emphasised to balance diversity as he teaches his students: "Even though we come from different ethnic, linguistic, and religious groups, we are one. One Indonesian nation. Therefore, we must love one another" (90). This story stresses that even the minority group needs to learn about tolerance. Indeed, tolerance in Indonesia is defined as "respect and acceptance of difference, not mere forbearance" (Laksana and Wood 2018, 4), different from what may be argued as the more negative connotation of tolerance in many Western countries, in which the notion of tolerance may be regarded as acknowledging difference rather than actively understanding it (Hoon 2017).

Apart from the recurring overt message of tolerance, *Kisah dari Banggai* is ground-breaking in two areas. First is its presentation of Confucianism, the latest addition in the officially state-recognised religions and one which, along with the associated Chinese cultures and traditions, had been prohibited in public expressions for more than 30 years. This ban has triggered ongoing prejudice towards its practice, primarily resulting from the lack of information regarding Chinese cultural beliefs and religion. As such, this book is innovative in that it is the first children's text that presents Confucianism as an equal belief with other religions in Indonesia (see Fig. 12.7).

The second ground-breaking aspect in the book is its advocacy of greeting different religious holidays, a sign of respect for diversity of beliefs but also a disputed gesture in an increasingly conservative society. In the 1980s, the MUI (Council of Indonesian Ulama), the respected Muslim authority in Indonesia, issued a *fatwa* (religious edict) that forbade Muslims from taking part in Christmas celebrations. The greeting of "Merry Christmas" to Christians and Catholics has also been a long-standing controversy among Indonesian Muslims (Hasyim 2011; Sirry 2013). Against this context, the narrative construct of the Muslim teacher in *Kisah dari Banggai* encouraging her students to not only make religious holiday cards, but also to openly accept friends from different faiths through the greetings, represents a significant departure from the conservative norms of the Muslim majority.

Kemudian, Pak Yesaya menuliskan semua agama yang ada di Indonesia agar seluruh siswa dapat melihatnya.
"Kristen Protestan, Katolik, Islam, Hindu, Buddha, Kong Hu Cu."
Untuk semakin melengkapi nilai toleransi, Pak Yesaya menambahkan tulisan "HARUS SALING MENGASIHI".
"Pak Guru, walaupun berbeda, kita harus saling mengasihi, ya?" ujar Kenza yang pernah mendengar kalimat itu dari mamanya.

Fig. 12.7 Illustration in *Kisah dari Banggai* (2017) depicts places of worship of six state-acknowledged religions in Indonesia, including the most recently recognised, Confucianism

The focus on the diversity of religions over ethnicities is lent further credence, given the region's recent history. Banggai is located in Central Sulawesi, a province that has been scarred by bloody communal violence between Muslims and Christians which erupted after the New Order ended in 1998, and such texts reflect the necessity of an interreligious bridge for the younger generation. Yet, even though the active and sprightly child characters suggest agency, it is the adults who still hold the key position in the stories as the messengers of religious tolerance.

The latest book in the series, *Kisah dari Sumba*, introduces readers to another under-represented region in Eastern Indonesia: Sumba island. All eight stories in the book place a heavy focus on Sumba's distinctive culture, traditions, and indigenous religion but, crucially, the child characters exercise their agency in solving the conflicts that arise from this diversity. Also of importance is that the message in the text is implicit, allowing the reader to reach his or her own conclusion without the somewhat clumsy, overt didacticism of the majority of books for children in Indonesia.

Marapu dan Kampung Tarung (Marapu and the Tarung Village) is a leap forward in Indonesian children's literature, as it becomes the first story in contemporary Indonesia that explicitly portrays the complexity of the indigenous religions still observed in the country. Many of these indigenous beliefs have been oppressed and marginalised, policies in direct opposition to a country which prides itself for being religious and tolerant (Afrianty 2012; Nurrohman 2014). For a long time, these *aliran kepercayaan* (cultural belief systems) were not legally recognised, and were open to discrimination. Only very recently were they finally acknowledged as equal to other major religions by the Indonesian government through the approval by the Constitutional Court to print them in the citizens' ID cards (Sapiie 2017).

In this text, Marapu, one of the indigenous religions, becomes a trigger for tension among the children of Sumba, most of whom observe the more mainstream religions of Catholicism, Christianity, and Islam. Meha, a boy from the village, faces a personal challenge when his classmates mock him as "the witch's child". He tearfully asks his mother: "They say Meha's religion is a witchcraft. Is it true?" (9). The boy is torn between peer pressure and defending his distinctive religious identity: "Of course, Meha is proud of his religion. However, he is sometimes embarrassed because his friends often equalise Marapu with dark magic" (9). In his explanation about Marapu, Meha's father reveals what must be felt by any number of people of native faiths: "The religion of Marapu has been practised by our ancestors in Sumba before Hinduism, Buddhism, Islam, Catholicism, and Christianity came into the archipelago. Today, Marapu and its followers are becoming more forgotten and marginalised" (10).

To resolve this tension, Meha invites his classmates to visit his village and learn about his religion directly from his grandmother, Apu Humba, an elder who teaches the native faith to the younger generation (see

Fig. 12.8). Apu Humba explains Marapu to Meha's school friends and stresses its message of tolerance:

> Every religion has its own belief and ways of praying. More importantly, whatever religion you believe in, you must own a kind, humble heart and always love each other. We must not underestimate or mock other religions and other people. (20)

Given the often rigid policies towards minority cultures and beliefs in Indonesia, it is encouraging that the story repeatedly mentions Marapu

"Agama Marapu adalah agama yang sudah dianut sejak zaman nenek moyang kita. Kata Marapu sendiri berarti 'yang dimuliakan' atau 'yang dipertuan' karena penganut agama Marapu memuja roh-roh nenek moyang dan percaya bahwa roh-roh ini adalah perantara mereka dengan sang pencipta. Jadi, biarpun penganut agama Marapu memuja roh-roh nenek moyang, kami percaya kepada Tuhan Yang Maha Esa. Karena agama ini sangat tua, jadinya memang terlihat seperti agama gaib. Namun, sumber agama ini adalah pencipta kita semua, yaitu Tuhan Yang Maha Esa."

"Agama Marapu tidak seperti agama Islam yang punya Al-Qur'an atau agama Katolik dan Kristen yang punya Alkitab. Apa yang diajarkan agama Marapu disampaikan secara lisan oleh para pemuka dan ahli agama Marapu saat acara keagamaan sambil diiringi nyanyian adat Sumba. Maka dari itu, banyak orang salah paham mengenai agama Marapu karena apa yang diajarkan itu tidak tercatat."

Fig. 12.8 Illustration for *Marapu dan Kampung Tarung* in *Kisah dari Sumba* (2018) explains one of the hundreds of indigenous faiths in Indonesia

as a religion, contesting the MUI's view that indigenous faiths are not equal to the more institutionalised religions (Marshall 2018). The following illustration (Fig. 12.9) supports this through its depiction of Marapu's religious leader hand in hand with the leaders from the more institutionalised religions.

As a country that has constantly witnessed the oppression of minority religions through the persecution of followers and attacks on their

Teman-teman Meha duduk dengan serius. Pikiran mereka menjadi terbuka mendengarkan cerita Apu Humba.

"Jadi agama Marapu itu bukan ilmu sihir, Apu? Mereka percaya Tuhan dan berdoa kepada roh-roh nenek moyang seperti agama Buddha? Begitu Apu?"

"Iya. Setiap agama mempunyai kepercayaan dan cara berdoa masing-masing. Tetapi yang lebih penting, apa pun agama yang kalian anut, kalian harus mempunyai hati yang baik, rendah hati, dan selalu mengasihi sesama. Tidak boleh meremehkan atau mengejek agama dan orang lain," kata Apu Humba.

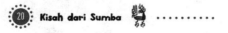

Kisah dari Sumba

Fig. 12.9 Illustration in *Kisah dari Sumba* (2018) shows a progressive image of a leader from a native religion in equal position as leaders from the state-acknowledged religions in Indonesia

places of worship (Parker 2010), contemporary Indonesian children's literature is moving towards a site of progressive discourse as it begins to embrace minorities through initial acknowledgement followed by approaches which encourage deeper understanding. Ignorance breeds prejudice, and this story models the ideal behaviour towards the minority: clear information is the critical first step towards tolerance.

Other stories in *Kisah dari Sumba* are equally rich in their portrayal of the Sumbanese cultures. In *Kado Kejutan untuk Ina Andu* (A Surprise Gift for Ina Andu), a little girl attempts to weave *tenun ikat* as a present for her mother and play an active part in keeping the cultural legacy of the traditional fabric. Rambu Kahi, the little girl, conscientiously learns all the stages of making *tenun ikat* from her grandmother: from harvesting cotton, understanding the fabric patterns and the philosophies behind them, dyeing the cloth with natural ingredients, to eventually weaving them (Fig. 12.10). By doing this, Rambu Kahi implicitly and inherently "owns" her culture as well as preserves it, without the explicit nationalistic imperative that she must unconditionally and unquestioningly "love" her culture. All female characters in the story—from the grandmother, mother, to Rambu Kahi—depict a strong chain of generations of guardians that unashamedly regard their culture as an integral part of their lives.

Another story worth mentioning for its representation of multiculturalism is *Perjalanan Meha ke Desa Wunga* (Meha's Trip to the Wunga Village). My previous reference to Bishop's metaphor of a mirror is relevant here, as Meha learns about the ancestry of the majority ethnic Javanese yet cannot find the history of his own people, an indication of how children from a minority group like Meha are often unable to locate themselves in the books they read and which seek to shape them with an identity outside of their immediate cultural history. Meha asks his grandmother to share with him the history of their ancestors, and Apu Humba recounts the legend of a pair of Sumbanese boys, and of how they created the first fire on the island to escape wild animals. The legend, albeit folklore, supports the overall theme of children's active agency in contributing significantly to their community in Sumba, a concept that views children as having the capacity to act independently (James and James 2012). Here, children make choices about their actions and express their ideas, becoming active constructors of their childhood experience instead of merely passive recipients of adults' received morals. Though rich in their authentic portrayal of Sumbanese culture, the stories in *Kisah dari Sumba* also depict the children in age-appropriate terms: curious, playful, and needing

Fig. 12.10 Illustration for *Kado Kejutan untuk Ina Andu*, a story from *Kisah dari Sumba* (2018), pictures a little girl exercising her agency in preserving her cultural legacy through the creation of *tenun ikat*

of acceptance. Such narratives are what Bishop (2012) deems "culturally conscious"—stories that depict both the distinctiveness of one group's cultural experiences and the universality of human experience. Thus, the narratives act as both "mirror" to the Sumbanese children, "window" to the rest of the archipelago (and hopefully the world), and also as "sliding glass doors" by introducing the social issues that affect the children in Sumba while raising awareness for children outside this specific group of their culture and authentic struggles.

Generally, multicultural books about children from Eastern Indonesia reveal the diversity of children from the region, even within one cultural group. In *Kisah dari Sumba*, Meha's indigenous religion distinguishes him from his classmates even though they are from the same ethnic group. Likewise, as shown in *Kisah dari Banggai*, the villages in Banggai have different dominant religions and ethnicities due to local migrations. For many years, the Eastern Indonesia region has also become what may be termed "the forgotten islands" in that it has suffered from ongoing conflicts and poverty. Geographically isolated from the more developed western regions—such as Sumatra, Java, and Bali—West Papua, Alor, Banggai, and Sumba are among the poorest provinces in Indonesia (Booth 2004). Both Alor and Sumba are located in East Nusa Tenggara, the southernmost province in Indonesia, which is claimed to be "the driest and poorest province in the Indonesian archipelago" (Cole 2008, 46). One region in the province, East Timor, disintegrated in 1999 and is now a sovereign state.

Against this sociopolitical context, multicultural books on Eastern Indonesia are expected to serve their roles as a "mirror" to the children from inside the community and to positively contribute to their construction of cultural identity as they see themselves represented in the stories. As Gopalakrishnan (2011) has posited, the inclusion of these disenfranchised people in multicultural literature is principally an attempt of "validation for all children's experiences" (5). Yet, as stated, it is also imperative that these multicultural books become a "window" for children in the archipelago as they learn about their peers in different areas through authentic portrayal, and for the "mirror" to serve as a "sliding glass door" for young readers to step into reality and not only acknowledge those who are different, but also take action to reduce the gap inequality caused by the differences.

LISTENING TO THE SILENCED

If the Eastern Indonesians have been forgotten, the Chinese Indonesians have been silenced. For decades, Indonesians of Chinese descent have been forbidden from expressing their culture and traditions through the implementing of various government regulations. One was the Presidential Decree No. 14/1967 by the New Order of Suharto, which prohibited the public expression of Chinese language, religious festivals, and cultural traditions. As Chee Kiong Tong (2010) explains, "The Chinese were marginalized and were pressured into assimilation by the *pembauran total* (complete assimilation) policy because Chinese cultural differences were deemed to be a threat to the national unity of Indonesia" (124).

Evidence of a Chinese presence in the archipelago can be found from the fifth century, although the bigger migration from China to Indonesia occurred four hundred years ago (Freedman 2000, 97). Today, Chinese Indonesians comprise less than 2 percent of the Indonesian population, and although they have assimilated and acculturated in various ways, the ethnic group has been a constant target for the social frustrations of the rest of the Indonesian people. Despite accepting the pressure to leave their distinctive culture behind to take up Indonesian identity, Chinese Indonesians remain victims of discrimination and prejudice (Kuipers and Yulaelawati 2009). The negative sentiment towards the ethnic group has invariably resulted in Chinese Indonesians choosing silence as a cultural strategy in direct response to, and in corroboration with, the regulation that "silenced" them. Only after the New Order ended and the well-known pluralist Abdurrahman Wahid became the first elected president in 1999, did Chinese Indonesians begin to slowly find voices. In 2000, Abdurrahman Wahid (or Gus Dur) annulled the discriminatory regulation, while his successor, Megawati Sukarnoputri, declared the Chinese New Year as a national holiday in 2003, further recognising the ethnic group's existence and the need "to liberate their long-suppressed identity and cultural heritage" (Hoon 2006, 154).

However, as Sai and Hoon (2013) have pointed out, "Chinese Indonesians continue to confront discrimination on a practical and day-to-day basis even after regime change" (16). Similarly, Tong's (2010) fieldwork in Indonesia reveals that "in daily life, the Chinese in Indonesia experience a high degree of ethnic discrimination" (135) while Mary Heidhues (2017) observes that Chinese Indonesians expecting to serve in public office face challenges from the "manipulation of anti-Chinese prejudices" and "when ethnic Chinese candidates are not Muslims, potential opposition on religious grounds" (608). It is within this context that multicultural children's books that feature Chinese Indonesians offer a potential remedy.

Bearing these considerations in mind, the first text to be assessed is *Cap Go Meh*, a picture book published by Litara, an independent publisher that has consistently produced high-quality children's literature on Indonesia's lesser-known cultures. The story opens with an inclusive invitation: "It's a celebration for everyone!" The accompanying illustration shows two girls who look very different, with no explicit mention of their ethnicity, yet Indonesian readers will readily identify them as representatives of two distinct ethnic and religious groups (see Fig. 12.11).

Nisa, who has slightly darker skin and round eyes, wears a green hijab and a tunic. Her name is most likely the short version for Annisa, a popular girl's name in Indonesia derived from Arabic which means "female", while the colour green that she sports is well-known in the archipelago as representative of Islam (in addition to white). As many Islamic centres and traditions choose green as their primary colour, readers will inevitably deduce that Nisa represents the Muslim Javanese. Nisa's friend Lily, on the other hand, is a typical Chinese-Indonesian with fair skin tone, slanted eyes, and the well-known traditional Cheongsam dress.

Nisa begins the story by describing the celebration of her religious holiday and her love of the Eid *ketupat*, a special dish that she eats on the seventh day of the religious period. Lily then shares her love of the Chinese New Year celebrations and a similar meal called Cap Go Meh, which

Fig. 12.11 Illustration from *Cap Go Meh* shows two girls from different ethnic and religious groups as friends who share similarities

means fifteen in Mandarin, and is thus eaten on the fifteenth day after the new year. Readers will notice that although Nisa and Lily look very dissimilar, there are more than a few similarities that they share. Both are cheerful girls who enjoy their special holidays and, most importantly, love the celebration of their cultural meal. Both festivals seem to "last forever" and are loved by children for the pocket money they receive ("Eid money" for Nisa and "lucky money" for Lily). The similarities between the two girls culminate in the special food enjoyed in their holidays as they both remark at the end of the story: "I don't care it's Eid or Chinese New Year, but our favorite food turns out to be the same!"

Through the vivid illustrations which depict not only the joy of Eid, but also the Chinese New Year, similarities are celebrated through the depiction of equality between the two cultures and beliefs. In these pages, Chinese Indonesians confidently embrace their distinct ethnic traits through open celebrations of faith and tradition and affirm their identity as both Chinese and Indonesian (see Fig. 12.12). Yet, such a scenario is contrary to a reality in which Chinese Indonesians are still reluctant to show their Chinese cultural heritage for fear of being considered as not assimilating, even after the repeal of New Order edicts (Arifin, Hasbullah, and Pramono 2017). Nisa and Lily's friendship, along with their families, who are seen as embracing each other in the background, models the ideal relationship between the dominant Javanese Muslims and the minority Chinese Indonesians, an encouraging image in the light of the anti-Chinese sentiments still prevalent in the country.

Recognition for the previously silenced Chinese Indonesians is explored further in *Misteri Kota Tua*, in which readers will find not only traditions and celebrations, but also representations of the oppression and the struggles of the ethnic minority. Beno, the main character, is a sixth-grader who has recently moved to Tangerang, a coastal suburb of Jakarta, because of his father's work. Beno's new home is an old Chinese settlement, and mystery ensues after he catches a man trying to break in. As he discovers more about the man, Beno learns more about the Chinese Indonesians in Tangerang. Together with Beno, readers "visit" important spots in the history of the Chinese Indonesians in Java, such as Teluk Naga (a coast in North Tangerang where the Chinese first arrived in the fifteenth century) and Klenteng Boen Tek Bio, the oldest temple in Tangerang, built in the seventeenth century, where the *potehi* puppet—a glove puppetry influenced by the Chinese and Javanese culture—is still

We have the dragon dance around town.

Fig. 12.12 Illustration from *Cap Go Meh* depicts the open celebration of the Chinese New Year that was previously banned in public during the New Order era (1966–1998)

performed. Throughout the story, readers also learn of the many acculturations between the Chinese and the Indonesians (see Fig. 12.13)—particularly the Betawinese, the Javanese and the Sundanese—resulting in Rumah Kawin (a building for wedding celebrations) and Gambang Kromong (a band of Chinese instruments and the Javanese gamelan). The cultures learnt by Beno are presented in a special section within the story, in the form of an illustrated fact sheet, showing readers that this part of the story is grounded in reality.

The story aims to eliminate prejudices that have for many generations been directed towards Chinese Indonesians. When Beno first meets Meylan, a Chinese Indonesian girl, he is bewildered to see that Meylan and her family do not look like the image he has in mind: "Perhaps Meylan and her engkong (grandfather) are not Chinese. They have dark skin. Their speaking manner is more like Si Pitung from Betawi" (36). This shows readers that the Chinese Indonesians are not homogenous

GAMBANG KROMONG

Gambang kromong adalah orkes yang memadukan alat musik Tionghoa dengan gamelan Jawa. Biasa dimainkan saat Imlek, upacara pernikahan, dan kematian.

gong

tehyan

suling

gambang

gendang

Diciptakan oleh Nie Hoe Kong, pemimpin komunitas Tionghoa (Kapitan China) yang diangkat oleh Belanda di Batavia di abad ke-18.

41

Fig. 12.13 Illustration from *Misteri Kota Tua* shows the various forms of acculturation of the Chinese and the Indonesian ethnic groups

nor do they always fit the prejudiced image of people outside the ethnic group. Chinese in Indonesia are indeed particularly heterogeneous, depending on where they live, the religion they choose, or how much they have assimilated or acculturated (Hoon 2006; Sai and Hoon 2013; Tong 2010). The portrayal of the Chinese Indonesians that Beno encounters in Tangerang is a promising model in dismantling the negative stereotypes often directed at the Chinese Indonesians: namely, that they are all wealthy and do not assimilate with the locals (Hoon 2006). Thus, the story attempts to bring to light a reality that is contrary to the ethnocentric labels put on them. The Cina Benteng—the Chinese Indonesians in Tangerang who have heavily assimilated with the Betawinese and the Sundanese, two ethnic groups in West Java—show that they are far from the stereotypes propagated by sections of Indonesia (see Fig. 12.14): they cannot speak Mandarin, are "married to the locals and look like most Indonesians" (37) and "work as fisherman, farmers, or even *becak* drivers, although there are also some who become traders" (38).

Misteri Kota Tua further explores the roles that Chinese Indonesians played during the nation's independence. *Sin Po*, the famous Mandarin newspaper during the colonial and independence eras, was "the first media that publishe[d] the lyrics of Indonesia Raya by Wage Rudolf Supratman" (40) which later became the country's national anthem. The newspaper also actively "promoted the name 'Indonesia'" which was critical for the new country (40). The Chinese Indonesian characters in the story are also portrayed as loyal to the country and strongly identify themselves as Indonesians. For example, the brother of the mysterious old man who arrives at Beno's house turns out to be a soldier who fought and died in the war for Indonesia's independence. As Tong (2010) posits, the Chinese Indonesians were not regarded as an important part of the nationalist movement even though they "supported the Indonesian revolution and helped in various ways" (120) and the long line of discriminatory policies towards the Chinese that had taken place since the Dutch colonial era had resulted in the ethnic group being labelled as foreigners. Moreover, the New Order regime "constantly questioned the position of the Chinese, their citizenship and their 'belonging' to the Indonesian nation" (Tong 2010, 126) and represented the Chinese as "the foreign 'Other' in order to prevent them from being accepted fully as 'Indonesians'" (Hoon 2006, 152).

CIRI-CIRI ORANG CINA BENTENG

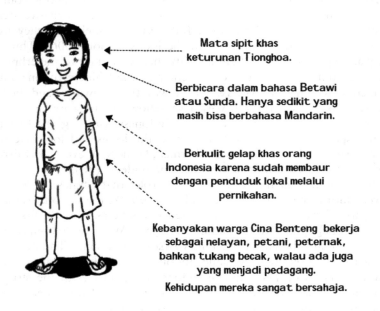

Mata sipit khas keturunan Tionghoa.

Berbicara dalam bahasa Betawi atau Sunda. Hanya sedikit yang masih bisa berbahasa Mandarin.

Berkulit gelap khas orang Indonesia karena sudah membaur dengan penduduk lokal melalui pernikahan.

Kebanyakan warga Cina Benteng bekerja sebagai nelayan, petani, peternak, bahkan tukang becak, walau ada juga yang menjadi pedagang.

Kehidupan mereka sangat bersahaja.

"Tapi tunggu sebentar" guman Engkong. "Rasanya Engkong mengenali beberapa huruf dalam surat ini," Engkong memiring-miringkan surat yang sejak tadi masih dipegangnya.

44

Fig. 12.14 Illustration from *Misteri Kota Tua* breaks down the appearance of a Chinese Indonesian who does not conform to stereotypes, revealing the heterogeneity of the ethnic group

When Beno tries to solve various mysteries with his new friends, he uncovers the tragedies suffered by the Chinese after Indonesian independence, such as the 1946 riots that resulted in the looting and burning of Chinese Indonesian houses and stores because the Chinese were accused of being Dutch spies. Beno also learns of the discriminatory presidential regulation in 1959, whereby the government issued a decree that forbade foreigners, including Chinese Indonesians who had not yet officially become Indonesian citizens, to conduct business in the country. Such discussion represents significant progress in Indonesian multicultural children's literature because these narratives do not merely expose the disenfranchised group's culture, but critically describe the group's authentic struggles and oppression. The text offers an important opportunity for children from outside the group to see different perspectives about the Chinese Indonesians and uncovers the social and historical dimensions that affect power structures in society (Cai 2002).

Cai (2002) emphasises the significance of multicultural literature in giving voice to and empowering the marginalised. A multicultural book that nurtures readers' agency fulfils potential through not only highlighting cultural diversity within Indonesia, but also empowering its diverse groups. Consequently, building agency, in addition to facilitating resilience and empathy, through the vicarious experience of reading has been rightly advocated by literacy scholars (Short 2012; Mathis 2015). Most crucially, Arief Budiman (2005) notes that the changing perceptions of Chinese Indonesians that take place after the New Order do not only happen to the majority ethnicity, but also to Chinese Indonesians' perception of themselves.

CONCLUSION

These selected texts reveal how multicultural stories in contemporary Indonesian society could become a space of inclusive potentiality—giving voice to the under-represented and marginalised, as well as validating diverse children's experiences across the archipelago. As products of society, they are important transmitters of values to the younger generation, in that they may both reflect and shape multicultural ideals, and this is recognised by the gatekeepers of the text, i.e. publishers and booksellers. With the escalation of intolerant cases in Indonesia, which may be argued to be the effect of an authoritarian regime, children's books have become important channels for the message of tolerance. Such books model ideal resolutions when tensions arise in encountering difference, by showing that knowledge of perceived "otherness" is the critical first step towards its understanding and acceptance. Yet, though diversity is often central to these narratives, it is not unaccompanied by the ever-important notion of unity. In the stories examined in this chapter which reference Eastern Indonesia, devices such as the presence of the national anthem and patriotic names in this remote area are critical to secure the unity of the archipelago. Likewise, the multicultural story of the Chinese Indonesians which features historical facts related to this ethnic group's active contribution to the fight for independence assures a broader national readership that this minority group, often viewed as unloyal and unpatriotic, is also an important component of the nation in its totality. Both aspects of multicultural children's literature—diversity and unity—are crucial to its acceptance and efficacy in Indonesia. Yet with such sentiments in mind, it is also worth noting Bishop's words, who argues that as noble as the goal of multicultural literature is, it still has its limits:

> It won't take the homeless off our streets; it won't feed the starving of the world; it won't stop people from attacking each other because of our racial differences; it won't stamp out the scourge of drugs. It could, however, help us to understand each other better by helping to change our attitudes towards difference. (1990, xi)

NOTES

1. "From Instruction to Delight" is the title of an anthology of early prose and poetry for children (Demers and Moyles 1982) that is considered a seminal work for the academic study of children's literature. The anthology reveals the changing conceptions of childhood as the role of children's readings has shifted from moral teaching ("instruction") to focus on engagement ("delight").
2. Religious education in Indonesia is confessional. Students learn the religion that they confess, and schools are obliged to provide the relevant teachers. This proves to be a challenge for certain schools, particularly those in rural areas that already struggle to have a sufficient number of teachers to facilitate the students. The danger of this "mono-religious model", as asserted by scholars (Nurwanto and Cusack 2017; Sterkens and Yusuf 2015), is the feeling of the superiority of one's religion due to limited knowledge about other religions, and the difficulty of accepting other beliefs as alternative perspectives.

References

Primary Sources

Dewayani, S. 2014. *Cap Go Meh*. Illus. E. Gina. Bandung: Litara.
Kurniawati, D.D., L. Sakilah, H.B. Sitio, D. Annisa, L.P. Syafri, Y.P. Pamungkas, and S.K. Marti. 2017. *Kisah dari Banggai*. Illus. K. Hanum. Jakarta: Bhuana Ilmu Populer.
Kusumawati, H. 2017. *Kisah dari Alor*. Illus. T. Lembong. Jakarta: Bhuana Ilmu Populer.
Ross, W. 2017. *Warna-warni Cerita Seru dari Raja Ampat*. Illus. M. Arum. Jakarta: Bhuana Ilmu Populer.
Siswati, Y. 2014. *Misteri Kota Tua*. Illus. I. Bayu. Jakarta: Kiddo.
Wihardja, M.M. 2018. *Kisah dari Sumba*. Illus. K. Rakhmavika and W. Haikal. Jakarta: Bhuana Ilmu Populer.

Secondary Sources

Afrianty, D. 2012. Islamic Education and Youth Extremism in Indonesia. *Journal of Policing, Intelligence and Counter Terrorism* (7)2: 134–146.
Arifin, E.N., M.S. Hasbullah, and A. Pramono. 2017. Chinese Indonesians: How Many, Who and Where? *Asian Ethnicity* 18(3): 310–329.
Aritonang, M.S. 2017. Indonesian Teachers Struggle to Promote Tolerance. *The Jakarta Post*, February 6. http://www.thejakartapost.com/news/2017/02/06/teachers-struggle-to-promote-tolerance.html.
Banks, J.A. 2009. Multicultural Education: Dimensions and Paradigms. In *The Routledge International Companion to Multicultural Education*, ed. J.A. Banks, 9–32. New York and London, UK: Routledge.
Banks, J.A. 2016. Multicultural Education: Characteristics and Goals. In *Multicultural Education: Issues and Perspectives, Eighth Edition*, ed. J.A. Banks and C.A.M. Banks, 3–23. Hoboken, NJ: Wiley.
Begler, E. 1998. Global Cultures: The First Steps Toward Understanding. *Social Education* 62(5): 272–275.
Bishop, R.S. 1990. Mirrors, Windows, and Sliding Glass Doors. *Perspectives* 6(3): ix–xi.
Bishop, R.S. 1997. Selecting Literature for a Multicultural Curriculum. In *Using Multiethnic Literature in the K-8 Classroom*, ed. V.J. Harris, 1–19. Massachusetts: Christopher-Gordon Publishers.
Bishop, R.S. 2012. Reflections on the Development of African American Children's Literature. *Journal of Children's Literature* 38(2): 5–13.
Booth, A. 2004. Africa in Asia? The Development Challenges Facing Eastern Indonesia and East Timor. *Oxford Development Studies* 32(1): 19–35.

Botelho, M.J., and M.K. Rudman. 2009. *Critical Multicultural Analysis of Children's Literature: Mirrors, Windows, and Doors.* New York and London: Routledge.

Bradford, C. 2010. Race, Ethnicity and Colonialism. In *The Routledge Companion to Children's Literature*, ed. D. Rudd, 39–50. London, UK: Routledge.

Brown, C.S., M. Tam, and F. Aboud. 2018. Ethnic Prejudice in Young Children in Indonesia: Intervention Attempts Using Multicultural Friendship Stories. *International Journal of Early Childhood* 50(1): 67–84.

Budiman, A. 2005. Portrait of the Chinese in Post-Soeharto Indonesia. In *Chinese Indonesians: Remembering, Distorting, Forgetting*, ed. T. Lindsey and H. Pausacker, 95–104. Singapore: ISEAS Publications.

Cai, M. 2002. *Multicultural Literature for Children and Young Adults: Reflections on Critical Issues.* Westport, CT: Greenwood Press.

Cai, M., and R.S. Bishop. 1994. Multicultural Literature for Children: Towards a Clarification of the Concept. In *The Need for Story: Cultural Diversity in Classroom and Community*, ed. C. Genishi and A.H. Dyson, 57–71. Urbana, IL: National Council of Teachers of English.

Christensen, N. 1999. Teaching Tolerance: A Comparative Reading of Two Danish Picture Books. *Bookbird* 37(4): 11–16.

Cole, S. 2008. *Tourism, Culture and Development: Hopes, Dreams and Realities in East Indonesia.* Clevedon, Buffalo, and Toronto: Channel View Publications.

Demers, P., and G. Moyles, eds. 1982. From Instruction to Delight: An Anthology of Children's Literature to 1850. Toronto: Oxford University Press.

Firdaus, E. 2018. The Learning of Religious Tolerance among Students in Indonesia from the Perspective of Critical Study. In *IOP Conference Series: Earth and Environmental Science* vol. 145, no. 1.

Freedman, A.L. 2000. *Political Participation and Ethnic Minorities: Chinese Overseas in Malaysia, Indonesia, and the United States.* New York and London: Routledge.

Gollnick, D.M., and P.C. Chinn. 2013. *Multicultural Education in a Pluralistic Society, Ninth Edition.* Boston, MA: Pearson.

Gopalakrishnan, A. 2011. *Multicultural Children's Literature: A Critical Issues Approach.* Thousand Oaks, CA: Sage.

Harjatanaya, T., and C.-Y. Hoon. 2020. Politics of Multicultural Education in Post-Suharto Indonesia: A Study of the Chinese Minority. *Compare: A Journal of Comparative and International Education* 50(1): 18–35.

Hasyim, S. 2011. The Council of Indonesian Ulama (Majelis Ulama Indonesia, MUI) and Religious Freedom. Irasec's Discussion Papers 12, December, Institut de Recherche surl'Asie du Sud-Est Contemporaine (Research Institute on Contemporary Southeast Asia, Irasec). Available online at http://www.irasec.com/documents/fichiers/47.pdf (accessed March 10, 2011).

Hefner, R.W. 2013. The Study of Religious Freedom in Indonesia. *The Review of Faith & International Affairs* 11(2): 18–27.

Heidhues, M.S. 2017. Studying the Chinese in Indonesia: A Long Half-Century. *SOJOURN: Journal of Social Issues in Southeast Asia* 32(3): 601–633.

Hoon, C.-Y. 2006. Assimilation, Multiculturalism, Hybridity: The Dilemmas of the Ethnic Chinese in Post-Suharto Indonesia. *Asian Ethnicity* 7(2): 149–166.

Hoon, C.-Y. 2013. Multicultural Citizenship Education in Indonesia: The Case of a Chinese Christian School. *Journal of Southeast Asian Studies* 44(3): 490–510.

Hoon, C.-Y. 2017. Putting Religion into Multiculturalism: Conceptualising Religious Multiculturalism in Indonesia. *Asian Studies Review* 41(3): 476–493.

Hunt, P. 2005. Introduction: The Expanding World of Children's Literature Studies. In *Understanding Children's Literature, Second Edition*, ed. P. Hunt, 1–14. London and New York: Routledge.

James, A., and A. James. 2012. *Key Concepts in Childhood Studies, Second Edition*. Great Britain: Sage.

Kanem, V., and A. Norris. 2018. An Examination of the Noken and Indigenous Cultural Identity: Voices of Papuan Women. *Journal of Cultural Analysis and Social Change* 3(1): 1–11.

Kuipers, J.C., and E. Yulaelawati. 2009. Religion, Ethnicity, and Identity in Indonesian Education. In *The Routledge International Companion to Multicultural Education*, ed. J.A. Banks, 449–460. New York and London, UK: Routledge.

Laksana, B.K.C., and B.E. Wood. 2018. Navigating Religious Diversity: Exploring Young People's Lived Religious Citizenship in Indonesia. *Journal of Youth Studies*. https://doi.org/10.1080/13676261.2018.1545998.

Marshall, P. 2018. The Ambiguities of Religious Freedom in Indonesia. *The Review of Faith & International Affairs* 16(1): 85–96.

Mashuri, Ali, and Esther van Leeuwen. 2017. Predicting Support for Reconciliation in Separatist Conflict. *Personality and Social Psychology Bulletin* 44(2): 173–185.

Mathis, J.B. 2015. Demonstrations of Agency in Contemporary International Children's Literature: An Exploratory Critical Content Analysis Across Personal, Social, and Cultural Dimensions. *Literacy Research and Instruction* 54(3): 206–230.

Mills, C. 2016. Heeding Rousseau's Advice: Some Ethical Reservations About Addressing Prejudice Through Children's Literature. In *Ethics and Children's Literature*, ed. C. Mills, 181–193. London and New York: Routledge.

Nurrohman. 2014. Pesantren Responses to Religious Tolerance, Pluralism and Democracy in Indonesia. *International Journal of Nusantara Islam* 2(1): 69–82.

Nurwanto and Carole M. Cusack. 2017. Addressing Multicultural Societies: Lessons from Religious Education Curriculum Policy in Indonesia and England. *Journal of Religious Education* 64(3): 157–178.

O'Sullivan, E., and A. Immel (eds.). 2017. *Imagining Sameness and Difference in Children's Literature: From the Enlightenment to the Present Day.* London, UK: Palgrave Macmillan.

Parker, L. 2010. Teaching Religious Tolerance. *Inside Indonesia.* October 4. Available online at https://www.insideindonesia.org/teaching-religious-tolerance?highlight=WyJseW4iLCJwYXJrZXIiLCJseW4gcGarya2VyIl0%3D (accessed February 15, 2019).

Parker, L. 2014. Religious Education for Peaceful Coexistence in Indonesia? *South East Asia Research* 22(4): 487–504.

Parker, L., C.Y. Hoon, and R. Raihani. 2014. Young People's Attitudes Towards Interethnic and Inter-religious Socializing, Courtship and Marriage in Indonesia. *South East Asia Research* 22(4): 467–486.

Partiningsih. 2016. Ideologi Pembangunan Orde Baru dalam Sastra Anak Balai Pustaka Tahun 80-an. *Atavisme* 19(1): 29–44.

Prinsloo, L. 2019. *Indonesian Publishing Industry: An Overview.* Presented at the London Book Fair 2019. Available online at https://www.londonbookfair.co.uk/PageFiles/379179/Laura%20Prinsloo%20presentation.pdf?v=636830784776458727 (accessed July 1, 2019).

Raihani, R. 2017. Education for Multicultural Citizens in Indonesia: Policies and Practices. *Compare: A Journal of Comparative and International Education* 48(6): 992–1009.

Ramdarshan Bold, M. 2019. *Inclusive Young Adult Fiction: Authors of Colour in the United Kingdom.* Switzerland: Palgrave Pivot.

Ramsey, P.G. 2009. Multicultural Education for Young Children. In *The Routledge International Companion to Multicultural Education*, ed. J.A. Banks, 223–235. New York and London, UK: Routledge.

Sai, S.-M., and C.-Y. Hoon. 2013. Introduction: A Critical Reassessment of Chinese Indonesian Studies. In *Chinese Indonesians Reassessed: History, Religion and Belonging*, ed. S.-M. Sai and C.-Y. Hoon, 1–26. London: Routledge.

Sapiie, M.A. 2017. Constitutional Court Rules Indigenous Faiths 'Acknowledged' by State. *The Jakarta Post*, November 7. Available online at https://www.thejakartapost.com/news/2017/11/07/constitutional-court-rules-indigenous-faiths-acknowledged-by-state.html (accessed June 24, 2019).

Short, K. 2012. Children's Agency for Taking Social Action. *Bookbird* 50(4): 41–50.

Sirry, M. 2013. Fatwas and Their Controversy: The Case of the Council of Indonesian Ulama (MUI). *Journal of Southeast Asian Studies* 44(1): 100–117.

Sterkens, C., and M. Yusuf. 2015. Preferences for Religious Education and Inter-group Attitudes Among Indonesian Students. *Journal of Empirical Theology* 28(1): 49–89.

Tong, C.K. 2010. *Identity and Ethnic Relations in Southeast Asia: Racializing Chineseness.* London and New York: Springer.

Wiwoho, B. 2017. Komnas PA Khawatir, Anak Mengolok Teman dengan Sebutan Kafir. *CNN Indonesia*, May 12. Available online at http://www. cnnindonesia.com/nasional/20170512190024-20-214439/komnas-pa-khawatir-anak-mengolok-teman-dengan-sebutan-kafir/ (accessed June 25, 2019).

Wooldridge, N. 2001. Tensions and Ambiguities in Critical Literacy. In *Negotiating Critical Literacies in Classrooms*, ed. B. Comber and A. Simpson, 259–270. Mahwah, NJ: Lawrence Erlbaum Associates.

Yokota, J. 1993. Issues in Selecting Multicultural Children's Literature. *Language Arts* 70(3): 156–167.

CHAPTER 13

The Paradox of the Filipino Child: Realistic Philippine Children's Stories (1990–2018)

Lalaine F. Yanilla Aquino

Most meanings are social; the values, beliefs, shared knowledge, pre-occupations, and ideologies of a community are coded in its language (Fowler 1996), be it oral or written, as in the case also of the language used in children's literature. Because writers cannot escape their milieu, the language style that they use embodies a particular view of the world, which comprises its activities, states, and values (Fowler 1996). It is this view of the world that this chapter aims to determine by analysing, inter-preting, and evaluating the language used in Philippine children's stories. Through close reference to Critical Stylistics, a contextualised linguistic approach to literature that aims to unmask the ideology found in written works, this chapter aims to assess how the Filipino child is represented in Philippine children's stories published between 1990 and 2018. In doing so, it will attempt to answer the following specific questions:

L. F. Yanilla Aquino (✉)
Department of English and Comparative Literature,
University of the Philippines, Quezon City, Philippines
e-mail: lyaquino@up.edu.ph

© The Author(s) 2020   289
B. Wilson and S. P. Gabriel (eds.), *Asian Children's Literature
and Film in a Global Age*, Asia-Pacific and Literature in English,
https://doi.org/10.1007/978-981-15-2631-2_13

1. What content words—nouns, adjectives, verbs—are used in the narratives to identify, describe, and characterise the child protagonist?
2. What kind of language do adult characters use with regard to the child protagonists and how does such language reflect the adults' view of the child?
3. What kind of language does a child protagonist use with the adults and how does such language reflect the child's view of her/himself?
4. What does the kind of language used in the stories reflect with regard to issues such as the child's agency, the protection of the child's rights, the child's role as a member of the community, and the child's challenges and opportunities in the global age?

THE STORIES

Selection Criteria

A total of 35 stories were selected based on the following criteria: the story is in a picture storybook format and is published from 1990 to 2018; it has been written by a Filipino and published in the Philippines; it tells a story in the realistic mode (whether contemporary or historical); it has a Filipino child as protagonist; and the child protagonist deals with a specific issue or challenge. The choice of the period of publication between 1990 and 2018 is to cover the three decades during which Philippine children's literature had become well established not just as a viable business concern (Paterno 1994) but also as a recognised genre and legitimate field of study. Most notably, the period covers the decades *after* these significant events in the history of children's literature in the Philippines: the establishment of the Philippine Board on Books for Young People (PBBY) in 1983 and the production of the Filipino version of the popular American children's television programme *Sesame Street*, called *Batibot*, also in 1983—a Filipino show which helped develop an audience and a market for children's literature in the country (Paterno 1994); the sponsorship of a workshop on writing for children by the Creative Writing Center of the University of the Philippines (UP) in 1983 and 1989; the opening of two new categories in the prestigious annual Palanca Awards for Literature—"Short Story for Children" in 1989 and "Poetry for Children" in 2009; and the offering of Children's Literature and Writing for Children as courses in various Philippine universities at the undergraduate and graduate levels, most notably in UP, which offers these courses in three colleges—College of Arts and Letters, College of Education, and Institute of Library Science.

Though I do not include an analysis of the illustrations (because that would require a different framework and a much longer essay), the picture storybook format was chosen because it usually targets younger children and therefore, usually also has protagonists who are approximately of the same age as the target readers. As indicated on the covers of the selected books, the age of the target readers ranges from three to eleven years old. Several books also indicate ages eleven and above as target readers. This study adopts the UNICEF definition of a child as a person who is under eighteen years of age (UNICEF, n.d.).

Why focus on stories that target young readers? As this study aims to unmask ideology related to the representation and treatment of children in a community, it is important to focus on the representation of the young child—the child who is still in her or his formative years—that is, the period crucial in the cognitive, social, emotional, and physical development of a human being. According to UNICEF (2005):

> Childhood is the time for children to **be in school and at play**, to **grow strong and confident with the love and encouragement of their family** and an **extended community of caring adults**. It is a precious time in which **children should live free from fear, safe from violence and protected from abuse and exploitation**. As such, childhood means much more than just the space between birth and the attainment of adulthood. It refers to the state and condition of a child's life, to the quality of those years. (Emphasis mine)

With regard to this, it is important to determine the kind of Filipino childhood represented and reflected in realistic stories. Since literature is an instrument of socialisation, this study also intends to find out what the stories have to say on how a child should behave in society and what representations of the "good child" the stories foreground.

Another practical reason for choosing the picture storybook format is because this is the format to which Filipino children—even those in the public schools and the remote areas of the country—will most probably have some kind of access, and therefore, exposure. With the Department of Education (DepEd) establishing library hubs in every school division in 2009 (Department of Education 2009), thousands of picture story-books were provided to public schools, with some divisions that have more than 800 schools receiving more than 50,000 picture storybooks (Department of Education, n.d.). Moreover, the shift to the K to 12 Basic Education Curriculum in 2012 paved the way for the implementation of the Mother Tongue-Based Multilingual Education (MTB-MLE), which also encouraged the use of literature-based literacy instruction, especially in kindergarten and the early grades, and therefore the use of stories written not only in the official languages of the Philippines (Filipino and English) but also in the major regional languages such as Tagalog, Kapampangan, Pangasinense, Iloko, Bikol, Cebuano, Hiligaynon, Waray, Tausug, Maguindanaoan, Maranao, Chabacano, Ivatan, Sambal, Akianon, Kinaray-a, Yakan, and Sinurigaonon (Department of Education 2012).

Genre and Sub-genre

My analysis focuses on realistic stories—both contemporary realistic sto-ries and historical realistic stories—because they portray a possible and more believable world that is usually centred on problems and issues faced by children in contemporary or historical times (Lukens et al. 2013). The target readers, therefore, would most probably be more familiar with the characters, conflicts, and settings of these stories; likewise, they will most probably be able to identify better with the child protagonists whose con-cerns and challenges are similar to theirs.

Of the 35 stories selected, 31 (89%) are contemporary realistic fiction while four (11%) are historical realistic fiction. Realistic fiction is not fantasy nor do the stories literally recount real life (that would be considered biographies or informational books); some realistic stories may be improbable but there are no details that are impossible (Temple et al. 2006). Both contemporary and historical realistic stories are valuable because they allow their target readers, the children, to develop empathy for other people and see life experiences beyond their own. The difference is that historical realistic fiction is often set in a time that, from the point of view of a child, is far removed from today (Temple et al. 2006); thus, adults may consider a story set during the EDSA People Power Revolution of 1986—the peaceful revolution that ousted the dictator Ferdinand Marcos—as still contemporary, but it is already historical as far as the young child is concerned.

Language

More than half of the 35 stories (51%, $n = 18$) were written originally in Filipino and published with an English translation. Ten of the stories (28%) were published only in Filipino. Five stories (14%) were written in English and published with a Filipino translation. Only one story—*Marvino's League of Superheroes* (Rival-Cosico 2014)—was written and published in English without any translation. Another story, *Water Lilies for Marawi* (Eusebio-Abad 2018), was originally written in English and published with a Maranao translation. A total of 33 stories (94%), therefore, were published in Filipino either as an original language or as a translation.

It is also important to note that this use of Filipino as a language in writing Philippine children's stories is quite a welcome development considering that in a study done on Philippine children's stories (Yanilla 1991), 71% of 625 stories published from 1960 to 1989 were written in English. The same study found that from 1980 to 1989, there was a big increase in the number of stories written in Filipino: 48% compared to only 6% in the previous decade. That trend in the 1980s must have continued in the decades that followed, judging by the number of realistic stories written originally in Filipino or published with a Filipino translation from 1990 to 2018. The language used in writing stories for Filipino children is one of the issues faced by writers and publishers of children's literature in the Philippines. Like other members of the Association of Southeast Asian Nations (ASEAN), the Philippines was colonised by a western country (the United States of America) and has adopted the language of the colonisers —i.e., English, as one of its official languages. This is the reason why the use of English, either as a medium of instruction (MOI) or as a language for writing Philippine literature, has remained a contentious issue (for more details on this, please see Yanilla Aquino 2012).

Categories

A story is an account of "what happened to particular people—and of what it was like for them to experience what happened—in particular circumstances and with specific consequences" (Herman 2007, 3). This definition is the basis used to categorise the stories selected for this study: the categorisation focused on what happened and *what* the nature of that event is—whether it was borne out of personal/family issues or issues that are mainly social, sociocultural, or sociopolitical. Thus, the 35 stories are grouped based on the major issues and challenges faced by the child protagonist. Some issues overlap, so the categorisation is based on the main or most prominent issue found in the story.

Seven stories have protagonists that deal with illness, developmental disorder, congenital disorder, or physical disability—either theirs or that of someone close to them. In *Two Friends, One World* (Sunico 1990) and *Sampu Pataas, Sampu Pababa* (*Ten Going Up, Ten Going Down*) (Molina 2007) one of the child protagonists (male in both stories) is blind while the other one—his friend (female in both stories)—serves as his "eyes" and guide; in *Ang Kuya ni Karina* (*The Elder Brother of Karina*) (De Los Angeles-Bautista 1996) the child protagonist has a deaf brother; in *Federico* (Evasco 1997) and *Big Brother* (Chong 2008) the child protagonist is close to someone with Down's Syndrome; in *Ang Pambihirang Buhok ni Raquel* (*Raquel's Amazing Hair*) (Gatmaitan 1999) the child protagonist has leukaemia; and in *There's a Duwende in My Brother's Soup* (Saguisag 2001) the child protagonist's younger brother has autism.

Eleven stories have child protagonists that deal with family issues. In *Ang Paaralan ni Fuwan* (*Fuwan's School*) (Anonuevo 2002) Fuwan does not want to miss her classes, but her father insists that she stay and work on their farm; in *May Kapatid na si Mungan* (*Mungan Already Has a Sibling*) (Del Castillo 2002) Mungan feels jealous of the baby in her mother's womb; in *Uuwi na ang Nanay Kong si Darna* (*My Mother Darna Is Coming Home*) (Samar 2002) the child protagonist problematises his first meeting with his mother, an Overseas Filipino Worker (OFW) who left him when he was still a baby; in *Yaya Niya, Nanay Ko* (*Her Nanny, My Mother*) (Remigio 2015) the child protagonist wishes that her mother would take care of her instead of the daughter of a rich family; in *Sandosenang Kuya* (*A Dozen Elder Brothers*) (Molina 2003) the child protagonist tells the story of how happy he is with his family in the orphanage—his twelve orphan elder brothers—only to realise that his elder brothers are leaving one after the other, as they come of age; in *Papa's House, Mama's House* (Patindol 2004) the child protagonists wonder why their parents cannot just live in one house like other families; in *Ang Lihim ni Lea* (*Lea's Secret*) (Rivera 2007) the child protagonist believes herself to have the power to go through walls, which turns out to be her way of coping with the sexual abuse she suffers from her own father while her OFW mother works abroad; in *Anong Gupit Natin Ngayon?* (*What Is Our Haircut for Today?*) (Molina 2012) the child protagonist complains about his barber-father never asking him what kind of haircut he wants when the father does so with all his other clients; in *Mantsa* (*Stain*) (Rivera 2013) the child protagonist hides the stains that appear on his skin every time he is verbally abused by his parents and other adults; in *Salusalo para kay Kuya* (*A Party for Elder Brother*) (Tinio 2015) the child protagonist tries to cope with the death of his elder brother; and in *Filemon Mamon* (Bellen 2004) Filemon is obese because his own parents encourage him to eat too much, and his obesity keeps him from realising his dream of playing the role of the muscular Philippine hero in the school play.

Seven stories have child protagonists that deal with social issues. In *BRU-HA-HA-HA-HA-HA ... BRU-HI-HI-HI-HI-HI* (Remigio 1995) the little girl realises that the woman she thought of as witch—because of "clues" she learned from people around her—is actually just an old woman who longs for care and companionship; in *Sampung Magkakaibigan* (*Ten Friends*) (Canon 2008) little Karlo realises that bullying his friends results in him being alone and lonely; in *Ang Ikaklit sa Aming Hardin* (*The Sunflower in Our Garden*) (Neri 2012) the little girl gets bullied in school simply because she has two mothers, but she stands her ground and makes her classmates know that there is nothing wrong nor shameful about having two mothers and not having a father; in *The White Shoes* (Chong 2013) poverty prevents a little girl from buying white shoes for the recognition programme—so she merely paints white an old pair of black shoes, but it rains during the programme and her white shoes gradually turn to black, much to her embarrassment; in *Ang Bonggang-bonggang Batang Beki* (*The Fierce and Fabulous Boy in Pink*) (Garlitos 2013) Adel, who is biologically male but very feminine in his mannerisms, finds acceptance within his family, but not with other people until he is able to prove that he has his own brand of courage; in *Marvino's League of Superheroes* (Rival-Cosico 2014) Marvino's poor family cannot afford the entrance fee to an art-toy museum until he befriends an old man to whom he shows his drawings, as a result of which the old man makes use of Marvino's drawings of Philippine heroes as a basis for his sculptures and gives him permission to enter the museum for free; and in *Ang Munting Opisina ni Nanay* (*Nanay's Little Office*) (Gonzales 2015) the child protagonist wonders why his mother does not dress like other office people nor has her own table and computer, until he goes to the office with her and discovers that she is an elevator operator.

Six stories have child protagonists that deal with sociocultural issues. In *Si Diwayen, Noong bago Dumating ang mga Espanyol* (*Diwayen before the Spaniards Came*) (Rivera 2001) Diwayen's village experiences famine and her family has no recourse but to have her serve as a slave in a rich family of the neighbouring village to pay their debts, but Diwayen is good and brave and saves the princess from danger, so Diwayen is given her freedom as a reward; in *Si Juanito Noong Panahon ng mga Amerikano* (*Juanito During the American Period*) (Rivera 2001) Juanito is recruited to work in Hawaii as a plantation worker, and though he misses his family, he opts to renew his contract to be able to send money back home; in *Si Segunda, Noong Panahon ng mga Espanyol* (*Segunda During the Spanish Times*) (Rivera 2001) Segunda wants to learn how to read and write like the son of a rich family, so she makes a bet with him on the condition that if she wins, he will teach her everything that his teacher is teaching him— which he does after he loses the bet; in *Ang Ibay ni Miana* (*Miana's Friend*) (Popa 2002) Miana is an Agta girl who is given the opportunity to go to school, but has to leave her family and stay with an ibay—a non-Agta friend—to be near her school; in *Bahay ng Marami't Masasayang Tinig* (*House of Many Happy Voices*) (Uson 2002) Palasia, a Badjaw girl who leaves her community near the sea to beg for food and money in the city, where she is almost always in danger, finds a house of many happy voices—a school where Palasia and her friend are warmly welcomed by the teacher; and in *Gustong Mag-aral ni Sula* (*Sula Wants to Study*) (Lemlunay 2002) Sula is a young Tiboli girl who wants to learn how to read and write, but wonders who will teach her when she has never seen her parents do these activities, until her mother comes home to tell Sula and her father that she has been attending an adult literacy school and she will also be teaching Sula what she learns.

Four stories have child protagonists that deal with sociopolitical issues. In *Si Jhun-Jhun, Noong Bago Ideklara ang Batas Militar* (*Jhun-Jhun Before the Declaration of Martial Law*) (Rivera 2001) Jhun-Jhun misses the past when his elder brother would spend time with him, so he follows his elder brother to find out what keeps him away from Jhun-Jhun, only to discover that his brother is working in a shoe factory whose workers are on strike and who have joined a rally against the dictator Marcos—and when the rally is violently dispersed by the military, Jhun-Jhun's brother is nowhere to be found; in *Si Pitong, Noong Panahon ng mga Hapon* (*Pitong during the Time of the Japanese*) (Rivera 2001) Pitong and his family must leave their house in the province after almost everything has been destroyed by the Japanese—they stay with his aunt in the city where they try to make do with whatever food and other necessities that can be found around them and where they personally experience the cruelty of the Japanese; in *Isang Harding Papel* (*A Garden of Paper Flowers*) (Rivera 2014) Jenny's mother is a political detainee during martial law, and she is seldom allowed to be visited by Jenny and Jenny's grandmother; each time Jenny visits, her mother gives her a flower made of old newspapers until Jenny's room becomes like a garden full of paper flowers; and in *Water Lilies for Marawi* (Eusebio-Abad 2018) ten-year-old Orak escapes from the terrorists who have invaded Marawi City and want to recruit him, by hiding for five days among the water lilies in Lake Lanao until government soldiers find him and take him to a hospital.

CRITICAL STYLISTICS

Stylistics can be defined as the use of the tools of linguistics in the study, analysis, interpretation, and evaluation of literature; it can also be defined as the study of style in language (Verdonk 2002). Style used to be seen as an inherent property of a literary text (Jakobson 1996), but it is now seen more as "a potential which is actualized in a (real) reader's mind, the product of a dialogic interaction between the author, the author's context of production, the text, the reader and the reader's context of reception— where context includes all sorts of sociohistorical, cultural, and intertextual factors" (Weber 1996, 3). Critical Stylistics is contextualised stylistics. As such:

> Critical stylisticians thus reject the mimetic view of language as a value-free transparent medium reflecting reality. They deny the possibility of a neutral representation of reality, and consequently see their own role as being demystificatory: to unmask ideologies, to denaturalize common-sense assumptions and, ultimately, to enable and empower readers. (Weber 1996, 4)

In using Critical Stylistics as a framework for analysing, interpreting, and evaluating the 35 realistic stories for children, I will attempt to determine the "common-sense" and naturalised notions of what a Filipino child is and the ideology regarding what it means to be a Filipino child in contemporary society. Ideology here is defined as "a body of norms and ideas that appear natural as a result of their continuous and mostly tacit promotion by the dominant forces in society" (Herman and Vervaeck 2007). In the children's lives, the dominant forces can well be the adults around them.

Since the Critical Stylistics method uses the tools of linguistics and focuses on particular linguistic units, this study focuses on the content words (nouns, adjectives, verbs, adverbs) that are used to characterise the child protagonists as well as the utterances addressed to them or made by them. Literature—the text that tells the narrative—is viewed as language itself (i.e., language is neither an object nor a medium of literature) and as a communicative interaction between the producer (the writer) and consumer (the reader) within relevant social contexts and, as such, the stories are a social basis of the formation of meanings (Fowler 1996). In other words, "all language use is value-laden" (Birch 1996), particularly the language used in stories for children.

THE CHILD PROTAGONIST

Identity Markers: Nouns and Pronouns

In order to determine the representation of the Filipino child in the Philippine realistic stories, it is imperative that the analysis focus on the child character. A character may be defined as a "story world participant" who is a part of the narrative domain rather than the narration domain and who is introduced in the text by means of referring expressions such as proper names, definite descriptions, and personal pronouns (Margolin 2007). An analysis of how the child character was introduced in the selected stories yielded these results: in 23 stories (66%), the child protagonist was introduced using a proper name; in the rest of the stories ($n = 12$, 34%)—most of which were told from the first-person point of view—the child protagonist was introduced using personal pronouns such as in the first sentence of *BRU-HA-HA-HA-HA-HA ... BRU-HI-HI-HI-HI-HI* (Remigio 1995): "Maniwala ka man o hindi, may kapitbahay akong bruha" ("Believe it or not, I have a witch neighbour). In this example, the first sentence seems to introduce the adult character (i.e., Mrs. Magalit, the neighbour-witch), but more importantly, it introduces the child character—the little girl—who tells the story from her point of view and introduces herself to the reader through the personal nominative pronoun *ako* (*I*).

Some of the proper names used to introduce the child protagonist do not only differentiate her/him from other characters in the story but also signify the community and the sociohistorical time to which s/he belongs; for instance, the name *Segunda* (Rivera, *Si Segunda, Noong Panahon ng mga Espanyol* 2001) is a Spanish word which literally means "second"—it identifies the child character as belonging to the time when the Philippines was still a colony of Spain (because *Segunda* is a Spanish word and a name that is very seldom used for Filipino girls today as it is already considered "old fashioned") and it likewise signifies the historical period when girls were considered *second*-class citizens and were not encouraged to study nor to pursue a career.

Aside from proper nouns, the child protagonists are also characterised using common nouns such as *anak* (daughter/son) (39% of the stories) or identified as *bata/musmos* (child) (22% of the stories) in the narration. These words foreground not only the age difference between child and adult but also the power relationship between them. A number of stories (22%) also made use of the child's cultural identity to refer to her/him: *Agta, Badjaw, Bontoc, Manobo, Maranaw, Tiboli*, which are words that refer to some indigenous people in the Philippines. A number of stories ($n = 9$, 25%) refer to the child protagonist as a *friend, playmate, classmate,* or *cousin*. Some stories ($n = 4$, 11%) identify the child protagonist as a member of a social group or as belonging to a particular social status: *alipin* (slave), *bakwit* (someone who evacuates, especially during the time of war), *binukot* (a girl who is secluded with the expectation that the seclusion will result in higher value placed on the individual by marital suitors in the future [Clark 2017]), *duma-an* (resident labourers in sugar plantations as opposed to the *sacada,* who is the migratory sugar plantation worker), and *gaon* or *pansangla* (a child who is temporarily given as a slave-mortgage to a rich family until her/his own family is able to pay their debts). Thus, the nouns used to refer to the child characterise her/him not only as a unique individual but also as a member of a family and the larger community, who may be expected to make some personal sacrifices, such as being a child labourer and serving as a mortgage for unpaid debts in order to help the other members.

Character Construction

Character construction is a process of continuous mental activity (Margolin 2007); thus, writers have to devise ways by which the target readers will recognise and distinguish a particular character. One such way is categorisation which can be biological (age, gender), cultural (ethnic), social, and behavioural or psychological.

Words that categorise the child protagonists biologically are used in the stories: the age of the main character is clearly given in nine stories and the gender is clearly indicated either through the name of the child protagonist or a word such as *iho* or *iha* (son or daughter) that is used to address the child. With the exception of one story—*Papa's House, Mama's House*—all stories clearly have a biologically female ($n = 20$, 56%) or male ($n = 23$, 64%) protagonist ($n > 35$ here, because some stories have both male and female protagonists). In the case of *Papa's House, Mama's House* (Patindol 2004), the child protagonist was the narrator who used only the pronoun *I* and the interlocutors that this *I* interacted with did not use any noun to address this narrator.

When the age or gender of the child protagonist is given, this information usually foregrounds the issue/challenge that the character faces. For instance, Orak in *Water Lilies for Marawi* (Eusebio-Abad 2018) is described as a ten-year-old Muslim boy and because he is already ten years old, he is deemed "old enough" to be recruited by the terrorists who invade the city of Marawi. On the other hand, Adel in *Ang Bonggangbonggang Batang Beki* (Garlitos 2013) is a biologically male child, so this is an issue in the story because his favourite colour is pink, he is very effeminate in his mannerisms, and he likes to stay at home doing household chores.

Words that categorise the child protagonist culturally or ethnically are used in eight stories. These are words that identify the child as belonging to a particular faith (*Muslim*) or an indigenous community (*Agta, Badjaw, Bontoc, Manobo, Maranao, Tiboli*). Such words serve not only to characterise the child protagonist but also to signal the complications in the plot. For instance, in the first paragraph of *Bahay ng Marami't Masasayang Tinig* (*House of Many Happy Voices*) (Uson 2002), the child protagonist is in a market with another Badjaw when somebody shouts, "Thief!" Though she and the other Badjaw are not guilty of theft and are there to beg for food and money, they run away for fear of being implicated. This occurs because the Badjaws are known to be "Sea Gypsies" and they actually live in the coastal areas of some parts of Mindanao but in the story, they are displaced and find themselves in the city, which poses danger to indigenous people. Thus, the mention of *Badjaw* in that setting identifies the child protagonist as outside of her natural element and therefore, experiencing difficulties such as poverty and hunger because of this.

The social categorisation of the child protagonists is indicated not just through the writers' use of nouns such as *alipin* (slave) and *duma-an* (resident labourers in sugar plantations), but through their use of descriptive phrases and clauses such as in these examples: *Ni hindi pinansin ni Miss Tabora ang marusing nilang damit* (Miss Nabora did not even pay attention to their dirty clothes) (Uson 2002), *Bitbit naman ng kaniyang amay ang kaniyang damit sa isang lumang bag* (His father is carrying her clothes in an old bag) (Popa 2002), *Kaya nagtitiis siyang lumakad nang ilang kilometro, nag-iisa, araw-araw papasok sa paaralan at pauwi sa kanilang bahay* (The reason she endures walking several kilometres, alone, every day to school and to their house) (Anonuevo 2002). Such descriptions foreground the poverty of the child protagonist and her/his family.

The behavioural/psychological categorisation of the child protagonist is also done through the use of descriptive words, phrases, and clauses. The descriptions can be further classified into those of positive behaviour ($n = 48$, 37%), negative behaviour ($n = 47$, 36%), and neutral behaviour ($n = 35$, 27%). Some examples of descriptions that denote positive behaviour are *brave, calm, happy, content, galing mag Ingles* (good at speaking English), *mas madaling matuto ang mga bata* (children learn things more easily), *masaya kami sa eskwelahan* (we are happy in school), and *pambihirang talento* (amazing talent). Some examples of descriptions that denote negative behaviour are *pinakamalikot* (most unruly), *pinaka-makulit* (most troublesome), *tila asong bahag ang buntot na kumaripas* (darted away like a cowardly dog), *nahiya akong magpakita kay Nanay* (I was too shy to show myself to Mother), *tila nayuping lata ang nguso niya* (his mouth is like a crushed tin can), and *walang oras magpahinga at maglibang* (no time to rest or enjoy things). Some descriptions that are rather neutral are *mini-triangle* and *maxi-circle* (pertaining to the shape of the face), *different, mahilig magbisikleta* (enjoys riding a bike), *maraming tanong ang aking kaibigan* (my friend has a lot of questions), *pink ang kulay na nagbibigay inspirasyon sa kanyang mga ideya* (pink is the colour that inspires his ideas), *dalawa ang aking nanay* (I have two mothers), and *gustong gumuhit ng mga tao* (likes drawing human figures). Based on the quantitative data, there is a balance between the positive and the negative among the 35 stories as to the behavioural/psychological descriptions of the child protagonists. The qualitative data, on the other hand, foreground a good mix of the positive qualities, strengths, talents, and abilities of the child protagonist on the one hand, and, conversely, children's behaviour and characteristics that are usually frowned upon or discouraged by adults in a community, such as being unruly and troublesome.

Interaction with Adults

To have a more holistic view of the representation of the Filipino child in these realistic stories, it is not enough to focus on the characterisation of the child as seen in the nouns, pronouns, and descriptive sentences that refer to the child protagonist. It is equally important to analyse and evaluate the child's interaction with the adult characters. Thus, the adults' utterances addressed to the child and the child's utterances addressed to the adults will serve as the linguistic data at this point.

Discourses within a narrative are in constant dialogue with social and ideological discourses (Thomas 2007). Thus, specific utterances made by a character to another character can reflect the central relationship between them and signify power relations, cultural differences, age difference, and so forth. An analysis of the pattern of utterances by adults addressed to the child protagonists in the 35 stories yielded the following results: there are around 100 utterances addressed to the child protagonists and these can be categorised as giving information or explanation (32%), expressing affection or concern (15%), praising the child or giving encouragement (13%), telling the child of her/his responsibility (12%), verbal abuse (7%), expressing amazement (6%), reminder (6%), direct command (5%), asking a question (3%), and apologising (1%). It should be noted that the quantitative data is very telling of how adults view children—for instance, almost one-third of the total utterances addressed to children provide some kind of information or explanation to help children understand certain things, such as in these examples: (1) *ganoon talaga, anak, naghahanapbuhay na kasi ang kuya mo* (that's the way things are, my son, because your elder brother is already working), (2) *hindi mahalaga kung babae o lalaki ang nag-aalaga ng mga (punla)* (it is not important if it is a woman or a man who takes care of [the seedling]), (3) *there's nothing wrong about wanting to have your favourite soup*, (4) *may pinipindot-pindot naman akong numero sa loob ng aking munting opisina* (there are also numbers that I press in my office). The first example is meant to explain to Jhun-Jhun why his brother no longer spends time with him; the second is addressed to Ikaklit, the girl with homosexual mothers, and is meant to tell her that there is nothing wrong about having two mothers as long as they take good care of her; the third is addressed to a girl whose young brother has autism, and is meant to make her see that there is nothing wrong with her brother wanting to have the same soup every day; the fourth is addressed to Bong, the little boy whose mother works as an elevator operator and whom he thinks is not like other people who work in an office. Such examples foreground that adults view a child as wanting in knowledge and information—thus, the need to explain things to her/him.

The quantitative data show that there is a good balance among utterances in which adults express their affection to the child protagonist, praise the child for something good that the child does, and tell the child what her/his responsibilities are. This is a "standard" upbringing for most Filipino children—they are given much love and encouragement, but they are also trained to be a responsible member of the family and of the community. These examples illustrate such upbringing: affection—(1) *Mag-ingat ka, Anak. Mahal kita.* (Take care, my son. I love you); (2) *di na beybi ang anak ko* (my son is no longer a baby); (3) *para na rin ito sa iyong kaligtasan, anak* (this is also for your own safety, my son); praise and encouragement—(1) *You are smart and despite all the work you do at home, you made it to the honor roll;* (2) *Anak, there is nothing to be ashamed of; there is everything to be proud of!;* (3) *then you must be good because people admire your work;* responsibility—(1) *try to help your brother with his assignments;* (2) *magsisilbi ka muna sa tahanan ni Datu Bulawan* (serve first in the home of Datu Bulawan); (3) *Tumulong ka sa pagdadamo sa bukid* (help in weeding the farm); (4) *mag-aral ka mabuti* (study well). Such examples foreground how adults view the child—s/he is an individual in need and deserving of love and encouragement, but also one who has to be trained to be a responsible and productive member of the family and the community. Such views are further reinforced by the examples of reminders and direct commands: *Maiksi ang kumot, Agapito. Kailangan ay matuto kang mamaluktot.* (The blanket is short, Agapito. You need to learn how to adapt.); *Importante ang mga dasal!* (Prayers are important!); *Huwag ka masyadong makulit ha* (Don't be too troublesome); *Now go to bed; Bumaba ka diyan!* (Come down!). A "good child", therefore, does her/his share in making the home environment and the larger community a better place to live in, follows the rules, and obeys the adults. These examples and the previous ones as well, give the impression that the adults are "always right". No wonder then that there is just one instance in which someone apologises to a child: "pasensiya ka na kung di man lang kita maipagtanggol minsan" (I am sorry if I am not even able to defend you sometimes).

The utterances children make to adults somehow match the utterances adults make to children. As mentioned earlier, a big percentage of the adults' utterances are meant to give the child some kind of information. Looking at the utterances made by children, a big percentage (34% of 97 utterances) asks questions such as *Bakit po kayo pinakulong?* (Why were you imprisoned?), *Hanggang kailan po ako doon, Ina?* (Until when will I stay there, Mother?), and *Bakit po wala akong tatay?* (Why don't I have a father?)—thus, if most of the child's utterances addressed to adults are questions, the adults are expected to answer or give some information. There is, however, a twist to this. In several instances, the adults do not give a direct answer as if expecting the child to "read between the lines". For example, in *Papa's House, Mama's House* (Patindol 2004) when the child protagonist asks the parents why could they not live in the same house like other families, the father replies, "Do you think trains and planes can travel together?" while the mother, on a separate occasion answers, "Let's mix white and yellow together. What color do you get?" In *Isang Harding Papel* (Rivera 2014), when the child protagonist asks her mother, a political detainee, "Bakit po kayo ipinakulong?" (Why were you imprisoned?), the mother jokingly says, "Paano pag may rally, lahat ng pinapalabas naming mga dula sa kalye, laban kay Marcos. Hindi niya siguro nagustuhan!" (When there is a rally, all the plays we perform on the street are against Marcos. Maybe he did not like them.) While the grandmother says, "Ang sabihin mo, pakalat-kalat kasi sa kalsada yang nanay mo, kaya napasama sa mga winalis" (The truth is, your mother was loitering on the street, so she was swept away like the others.). In *Ang Ikaklit sa Aming Hardin* (Neri 2012), the homosexual mothers answer the question of the child protagonist by using a metaphor—that of taking care of a seedling. In *Uuwi na ang Nanay Kong si Darna*, the father tells the child protagonist that his mother is a real superhero whose services are needed by the people in Hong Kong—this is to justify all those years when the mother was away from home and from her own child. Why do adult characters (like adults in real life), when asked by children about serious issues such as the separation of parents, the imprisonment of a parent, or the homosexual relationship of parents, respond by offering another question, a joke, or a metaphor as a reply? Is it because they do not trust the child's comprehension enough or is it because they want to protect the child from the harsh realities in life?

Interestingly, in nine (26%) of the 35 stories the child protagonist does not have any speaking line addressed to adults; two protagonists (Karina and Sula) do not speak at all in the story while the other child protagonists speak only to other children and never to adults. Thus, the representation of a child in these realistic stories can be gleaned not only from the linguistic evidence that is there but also the linguistic evidence that is *not* there in the narrative. It is curious how these stories supposedly focus on the child protagonist, but the child's voice is literally seldom heard by the adult characters. As for the other utterances, they are mostly a few examples of greetings ($n = 4$) such as "Magandang umaga po, Miss Pilar" (Good morning, Miss Pilar), short replies ($n = 6$) to questions such as "Hindi ko po napansin ang pinto" (I did not notice the door), complaints ($n = 2$) such as "This is too tight and short!", jokes ($n = 2$) such as "Pero, nanang, bata pa po ako. Hindi pa ako pupunta sa langit!" (But mother, I am still too young. I am not yet going to heaven!), expression of affection ($n = 4$) such as "Lab yu, Nay" (I love you, Mom), stating one's ability ($n = 4$) such as "Maari na akong magtanim sa hardin!" (I can now plant in the garden!), refusal ($n = 5$) to do something such as "Nay, ayoko na po pumasok sa eskwela" (Mother, I don't want to go to school anymore), and apology ($n = 3$) such as "Sorry po, Nay" (I am sorry, Mother). It should be noted here that the child protagonists have three instances of apology compared to only one made by the adult characters, thus showing the power relation between the child and the adult, in which the child more readily apologises.

The Representation of the Filipino Child

The linguistic evidence in the stories examined shows the paradox that is the Filipino child. On one hand, adults believe in her/his ability to do things, so s/he is given relatively heavy responsibilities such as caring for a sick father, taking care of an older brother with autism, weeding the farm, taking care of a blind friend, serving as payment for a family debt, and earning a living for the family as a child labourer. But on the other hand, the child's questions are sometimes not taken seriously, s/he is viewed as needing much protection from the harsh realities of life, and is often just seen rather than provided with a realistic voice.

Part of the paradox that is the life of the Filipino child is that the very people—the adults—who are supposed to protect her/him can be the same people who do her/him harm or cause her/him grief. It is rather difficult for the Filipino child to believe adults when they say that they do things for her/his sake, as may be evidenced by the depictions of the working mothers in *Uuwi na ang Nanay Kong si Darna*; *Yaya Niya, Nanay Ko*; and *Ang Lihim ni Lea*, who have unwittingly caused their children grief. As guiding points in these particular narratives, when the adults closest to the child such as the fathers in *Ang Paaralan ni Fuwan* and *Ang Lihim ni Lea* fail to give her/him the protection and nurturing s/he needs, other significant adults such as her/his teachers step into offer help.

It is also part of the paradox of a Filipino child's social and familial existence that though s/he is supposed to be the first to be protected when misfortunes, calamities, and tragedies happen in the family and in the community, such as famine in the village, terrorism in the city, or the death of a family member, s/he is also the first to be "sacrificed" because s/he has the least power in the family and the community.

Part of the paradox of the average Filipino children is that though their common life circumstances, which may potentially include poverty, war, and/or disabilities, prevent them from truly enjoying their supposed rights as children (to play and enjoy recreation, to live in a peaceful community, to be given enough education to improve themselves, and to be protected from abuse and violence) they still manage to be resilient, to show their own kind of courage, and to rise above the circumstances that tend to pull them down.

The research undertaken on this set of Philippine realistic stories for children has allowed a number of observations to be made. The use of Filipino in writing most of the realistic stories in this survey may be taken as recognition of the child's right to be taught in a language more familiar to her/him, just as the production of the picture storybooks may be taken as recognition of the Filipino child's need for leisurely reading. The proper names used to identify the child protagonists may be taken as recognition of the child's uniqueness and her/his right to a name and a nationality, and the varied family setup in the stories may be taken as an acknowledgement of the child's right to have a home and nurturing family. Yet, despite these positive social connotations, the word choices, the descriptions, and the utterances made in the stories still foreground the adults' ambivalence towards the child—whether to allow the child to be playful and carefree or to burden her/him at this early age with heavy responsibilities as a preparation for adult life. Though the picture storybooks are supposed to be produced for the benefit of the Filipino child, the ideology that they contain regarding the notion of the "good" child who is obedient to adults, lacks in knowledge and experience, and is better seen than heard, will not really benefit the Filipino child if s/he is to be a truly responsible and productive member of the community. It may be argued that protagonists who are more independent, self-reliant, and assertive can serve as better role models to young children. Yet from a close analysis of the language used in these narratives, it may also be argued that Filipino adults (such as the writers of these stories), while overtly acknowledging that the courage and inner strength of the child is paramount, are perhaps subconsciously invested in maintaining the status quo—to keep the child in her/his "lower", "less privileged", and "less powerful" place in the family and in the community.

References

Anonuevo, Victoria. 2002. *Ang Paaralan ni Fuwan*. Quezon City: Adarna House, Inc.

Bellen, Christine. 2004. *Filemon Mamon*. Quezon City: Adarna House, Inc.

Birch, David. 1996. "'Working Effects with Words'—Whose Words?" In *The Stylistics Reader: From Roman Jakobson to the Present*, edited by Jean Jacques Weber, 206–221. London: Arnold.

Canon, Kristine. 2008. *Sampung Magkakaibigan*. Quezon City: Adarna House, Inc.

Chong, Grace D. 2008. *Big Brother*. Mandaluyong: OMF Literature, Inc.

———. 2013. *The White Shoes*. Mandaluyong City: OMF Literature, Inc.

Clark, Jordan. 2017. *BINUKOT: Women Secluded and Veiled in Philippine History*. 8 December.

De Los Angeles-Bautista, Feny. 1996. *Ang Kuya ni Karina*. Mandaluyong: Cacho Publishing House, Inc.

Del Castillo, Grace. 2002. *May Kapatid na si Mungan*. Quezon City: Adarna House, Inc.

Department of Education. "DepEd Orders." *Department of Education*. 15 June 2009. https://www.deped.gov.ph/2009/06/15/do-64-s-2009-institutionalization-of-deped-library-hub-project-in-all-regions-and-schools-divisions-nationwide/ (accessed July 17, 2019).

———. *Guidelines on the Use of the Mother Tongue-Based-Multilingual Education (MTB-MLE)*. 12 February 2012. https://www.deped.gov.ph/wp-content/uploads/2012/02/DO_s2012_16.pdf (accessed July 17, 2019).

————. *Overview of the Library Hub Project*. n.d. https://slideplayer.com/slide/8156376/ (accessed July 17, 2019).

Eusebio-Abad, Heidi Emily. 2018. *Water Lilies for Marawi*. Makati City: The Bookmark, Inc.

Evasco, Eugene Y. 1997. *Federico*. Quezon City: Adarna Book Services, Inc.

Fowler, Roger. 1996. "Studying Literature as Language." In *The Stylistic Reader*, edited by Jean Jacques Weber, 196–205. New York: Arnold.

Garlitos, Rhandee. 2013. *Ang Bonggangbonggang Batang Beki*. Quezon City: LG&M Corporation.

Gatmaitan, Luis P. 1999. *Ang Pambihirang Buhok ni Raquel*. Quezon City: Adarna House, Inc.

Gonzales, Fernando Rosal. 2015. *Munting Opisina ni Nanay*. Quezon City: Lampara Publishing House, Inc.

Herman, David. 2007. "Introduction." In *The Cambridge Companion to Narrative*, edited by Herman David, 3–21. Cambridge, UK: Cambridge University Press.

Herman, Luc, and Bart Vervaeck. 2007. "Ideology." In *The* Cambridge *Companion to Narrative*, 217–230. Cambridge: Cambridge University Press.

Jakobson, Roman. 1996. "Closing Statement: Linguistics and Poetics." In *The Stylistics Reader: From Roman Jakobson to the Present*, edited by Jean Jacques Weber, 10–35. London and New York: Arnold.

Lemlunay, Nieves. 2002. *Gustong Mag-aral ni Sula*. Quezon City: UNICEF and Adarna House, Inc.

Lukens, Rebecca J., Jacquelin J. Smith, and Cynthia Miller Coffel. 2013. *A Critical Handbook of Children's Literature*. 9th edition. Boston: Pearson Education, Inc.

Margolin, Uri. 2007. "Character." In *The Cambridge Companionto Narrative*, edited by David Herman, 66–79. Cambridge and New York: Cambridge University Press.

Molina, Russell. 2012. *Anong Gupit Natin Ngayon?* Quezon City: Adarna House, Inc.

————. 2007. *Sampu Pataas, Sampu Pababa*. Quezon City: Adarna House, Inc.

————. 2003. *Sandosenang Kuya*. Quezon City: Adarna House, Inc.

Neri, Bernadette Villanueva. 2012. *Ang Ikaklit sa Aming Hardin*. Pilipinas: Twamkittens.

Paterno, Maria Elena. 1994. "A History of Children's Literature in the Philippines." In *Bumasa at Lumaya: A Sourcebook on Children's Literature in the Philippines*, edited by Virgilio S. Almario, Maria Elena Paterno, Ramon C. Sunico and Rene O. Villanueva, 9–23. Pasig City: Anvil Publishing, Inc.

Patindol, Jean Lee C. 2004. *Papa's House, Mama's House*. Quezon City: Adarna House, Inc.

Popa, Allan. 2002. *Ang Ibay ni Miana*. Quezon City: UNICEF and Adarna House, Inc.
Remigio, Ma. 1995. Corazon. *BRU-HA-HA-HA-HA-HA...BRU-HI-HI-HI-HI-HI*. Quezon City: Adarna House, Inc.
———. 2015. *Yaya Niya, Nanay Ko*. Manila: UNICEF.
Rival-Cosico, Rae. 2014. *Marvino's League of Superheroes*. Quezon City: Adarna House, Inc.
Rivera, Augie. 2007. *Ang Lihim ni Lea*. Baguio City: Soroptimist International of HOPE Baguio.
———. 2014. *Isang Harding Papel*. Quezon City: Adarna House, Inc.
———. 2013. *Mantsa*. Makati City: Plan International.
———. 2001. *Si Diwayen, Noong Bago Dumating ang mga Espanyol*. Quezon City: UNICEF and Adarna House, Inc.
———. 2001. *Si Jhun-Jhun, Noong Bago Ideklara ang Batas Militar*. Quezon City: UNICEF and Adarna House, Inc.
———. 2001. *Si Juanito, Noong Panahon ng mga Amerikano*. Quezon City: UNICEF and Adarna House, Inc.
———. 2001. *Si Pitong, Noong Panahon ng mga Hapon*. Quezon City: UNICEF and Adarna House, Inc.
———. 2001. *Si Segunda, Noong Panahon ng mga Espanyol*. Quezon City: UNICEF and Adarna House, Inc.
Saguisag, Lara. 2001. *There's a Duwende in My Brother's Soup!* Quezon City: Lampara Publishing House, Inc.
Samar, Edgar. 2002. *Uuwi na ang Nanay Kong si Darna*. Quezon City: Adarna House, Inc.
Sunico, Ramon C. 1990. *Two Friends, One World*. Mandaluyong: Cacho Publishing House, Inc.
Temple, Charles, Mariam Martinez, and Junko Yokota. 2006. *Children's Books in Children's Hands: An Introduction to Their Literature*. 3rd edition. Boston: Pearson Education, Inc.
Thomas, Bronwen. 2007. "Dialogue." In *The Cambridge Companion to Narrative*, edited by David Herman, 80–93. Cambridge: Cambridge University Press.
Tinio, Ergoe. 2015. *Salusalo para kay Kuya*. Quezon City: Adarna House, Inc.
UNICEF. 2005. https://www.unicef.org/sowc05/english/childhooddefined.html (accessed July 30, 2019).
———. *UNICEF for Every Child*. n.d. https://www.unicef.org/child-rights-convention/what-is-the-convention (accessed July 30, 2019).
Uson, Ricardo. 2002. *Bahay ng Marami't Masasayang Tinig*. Quezon City: UNICEF and Adarna House, Inc.
Verdonk, Peter. 2002. *Stylistics*. Oxford and New York: Oxford University Press.

Weber, Jean Jacques. 1996. "Towards Contextualized Stylistics: An Overview." In *The Stylistics Reader: From Jakobson to the Present,* edited by Jean Jacques Weber, 1–8. London and New York: Arnold.

Yanilla, Lalaine F. 1991. *Values as Reflected in Philippine Children's Stories from 1960–1989.* Quezon City: University of the Philippines.

Yanilla Aquino, Lalaine F. 2012. "English Language as Auntie: Of 'Good Intentions' and a Pedagogy of Possibilities–ELT in the Philippines and Its Effects on Children's Literacy Development." In *English Language as Hydra: Its Impact on Non-English Language Cultures,* edited by Vaughan Rapatahana and Pauline Bunce, 158–174. Bristol, Buffalo, and Toronto: Multilingual Matters.

CHAPTER 14

Through Screens and Streams: Digital Liminality and Identities in Philippine Young Adult Speculative Fiction

Gabriela Lee

INTRODUCTION

The increasingly interconnected world we live in has given rise to new and diverse ways of creating and constructing information across various modes of communication. Young adults who have grown up during the ubiquitous rise of accessible home Internet connections and the popularity of social media have access to different lines of communication, many of which did not exist some twenty-odd years ago. In the latest survey from the Pew Research Center, data shows that over 95% of the surveyed teens owned, or had access to, a smartphone (Pew Research Center 2018). Such access to portable communication devices has created a space for young adults to maintain connections with their peer groups, which is reflected in another Pew survey that indicates that over 81% of

G. Lee (✉)
University of the Philippines Diliman, Quezon City, Philippines
e-mail: gdlee@up.edu.ph

B. Wilson and S. P. Gabriel (eds.), *Asian Children's Literature and Film in a Global Age*, Asia-Pacific and Literature in English, https://doi.org/10.1007/978-981-15-2631-2_14

surveyed teens use their smartphones to keep in contact with their friends and acquaintances through social media (Pew Research Center 2018).

In the Philippines, information regarding Internet usage comes through the Philippines Statistics Authority's Functional Literacy, Education, and Mass Media Survey (FLEMMS). The latest information was released in 2013, in which the survey described the general Internet usage of Filipinos, with 16% of Filipinos using social media daily, and 13.9% using the Internet for research, work, or school (Philippine Statistics Authority 2013). Furthermore, according to the survey:

> [y]ounger Filipinos had more exposure to the internet than the older ones. Almost two in every three Filipinos 15 to 19 years old had exposure to the internet: surf the internet for social media/interaction (67.8%) and surf the internet for research work (65.3%), compared with only 24.2 per cent and 24.0 per cent of those aged 40 to 49 years, respectively. (Philippine Statistics Authority 2013)

However, this does not take into account the rise of Internet usage, especially in the last few years, nor does it take into account smartphone access or other means of using or connecting to the Internet.

The 2017 National Book Development Board (NBDB) Readership Survey contains a more recent data set that tracks the reading habits of Filipinos, divides the usage between children (7–17 years old) and adults (18–64 years old), and has included online reading habits. According to this more recent survey, at least 35% of the adult respondents read online, while 37% of the child respondents read online. Furthermore, at least 69% of the child respondents declared that they use a smartphone to read online (2017), which implies that most of their reading experience still takes place on screens (National Book Development Board 2017).

This experience is symptomatic of the rapidly changing and diversifying ways of consuming narratives—not just books, but also films, TV shows, videos, and other forms of narrative media. Unlike the technology of the television screen, where there is a one-way journey from TV station to individual viewer, the digital screen is permeable and allows for an interconnected response to the media being projected on the screen. This form of two-way exchange allows for both the narrative and the audience to participate in a conversation, so to speak, yet these kinds of exchanges may be posited as either productive or insidious, depending on the situation and perspective. Bearing these factors in mind, further elucidation regarding such exchanges is needed in order to imagine their possibilities and potential.

For these reasons, this chapter seeks to investigate the ways in which digital technologies, in particular computer screens and digital streams, act as both portals between and spaces in which identities are negotiated in two ongoing Philippine young adult speculative fiction (PH YA SF) novel series: *Jumper Cable Chronicles* (2018) by E. K. Gonzales, and the *Janus Silang* series (2014–2017) by Edgar Calabia Samar. While focusing on the first volume in both series, this chapter will examine how the digital aspects of the storyworlds—the TALA Online MMORPG in *Janus Silang* and the crossing of digital streams and dimensions in *Jumper Cable Chronicles*—become portals from which the protagonists make "the transition between this world and another; from our time to another time" and metaphorically, "from youth to adulthood" (Mendlesohn 2008, 55). As such, these kinds of portal narratives may be read as useful analogies of young adult experiences.

In particular, by examining these narrative devices and how they disrupt the world of the protagonists by shifting from the *known* to the *unknown*, the reader can map the fluctuations in both the identities and positionalities of these characters which, in turn, mimic the kind of shifting identities Filipino young adults employ online. This can be articulated using the concept of digital liminality, which refers to the use of "digital technologies in which [young adults] are so invested" and its "[tendency] to create, and replicate, a splintered sense of self. That self may have cohesion within the network of a particular social media, but it does not usually translate well beyond the medium" (Stephens 2016, 28). Moreover, this liminality may also describe a sense of "temporary freedoms [that] are only a means of breaking old habits, and preparing [young adults] to accept the responsibilities (and hence the confinements) of adulthood" (Stephens 2016, 27).

DIGITAL LIMINALITY AND YOUNG ADULT LITERATURE

The concept of "digital liminality" as a term may have first been used by Gregory Stephens to describe the state of in-betweenness of young adults who use the Internet and social media in "achieving separation and liminality through digital technology in ways that were unimaginable for prior generations" (Stephens 2016, 20), in particular through his observations of students from Saudi Arabia as they underwent scholastic rites of passage through his freshman English class, in which they grappled with their conservative culture and the liberal atmosphere and attitudes they discovered online, particularly through the screens of their mobile phones. Stephens observes, through this ethnographic study, that there was difficulty in reconciling his students' online attitudes and identities with the restrictive cultural practices of their home country. Yet, because of their positions as well-educated and well-connected young people, they remained in a state of liminality, in which they struggled to maintain a balance between the world in which they grew up and the world experienced through their screens.

Furthermore, Stephens notes that "the individuation process [takes] place in a liminal space" (Stephens 2016, 26) in which individuals begin to explore the worlds accessible to them—and in the twenty-first century, this access has been shaped by the Internet and the mobile phone. While he acknowledges that the students have opportunities to engage with both the online and offline worlds, and to create connections in both spheres, in the end:

> all forms of liminality eventually must dissolve. Usually the individual returns to a social structure—with both individual and structure transformed. But if that structure cannot integrate the transformed individuals, then these "non-normative" individuals with their non-assimilated liminality may develop their own more or less autonomous social structure. (Stephens 2016, 26)

Using Stephens' real-world observations and initial definition of digital liminality as a starting point, I would like to extend his argument further and posit that digital liminality is a necessary experience in identity-making for young adults, and that this experience is modelled and expanded in young adult literature. Because this "rite of passage has been transformed by technology" (Turkle 2011, 146) this will also be reflected in the kind of literature that young adults consume. Furthermore, Sherry Turkle observes:

> The network's effects on today's young people are paradoxical. Networking makes it easier to play with identity (for example, by experimenting with an avatar that is interestingly different from you) but harder to leave the past behind, because the Internet is forever. The network facilitates separation (a cell phone allows children greater freedoms) but also inhibits it (a parent is always on tap). Teenagers turn away from the "real-time" demands

of the telephone and disappear into role-playing games they describe as "communities" and "worlds." And yet, even as they are committed to a new life in the ether, many exhibit an unexpected nostalgia. (Turkle 2011, 142)

While these paradoxes are already experienced in real life, especially with the way that our everyday lives are tethered to the Internet, they are highlighted and exposed in literary narratives, in which there is an awareness that such paradoxes can be manipulated and reworked in order to provide particular commentaries on human existence.

Science fiction, as a genre, seems particularly suited to exploring the liminal nature of growing up and figuring one's position within and beyond the digital sphere, since it posits that the construction of the narrative is based on existing foundations of scientific understanding and, extrapolating from there, the infinite possibilities of story. In particular, science fiction that focuses on "technology as a motif for exploring new relationships between the mind and the body" (Flanagan 2014, 12) is vital in providing ways to elucidate the potential strengths and pitfalls of digital liminality. In fact, Victoria Flanagan's explorations of posthumanism, technology, and identity in young adult fiction is a useful text with which to examine the possibilities of digital liminalities in young adult texts. This is because:

the emphasis on subjectivity in posthumanism [...] complements YA fiction's thematic and ideological preoccupation with subject formation. Adolescence is often constructed in terms of its 'otherness' or liminality within this genre... [t]here are obvious parallels between the 'otherness' of robot and cyborg characters and the liminality of adolescence as a category of identity, making narratives about the development of 'othered' subjects appealing to young adult readers who see themselves as falling outside the constructs of either adulthood or childhood. Novels for adolescent readers also pursue this issue in less literal terms, however, frequently using virtual reality as a means for exploring the fragmented, tenuous, and collective sense of self that arises out of regular experiences in cyberspace. (Flanagan 2014, 18–20)

In particular, I would like to examine the presence of the screens in the two young adult novels that I will be analysing, and will interpret these screens as portals through which the teenage protagonists are able to experience liminality through the digital worlds which the stories explore.

As Farah Mendlesohn notes, portals are more commonly associated with fantasy stories, in which "the portal fantasy allows and relies upon both protagonist and reader gaining experience" (Mendlesohn 2008, 37) and commonly relies on quest narratives as the structural support upon which the novels are usually built. Furthermore, she notes that "portal fantasy is about entry, transition, and negotiation" (Mendlesohn 2008, 37) and it is during the transitory phase that I am most interested, as this corresponds to the liminal experience of the protagonists within the narrative, and it is within this space that identities are in flux and dependent on the decisions and actions of the characters.

It is also important to note that, particularly in genre fiction for young adults, the very notion of fantasy and science fiction as separate genres can be blissfully ignored by writers. As Jessica Yates notes, "science-fictional motifs may appear [...] in works whose overriding ethos is magical" (Yates 2004, 519) and vice versa. This may be because, while fantasy for children and young adults has a longer and more robust tradition, science fiction narratives for children and young adults typically have contained either magical or magic-like elements, and have invariably emphasised themes of youthful exploration, similar to the boys' adventure stories that were popular during the eighteenth and nineteenth centuries in the United Kingdom and the United States. As such, "there has been no tradition of children's science fiction comparable to children's fantasy" (Yates 2004, 521). For these reasons, it is important to assess speculative fiction—the umbrella term used to refer specifically to narratives written in the non-realist genre, particularly fantasy, science fiction, and paranormal horror—as genre nomenclature in order to take into account the shifts between science fiction and fantasy in YAL.

In the Philippines, there has been little to no critical or genre studies in either science fiction, which has historically occupied a niche position in the largely social realist traditions of Philippine literature in English, or young adult literature, which has only begun to be recognised as a separate category from children's literature in recent years. In their seminal essay, "Filling the Gap: Young Adult Literature in the Philippines", Carla M. Pacis and Ramón C. Sunico attempt to chart the development of YAL in the Philippines. This is still primarily considered a new genre, tracing back its genesis to 1998, when the Philippine Board on Books for Young People (PBBY) and the Asia-Pacific Cultural Centre for UNESCO (ACCU) conducted a writing workshop, spearheaded by Australian writer Jackie French, specifically designed to create novel-length narratives for teenage readers. This resulted in the first spate of novellas from writers such as Carla M. Pacis and Lin Acacio-Flores, which were continuously published from the late 1990s to the early 2000s, by Cacho Publishing House (Pacis and Sunico 2016, 118).

Around this time, the children's publishing company, Adarna House Inc., began to venture into young adult literature by hosting the Pilar Perez Medallion for Young Adult Literature, along with Filipinas Heritage Library (FHL), beginning in 2001. The competition was short-lived and only ran for two years, producing four novels (two in Filipino and two in English), all of which were written in the realist mode, and which explored the experiences of Filipino teenagers from the past and the present, from urban Manila to far-flung Sulu in the Mindanao region. Only one of the four novels, *Anina ng Mga Alon* (*Anina of the Waves*) by Eugene Y. Evasco, is still available for purchase. However, Pacis and Sunico's essay also bemoans the lack of manuscripts fit for publication, citing that "several books later, it seems we have lost steam. The annual release of YA books is more the exception than the rule. At least two of the publishers [...] agree on the lack of publishable submissions" (Pacis and Sunico 2016, 119–120). There is also the question of book sales from local YA authors, with the essay observing that "in the Philippines, books written by Filipinos for Filipino adolescents have still to make a sizeable impact in terms of both sales and readership... [t]here are many complicated issues behind this, not least the poverty of our populace" (Pacis and Sunico 2016, 120–121).

Furthermore, the essay also observes the conservative gatekeeping of places such as schools and church communities, who control much of the reading material that young adults are exposed to in the classroom, particularly since "there are themes and subjects that interest [young adults] that may be considered taboo by educators, especially in a conservative country such as ours... [w]hat seems to be preferred here would be novels that deal with history or contemporary social realities. YA novels of fantasy and science fiction still have to be published here — never mind their being taken up in school" (Pacis and Sunico 2016, 122–123).

Though some of the information here can be easily taken for granted—after all, this chapter is discussing two novels that can be classified as falling within the science fiction genre—the lack of diverse literary choices in the Philippines aimed for young readers, children, and young adults alike, is clear in the kinds of narrative themes that are usually pursued by writers. According to a study by Myra Garces-Bacsal of award-winning children's books in the Philippines from 1991 to 2011, statistics reveal that at least 54% of works were contemporary realist fiction, and only 19% could be considered non-realist or fantasy works (Garces-Bacsal 2013, 95). Garces-Bacsal also notes that there has been "a considerable increase in contemporary realistic fiction during the last ten years [...] as opposed to fantasy, which has dropped significantly" (Garces-Bacsal 2013, 96). This is also echoed in the Pacis and Sunico essay, in which they note that aside from a lack of written output, there is also a lack of support from the establishment, including universities and other publishing houses, to encourage, diversify, and promote young adult literature written in the Philippines.

Despite these limitations and restrictions, it has become clear that the access to digital technology and to more diverse narratives and platforms for creation and negotiation necessitates a new discussion of the kinds of realities that young adults may be encountering. This is perhaps one of the strengths of science fiction as a genre in that it explores what these new realities might look like for the teenage reader, and how they can engage with it.

Portals and Screens in Philippine Speculative Fiction for Young Adults

I have chosen to analyse two science fiction young adult novels written by Filipino authors which exemplify the kind of digital liminality and negotiation of identities discussed in the previous sections of my essay. As mentioned earlier, these novels are written in the vein of speculative fiction, which provides this analysis with a more complex layer to consider in terms of the negotiation of identities in the digital spaces that these novels contend with. Both books have been published by the same Philippine publishing company, Adarna House Inc., which has been a constant presence in the Philippine children's publishing industry since the late 1970s, and has established its identity as one of the leading publishers of children's picture books and instructional books. In the early 2000s, Adarna expanded its oeuvre to encompass the then-nascent genres of young adult and middle-grade literature. The novels *Jumper Cable Chronicles: Si Santa Anita* by E. K. Gonzales (translated into Filipino by Xi Zuq) and *Si Janus Silang at ang Tiyanak ng Tábon* by Edgar Calabia Samar are results of that expansion. Both novels are published in Filipino, and are first volumes in separately planned series.

The first edition of *Si Janus Silang at ang Tiyanak ng Tábon* (referred to as *Si Janus Silang* from this point onwards) was published in 2014, and is the first book of an ongoing series centred around the titular character, Janus Silang, of which there are currently three volumes in print and a fourth volume to be launched in 2019 at the Manila International Book Fair. The author, Edgar Calabia Samar, has previously written two other novels for adult readers, but this is his first foray into young adult fiction.

Similarly, author E. K. Gonzales previously wrote short stories set within the same world as *Jumper Cable Chronicles* but *Jumper Cable Chronicles: Si Santa Anita* (henceforth referred to as *Santa Anita*), which was published in 2018, was her first novel. *Santa Anita*, which was originally written in English as *Jumper Cable Chronicles: Miracle Girl*, was completed as part of the requirements of the Ateneo AILAP Writing Lab for the Young Adult Novel in 2015, for which Samar was one of the facilitators.

Both *Si Janus Silang* and *Santa Anita* share many overlapping qualities: both of their protagonists are male, both novels are set in the near future as opposed to the far future of many science fiction novels, and both of them emphasise the presence of digital technologies as central forces that propel the narratives forward. In fact, both novels show the ease in which Filipino teenagers dive into the digital worlds of social media and technological advances as ways of gathering information, communicating with the other characters, and showing how—by traversing the worlds within the screens and beyond the screens—they are able to build and negotiate particular identities for themselves.

Si Janus Silang lays the foundations of the entire series as well as the journey of the main character, Janus Silang. He is 13 years old when the novel begins, and he is described as someone on the cusp of adolescence—his concerns centre on winning the championship for TALA Online, a Filipino-made MMORPG (Massively Multiplayer Online Role-Playing Game) that uses Philippine mythologies as a foundation for its digital world, and using the prize money to purchase gifts for his family and Mica, the girl he has a crush on. However, during the last qualifying round at the Internet rental shop where the competition is being held, he realises that the five other boys that he was playing with died in the middle of their round. Even the deaths seemed supernatural—the dead boys' bodies all turned to ash, as though they had been incinerated from within. The mystery deepens when Janus learns, through snippets from online news forums, social media websites such as Facebook and Twitter and the game's own fan-run website TALArchives.com, and local news shows, that there were more players dying in computer shops all across the Philippines—all while playing TALA Online.

TALA Online is the crux upon which the entire first novel is built. The acronym TALA stands for "Terra Anima Legion of Anitos". It is described as a:

> strategy game… dalawa ang kalaban dito. Una, ang computer-generated na Legion of the Soulless na iba't ibang nilalang ng dilim sa mga mito't kwentong bayan at kahit sa ilang urban legend. Iba-iba ang pakana ng bawat isa para pigilin ka sa paglampas sa isang level. Ikalawa… ang mga kapwa mong gamer na bumuo ng sari-sarili nilang Bayani at Anito na nakikipag-unahan sa iyong matagpuan sa Tala, ang Bathaluman ng Liwanag. Isa lang ang mauunang makatagpo kay Tala. Komplikado ito dahil kahit kalaban mo sila, katulong at kasangga mo sila sa paglaban ng mga Soulless, hangga't di kayo nakararating sa dulo. (Samar 2014, 2–3)

*

> *strategy game… where there are two enemies. First, the computer-generated Legion of the Soulless, comprised of the different creatures of darkness coming from Philippine folktale and myths and even urban legends. These creatures have different ways of preventing you from completing a level. Second… your fellow gamers who formed their own Bayani and Anito, and who are racing against you to find Tala, the Goddess of Light. Only one of you will find Tala. This makes it complicated because even though the other players are your enemies, you need their help in getting past the Soulless, at least while you haven't reached the end.*[1]

In the novel, the game is initially compared to DOTA or Defense of the Ancients, a popular MMORPG based on Blizzard's *World of Warcraft* series, perhaps as a way to assist the reader in understanding both the visuals and mechanics of the game. However, unlike the menagerie of pre-built characters in DOTA, TALA Online requires the player to choose from two heroic archetypes or Bayani: Bagáni or Púsong. The Bagáni is rooted in the physically gifted or masculine hero, while the Púsong is based on the trickster hero, the one who could change shape or form (Samar 2015, 61 and 79). These choices are already asking the player to adhere to a particular kind of identity with the question: what kind of hero do you want to be?

Furthermore, it is also interesting to note that there seems to be a clear gender-based perception of the two roles provided by the game. When Janus recounts his experience in choosing a character, he remembers that:

> [b]ibihira pa ang gumagamit ng Púsong sa mga naglalaro sa Malakas, sa pagkakaalam niya. Marami sa mga pumipili ng Púsong bilang Bayani, hindi nagtatagal... "Nasa Malakas ka," sasabihin ni Harold noon. "Dito, ang Bayani e Bagáni. Doon ka maglaro sa Rainbow!" Sabay tawanan. Rainbow Network ang Internet shop na mas tinatambayan ng mga babaeng teenager, para mag-FB, mag-chat, maglaro ng Fashion World, mag-Candy Crush, manood sa YouTube. Walang nagta-TALA na mahuhuling nag-i-Internet sa Rainbow Network. (Samar 2014, 13–14)

*

> *it was rare for the players at Malakas [Internet Shop] to use a Púsong as a player character. Many of those who chose the Púsong as their Bayani never last long... "You're playing in Malakas," Harold said before. "Here, everyone plays the Bagáni, as their Bayani. Otherwise, you might as well play at Rainbow!" He laughed. Rainbow Network was the Internet shop where most of the female teenagers hung out to use Facebook, chat, play Fashion World or Candy Crush, or watch YouTube. Nobody who played TALA would be caught dead at Rainbow Network.*

Another choice that a TALA Online player needs to make is the *anito* who will accompany his or her in-game character. In Philippine mythologies, the *anito* is a crafted artefact that represents specific deities in local pantheons or objects of worship. In the game, the Anito functions as the spirit guide of the player. Aside from choosing their player identity, TALA Online also requires the player to choose an Anito. Once again, it provides a secondary choice to build on the identity of the player. Similar to the player type, TALA Online provides only two choices for the Anito: the Diwata or the Nuno. Once again, the novel draws from Philippine mythology to establish particular ways of thinking about identities; the *diwata* refers to minor female deities or nature spirits, while the *nuno* refers to small, forest-dwelling old spirits who act as guides or guardians to adventurers (Samar 2015, 19 and 97). In the game, "[t]he power of the Nuno deepens as the game progresses... meanwhile, the power of the Diwata widens" (Samar 2014, 24) though this is never elaborated on with relation to the gameplay. Here, the characters still need to make a choice regarding the relationship between their player character and the spirit guide:

> Sa isip ni Janus noon, mas kailangan ng Púsong niya ang lalim ng Nuno, kailangang may pinaghuhugutan ang liksi ng Púsong ... [k]aya nga nang namimili siya ng Anito, malinaw kay Janus na Nuno ang pipiliin niya. *Lalim.* Kahit naglalakbay palayo... alam niyang hindi laging pagpapalawak ng mundo ang layunin. Minsan, kailangan pumailalim. (Samar 2014, 25–27)

> *

> *In Janus' mind before, his Púsong needed the depth of the Nuno because it needed somewhere to draw its litheness from... that was why when he was choosing his Anito, it was clear to Janus that the Nuno was his only choice. Depth. Even if he traveled far and wide... he knew that he wasn't really traveling farther. He was traveling further.*

Together, the Bayani-Anito Tandem, or BAT, establishes the unique player identity within TALA Online. The player's BAT dictates how well they are able to navigate each level of the game, which uses particular Philippine mythical creatures and monsters in order to challenge the players. If your character dies within the level, you are returned to Level 1 and you need to recreate your BAT all over again. There is the implication that the longer a player maintains their BAT, the Anito "learns" how to play alongside your Bayani character, and knows the best way to assist you in beating each level. Furthermore, there is a level of cooperation between all the players playing within that level that dictates how easy or how difficult it would be to beat the monsters of that level.

As such, once Janus enters the digital world of TALA Online, he navigates not only the levels created by the game designers, but also how he relates with the other players in-game, and how he projects his own personality through his constructed BAT. Janus' justifications of his in-game choices are based on how he recognises himself as an individual, and brings these choices into the game world. Despite the fact that the game world of TALA Online exists only online as an MMORPG, Janus sees it as another aspect of his identity—the digital is not separate from the analog, but rather becomes another space for being which he accesses through a computer screen. This makes the world of TALA Online a liminal space where players move from their digital avatars as representations of themselves in-game to their real-world engagement with the game itself.

All of these game elements can be traced back to Russell W. Belk's analysis of the extended self within a digital world. According to Belk, "the possibilities for self-extension have never been so extensive" (Belk 2013, 477) as with the advent of digital technologies. His theory of the extended self has been further expanded to encompass current digital technologies and how these are incorporated into an individual's sense of identity and self. He notes that there are five things that have changed because of an increasingly digitised world: dematerialisation, re-embodiment, sharing, co-construction of self, and distributed memory (Belk 2013, 477). In particular, Janus exemplifies re-embodiment, or a significant attachment to an online identity or avatar, in which "avatars affect [the] offline self" (Belk 2013, 478) as well as distributed memory, in which there are online narratives of the self, as though the physical self has gone through the digital experience within the world of the game. As such, Belk observes that in online games, "virtual goods occupy a liminal category between the material world and the imaginary world" (Belk 2013, 479) with the term "goods" potentially referring to not just objects but any kind of transactional activity enacted by the player within the game—including playing the game itself.

Even the space where he plays TALA Online can be considered a liminal space. Malakas Computer Shop is the name of the computer rental place where Janus and his male friends play—and the text emphasises that most of the players at Malakas are male students from all over Balanga, a town in Batangas, a province south of Metro Manila. Most of the computer users of Malakas are MMORPG players, either of DOTA or of TALA Online. As mentioned earlier, the other Internet shop in town, Rainbow, is considered too feminine by many of the TALA players, who mostly identify as male.

The existence of a physical space that allows people to access a digital space through a computer screen becomes a portal through which the players quite literally traverse two worlds: the world of the game and the world their physical bodies reside in. Through this space, not only are identities explored in-game but also within the real world in which their game usage is observed and commented upon by those who observe their physical selves but do not have access to their digital selves. The novel explores this conversation through the lens of technophobia, and grapples with the inaccessibility of this digital liminal space to particular audiences—in this case, addressing the generation gap between those who play online games and those who do not.

Janus himself can be considered a liminal character as well, as not only does he exist within the physical world, but his lineage connects him to the metaphysical story world of the novel. In the course of uncovering the mystery of the deaths of TALA Online players, Janus learns of a grand battle between the forces of darkness and the forces of light, represented by the Tiyanak, a malevolent being cursed by its dying mother to destroy family units where children have died, and its twin, Tala, whose father is the supreme god Bathala, and is the only being who can permanently destroy the Tiyanak.

Drawing from Philippine mythology, the *tiyanak* is said to be a small creature that takes the shape and sound of a baby and lures travellers into the forest with its cries, which sound like that of a lost child. However, once the traveller picks up the *tiyanak*, it devours the person and walks away. It is said that the *tiyanak* is a kind of shape-shifter, but it can only take on the voice and shape of a child (Samar 2015, 10–11). In *Si Janus Silang*, these folk tales are deepened and expanded by tying the Tiyanak and Tala together to form another kind of duality, echoing the choices made within the game and pulling Janus in two directions. On the one hand, he is desperate to separate himself from his lineage, the legacy of a Pusong who has the capability to track down the missing Tala both in-game and in real life; on the other hand, he is desperate to help as well, and to do the right thing—even if it seems difficult. It is this kind of decision-making that leads to the final third of the novel and its climax.

As we can see in many young adult novels, this kind of turning point—a choice thrust upon the main characters in order to highlight the importance of their place in the world and how their decisions impact the people around them—is heightened by the fact that in *Si Janus Silang*, the main character connects his identity to a kind of fantastical game reality that is initially only accessible through a computer screen. It is through these kinds of digital experiences that the main character is able to come to terms with the disparate parts of his identity and begin forming a new whole.

Similarly, in *Santa Anita*, the narrative begins with the 16-year-old main character, Dino Soriano, sitting in front of a screen. He has recalibrated his laptop to watch the international streaming match of Manny Pacquiao, which is being broadcast on pay-per-view channels. Since he does not have access to legitimate forms of watching the boxing match, he has decided to hack the Internet signal and reprogramme it so that he can watch the stream. However, due to this course of action, he has inadvertently allowed a dimension engineer and agent named Haya Project to enter this dimension through the temporary stable connections that Dino establishes. Haya Project introduces himself as part of a Bioenhancement Project in his dimension, and informs Dino that a multiverse exists, and that the world that Dino belongs to—which is posited to be the world to which the reader also belongs—is being accessed for the first time by beings outside of this dimension.

Haya Project is characterised as a boy on a mission: he has entered Dino's dimension to look for his missing partner, Anita Project, whose last known coordinates were in Dino's dimension. Dino is understandably confused by Haya's presence in his world—his previously stable and easy-to-understand world—and initially rejects the reality of Haya's presence.

> When I saw the kid suddenly 3D-print in my room, I think I did what any self-respecting Pinoy would in that situation: I ran to the farthest corner, the area farthest away from a ghost… I pulled out all the wires and cables that attached to my laptop, hoping to stop any remaining data flow, hoping to make that apparition disappear.
>
> But the boy was still there, in front of me, in the early afternoon dimness. He patted his arms and legs, as if checking if they were really there. He pulled back at a sleeve and observed a watch there. He grinned. He looked up at the ceiling, down at the floor, around at the bare walls and the one bookshelf, and at my bed. He looked at me.
>
> I did what any self-respecting Pinoy would do next: I stood up and raised my hands, placing them behind my back. "You can take the laptop. There's not a lot of money in my wallet, but you can have that, too. Just don't hurt my parents". (Gonzales 2018, 4–5)[2]

Here, the digital screen is used as a portal in both a literal and metaphorical fashion. Haya is able to bring superior technological materials from his dimension to ours by using portable 3D printing technology attached to his wrist screen to copy them from his home dimension to Dino's room. Similarly, Anita Project is also able to bring large numbers of superior medical treatments from her dimension to ours by using a similar portable digital device that she calls a dimension kaleidoscope.

The screens brought over by Haya Project and Anita Project when they moved from one dimension to the next provide them with access to their home dimensions.

This is further expanded when, as the narrative progresses, both Dino and the reader discover that their initial meeting in the Haya Project turns out to be nothing more than a projection of Haya's bio-enhanced consciousness. Through the hot-wired cables that Dino initially used to stream a boxing match, Haya has been able to tap into the coordinates of this dimension and, essentially, 3D-print himself an avatar to move around our world, leaving his physical body connected to the digital devices that powered his avatar and enhanced his search for Anita Project:

> She lunged and quickly swiped at Haya's arm. I saw a small blade in her hand.
>
> But as the blade separated from the boy, it had no blood. There was no blood on Haya, either, not even a scratch, not even a welt that a blade had passed. There was only surprise on his face.
>
> Anita held the same blade over her forearm. She made a quick and light cut across. It immediately drew a red line, which quickly spilled a trickle of thick red fluid.
>
> Anita spoke again. "I want to talk to YOU, Haya. Not an avatar."
>
> "What...do you mean?"
>
> "You're smarter than that," the girl said.
>
> I stared at both kids in front of me. Both of them looked as solid as the other. But apparently I was staring at a real dimension-hopping girl at my right, and the most impressive 3-D printed live-action hologram I have ever seen in my life, on my left. (Gonzales 2018, 71–72)

However, as Mendlesohn notes, portals open in both directions (Mendlesohn 2008, 59). In *Santa Anita*, this can be seen in the way that Dino is 3D-printed from our world to Haya's world as he finds himself essentially projected in another dimension. His avatar meets the physical body of Haya, who is now in a state of unconsciousness following his extended travels through his avatar in Dino's world, and he learns more about the Bioenhancement Project and why Haya was desperate to find Anita. It is also here, when he enters the portal that was previously only opened by Haya, that he begins to accept a new identity, that of a dimension agent.

In fact, the question of identity is seeded throughout the narrative: Dino's insistence of the singularity of his identity as a teenager who is about to enter junior high and who wants nothing to do with Haya's mission; Haya's insistence of his identity as a dimension agent and his mission to bring Anita home; and Anita's insistence of her identity as a free agent who can use her access to the multiverse as a way to help the sick and the less fortunate. But as the story progresses, and the characters shift from one dimension to another, the reader can see how each character begins to negotiate their identities and discover that they are capable of change.

In particular, the negotiation of identities through the experiences of the digital liminalities of Dino, Haya, and Anita provides the reader with a way to see how the young adult characters use the digital shift in order to expand and grow from their current capabilities to new and more positive aspects of their identities. This is particularly seen in Dino, as he is the main protagonist as well as the narrator, and since the novel is told from the first-person point of view, the information that we receive about Haya and Anita is filtered through Dino's limitations of understanding. This is a useful literary technique to show the reader how the characters' travels through dimensions provide a way to expand their knowledge of the world around them:

Apparently there are at least 200 confirmed spacetime dimensions. There are others, of course, many more, according to the Many Worlds, or multiverse, theory. But only 200 are stable and moving at a regular pace, with stable application of classic, quantum, and relative physics. That is, only 200 are stable enough to sustain life and maintain science. Haya comes from the forty-eighth known dimension, and I'm from one of the last stable ones.

Haya's world has long been aware of the many spacetime dimensions, and it is now able to enter and explore the others, to learn from them, to know how they are different. Maybe they will get the learning and apply them to their own world.

Haya was a dimension engineer, someone specializing in making this dimension-traveling thing stable and safe for others. Haya was also one of those tasked to do the dimension-traveling himself, a dimension jumper.

I did show him my textbooks, showing him what my world knew about other dimensions.

Haya pointed to this quantum theory and that special relativity principle, things that the junior high textbooks summarized in several paragraphs but did not explain too deeply yet. I also showed him the deeper explaining one textbook did for Einstein's general relativity principles.

"Basic information," he said.

I stared at him. "Basic?"

He nodded. (Gonzales 2018, 19)

Furthermore, in both *Si Janus Silang* and *Santa Anita*, the characters are shown as adept in navigating the online world in order to uncover the mysteries that surround them. Both Janus and Dino use their Facebook contacts to learn more about the goings-on in the world; Dino uses YouTube in order to learn more about the mysterious girl who seems to be able to heal the sick and the dying through a magical pill; Janus filters through Twitter hashtags and memes about TALA Online, as well as checks the wiki-like TALArchives.com for more information about both the game and the deaths surrounding the game. Both characters rely on their mobile phones to tether themselves to the world of digital information. This exemplifies how Stephens initially conceived digital liminalities, particularly the movement of individuals through streams of information.

However, both novels go beyond the initial notion of digital liminality provided by Stephens as they elevate the notion of entering/existing/identifying the self through a screen and into a digital world from the practices of real-life teenagers using these screens as a way of literally entering a world that was initially beyond their understanding. As such, it is important to note that by writing these novels within the non-realist genre, the narratives move us from reality to speculation, and allow us to more fully explore what it means to be able to traverse spaces that are both physical and digital—that is, to say, liminal.

BEYOND SCREENS AND PORTALS

Suffice to say, the screens-as-portals used in both *Si Janus Silang* and *Santa Anita*, which allow the protagonists to move through worlds familiar and new, both literally and metaphorically, function as a narrative device and as a significant motif within the novels. The screens themselves become liminal spaces where both Janus and Dino exert a kind of agency that they do not have once they have passed through either side. These screens become emblematic of the choices these characters make—a kind of threshold that, once entered, can no longer be removed from experience or memory. Janus chooses to log on to TALA Online for the final time in order to follow the instructions of his mentor, Manong Joey, in their desperate search for the Tiyanak. Dino chooses to accept the invitation of the Haya Project to enter another dimension and learn about the dangers and degradation experienced by bio-enhanced children. These decisions illustrate the power of choice, choices that engage with the reality of the world beyond the screen, and show the reader how each character determines the kinds of identity that they take upon themselves.

The screens-as-portals, which provide a threshold which the main characters must choose to cross, may correspond to Joseph Campbell's identification of the Threshold stage of the Hero's Journey (Campbell 2008, 27–30) in his seminal work, *The Hero with a Thousand Faces*, which traces the archetypal hero's narrative culled from his research in comparative mythologies. While Campbell's work has largely given way to more fragmented and postmodern narrative techniques, in many non-realist YA narratives, the arc of the hero's journey is still a useful narrative tool to chart the progress of the YA hero as he responds to the call of adventure. To a certain extent, the narrative Threshold is the first portal upon which the hero enters and faces his first challenge (Campbell 2008, 64). It is not surprising here, in these two novels, that the screens function as portals through which the characters gain entry to another world—a world where they are required to take on the mantle of a new identity and to eventually incorporate that into their present identity. But it is the moment when they choose to enter the digital portal that becomes a moment of liminality that could not be achieved in any other way, because the portal itself is liminal; it shifts from a physical space to a digital space and then back again.

As such, the threshold to move from one stage of life to another, to take on a new identity that we incorporate into our own, also shifts. As

Engel notes, "[t]his passage through the ritualized threshold, whether part of a coming-of-age ritual or a graduation, is a point of no return. Participants have been permanently altered, either in their own eyes or in the eyes of their culture. After temporary dissolution, those who undergo threshold rituals return not to their old selves but to new ones—albeit embedded within the same society" (Engel 2017, 2). Similarly, both Janus and Dino are changed by what they see and experience through the portals that they enter, the thresholds that they cross, and they both return from their time in the world beyond the screen as different people.

Janus, who learns that the game world of TALA Online has very real consequences in the grand scheme of his own world, decides to do his part and re-enter the game world after avoiding it following the mysterious deaths of other players. However, as he refamiliarises himself with the game and feels himself capturing the adrenaline of success, his entry into the digital world comes at a price vis-à-vis his real world. His search for Tala in-game allows the Tiyanak and his minions to track him down and destroy his family as the price for interfering with the Tiyanak's plans, and his identity shift, which began as a gamer trying to find the answers to the mystery of the game and its impact on players, takes a downward turn as he is forced to reckon with the broader personal consequences of his choices, and the loss that he faces at the conclusion of the narrative in the first book. However, as this is the first novel of the series the reader is also assured that, perhaps somewhere down the line, Janus will be given the chance for retribution. As such, the text shows the consequences of action and choice in both virtual and real spheres and recognises these as powerful intertwined elements within the young reader's (and gamer's) worlds. It acknowledges the blurred and overlapping boundaries between the two existences, while also highlighting the continuing open-ended narratives which teenagers and young adults must engage on multiple levels in contemporary digitalised society.

Dino, who learns that there are other dimensions of reality beyond our own, and who learns how to access them through advanced technology, finally stops asking questions and instead takes action by assisting Haya Project in liberating Anita Project from both her naivety and the overbearing local politician who seems to have taken control of her medical "miracles". This choice is cemented after he learns that the Haya Project that he encountered in our world was an avatar projected by screens into the world in which Dino lives; crucially, midway through the novel, Dino must himself take on an avatar and be transported to Haya Project's world in order to find out the true purpose of the other boy's search for Anita Project. His identity shift, which begins as a student trying to enter a prominent senior high school, takes on more altruistic dimensions as he assists in saving Anita and Haya from the dramatic stampede at the climax of the novel and embraces his new identity as Dimension Agent 001 for Dimension 196, our dimension. Similarly, as this is the first novel of the series, the reader is allowed to posit new adventures after the end of this narrative. Again, real choices and consequences—concepts that may often be considered separate to virtual reality and gaming—are central to the narrative and reinforce the idea that decisions made, even in imaginary spaces, have clear ramifications in terms of actual self-perception and actions in the real world.

Further, both novels emphasise the necessity of digital worlds as vital places of agency where the young adult can explore experiences without the traditional presence of a mature adult to shape such moments. The symbolic nature of the screen-as-portal serves as a vital moment of liminality through which the characters must choose whether they decide to pursue their goals or remain in the relative safety of their current, known world. In the Philippines, this constitutes a crucial recognition of the need for the independence of Filipino teenagers, who often still live within particularly conservative cultural mores and family structures. For the Filipino young adult, such texts become valuable moments in which neither gatekeepers nor peers have control, but which revolve around individual choice, and it is the young adult who makes these choices and accepts the consequences. As such, both *Si Janus Silang* and *Santa Anita* advocate digital worlds as places of discovery and self-awareness, suggesting that the digitalised screen is not merely a reflection, but also a portal through which one can pass into an existence which promotes imagination, social responsibility, and a clear moral stance.

NOTES

1. All translations from the original source material by Gabriela Lee.
2. Original text in English provided by the author through email on July 7, 2019.

REFERENCES

Belk, Russell W. 2013. "Extended Self in a Digital World." *Journal of Consumer Research*, Vol. 40, No. 3 (October): 477–500. https://www.jstor.org/stable/10.1086/671052.

Campbell, Joseph. 2008. *The Hero with a Thousand Faces*. Novato, CA: New World Library/Joseph Campbell Foundation.

Engel, Adam J. 2017. "Between Two Worlds: The Functions of Liminal Space in Twentieth-Century Literature." PhD diss., University of North Carolina at Chapel Hill.

Flanagan, Victoria. 2014. *Technology and Identity in Young Adult Fiction: The Posthuman Subject*. New York: Palgrave Macmillan.

Garces-Bacsal, Myra. 2013. "Narrative Themes of Award-Winning Stories for Children in the Philippines from 1991–2011." In *Beyond Folktales, Legends, and Myths: A Rediscovery of Children's Literature in Asia*, edited by Myra Garces-Bacsal and Jesus Federico Hernandez, 93–102. Singapore: AFCC Publications.

Gonzales, EK. 2018. *Jumper Cable Chronicles: Si Santa Anita*. Translated by Xi Zuq. Quezon City: Adarna House, Inc.

Mendlesohn, Farah. 2008. *Rhetorics of Fantasy*. Middletown, CT: Wesleyan University Press.

Pacis, Carla M., and Ramón C. Sunico. 2016. "Filing the Gap: Young Adult Literature in the Philippines." In *Bumasa at Lumaya 2: A Sourcebook on Children's Literature in the Philippines*, edited by Ani Rosa Almario, Neni Sta. Romana Cruz, and Ramón C. Sunico, 117–129. Pasig City: Anvil Publishing.

Pew Research Center. "Teens' Social Media, and Technology 2018." Last modified May 31, 2018. Last accessed July 15, 2019. https://www.pewinternet.org/2018/05/31/teens-social-media-technology-2018/.

Pew Research Center. "Teens' Social Media Habits and Experiences." Last modified November 28, 2018. Last accessed July 15, 2019. https://www.pewinternet.org/2018/11/28/teens-social-media-habits-and-experiences/.

Philippine Statistics Authority. "2013 FLEMMS Functional Literacy, Education, and Mass Media Final Report." Last accessed July 15, 2019. https://psa.gov.ph/content/functional-literacy-education-and-mass-media-survey-flemms.

Philippine Statistical Research and Training Institute. "2017 National Book Development Board (NBDB) Readership Survey." Last modified September 28, 2018. Last accessed July 15, 2019. http://booksphilippines.gov.ph/wp-content/uploads/2018/10/Presentation_DMapa_NBDB_Readership_Survey_28SEPT2018.pdf.

Samar, Edgar Calabia. 2014. *Si Janus Silang at ang Tiyanak ng Tabon*. Quezon City: Adarna House.

Samar, Edgar Calabia. 2015. *101 Kagila-Gilalas na Nilaláng*. Quezon City: Adarna House.

Stephens, Gregory. 2016. "Digital Liminality and Cross-Cultural Re-integration in the Middle East." *The CEA Forum* (Winter/Spring): 20–50. https://journals.tdl.org/ceaforum/index.php/ceaforum/article/view/7085.

Turkle, Sherry. 2011. *Alone Together: Why We Expect More from Technology and Less from Each Other*. New York: Basic Books.

Yates, Jessica. 2004. "Science fiction." In *International Companion Encyclopedia of Children's Literature*, edited by Peter Hunt, 519–531. New York: Routledge.

PART IV

Diaspora

CHAPTER 15

Symbiotic Cultural Landscapes: Retelling Chinese Folktales in Ed Young's Picture Books

Fengxia Tan

INTRODUCTION

A comprehensive view of picture books created by ethnic Chinese in the Western world reveals that folktales are a common resource in their creation. This inclination relates to both the characteristics of the folktales themselves but also to the creators' cultural identities. In terms of the folktales themselves, each shows specific regional landscapes and customs combined with distinct local or national characteristics but also, apart from the political ideology, each invariably contains universal motifs of moral and cultural significance which extend across national boundaries; as collective generational expressions, the contents and structures of folktales are often embedded with Carl Gustav Jung's "collective uncon- sciousness" through which a deep psychological consensus of readers across cultures and nations may be invoked. In his study of picture books published in the United States, Leonard Marcus notes: "Characters in

F. Tan (✉)
School of Chinese Language and Literature, Nanjing Normal University,
Nanjing, Jiangsu, China
e-mail: njtanfengxia@sina.com

© The Author(s) 2020   337
B. Wilson and S. P. Gabriel (eds.), *Asian Children's Literature
and Film in a Global Age*, Asia-Pacific and Literature in English,
https://doi.org/10.1007/978-981-15-2631-2_15

folk stories so often represent universal types – the trickster, the fool – that add up to a kind of inventory and philosophy of human potential" (Marcus 2012, 34). Importantly, folktales which express imagination can readily stimulate a child's interest in reading and those folktales emerging from different ethnic groups may also aid readers to find the similarities and differences in and between seemingly disparate national cultures. In terms of creation, production and dissemination, folktales represent an important component of the collective memory of ethnic cultures. In this sense, folktales handed down over generations attain characteristics similar to classic literature which, as Yiheng Zhao has noted, "are like the totem of the ancestors, from which the tribal people can find cohesion and a sense of belonging" (Zhao 2011, 386). Significantly, there is a common phenomenon whereby folktales are frequently used in adult fiction by Chinese American writers, often functioning as a touchstone for cultural origin and a path towards a more hybrid present and future:

> Myths and folktales can help construct Chinese contexts in the narrative of novels, which not only reflect the traditional Chinese culture extending to overseas in a unique way but also show a way of Chinese cultural identity in Chinese American literature. (Hu 2003, 172)

The creation of such children's picture books based on folktales by the Chinese diaspora also reflects the cultural attitudes, values and aesthetic orientations of the authors. Original national cultural scenes reappear, are reconstructed and are even transformed in these works.

Ed Young (杨志成), a Chinese American writer and illustrator, is a distinguished representative in this field. His career in picture books started in 1962 and he has been continuously creating children's picture books for more than fifty years, now totalling approximately one hundred published texts. He has been nominated for the International Hans Christian Andersen award twice as an outstanding creator and, in 2016, was the winner of the lifetime achievement award in the field of American illustration. Though traditional Chinese folktales are the main subject resource of his picture books, his abundant and creative interpretations of the ideology of these folktales blend Eastern and Western cultural ideas and artistic techniques, providing a conscious, open-minded exploration of a cultural landscape that represents mutual integration and symbiosis.

THE RENEWAL OF THE TRADITIONAL FOLKTALE THROUGH THE ENHANCEMENT OF CONFLICT AND TENSION

The origins of Young's symbiotic approach to his work may be discerned from his biography. Having accepted Western culture in the United States in his youth in order to be, in his own words, "a full American", he later became strongly interested in Chinese culture, especially after he began to learn the Chinese sport of Tai-Chi. He chose picture books as the medium through which to spread the culture and art of China. Young melts what I term the "salt" of culture into the "water" of stories and believes that children's stories must contain a combination of excitement and emotion, while the illustrations should project novel but compatible images in order to attract readers and stimulate their inner perception and mental growth. In his design of stories, he endeavours to create a particular tension which represents the "conflict or fraction between complementaries, converses, opposites" (Flower 1973, 192). He also endows his images with intriguing symbolic connotations, thus combining the didactic function of traditional folktales with modern ideas through a highly aesthetic technique that provides a strong visual impact.

This bold innovation is especially successful in *Lon Po Po: A Red-Riding Hood Story from China* (1989), which won the Caldecott Medal.[1] Young's story is based on the Chinese folktale *Wolf Grandma* (*Lang Wai Po*《狼外婆》), and to acknowledge this Chinese cultural influence in the first instance, Young directly adopts the Chinese rendition of "wolf grandma" for the title. This folktale relates the story of three children who fight against a disguised wolf but its principal difference from the Western story, which focuses on the titular female, is that these children are neither eaten by the wolf nor saved by the hunter, but instead save themselves through their own courage and wisdom. Young's dedication to this book reads, "To all the wolves of the world for lending their good name as a tangible symbol for our darkness". The illustration on this page is both ingenious and strange in that it provides a perfect combination of a wild wolf and a grandmother in blue clothes, a compelling mixture that leads the reader to ponder if evil resides within us or in our perception of the world. Young's dedication shows a sensibility that is conscious of contemporary social concerns through its promotion of animal rights and environmental awareness; since the image of the wolf is created in a realistic way and the violence by which the three children kill the wolf may offend animal protection activists and young readers, the author claims to "borrow" the image of the wolf from traditional fairy tales. Compared to the connotation of the original Chinese folktale, this special dedication adds the ecological ethics of respecting animal life to the overall theme and also implies the symbolic association of the image which refers to the evil force in disguise.

Young's deliberate use of contrasting colours lends new power to the story. Compared with the native Chinese picture book *Wolf Grandma* (adapted by Zhou Zhengliang, illustrated by Tian Yuan 2010) which has a traditional style, Young's artwork and imagery provide fresh impetus to a traditional story. The cover of the Chinese version shows the protagonists, including both children and the personalised wolf grandmother, in bright colours, soft lines and a balanced composition, thus conveying a light, cheerful tone and a sense of security. In contrast, Young's brush provides dark, realistic images. The sole figure on the cover of his book is the wolf, drawn to look fierce and menacing; its solitariness, huge, black body and the white light from its eyes force readers to face up to its inherent cruelty. The first page of the text reveals the scene of the mother leaving home to visit the children's grandmother. Yet, upon closer inspection, one may discern the image of the wolf hidden in the landscape, indicating the potential danger lying in wait. When the wolf grandmother knocks on the door in the evening, the three children's faces appearing at the door and the wolf's face outside the door are paralleled in the two vertical sections within the page. The children in the red candlelight and the ghostly wolf grandma in the overwhelming dark night are in stark contrast, conveying to the reader the potentiality of brutality and murder. The dark colours and heavy atmosphere of the first half of the narrative correspond to the crisis introduced by the disguised wolf; the colour in the latter half, which depicts the children's fight against the wolf, gradually becomes lighter and brighter, symbolising the emergence from danger into safety and the children's courage, confidence and joy in victory. Yet, unexpectedly, the colour and shadow at the end of the story break with convention again. Instead of the expected saturation of bright colour to depict a cosy family reunion in keeping with traditional resolutions in children's narratives, Young employs a double-page spread depicting their house surrounded and all but engulfed by a dim and enigmatic environment, and again the wolf's body becomes an integral part of the landscape. This page corresponds with the opening page of the narrative and implies not only the inscrutability of nature, and that evil remains ever-present in the world, but also speaks to our primal, subconscious fears.

Young creates new meaning through his extraordinary illustrations; the explicit and implicit visual metaphors of the wolf throughout the narrative provide an ideological force that counters the happy, more simplistic, conclusion of the original folktale.

Young explores the serious themes contained in folktales through the use of a large number of contrasting colours to reflect the inherent contradictions in his subject matter. In *Cat and Rat: The Legend of the Chinese Zodiac* (1995), he uses thick and heavy pastel illustrations throughout the book. Despite the close friendship of the cat and the rat being the focus at the outset of the story, the narrative is offset by the choice of cold colours such as dark blue and black to express the background, implying that their "friendship" is inflected by a dark conspiracy. The implication of these illustrations functions in opposition to the text, thus resulting in the underlying tension that is conveyed to the reader. Another example of Young's subversion of the traditional folktale narrative arc is *White Wave: A Chinese Tale* (text by Diane Wolkstein: 1979), which is titled *The Snail Girl* (《田螺姑娘》) in the original Chinese folktale, and which marks Young's first use of solely black and white illustrations. The cover of the first edition depicts a large grey snail shell, the black shadow of which features an inanimate object rather than the "moon goddess", a creature who lived in the snail shell as the mysterious key figure of the original story. Thus, the illustration immediately introduces a sense of suspense but also an emotional neutrality to the story. In the redesigned version (1996), a large black snail shell occupies almost the entirety of the cover on a much blacker background, marking the gravity of the story which is about to follow. This text, adapted by the American author Diane Wolkstein, tells a story of unfulfilled love, which differs from the happy ending of the Chinese folktale in which the fairy girl remains on earth and marries the farmer. In this adapted version, the young farmer finds that it was the moon goddess who emerged from the snail shell and cooked for him. Although he knows he is forbidden to touch the goddess, he cannot resist, resulting in the goddess, White Wave, departing but leaving him the snail shell as a gift. The farmer, who has fallen in love with the goddess, wants to build a shrine to bring her back and ignores his farming duties, which results in his starvation. After calling the goddess's name in his great need, he survives on rice emanating from the snail shell, tempers his extravagant expectations, and accepts that he must again begin to farm and live as an ordinary mortal. Both the shrine and the shell disappear when the farmer dies. Compared with the original narrative, this retold text has a richer connotation, implying that love and desire may never be fulfilled, while introducing the idea that, after death, all that remains is the narrative. Young uses black and white paintings to express the emotional resonance of this story, which focuses on the insurmountable boundary between heaven and earth, and conveys the guilt and sorrow of irreparable human limitations. What is particularly remarkable is the deliberate vagueness of the image of the big snail shell, which is illustrated in light lines throughout the book. The spiral pattern on the shell becomes representative of the protagonist's life and the path he will follow and Young uses large blank spaces to convey a form of ethereal nihilism which may be associated with Taoist thought. He has commented in an interview that he did not agree with the stereotypical happy ending of the original story because such conclusions are not necessarily representative of life and children should also be exposed to the possibility of sadder outcomes. In keeping with this point of view, Young's picture books do not shy away from the imperfections of life and the darker side of human nature, much of this being achieved through the unconventional use of contrasting colours, which may involve emotive associations but also lend his books a texture of flexibility and toughness.

Creating tension through conflict is one of a number of Young's aesthetic strategies to break through what I term the "bottleneck" of traditional Chinese illustrations, which often emphasise artistic conception but lack inner tension. The tension of Young's narratives is reflected in his composition of pictures, and the juxtaposition of images. As one such example, he adopts the form of the Chinese screen (Ping Feng 屏 风) to structure the pictures in *Lon Po Po*. The double-spread pages are composed of screens in the groups of 2 + 1, 1 + 2, 1 + 1, 2 + 2 and so on, and the perspectives of different widths form the up-down rhythm of the narration. In the first half of the story, the images of the wolf are huge and tower over the far smaller images of the children, emphasising the threat they face from the wolf. In the second half of the story, the size and position of the images of the children and the wolf are reversed as the illustrations take the perspective of the children, who have climbed up a tree and look down at the small wolf, thus signifying the children's proactive response and increasing dominance. In the Chinese version *Wolf Grandma*, illustrated by Tian Yuan, the size and position of these symbolic representations of good and evil are not particularly dissimilar, the balance of power and the peaceful atmosphere between the two sides reflecting the traditional aesthetic orientation of harmony. Young's painting style, conversely, provides a strong sense of contrast and focuses more on the cross-cultural aesthetic of conflict, while also paying close attention to the resolution of that same conflict: that is, towards balance despite the conflict. As one such example of this attention to conflict and resolution, in the story *Little Plum* (1994) Young adopts softer pastels to outline the images and to portray the scenery combined with a large area of colour blocks and superimposed lines. The exaggerated contrast in the slight size of *Little Plum* in comparison to the enemy troops juxtaposes symbols of oppression against the little boy's extraordinary courage and wisdom in fighting against the enemy despite his diminutive size and the magnitude of the odds he faces. The intersectional arrangement of long shots and close-up scenes reinforces the grand contradictions that lend this story its power and philosophical depth.

Such tension allows for an abundant aesthetic space, equal to that of other forms of literature and expression, as has been noted in Cleanth Brooks's theory of paradox which, as Roger Flower has observed, "posits the power of the tensions involved in poetry as an evaluative criterion in accord with the notion of a poem as drama" (Flower 1973, 193). This standard of poetry evaluation is readily applicable to picture books and in Young's works the contradictions between words and pictures, between the intensive colours and the compositions of the pictures, often evoke a sense of mystery—of strangeness but also of strength. The soothing rhythms of the original Chinese folktales are transformed, given renewed excitement and even a thrilling charm through the symbolic use of colours and images. The majority of contemporary native Chinese picture books of folktales follow traditional themes and aesthetics, but Young, who lives in America, has consciously changed this moderate and light-spirited traditional aesthetic by absorbing and melding the more common Western artistic pursuits of fancy and mystery. In doing so, he has transformed the conventional temperament of Chinese folktales, introduced a dramatic power not seen in the original stories, and through his innovations brought new challenges to readers.

Blending the Intangible with the Abstract to Enrich Artistic Charm

The art in the picture books of different nations may often be said to be representative of the national characteristics from which it emerges. In keeping with his transcultural emphases, Ed Young's illustrations employ a range of artistic methods and styles, including the use of pencil, crayon, papercutting, collage and ink, among other materials and techniques. Many of his works show a relationship to Chinese traditional principles, but they also creatively integrate a number of Western artistic techniques which give these folktales of Chinese origin a new and innovative outlook. For example, his illustrations draw heavily on Chinese freehand brushwork (Xie Yi 写意) but also incorporate the more subjective colours of Western impressionism together with abstract representations of modernism. What these three artistic genres have in common is that they all attach particular importance to conveying the intrinsic spirit or charm of the images themselves, a fusion of Eastern and Western art forms which allows Young to "render the spirit" implicitly, emphasising the verve and feeling that may often be associated with Eastern art while employing the emphasis on thematic importance to which, it may be argued, Western art attaches considerable value.

Young's attractive illustrations often blend freehand watercolour and crayon lines in different textures, creating a mysterious—and often incongruous—beauty. His freehand brushwork involves simple strokes in order to evoke a deep, lingering interest in the images and bears similarities to impressionist techniques in terms of the atmosphere it seeks to create. Young employs "dots", a technique commonly used by Impressionists, to replace lines in traditional paintings, while also borrowing from the Impressionist predilection for the use of "paint to create a broken or reflected sense of light, which captures a sensory impression of life rather than a detailed portrayal of reality. Bright colours and swift brush strokes often mark impressionist art" (Matulka 2008, 80).

The Hunter: A Chinese Folktale (text by Mary Casanova **2000**) is one such example in which the emotive illustrations vividly convey the solemn sentiments of the story. In order to persuade the villagers to leave home to save themselves from the coming flood, the virtuous hunter Hai Li Bu decides to reveal the secret of the pearl from the Dragon King, who warned him never to do so, and which results in his being turned permanently to stone. To reinforce the portentous atmosphere of such a tale, each page is set against a rocklike, dark brown background dotted with black points, the main images being depicted in light or dark ink, while Young also only outlines the general shapes of the villagers instead of specific facial detail, and uses an impressionistic colour block to render the environment. In addition to the two main colours of brown and black, he occasionally adds a small number of white, red, indigo or cyan dots as special signifiers, combined with images that alternate between impressionism and realism, to suggest the psychological state and emotional shifts of the characters.

While traditional Chinese folktales generally focus on plot, Western narratives are often inclined to pay equal attention to the characters' personalities and psychological motivations. Young integrates these two schools of thought in his imagery and seeks to convey the visualisation of a hidden mental world, a world in which the depiction of eyes, symbolising a "window to the soul", becomes one of his principal concerns. To visually represent this, Young often uses line-drawing skills to depict eyes highlighted by white. For example, in *Lon Po Po*, the eyes of the wolf and children are emphasised on several occasions, just as the prominent emotive facial expressions in the climax of *The Hunter* represent Hai Li Bu's conflicted and highly emotional inner world. Young portrays the tears in the central character's eyes and the big pearl in his palms with white crayon, contrasting this texture with tan pastels in the background. Such illustrations in picture books serve a crucial function in that they contribute to the narrative beyond merely visualising the written text. In this instance, Young's depiction of eyes reflects the inner motivations and psychology of the characters and in so doing supplements but also transcends the text, in that it expands a psychological space not covered by words and reinvents a Chinese painting tradition that is more likely to convey its characters' temperaments in a vague, ambiguous fashion.

Young combines freehand brushwork with abstraction and symbolism to create indistinct yet complex aesthetic effects. *Yeh-Shen: A Cinderella Story from China* (text by Al-Ling Louie 1982) is another such masterpiece that exhibits these qualities. In this story, in addition to a surfeit of blank space designed to render a dreamlike atmosphere, Young employs a unique expressionist style to evoke a balance between reality and illusion. Yeh-Shen is the oldest version worldwide of the Cinderella story, dating back to the Tang Dynasty in China in the nineteenth century BC, and over a thousand years earlier than the oldest-known version of the Cinderella story in Europe.[2] Yet Young has observed that, when taken from a cross-cultural perspective, one perceives shared truths in both versions, which exist alongside each other, but also draw strength from these differing cultural perspectives: "When you take two Cinderella stories and put them side-by-side, you start to see both the universal truth across cultures and the uniqueness of each culture" (Young 1996). Such symbiosis is clearly reflected in Young's illustrations in which the old man, transformed by the soul of the carp, is equivalent to Cinderella's European godmother. In Young's version, the charming image of the fairy carp, which first appears on the cover, continues through almost the entirety of the narrative; its various guises are embodied with soft, light watercolour shades to reflect the different atmosphere of the setting or the protagonist's mood, an expressionistic style which results in a graceful aesthetic effect. Such a mixture of reality and illusion invites readers to enter an ethereal and imaginative world.

Even in *The Emperor and the Kite* (text by Jane Yolen 1967), which uses a simple paper-cutting technique, Young not only pursues the delicacy of what the traditional Chinese paper cutting emphasises in its shape but also incorporates Western symbolism in its details. For example, when the little princess's four elder brothers line up to worship their royal father, four suns of different shapes and heights are arranged on the spread page, because the brothers resemble four rising suns in their father's eyes; when her three elder sisters go to serve food to their father, three moons in varying degrees of wax and wane also symbolise their significance in their father's eyes. The shape and position of the suns and moons, and the varying degrees of light emanating from them imply the different ages, positions and even the personalities of the princes and princesses. The facial expression of the dragon-face kite, made by the ignored little princess, indicates her loneliness and her desire to be valued, a symbolic strategy which Young often employs to implicitly show the unuttered feelings and thoughts of his characters, and which forces readers to closely consider the characters' motivation and psychological makeup.

While the narration of traditional folktales is invariably chronologically linear and relatively straightforward, Young's narration of the folktales through illustration, imagery, and visual symbolism breaks these stereotypes through the introduction of multiple aesthetic elements. Generally speaking, in the illustration of a folktale it is inevitable that one must closely consider the specific folk style for, as Denise Matulka has noted,

Folk art expresses traditions passed from generation to generation and reflects commonly held beliefs, values, and customs. Although similar to naïve art, what makes folk art distinct is the sense of place often inherent in the illustrations. The artist spends a lot of time researching costumes, mood, and spirit. The finished illustration has a homemade or handcrafted look. (Matulka 2008, 80)

Young's illustrations are based on a figurative folk style, which foregrounds national or regional characteristics, and which is blended with abstract and symbolic elements together with aspects of modernism and, on occasion, postmodernism. In *The Cat from Hunger Mountain* (2016), for example, he adopts an exquisite mixed-media collage, which comprises a large number of traditional Chinese elements, to visualise the decoration of the cat's house and the pattern of its clothing. Young organises the paper, cloth, bamboo and other materials of different textures into an elaborate collage which creates a multifaceted effect and enhances the visual stimulus for the reader. The imagery employed to create the characters is also unusual. This folktale relates the narrative of a rich lord who, having lived a luxurious and wasteful life, endures a famine, and repents of his former lifestyle after begging rice from a monk who had saved the lord's previously wasted rice. Interestingly in this tale, Young makes use of animal rather than human images, a number of which are borrowed from the famous American animated movie *Kung Fu Panda* (2008), including the panda, peacock, leopard, and which lend a sense of playfulness and contemporary fashion. Young complements the moral lesson in the original folktale with the philosophical binaries of possession and loss, and of existence and absence, which are underscored by an imperative to cherish the seemingly mundane aspects of our daily life, as is evidenced by the dedication: "To the strange virtue in deprivation, an unwanted and the least understood gateway to humanity and life's riches". The rice in this story symbolises the preciousness of the ordinary, both the tangible and intangible, which are so often ignored in our daily lives and Young turns the somewhat tedious didacticism of the original fable into a deeply affecting and thought-provoking modern story. His collage illustrations combine exaggerated close-ups of characters set upon an idyllic background scenery and juxtaposes rough and delicate styles, humour and sorrow, together with multidimensional perspectives, to completely reimagine the original story.

Young's picture books are invariably amalgams of the concrete and the abstract, but it is these abstract elements, I would suggest, which can especially ignite a child reader's imagination and comprehension because such art seeks to attain philosophical truths through focusing on internal quality and external form, through exaggerating or simplifying objects and their forms, and through highlighting the expression of emotions and feelings: "Abstractionism is the progress of art and aesthetic ideas, which is no longer a direct expression but an indirect expression. While we are creating, observing and appreciating, it has already started to think about it" (Chu 2011, 102). In this sense, Young has a close awareness of the needs of his young readers:

> When the children read my books, I want [my books] to excite the children. I want their imagination to roam. I want to encourage their participation. I want them to find something which they cannot see immediately. (Young 1996)

The author's expectation of his readers' responses orientates his creation, and ensures that his abstract approach to his subject aligns closely to children's participation and thought processes, the intent of which is to form a symbiosis between the author and the young reader. Young's artistic methods, which blend Chinese traditional painting skills and modern artwork, invite the reader to consider the concepts expressed in the story at multiple levels but also, in his retelling of folktales through image narratives, there may be witnessed a sensitive rendering of Eastern aesthetics melded with the intellectual erudition of the Western style. The result is both delicate and wild, agile and profound. Thus, the subtle synthesis of Chinese and Western artistic methods greatly enriches his retelling of traditional narratives, attracting readers into broader and richer spaces and expanding their aesthetic visions and emotional experiences.

ENCODING CULTURAL MEMORY
AND PURSUING SYMBIOTIC AESTHETICS

As a cross-cultural Chinese American author and illustrator, Young consciously embraces the responsibility of carrying forward traditional Chinese culture and art. Yet his retelling of Chinese folktales is not only for readers of "all ages", as he explains in *The Lost Horse: A Chinese Folktale* (1998) but also for readers of "all ethnic groups" precisely because what is closely related to cultural communication from creators is the cultural acceptance of their readers. The French thinker Pierre Bourdieu defined the essence of this cultural acceptance in the following terms: "The manner in which culture has been acquired lives on in the manner of using it. [...] A work of art has meaning and interest only for someone who possesses the cultural competence, that is, the code, into which it is encoded" (Bourdieu 1984, 2). Considering these sentiments in relation to picture books that rely heavily on image narration, it may be seen as crucial to make full use of the images, and the deeper symbolism contained within those images, to convey cultural information and to help readers to receive such information as effectively as possible. Karen Coats points out that a key issue in the process of reading images in picture books is as follows: "Images speak to us emotionally, intellectually, and socially, but their messages are not transparent; they are mediated through our embodied memories and experiences as well as our experiences with other texts in our culture" (Coats 2018, 158). Thus, in order to address readers beyond purely national boundaries, Young's picture books on folktales are not only encoded with national culture internally but also with ethnic cultural codes and manners externally. For instance, he often overtly positions information about Chinese culture and associated interpretations directly before or after the main body of the picture book, a tactic used to facilitate the perception and comprehension of a non-Chinese readership.

Young attaches great importance to the use of paratext, a theoretical concept first put forward by the French structuralist critic, Gérard Genette, before and after the central text, making significant use of it to disseminate cultural coding.[3] In comparing it to a "threshold", rather than the more restrictive qualities of a "boundary", Genette deemed that the most essential component of a paratext is what he terms its "functionality":

> Whatever aesthetic intention may come into play as well, the main issue for the paratext is not to "look nice" around the text but rather to ensure for the text a destiny consistent with the author's purpose... [T]he paratext provides an airlock that helps the reader pass without too much respiratory difficulty from one world to the other, a sometimes delicate operation, especially when the second world is a fictional one. (Genette 1997, 407–408)

In other words, the paratext is designed to make readers approach the meaning of the text and its didactic intentions through accessing its coded hints and implications—encoded cultural information which Young makes considerable effort to embed in an aesthetically pleasing and readily approachable format.

With regard to his approach to folk stories recorded in ancient Chinese literature, Young usually sets a page at the beginning of the picture book and copies the original story with Chinese brush calligraphy, which provides a direct display of the national cultural landscape. Calligraphy, drawing and seals[4] are integrated to form a cohesive whole in Chinese painting and Young is especially fond of using seals as special cultural codes in order to remind readers of the story's original language. In *Cat and Rat*, he reveals the Chinese zodiac animal names with seals and explains the personality of each animal in order to arouse readers' curiosity about their year of birth and its correspondence to the characteristics of that zodiac sign. Cultural annotations of this nature assist readers in accessing cultural detail at both specific and broader levels. Another example, *The Sons of the Dragon King* (2004), restates the Chinese folktale regarding the nine sons of the dragon by infusing it with the modern connotation of rearing someone according to his or her natural ability. Before the text, Young introduces the Chinese legend of the dragon in an "author's instruction" and employs unusual seals to demonstrate the names of the nine sons of the dragon king, as well as the cause of the story. Moreover, this use of seals in his work sometimes has a specific narrative function. In *The Hunter*, for instance, the seals on the right-hand corner of each right page are similar to the chapter titles seen in ancient Chinese novels, but these seals also function as a second narrative, which not only summarises the main plot of the double-page spread, but "comments on the nexus of illustration/story [for] just as the second narrative creates a polyvocality to the text of the picture book, so does the second narrative create a polyvocality to the illustrations" (Stewart 2003, 46). Thus, the illustrations with seals present multiple perspectives and allow for multiple interpretations and it is through narratorial strategies such as this that Young consciously and symbolically highlights national cultural codes and endows his stories with multiple meanings and functions from content through to form.

The strategy of coding national cultures can also be further reflected upon in Young's picture books of folktales from other countries, nations and regions. In each instance, Young studies and applies the respective national artistic techniques to his interpretations to convey cultures and aesthetic landscapes into which Chinese cultural codes and aesthetics are also appropriately melded. One such example, *Moon Mother* (1993), is adapted according to a native Indian legend regarding the creation of animals and humans. The text lyrically describes the relationship among immortals, humans and nature. It foregrounds the intimate relationship that indigenous people share with nature, which bears some similarities to the Chinese Taoist philosophy regarding "the union of heaven and human". The hazy colour of its illustrations evokes the sense of mystery inherent in the Indian legend, while combining it with the "artistic conception" (意境) seen in Chinese traditional art. A further example, *I, Doko: The Tale of the Basket* (2004), relates to a Nepali story, yet Young cites a famous Confucian saying before the principal text: "What one wishes not upon oneself, one burdens not upon another.—Kung Fu Tze, Sixth Century B.C." The growth and decline of life are represented from the perspective of the basket's narrative, which criticises the unfilial and heartless behaviour of abandoning the elderly. This story relates particularly to family ethics that may be associated with East Asian cultures. The Nepali clothing, accessories and living customs are vividly depicted and the distant vistas are represented through light colour redolent of Chinese freehand brushwork, while the characters' facial features, which reflect their intense emotions, are portrayed in close-up, a technique often associated with Western art. Thus, both harmonious and contradictory images are interwoven in the text to correspond to the highs and lows of the plot itself, a method of storytelling which evokes an emotive response through the manifestation of internal and external narrative tension. Young's recreations of geographically and culturally diverse folktales can be regarded as an extension of his retelling of Chinese folktales, and further expands his cultural empathy and artistic techniques. These works have an intrinsic consistency in their thoughts and art; namely, they embrace a consideration of national culture and universal individuality, compose multicultural codes on the basis of respecting a variety of art forms and consciously or unconsciously synthesise the creator's own cultural orientation, artistic techniques and style. All of these factors combine to produce a new or revised understanding of folktales, offering a unique contribution to the promotion of cultural diversity in children's literature in the contemporary world.

In his work on folktales, Young encodes a large number of overt and covert cultural elements, thereby constructing a national cultural memory which retains a unity but can also represent, where appropriate, the hybridity and diversity of its components. Such an approach reflects his consideration of ethnic cultural identity in the context of different cultures and is an important artistic position to embrace in the modern, transcultural world because, as Jan Assmann, a scholar of ancient Egyptology in Germany who studies cultural memory argues, cultural memory and globalisation often work in opposite directions:

> Memory functions in the direction of identity which, in all of its fuzziness, always implies a notion of difference. Globalization, on the other hand, works in the direction of diffusion, blurring all boundaries and bridging all differences. (Assmann 2010, 123)

The motivation for Young to reimagine Chinese folktales, I would argue, stems from his awareness of what I term the "identity" of the mother culture and the "alterity" of the immigrant culture, the tension between which is one of the main consequences of globalisation. Young reimagines folktales and uses them as instruments of renewal which embrace a new spirit, stories in which cultural "identity" and "otherness" are neither completely separated nor opposed, but which show the multiple possibilities of integration. The context of culture comprises, in part, a vertical time flow and horizontal space and in Young's works, this time flow is mainly demonstrated as a transformation from tradition to modernity, while space is manifested as a juxtaposition of the East and the West. To explain this in more detail, it is helpful to note the work of Liu Guanzhong, a Chinese scholar of design who has put forward the concept of "symbiosis aesthetics", which emphasises the integration of different elements, including vertical inheritance and horizontal communication:

> Tradition and innovation coexist. Science and art coexist. History and present coexist. Nature and humans coexist [...] The symbiosis also covers the coexistence of different cultures and different aesthetic views. The separated elements are synthesized into a complete and infinite system by overlapping, paralleling, composition and combination to construct the unity in the contradiction. (Liu: 30)

Under these circumstances, the elements of disparate time, space and nature seek harmony and unity through difference and produce multiple meanings in this newly built aesthetic system. Yet the sublimated effect through this interaction is more complex and far richer than the simple sum of several elements for this aesthetic view of symbiosis reflects positive, creative and multidimensional philosophical views and provides an ideological basis for contemporary multicultural symbiosis.

As an active organism, all culture(s) must constantly adapt, and such adaptation and alteration necessarily require a constant and collective revision of historical memory together with an allowance for new realities and ideas. The innovation in, and development of, any given culture must also be derived from its exchange and complementarity with other cultures.

Under these terms, Young's creative picture books, based on folktales, provide an essential cross-cultural synthesis through his lived experience of dual cultural identity. The collision and intersection of experiences in this heterogeneous space, and the mutual adjustment between traditional and modern art forms and ideas from East and West, ensure that his creations comprise open-minded cultural visions and ideas that are both active and constantly evolving. His works reflect a range of mixed cultural images encoded in an abundance of cultural information and meanings, but also demonstrate a tonality beyond his own ethnic traditions, as John Stephens and Robyn McCallum argue in *Retelling Stories, Framing Culture*:

> [F]ew retellings are simple replications, even when they appear to reproduce the story and point of view of the source. In such cases, the purpose is generally cultural reproduction, in the sense of transmitting desired knowledge about society and the self, modes of learning, and forms of authority. (Stephens and McCallum 1998, 4)

Young's creative retelling of Chinese (and other) folktales, then, combines not only the distinct marks of national culture, but also embeds cultural and artistic codes in the narratives to form a symbiosis of diverse society(ies) and the heterogeneity that drives such societies forward.

To extend this idea further, the theory of symbiotic aesthetics proposed by Liu Guanzhong also speculates upon the relationship between artists and recipients:

> Arts need to go beyond the artist's own narrowness and limitation to give the power and opportunities to the masses, to participate in art by opening the door of the art palace, and to inspire, as well as to induce, the receivers' association/imagination to reach the reinvented realm through communicating and supplementing with each other. (Liu 2008, 30)

This is a crucial and non-negotiable aspect of art and its creative process, and one which is further underlined by Wang Yuechuan, a scholar of literary theory, who interprets the essence of "understanding" in his *Art Ontology* (1994) in the following terms:

> It is not only the emotional and rational communication between one person and another but also my existence and my way of existence. It drives my consciousness and all the unconsciousness in my primal energy to pursue a new life. (Wang 1994, 260)

Thus, the process of understanding a text necessarily requires the active search for meaning in the text itself, a process which also involves the individual reader forming the meaning of the text in concert with the reader's own lived experiences and life philosophies. Given these considerations, Jack Zipes's observations on the purpose of such tales in *Breaking the Magic Spell: Radical Theories of Folk and Fairy Tales* are of particular relevance:

> Paradoxically the magic power of folk and fairy tales stems from the fact that they do not pretend to be anything but folk and fairy tales, that is, they make no claims to be anything but artistic projections of fantasy. And in this non-pretension they give us the freedom to see what path we must take to become self-fulfilled. They respect our autonomy and leave the decisions of reality up to us while at the same time they provoke us to think about the way we live. (Zipes 1979, 18)

Young's picture books transmit Chinese cultural landscapes to a broad readership while also transforming this same landscape by way of the autonomous freedom that his bicultural sensibilities engender. This inspires readers to actively participate in decoding the cultural connotations inherent in the retold tale, but to also consider new landscapes at internal (through text and images) and external (through lived experience) levels of engagement. During such a subjective process, readers are likely to begin to encode their own understanding into the text to complete the production of the meaning of the text, and in so doing achieve the goal of symbiotic aesthetics advanced by Liu. Undoubtedly, reading picture books is helpful not only in shaping children's aesthetic sensibilities but also in forming their ideologies and identities, an argument that Coats also affirms:

> Illustrations tell powerful stories that are meant to appeal to the viewer's emotions and convey cultural values [and] it is important to understand how illustrations in children's and YA texts participate in the emotional and ideological structuring of contemporary enculturated subjects. (Coats 2018, 150)

Appreciation and understanding of picture books that bear external national/cultural memories are highly likely to have an impact on the attitudes towards these national cultures of those children who may be experiencing them for the first time or who may live outside of these cultural parameters, and may strongly influence their own ideologies and even their own worldview and identity. As for readers approaching such texts from within their own nation or ethnicity, these experiences may contribute to reaffirming—and in some cases challenging—their national/ethnic cultural identity, while for foreign readers this may also contribute to a more open-minded cultural vision. Through this organic integration of the characteristics of different national cultures, as well as the intangible synergism between author and reader(s), Young has created a multidimensional example of symbiotic aesthetics in his picture books, which provides young readers with an essential tool for their mental development.

Conclusion

As Nancy L. Hadaway argues in her introductory article "Building Bridges to Understanding" in *Breaking Boundaries with Global Literature*:

> Literature reflects the experiences, values, and beliefs of a group of people. As such, it can provide insights into a culture, promote empathy, and support a developing sense of identity. Through literature we can extend our knowledge as well as our personal boundaries, developing new perspectives and expanding our understanding of who 'we' are. (Hadaway and McKenna 2007, 1)

Hadaway suggests using the term "global literature" in preference to either "multicultural literature" or "international literature" (2007, 5). Folktales, so many of which seem to have been conceived across cultures and bear universal thematic connections and narrative structures are, I would suggest, prime examples of global literature. And it is these components of global folktales, which embrace unity but also celebrate diversity, that provide crucial ideological points of connection and comprehension across culture and chronology. As Ashley Bryan, an illustrator and folklore expert, has noted, "I came to feel that the stories of the world tend to bring us together. I speak of folk stories as a 'tender bridge,' as a way of connecting past cultures and times to the present" (Quoted in Marcus 2012, 35).

Ed Young has a similar view: he regards picture books and children's literature as singularly important, for these works can help children find where they belong in their society and in the world. He creates picture books of folktales which draw from a national context but are expanded to include symbiotic aesthetics in order to give children in the era of globalisation a broader vision through which to seek their cultural identity. He has transformed, regenerated and sublimated Chinese national cultural memory into a more universal and modern one, and one which provides a reference point for the children's literature of various countries in how to activate local cultural resources, how to explore and represent the relationship between immediate national considerations and broader global concerns, and between tradition and modernity. In closing this discussion, it is pertinent here to reference Mitsumasa Anno, a distinguished Japanese master whose creations have also garnered international recognition, and which bear some connection with Young's work. In creating *Anno's Journey*, a series of picture books about the landscapes of many countries, Anno notes that he unconsciously adopts the traditional Japanese picture-scroll form, but that his core idea is:

> [E]verywhere in the world, if there is a road and a river, there is always a bridge. In making my books, I have been seeking archetypes that transcend any particular culture. I have looked for images that people everywhere would know. (Quoted in Marcus 2012, 13)

Though Young's work differs in many aspects from that of Anno, and each has his own artistic approach to cultural awareness and universality, both roads lead to the same destination. In this era of globalisation, it is the open-minded pursuit of symbiotic aesthetics and the creation of children's texts that embrace this understanding, and that hold true to the philosophy of Fei Xiaotong, a Chinese scholar of sociology and anthropology, who advocates that "various beauty can coexist and be harmonious but different" (2013, 458). Such a concept is particularly important for children's literature that aims at cultivating future citizens cognisant of their national heritage but also of their global responsibilities. Ed Young's work embodies this ideal.

NOTES

1. The Caldecott Medal: The Caldecott Medal was founded in 1937. It is awarded annually by the Children's and School Librarians' Sections of the American Library Association and is named in honour of the nineteenth-century English illustrator Randolph J. Caldecott. The Caldecott Medal is

awarded to the artist of the most distinguished American Picture Book for Children published in the United States during the preceding year and goes to the artist, who must be a citizen or resident of the United States, whether or not he or she is the author of the text. One winning picture book and four honour picture books are selected every year (http://www.ala.org/alsc/awardsgrants/bookmedia/caldecottmedal/aboutcaldecott/aboutcaldecott).

2. There are thousands of variants of the Cinderella stories over the world. The first literary European version of this story was published in Italy by Giambattista Basile in his *Pentamerone* in 1634; and the version in French by Charles Perrault in *Histoires ou contes du temps passé* in 1697. Another version in German was published by the Brothers Grimm in their folk tale collection *Grimms' Fairy Tales* in 1812.

3. Paratext is a concept in literary interpretation which is often associated with books, including a cover, title, front matter, back matter footnotes and many other materials. Editorial decisions can also fall into the category of paratext, such as the formatting or typography. The added elements form a frame for the main text, and might change the reception of a text or its interpretation by the reader.

4. A seal in Chinese arts is a special printing stamp which usually represents a name.

References

Assmann, Jan. 2010. "Globalization, Universalism, and the Erosion of Cultural Memory". In Assmann, Ali & Conrad, Sebastian (eds.), *Memory in a Global Age: Discourses, Practices and Trajectories*. London and New York: Palgrave Macmillan.

Bourdieu, Pierre. 1984. *Distinction: A Social Critique of the Judgement of Taste* (1979). Trans. Richard Nice. Cambridge, MA: Harvard University Press.

Casanova, Mary & Young, Ed. 2000. *The Hunter: A Chinese Folktale*. New York: Atheneum Books for Young Readers.

Chu, Xiaoqing. 2011. "Design, Human and Contemporary China: An Interview with Professor Liu Guanzhong". *Yi Shu Bai Jia*, 123(6): 96–112. [楚小庆:《设计与人类以及当代中国——清华大学美术学院柳冠中教授访谈录》,《艺术百家》2011(6): 96–112。]

Coats, Karen. 2018. *Bloomsbury Introduction to Children's and Young Adult Literature*. London and New York: Bloomsbury.

Fei, Xiaotong. 2013. "Diverse Aesthetics Together and Human Civilization". *Globalization and Cultural Self-Awareness*. Beijing: Foreign Language Teaching and Research Press. [费孝通:《"美美与共"和人类文明》,《全球化与文化自觉》, 北京:外语教学与研究出版社, 2013年。]

Flower, Roger (ed.). 1973. *A Dictionary of Modern Critical Terms*. London and Boston: Routledge & Kegan Paul.

Genette, Gerard. 1997. *Paratexts: Thresholds of Interpretation*. Trans. Jane E. Lewin. Cambridge: Cambridge University Press.

Hadaway, Nancy L. & McKenna, Marian J. (ed.). 2007. *Breaking Boundaries with Global Literature: Celebrating Diversity in K-12 Classrooms*. Newark: International Reading Association.

Hu, Yong. 2003. *Cultural Homesickness: Cultural Identity of Chinese American Literature*. Beijing: China Drama Press. [胡勇：《文化的乡愁——美国华裔文学的文化认同》, 北京：中国戏剧出版社, 2003年。]

Liu, Guanzhong. 2008. "Symbiotic Aesthetics: An Exploration of Contemporary Design and Art Philosophy". *Decoration*, 186(10): 28–30. [柳冠中：《共生美学观——对当代设计与艺术哲学的初探》,《装饰》2008年第10期, 第28–30页。]

Louie, Ai-Ling & Young, Ed. 1982. *Yeh-Shen: A Cinderella Story from China*. New York: Philomel.

Marcus, Leonard S. (ed.). 2012. *Show Me a Story! Why Picture Books Matter: Conversations with 21 of the World's Most Celebrated Illustrators*. Somerville, MA: Candlewick Press.

Matulka, Denise. 2008. *A Picture Book Primer: Understanding and Using Picture Books*. Westport: Libraries Unlimited.

Stephens, John & McCallum, Robyn. 1998. *Retelling Stories, Framing Cultures*. New York and London: Garland Publishing.

Stewart, Michelle Pagni. 2003. "Emerging Literacy of (An)other Kind: Speakerly Children's Picture Books". *Children's Literature Association Quarterly*, 28(1): 42–51.

Wang, Yuechuan. 1994. *Art Ontology*. Shanghai: Shanghai San Lian Bookshop. [王岳川：《艺术本体论》, 上海：上海三联书店, 1994年。]

Wolkstein, Diane & Young, Ed. 1979. *White Wave: A Chinese Tale*. New York: Crowell.

———. 1996. *White Wave: A Chinese Tale* (redesigned edition). San Diego: Harcourt Brace.

Yolen, Jane & Young, Ed. 1967. *The Emperor and the Kite*. New York: Philomel.

Young, Ed. 1989. *Lon Po Po: A Red-Riding Hood Story from China*. New York: Philomel.

———. 1993. *Moon Mother*. New York: HarperCollins.

———. 1994. *Little Plum*. New York: Philomel.

———. 1995. *Cat and Rat: The Legend of the Chinese Zodiac*. New York: Henry Holt.

———. 1996, July 23. *Interview with Jui-Yi Huang* [Cassette Recording]. New York: Hastings-on-Hudson.

———. 1998. *The Lost Horse: A Chinese Folktale*. San Diego: Harcourt Brace.

———. 2004. *I, Doko: The Tale of the Basket*. New York: Philomel Books.

————. 2004. *Sons of the Dragon King.* New York: Atheneum Books for Young Readers.

————. 2016. *The Cat from Hunger Mountain.* New York: Philomel Book.

Zhao, Yiheng. 2011. *Semiotic Principles and Deduction.* Nanjing: Nanjing University Press. [赵毅衡:《符号学原理与推演》, 南京: 南京大学出版社, 2011年。]

Zhou, Zhengliang & Tian, Yuan. 2010. *Wolf Grandma.* Guizhou: Guizhou People Press. [周正良改编、 田原绘画:《狼外婆》, 贵州: 贵州人民出版社2010年。]

Zipes, Jack. 1979. *Breaking the Magic Spell: Radical Theories of Folk and Fairy Tales.* London: Heinemann.

CHAPTER 16

Hyphens, Hybrids and Bridges: Negotiating Third Spaces in Asian-American Children's Literature

Susan Ang

In *The Location of Culture* (1994), Homi Bhabha theorises the Third Space, a dialogical site in which the asymmetries of power and culture between two groups might be set aside for them to encounter one another. That encounter, which displaces both groups from their origins, results in the "dissemination of both cultural traditions", and the emergence of a new, hybrid, identity which is "neither the one

---

There are certain Third spaces that are more productive and meaningful than others. One of these is the classroom and all the virtual versions that grow from it. Here, asymmetries of power dissolve and ideas hybridise, then to be disseminated. I am very grateful to students past and present: Lim Zhan Yi, Justin Goh, Rebecca Seah and Joycelyn Lee who have in various ways helped to shape this piece.

S. Ang (✉)
Department of English Language and Literature, National
University of Singapore, Singapore
e-mail: susan_ang@nus.edu.sg

B. Wilson and S. P. Gabriel (eds.), *Asian Children's Literature
and Film in a Global Age*, Asia-Pacific and Literature in English,
https://doi.org/10.1007/978-981-15-2631-2_16

or the other" (Ikas and Wagner 2009, 2). That Third Space is thus a *dis*comfort zone, a space outside and beyond the clarities, certainties and essentialisms of either group, a space of the provisional, the tentative, the unknown, and therefore a negotiatory space in which one feels and navigates one's way towards new knowledge. In this sense, the Third Space is a meta-epistemological space, one in which one becomes aware of the inadequacies of former knowledge and ways of knowing. It is also an empirical space, in the sense that it is here that the truths of lived experience—what Henri Lefebvre might align with his own version of "Third space", i.e. *espace vecu* (lived space)[1]—come to supplant those of inherited and theoretical knowledge about the other. The in-between-ness, outside-ness and beyond-ness of Third space is thus what Bhabha theorises as providing the "terrain for elaborating strategies of selfhood – singular or communal – that initiate new signs of identity, and innovative sites of collaboration, and contestation, in the act of defining the idea of society itself" (Bhabha 2004, 2).

This is perhaps a useful set of observations with which to begin an investigation of Asian-American children's literature, one of whose main concerns is the hyphenated and hybrid existence of its subject (Asian-American culture/individuals), and the way in which its protagonists venture the terms of that existence, the terra incognita between cultures and/or the edgy interface between ethnicity and nationality. That venture, as this chapter argues, is, in many works of children's literature, channelled through Third space, whose ambivalences and ambiguities create the conditions for the state of not-knowing that must precede the formation of new knowledge, which is often arrived at and expressed through the shuttling or migration of the sign.

Many of the texts this chapter will be referring to could be described as *Bildungsromane*, which is perhaps to be expected, given the elective affinity between the intended reader, literary form and Asian-American writing; I speak of their mutual concern with matters of formation and identity. The features of the Asian-American *Bildungsroman* derive from the particularities of the Asian-American experience, which, whether that of the "FOB" ("Fresh off the boat") or "ABC" (American-Born-Chinese), whether that of *issei, nisei* or *sansei* (first, second and third-generation Japanese-Americans), and their correlatives in other immigrant ethnic groups, is, as Shirley Geok-Lin Lim has noted, that of the ethnic minority which lives as a permanent stranger in the eyes of the majority (Lim 1986, 58) with all that this entails. The Asian-American immigrant may have two homes or none, as seen, for example, in Lensey Namioka's *Ties That Bind, Ties That Break* (1999) which details the experiences of a Chinese girl, disowned by her family, who emigrates to America, or Cynthia Kadohata's *A Place to Belong* (2019) whose protagonist, an American-born-Japanese, is (re)patriated to Japan after the war. That "home" can be provisional and shifting, as seen in Kadohata's *Outside Beauty* (2008), and the experience of unsettled liminality that Bhabha notes as characterising our times might in fact be said to mark the "restless mobility" (Bhabha 2018, 2) of the Asian-American experience in which there is often the same

> sense of disorientation, a disturbance of direction, […] an exploratory, restless movement caught so well in the French rendition of the words *au-delà* – here and there, on all sides, *fort/da*, hither and thither, back and forth. (Bhabha 2004, 2)

The immigrant's children or grandchildren might be simultaneously "a part of" while yet being "apart from". They might have two names (Joseph/Precious Light, Mary/Third Sister Yang[2]) or even more, as mused upon by the protagonist of Grace Lin's *Dumpling Days* (2012) as she gazes on her new name chop, carved for her during her visit to Taiwan:

> The crisp red square, the Chinese characters, and GRACE PACY in block letters. Should I have gotten Grace Pacy Lin, since that was my whole name in English? Hmm. Well, some of the Chinese characters meant Lin, but none meant Grace. So maybe it was okay. Maybe it made things kind of equal. Grace was the part of me that was all American, Lin was the part that was all Asian, but Pacy was both. (Lin 2019, 236)

Yet, no matter the names or their number, the protagonists of many Asian-American works for children struggle with the lack of a clearly defined sense of self, as seen, for example, in *Who's Hu?* (1980) the cultural-national-ethnic "identity crisis" (Namioka 1980, 8) of whose 1950s Chinese-American protagonist, Emma Hu, is amplified by gender issues as she attempts to work through the seeming contradictions of being a girl *and* a maths genius, two things considered incompatible by many of her peers both American and Chinese-American.

The Asian-American experience in children's literature often begins with discomfort and asymmetry, which are confronted, worked through and worked out in environments and locations which are, effectively, Third spaces. While Bhabha's Third space is an abstraction, a metaphorical space, a conceptual space, the concept is often mobilised in Laurence Yep's fiction via actual literal spaces, which are simultaneously a part of and apart from the social space of the community, as are the individuals that they host. Examples from Yep's *Golden Mountain Chronicles* may be found in the cemetery in *Mountain Light* (1985) where Cassia and Squeaky, from communities hostile to each other, for lack of any other safe meeting space, come to converse or the cave in *The Traitor* (2003) where Michael and Joseph—outsiders to their own communities—encounter each other, the railway tunnels where Otter shares food and conversation with Seth in *Dragon's Gate* (1993), and the boarding house in *Dragonwings* (1975) where Miss Whitlaw, her niece Robin, Moon Shadow and Wind Rider learn to see the shape of each other's constellations in the same stars. Other examples of the literalised Third space may be found in Cynthia Kadohata's work, for instance in the Kazakhstani orphanage from *Half a World Away* (2014) in which the Romanian child adopted by American parents finally makes accommodation with them as they prepare to adopt a second, Kazakhstani, child. Further examples exist in the mobile trailer and harvesting fields of *The Thing About Luck* (2013) and in all the other temporary homes and micro "floating worlds" constituted by internment camps and other such spaces of *Weedflower* (2009) and *A Place to Belong* (2019) in which the child, stepping outside the known safety of its own space, encounters the stranger, and in doing so, finds himself.

The importance of the literality or concreteness of these Third spaces inheres in the fact that it is sociospatiality which gives shape and dimensionality to the sociohistorical and sociopolitical, hence sharpening and giving force to the symbolics of Third space. The concreteness of the spatiality both activates and "actualises" the sociohistorical and sociopolitical, in both senses of the word "actualize", enabling the realisation, manifestation and action of those forces, turning, as Justin Goh has observed, "theory into practice, ideology into reality and epistemology into phenomenology".[3] If the discourse of power can draw so intuitively on spatial metaphors, such as that of marginality, it is because the literal expressions of space are—in a quite non-symbolic way—expressions of power, and also their asymmetries. The experienced limits of personal space often correspond to the felt limits of personal power, the allocation and location of space within a larger geopolity being likewise an index of sociopolitical power; the jostling for space and position in the locked hold, within the micro-polity of the ship bringing Tiny and Squeaky over from China (*Mountain Light*) is a clear demonstration of the relations between power, location and spatiality. "Small" may not in itself symbolise disempowerment, but "small", in spatial terms, tends to signal constrained economic power which has its own correlation to other forms of power. The spatial experience of the Asian immigrant in America, as depicted in Yep's novels, is largely one of small constricted spaces, the point sharpened when set against the plenitudinous availability of space in America. Otter, seeing the American landscape from the train, hears a fellow Chinese traveller comment "You could grow anything here ... And they use hardly any of the land" (Yep 2001b, 74). The dangerously cramped boat from China to America (*Mountain Light*), the squashed cabins and narrow tunnels for the railroad workers (*Dragon's Gate*), the tiny apartments in Chinatown (*Child of the Owl*) are just some of the sociospatial indicators of sociohistorical power-patterning seen in the novels.

In the same way that the power of the Foucauldian heterotopia derives from its dual ontology, exemplified by way of the mirror whose virtual dimension exists as an extension of the real with each dimension exerting traction on the other, the symbolic acquires force when affinitively (and hyphenatively) yoked to the literal, the symbolics and mechanics of Third space visibilised and illuminated through its concrete manifestations. That visibility is heightened especially when set against the backdrop of the larger literal-symbolic economy of the [Asian]-American landscape whose depiction in *The Traitor* I propose to close-read as sharpening the novel's use of Third space. Michael Purdy, the white American boy, illegitimate child of Mary Purdy, laundress, lives in a small Wyoming town in a shack "called a shotgun, because you could stand at the rear door and blast a shotgun out of the front door and not hit anything" (Yep 2004, 9). The shack has "no hallway, just doors opening from one tiny room to the next", the lack of hallway suggesting the lack of passage, the impasse. The Purdy shack is notable not just for its small cramped conditions—the front room serves both as parlour and Michael's bedroom (Yep 2004, 9) but also for its emptiness and the pencilled outlines of a fireplace, rug, pictures, dog, flowers and fence on the walls which attest simultaneously to the socioeconomic state of the Purdys and to their dreams, signs of what they have, wish to have and do not have, the double ontology of the shack thus functioning as a concrete emblem of the literal-symbolic economy spoken of earlier.

Michael's outsider status within the white American community is manifested through his relations with space, his illegitimacy providing a spurious reason for Miss Virginia to bar him from the church on Sunday. Spatial metaphor is used to further inflect and sketch the map of his social relations as when Michael observes that his white neighbour, Seth, and he "got along like two wildcats tied together by the tail and dumped inside a small bag" (Yep 2004, 10). The problems of an enforced hyphenated existence especially in relation to the limitations of space are flagged up by the image of the wildcats, which however complicates in advance the presumed Asian-American sociological map, by exposing the Asian-American dyad as already-bifurcated by other, less easily named, fault lines. The seeming clarity of the binary (Asian/American) is blurred, in the same way that the pencil outlines on the Purdy shack are scuffed and smudged, by the transferability of the image, whose double applicability (to Asian-American coexistence, to Michael-Seth coexistence), problematises any epistemology, any way of knowing and making sense of the world, that might be constructed purely along ethnic lines.

It may be useful before proceeding to examine the Third space encounters in *The Traitor* to clarify the logic of the "third" in "Third space" by way of Edward Soja and Lefebvre. Lefebvre's observations, in *La Présence et l'absence* (1980) to the effect that the dyad has long governed or structured philosophical thought, proceed to tender the "third" as a term that offers, as Soja says, to break apart the closed logic constituted by the binary.

> This dimension, a third possibility or moment that partakes of the original pairing, is not just a single combination or an "in-between" position along some all-inclusive continuum but can be understood as critical thirding-as-Othering. It is the first and most important step in transforming the categorical and closed logic of either/or to the dialectically open logic of both/and also. Two terms are never enough: *Il y a toujours l'Autre*. There is always the Other, a third term that disrupts, disorders, and begins to reconstitute the conventional binary opposition into an-Other that comprehends but is more than just the sum of two parts. (Soja 2009, 52)

Thirdspace,[4] then, rebukes the binary, not just by offering a third place in which to stand, but, by virtue of its ability to articulate a position not encompassed by the dyad, calls both the epistemological model, and the knowledge produced by it, into question. The knowledge produced by the antithesising machinery of the dyad is challenged by that which is neither a term nor its opposite, and which might not even be a convenient convergence of the two. It is this that lays the ground for Bhabha's Third space in which inherited wisdom and "knowledge" are set aside in favour of unknowing with all its attendant hesitations and humility.

The Third space, then, is a cave of epistemological (and perhaps even ontological) making and unmaking, and as Michael and Joseph step outside the actual spatial territories of their respective groups, which represent an either/or, Asian/American, we may see Third space begin to take abstract form even before it coalesces in the literal form of the cave they will call "Star Rock". Michael, leaving town, crosses a bridge and heads west:

> For my landmark I picked out the pinnacle that towered over the hills. It reared upward from the soil like the Leviathan in the Bible, like some monster punished by being turned into stone. I'd learned every fold and fissure, just as I knew every worry line on my mother's face.
> It was already so hot, it was hard to recognize things at a distance. The heat made their shapes all wavy. For a moment I thought they were the ghosts of the Shoshone Indians we white folks had driven away from here. I bet the Shoshone would have had something to say about the town's claim that this was "our" land. And I bet the Shoshone would have wanted to drive us out back then just like we were trying to do to the Chinese right now. (Yep 2004, 23–24)

What may be noted here is the way in which what is "known" subtly shifts, metamorphoses and is destabilised. The landmark, functioning as a signpost whereby to map the territory, quickly becomes unstable, analogised first to the Leviathan, then re-analogised to a petrified monster, framed first explicitly via Biblical knowledge, then implicitly and less clearly via Greek myth as Andromeda's sea monster petrified by Medusa's head. Despite Michael's claim to detailed, intimate and stable knowledge—that he knows the terrain as well as he knows his mother's face—the very instability of the description and episteme symbolically undermines the assertion. And in the landscape's wavering outlines and metamorphosis in Michael's fancy into the ghosts of the Shoshone, we may trace two points: a further deformation of what has hitherto been firm, and a questioning of the grounds on which the "white" American bases his claim to America. In the description of the literal-symbolic territory Michael traverses, we see Third space taking preparatory shape, as received wisdom that perhaps forms the substratum of being is interrogated. Michael, here, is no longer, either literally, or symbolically, in "his" own territory, "his" space, but in an "other space". That "other" space is both a part of and apart from the territory claimed by the (white) American, in the sense that this is unsettled land; while considered to be part of (white) American possessions, it has to be approached by way of a bridge, a tenuous hyphen.

The reference to an "other space" invokes the heterotopia sketched out in Foucault's "*Des Espace Autres*" (1967), translated into English as "Of Other Spaces", whose place in the argument and analysis should be clarified. The "heterotopia", while not strictly conceived of as a "*third*" space in the same way that Bhabha's, Lefebvre's or Soja's are, shares something of its contestive function, and maps fairly easily to Third space; all of the above, as with Foucault, essentially mean by "space" a set of relations, Foucault observing that

> ... we do not live in a kind of void, inside of which we could place individuals and things. We do not live inside a void that could be colored with diverse shades of light, we live inside a set of relations that delineates sites which are irreducible to one another and absolutely not superimposable on one another. (Foucault 2010, 231)

The heterotopia—the "other space"—has an ambiguous relation to what we might call "this-space", being both situated within "this-space" while being what Foucault calls a "countersite", representing, contesting and inverting the other "real" sites within the culture (Foucault 2010, 231). Its hyphenated "a part of/apart from" relation to "this space" correlates the heterotopia to the Asian enclaves within the American geopolity, as well as to the liminal figure of the insider–outsider which is represented by the Asian-American in many Asian-American texts, and also, in *The Traitor*, by Michael, who inhabits the margins of the white ethnic community. But the heterotopia has yet another implied function which is brought into play by Foucault's exemplification of the heterotopia-as-mirror:

> The mirror is, after all, a utopia, since it is a placeless place. In the mirror, I see myself there where I am not, in an unreal, virtual space that opens

up behind the surface; I am over there, there where I am not, a sort of shadow that gives my own visibility to myself, that enables me to see myself there where I am absent: such is the utopia of the mirror. But it is also a heterotopia in so far as the mirror does exist in reality, where it exerts a sort of counteraction on the position that I occupy. From the standpoint of the mirror I discover my absence from the place where I am since I see myself over there. Starting from this gaze that is, as it were, directed toward me, from the ground of this virtual space that is on the other side of the glass, I come back toward myself; I begin again to direct my eyes toward myself and to reconstitute myself there where I am. The mirror functions as a heterotopia in this respect: it makes this place that I occupy at the moment when I look at myself in the glass at once absolutely real, connected with all the space that surrounds it, and absolutely unreal, since in order to be perceived it has to pass through this virtual point which is over there. (Foucault 2010, 232)

The heterotopia here is implicitly assigned a function deriving from certain of its properties: it is speculative, reflective, that which enables self-visibilisation and thus, self-knowing. But it also interrogates the grounds of one's being in the world while offering to serve as the starting point for self-(re)construction, and it is these functions, accreted to those negotiatory, exploratory, interpretive ones of Third space, which facilitate the elaboration of "strategies of selfhood – singular or communal – that initiate new signs of identity, and innovative sites of collaboration, and contestation, in the act of defining the idea of society itself" (Bhabha 2004, 2), as described at the outset of this chapter.

The approach to Third space, then, as seen in the excerpt from *The Traitor*, is marked by the dismantling, complication and reconstruction of self-image in a series of viewings which reflect, contest and invert it. Michael's comment that "the Shoshone would have wanted to drive us out back then just like we were trying to do to the Chinese right now" (Yep 2004, 24) first views the communal self through a gaze which is both self-reflexive and self-othering, from the imagined point of view of the Other (the Shoshone) before swinging back to view self and Other (the Chinese) through his own, western, eyes. That diachronic view which spectates and speculates self both as self and other, as legitimate occupier and as illegitimate invader, provides a stereoscopic view of the self, both rending the self-image but also rendering it in depth. At the same time, it inaugurates the process of negotiation with the Asian other; one cannot view oneself stereoscopically without there being some commensurate change in the way one views the other and one's relations with the other. It might, incidentally, be noted that this re-visioning of self and other has been made possible by the introduction of a third, the Shoshone, whose g(host)ile presence, both historical and perceptual, haunts and complicates the dyadic oppositionality of Chinese and American and the grounds upon which that oppositionality is based.

Bhabha's Third space, as earlier sketched, is the space of encounter in which the received wisdom of "pre-given ethnic or cultural traits set in the fixed tablet of tradition" (Bhabha 2004, 3) is set aside along with stereotypes and other forms of essentialism, in favour of an openness to the truth of that which *is*. It is an "interstitial passage between fixed identifications [which] opens up the possibility of a cultural hybridity that entertains difference without an assumed or imposed hierarchy" (Bhabha 2004, 5). Third space, then, is the womb of the hybrid, a place of epistemological unmaking. The price of admission to the actual Third space of the cave itself is the admission of imperfect knowledge, exemplified by Michael suddenly seeing the hole in the wall: "I didn't know the pinnacle as well as I had figured" (Yep 2004, 25). In the darkness of the cave, he hears a sound which he cannot interpret: "Was it a wolf? I didn't know which was worse: a wolf or Seth" (Yep 2004, 25). The darkness is replaced by a dim light in which he sees "a Chinese about my age", who "spoke English clear as a bell... I'd thought he'd talk broken, like the other Chinese". "You speak good", I whispered, blinking my eyes in surprise. "I speak English well", he corrected me, "all high-and-mighty-like" (Yep 2004, 26).

While this initial exchange addresses and redresses asymmetries of culture and power in a fairly unsubtle way—the Chinese speaking better English than the Caucasian—and begins, unpromisingly, with rocks threateningly poised, it progresses, as the interpretative reflex is stilled and inquiry installed in its place. Existing assumptions about the Other, for example that all Chinese speak broken English, that all miners desire sunshine, that all white Americans are monsters, that all Chinese are thieves and invaders, are slowly dismantled, whittled away bit by bit in the same way that Joseph taps patiently at the wall of the cave with hammer and chisel to free the fossils from the rock.

It might be noted, however, that what this Third space encounter stages could also be described as "ghostpitable", my use of the term inspired by, rather than strictly adherent to, the play on meanings brought to "hauntology" and "hospitable" by Derrida, and then Coughlan and others after him. The encounter is haunted, as it were, by several things: past occupancy, present politics, by fathers and by the byzantine intricacies of "hospitality" and its etymological origins. The opening claim and counterclaim: "This is my hiding place" and the response "I was here first" (Yep 2004, 26) are ghostly rehearsals, in small, of claims to territory and their basis, of the world outside this Third space, both past and present. They repeat the historical claims of Shoshone priority and white American invasion, the sociodynamics of that relationship reiterated, contested and inverted in the Asian-American engagement of the novel's present. That history, like "tradition" with its rituals and set ways of thinking, is a sign of the father. Yet, that Michael and Joseph disarm, to approach each other with empty hands, that they abandon the "fixed identifications" each has of the other's ethnicity, constitutes a break with "tradition" and the cultural "father". It is this, rather than in any other, more literal, sense they are "traitors", "traitor" and "tradition" ironically deriving from the same etymological root, "*trădĕre* to deliver, hand over"; "treachery" here marking a failure of the affiliative, a break with the "handing over" of values, ways of doing, ways of being. It is a passing over (elision) rather than a passing over (transmission), although that "treachery" may also be, as I will attempt to show, a tenuous bridge providing passage over and passage through.

"Ghostpitality", however, is more than a matter of iterative haunting, absent-presence, or of welcoming the ghost. Entwined with the claims of ownership and priority are also the ghostly dynamics of guest and host with their attendant, ambivalent, asymmetries of power and obligation: to extend hospitality, to eschew hostility, hospitality being more than a proffering of food and drink, but also of shelter and protection. The very ambiguity of whose claim it is that holds good (and who thus owes what to whom) a/voids (or passes over) the disparity of the power dynamic involved in guest/host relations, in fact restoring the peculiar equivalence of the originary relation which has been remarked by many. J. Hillis Miller, for example, observes:

> The words "host" and "guest" go back in fact to the same etymological root: ghos-ti, stranger, guest, host, properly "someone with whom one has reciprocal duties of hospitality." The modern English word "host" in this alternative sense comes from the Middle English (h)oste, from Old French, host, guest, from Latin hospes (stem hospit-), guest, host, stranger. The "pes" or "pit" in the Latin words and in such modern

English words as "hospital" and "hospitality" is from another root, **pot,** meaning "master." The compound or bifurcated root **ghos-pot** meant "master of guests," "one who symbolizes the relationship of reciprocal hospitality," as in the Slavic **gospodi,** Lord, sir, master. "Guest," on the other hand, is from Middle English **gesl,** from Old **Norsegestr, from ghos-ti,** the same root as for "host." A host is a guest, and a guest is a host. (Hillis Miller 1977, 442, emphasis in original)

The common origin of "host" and "guest" is intriguing in itself, but it is the implications of that commonality, and of their relation to the further labyrinthine network of cognate meanings, which illuminate the ambivalent relationship between guest and host (and, by extension, Asian and American), that need to be teased apart if a generative hybridity is to result. "Host", as various scholars have pointed out, is both host and hostage to a host of other meanings. The Latin *hostis,* a form related to "*ghosti*"[5] has at various times signified "stranger" and "enemy", Liberman further refining the meaning: "Latin *hostis* meant 'public enemy,' in distinction from *inimicus* 'one's private foe'" (Liberman 2013). Both the proximity to, and shift of, "stranger" to (public) "enemy" inflect (and infect) the sociodynamics of Asian-American relations as seen in *The Traitor,* and various other Asian-American works for children dealing with a history of racism or xenophobia, that shift also traced in the first two of Yep's *Golden Mountain Chronicles, The Serpent's Children* (1996) and *Mountain Light,* both set in China. In both these novels, those of Hakka origin in the Cantonese communities of Guangzhou, to whom Yep appends the name "Strangers", are the victims of hostile sentiment directed at the stranger-become-enemy in times of hardship, Otter's mother Acacia being one of those killed during the riots. "Hakka", however, is more properly translated not as "stranger" but as "guest", as its Chinese characters, 客家 (*ke⁴jia¹*), indicate. That the Chinese in Yep's novels are described as the "guests of the Golden Mountain" invokes, then, and sets catenating, the g(host)ly trinity of guest-stranger-enemy.

Yet, if "guest" is capable of sliding along the spectrum of meanings towards "stranger" and "enemy", it is equally capable of pulling in the other direction, towards "friend":

West Aryan **ghosti-s,* represented also by Latin *hostis,* originally "stranger", in classical use "enemy" (whence the compound **hosti-pot-,* contracted *hospit-, hospes* guest, host) and by Old Church Slavonic *gosti* guest, friend. (*OED Online,* s.v. "guest, n.")

And that "guest" and "host" draw on the same root points us in the direction of commonality and equivalence, rather than oppositionality, the resolution of the apparent paradox lying in the (ideal) reciprocality of the relation that is implied by the interchangeability of the two:

> The words "host" and "guest" go back in fact to the same etymological root: *ghos-ti*, stranger, guest, host, properly "someone with whom one has reciprocal duties of hospitality." (Hillis Miller 1977, 442)

Reciprocity is another means whereby to even out imbalances of power, and indeed, Hillis Miller suggests that it is this which converts the asymmetries of the parasite-host relationship into the equivalences of the guest/host one. The g/hostly relation is recuperated in Third space through the encouragement of the reciprocal instinct. After the opening truce, followed by a brief resurgence of hostility (which Derrida reminds us is always incipient in hospitality) during which inherited assumptions about the other are voiced, and exorcised, Joseph proceeds to chisel a pyritised ammonite out of the rock, a golden star. While Michael thinks of fighting him for it, Joseph suddenly gives it to him, and Michael, "overwhelmed by his kindness" (Yep 2004, 32) demurs: "I don't have anything to give you back". Despite Michael's scruples, the encounter is marked by the reciprocity of gifts given and received: the two exchange knowledge, about themselves, fossils, the history of the cave and region, and before they leave the cave, they exchange names; the second meeting in the cave involves a more obvious form of reciprocal hospitality as they give and (par)take of Chinese tea, Chinese jerky and American hardtack.

This new economy of ghostpitality, which has been quickened and nurtured in the nowhere and now here of Third space, stands in reflective contrast to that of the world outside, in which white and Chinese miners and laundries compete for space, resources and customers. That competition fuels and triggers the race riots which, in the historical event (1885) in Rock Springs, Wyoming, on which the events of Yep's novel are based, ended with 28 Chinese dead and 15 injured, and 78 Chinese homes burned down. The ghostpitable economy of this Third space on the other hand, is both generous and generative, engendering not just "new signs of identity, and innovative sites of collaboration, and contestation" (Bhabha 2004, 2) in the process redefining the shape of the ideal society but also activating the symbolic economy of the text.

The literal, as earlier argued, is important because it gives shape and force and visibility to the symbolic. But the symbolic has an equal importance if for no other reason that it attests to a surplus, of that which lies beyond the literal and gives it meaning; like "guest" and "host", "literal" and "symbolic" are ideally reciprocal. In a world which is depicted as impoverished, a wasteland, the excess, or "something more" that is symbolised by the symbolic has a luxury value; we saw this in the empty pencilled outlines of fireplace and flowers, the pencilled rug and the dog on the rug in Mary Purdy's shack. The world outside the cave, as analysed earlier, is a wasteland in which the metaphorical and symbolic is largely dormant, inert, desiccated. Images, for instance, such as that featuring in Michael's observation, en route to Star Rock, that "[i]n the town, surrounded by houses and people, the sky felt all closed up like a clam" (Yep 2004, 15), are initially as unyielding as the image itself. Yet, their meanings are fully activated by the ghostpitable energies of the cave, not just individually, but as a system. The fossil, for example, that Joseph first digs out and shows to Michael, is a clam. It is closed up, and fossilised, like both Asian and American communities, their values and assumptions. Yet, when dug out of the rock, it is seen to gleam gold. As Joseph explains, it is really iron pyrite, fool's gold, the mineral which has over the millennia slowly replaced the cells of the real shell. The sealed and inert image of the clam, at this point, however, ceases to be merely a simple simile for constriction, but is activated to bring together the notions of constricture and fossilisation, and additionally the promise that over time things can change, even fossils, even fossilised clams, and by extension even fossilised clammed-up communities and societies, which, infiltrated by migrant minerals, will gleam gold. The closed and dormant image, then, becomes dynamised, a symbol of how societies evolve and alter as they become hosts to new elements, the sealed image opening up. Joseph describes the cave of gleaming pyritised clamshells as a "whole ocean of stars", the images triggering Michael's memory of his father's notes on how the whole area millennia ago had been an ocean. The knowledge that this terrain was once aquose revisits and revises the earlier odd image of the rock formation as resembling Leviathan rising from the soil, the image of the "ghost sea" (Yep 2004, 105), which the boys fancy they hear, naturalising the monster by returning it to its proper element and making it at home as it were. With the reintroduction of the ghost sea, things—meanings, values, traditions and so on formerly affirmed—are symbolically softened and made fluid, this suggested in the boys' second meeting during which the rituals of hospitality are enacted in the giving and receiving of food and drink, both chewing at Chinese dried beef jerky and American hardtack to moisten and soften them.

The images continue to accrue meaning; the fossilised golden clam which the boys fought for is replaced by the already-mentioned hospitable gift to Michael by Joseph of a fossilised golden ammonite, whose radiant form points outwards rather than being clammed up. And Michael, lying back and staring up at the shining cave ceiling, imagines himself "floating on an ancient ocean", then, closing his eyes, tries to picture "nothing but water. No mountains. No town. No bullies. Just me and Joseph drifting under the stars of a lost sea" (Yep 2004, 107).

That ancient ghost ocean, amniotic fluid in the womb of Third space, an absent–present sign of a time and space before either America or China even existed, rebirths the boys as simple equals, "Michael" and "Joseph" without their pre-identifications of "Chinese" and "white". The black and white of polarised opposites, which finds a serendipitous literalisation in the coal and laundry which form the sites of economic tension and contention between Chinese and white American communities in Rock Springs, is dissolved in a complex image that sees the hatred that Michael feels for the Chinese invader "melted away like dirt under [his mother's] strong soap" (Yep 2004, 31).

When the race riots break out it is the ghostpitality of Third space that saves Joseph and his father, Otter. Michael's allusion to his house and its fading pencilled "ghost garden" (Yep 2004, 223) lets the Youngs, contemplating flight to the "wastelands", recognise the sign of a possible refuge. While hating the Chinese, Mary Purdy sees in Joseph Michael's double, and invites them in, her apron, in her tension, "twisted [...] tighter and tighter in her hands till it was a rope" (Yep 2004, 225). Earlier, Joseph has angrily sawn off his queue, his "rope of hair" (Yep 2004, 164) and with it his links to China; as Otter reminds him, if he cuts it off, he can never go back to China: "The Manchus would kill you as soon as you got off the boat" (Yep 2004, 163). To borrow the words of a Namioka title: "Ties that bind. Ties that break". Now, the new "rope" ties him to America. (Ties that bind.) The rope is simultaneously lifeline, tether and umbilical cord.

The Youngs thus enter a second Third space, the "ghost house" (Yep 2004, 235) as "guests" (Yep 2004, 238), fed and protected by Mary and by the "ghost boy" as Michael names himself. Here, Joseph and Otter put aside their misconceptions of each other's "old-fashionedness" and "modernity" (Yep 2004, 256), and the Purdys and Youngs, emblems of Asia-America, renew the covenant of the hyphen. This is recuperated by the reciprocities of the g/host relation that exorcise other ghosts. The pencilled-in garden, a hauntological sign of an unrealised future, is filled in by the papercuts of flowers and butterflies created by Otter and Joseph as gifts wherewith to thank their hosts. But the papercutting has a further significance, which lies in its having been a skill passed on to Otter by his uncle Foxfire (*Dragon's Gate*), and which Joseph, Americanised and scornful of "old-fashioned" Chinese skills and crafts, has refused, until now, to learn. That he now does to repay the Purdys' hospitality may therefore be understood as simultaneously a bridging and hybridging across cultures and across generations, reinstating the "traitor" within the "tradition", which is however, now understood not as a static body of forms and ideas, but a necessarily evolving one. As Eliot observes in "Tradition and the Individual Talent" (1919), "tradition" is constantly evolving and modified by means of what the individual talent adds and brings to it; in other words, and paradoxically, it is the traitor who enriches and modifies tradition.

The ghost-as-sign has, throughout *The Traitor*, undergone an almost imperceptible metamorphosis from hostility to hospitality to emerge in imago form in the closing scenes of the text. Both hostile revenant, a sign of the past, and melancholic haunt of an unrealised future are trans-formed and exorcised through the offices of Third space. In restoring the proper reciprocal relations of "guest" and "host" to conflate the two as "g/hosts" with a common (etymological) past, Third space has shaped a hybrid with a hoped-for common future. The ghost cave transforms into the ghost house, which develops into a proper home, this enabled by the exercise of hostly obligations—not just to feed but also to shelter and pro-tect. The mob, threatening to invade the Purdy household to check for Chinese fugitives, is deflected by Mary and Michael, who endure insults, abuse and beating; we are reminded of the proximity of *hostis*, relative of *ghosti*, to *hostia*, and hence of the relations binding and holding "ene-my", "stranger", "guest", "host" and "sacrifice" hostage to each other. As Liberman observes, "[*h*]*ostia* ['sacrificial victim'] is a derivative of *hostis*" and "the etymon of *host* 'consecrated wafer'", and Michael's suffering himself to be physically beaten in order to protect his guests is an enaction of hospitable ritual that transforms the ghostly shack into ho(st)ly sanctu-ary: "We'd found our sanctuary at last" (Liberman 2013; Yep 2004, 225). The home, sanctified by sacrifice, is fleshed out and realised in images of the hybrid family, Asian and American, eating together, doing laundry together and playing cards together, the house pyritised (rather than piratised) into a fully lived-in Lefebvrean Thirdspace, the *espace vécu* of human interaction. What card game is played is left unspecified, an empty sign, its ambiguity accommodating the games of both cultures though one is reminded, briefly, of that moment in Yep's *Child of the Owl* (1977), in which Casey's grandmother, searching for the name of her son Phil's preferred card game, asks, "what's that word for a road that goes over water?" (Yep 2001a, 46).

The wasteland has, with giving and compassion, flowered. The shack, architected without corridors and thus, as earlier suggested, an impasse, an aporia, is transformed into a way forward, a way through, a way out. Otter and Joseph offer to leave secretly, through the back door, so as not to expose the Purdys to the hostility of their neighbours. Mary Purdy, however, refuses: "*You're guests. You'll use the front door*" (Yep 2004, 285, italics in original), and the Youngs exit the womb of the Third space legitimately birthed, as it were, and publicly owned. The earlier empty parlour with the golden watch on the wall was a distorted double of the cave with its golden fossils, the cave's felt timelessness finding an eerie echo in how, metaphorically speaking, time has not moved on for the Purdys since Michael's father died. Yet, the ghostpitality, extended and enjoyed by the Purdys and Youngs, has made Mary Purdy aware how she is in danger of fossilising, and, tired, as she says, of "the old ghosts of past wrongs just haunting folks and driving them on like they're possessed" (Yep 2004, 283), she decides to move out and move on, selling the gold watch to fund their peregrinations in the search for a new home.

What we have been tracing, in this reading of Yep's *Traitor*, may be understood as an allegory of Asian-American relations as developed from hostility through hospitality into hybridity through the vehicle of a translative Third space.[6] That Third space is both constructed and inhabited by the shuttling sign whose movements describe and bring into being the figure of the bridge. The significance of this becomes clearer if we recall Bhabha's descriptions of stairwells, bridges, corridors and passageways, as "connective tissue" (Bhabha 2004, 5) facilitating the symbolic interaction which resists the tendency of identifications and meanings to settle and stagnate. It is this to-and-fro, then, that keeps dialogicity alive. This is demonstrated in Bhabha's masterful reading of the worsted in Joseph Conrad's *Heart of Darkness*, that reading trading on the migrations of the "arbitrary sign" which shifts "across the open frame of signification" (Bhabha 2009, xii) marking both distance and cultural difference, enabling entry into the openness of Third space. The moving sign, first losing "familiar origin" and then passing "through an estranging realm of untranslatability", finally emerges ready to be "raised anew" (Bhabha 2009, xii).

Examples of the migratory sign may be found in the figure of the owl in *Child of the Owl* whose different cultural meanings, and how they illuminate parent–child relations, shuttle in debate between Chinese grandmother and Americanised granddaughter, and whose protean undecidability is depicted in the carved owl belonging to Paw-Paw:

> It was like someone had taken a full, frontal view of an owl and slit it down the middle and spread the parts out across the charm. And every little part had come to life and was playing a violent game with the other parts: an eyebrow was more than an eyebrow, it was also a little scaled dragon that was trying to swallow up the eyes which weren't just eyeballs – they were also miniature snakes swallowing their own bodies before the dragon could get them. But it was the smiling beak that caught my attention – it seemed at any moment ready to crawl off the charm and down over my arm. The smiling beak, sinuous and twisting, was a tiger, dangerously playful as it stretched its paws and tail ever so slightly upwards...... (Yep 2001a, 74–75)

It is also found in the words-as-signs which are batted back and forth in translative enquiry in Lensey Namioka's *Yang the Youngest and His Terrible Ear* (1992) which echo the to and fro of the baseball and the movements of the musical bow which, as stereotyping signs of the American and Asian child, first separately metonymise Asia and America, but which also, as "languages" extending and yet distinct from either culture, together form the Third space and (hy)bridging metaphors of the work. The shuttled sign is also present in the figure of the bridge itself, which manifests typographically as hyphen, figuratively as metaphor and mythically as the bridge of birds that recurs in more than one Asian-American text, for example Yep's *Dragons of Silk* and *Dragonwings*, and Grace Lin's *Where the Mountain Meets the Moon* (2009). And finally, it is present in the figure of the hybrid itself, who is at once migratory sign and bridge, as seen for example in Namioka's *Half and Half* (2003) and Yep's *Thief of Hearts* (1995) whose Eurasian protagonists work through the issues that come with their racial hybridity.

If the idea of the migratory sign maps easily to Asian-American writing, it does so because of the migratory narrative of America as "a land of transients and transience, of movements *to* and *across*" (Paglia 1990,

573), in which the ever-moving frontier is a boundary constantly under construction, under erasure. The story of the loss of familiar origin (in both senses of "familiar") and the passage through estrangement and difficult "translation" (again in both senses of the word) is also the story of the migrant, which is traced in works such as Yoshiko Uchida's *Jar of Dreams* (1981), Namioka's *Ties That Bind, Ties That Break* (2003) and Yep's *Mountain Light* and *Dragon's Gate*. Both narratives of migration (of sign and migrant) come together in works such as Jean Kwok's *Girl in Translation*[7] (2011) in which the difficulties of translation—Hong Kong to America, childhood to adulthood—are reflected in the novel's representation of English heard by the 11-year-old protagonist, Kimberley Chang:

> "Our new student *eye-prezoom*?" (Kwok 2011, 25, italics in original)
> "This is a *pop quick*," he said. "Fill in *allde captal see T's*." (Kwok 2011, 26, italics in original)

In a world in which the eye has already "pre-zoomed" (and the I's shape consequently presumed), the sign remains untranslated and unmoving, the singularity of its meaning unchallenged, unnegotiating. Making a mistake on her first day in school, and fearing to cross it out, Kimberley crosses over to the teacher's desk to request a "rubber". The ensuing mirth and ribaldry are to her untranslated, inexplicable, until the girl at the next desk leans over:

> "It's called an eraser here," she whispered. She tucked a strand of her feathery hair behind her ear and pushed a pink eraser across the gap between our desks. (Kwok 2011, 51)

The gap between desks is bridged by the translation of the "rubber" across it, and that between Annette and Kimberley, Asian and American, similarly erased. The migrations of the "rubber" establish a dialogic Third space which is translative in both senses, correlating the locutions of culture—what a thing is called *here* with what it is called *there*—so as to ease the passage of the migrant individual across locations. In the to and fro, "rubber" alters from being the inert non-conductive material with high resilience and elasticity which first entered the text in the opening sentence of the first chapter in the form of Kimberley's boots, to prophylactic and then to eraser, shifting from that which insulates and prevents passage—of electricity, heat, sperm—to that which erases boundaries by crossing them, a sign of the migrant itself, and also a bridge, a sign of new friendship. "Rubber", then, in its migrations not only constructs Third space but is semiotically activated, becoming polysemic in the same way that "clam" and "rope" were in *The Traitor*. Its continued migration through the text sees it reappear eventually in the form of the two condoms the adult Kimberley insists Matt use the first time they have sex; both "condoms had rubbed against each other and they'd both torn" (Kwok 2011, 252), the result of which is the child, Jason. The sign, even in its rupturing, proves generative.

What should be remembered at this point is that Bhabha's notion of hybridity which, along with the dissemination of cultures, is one of the desired end results of the sojourn in Third space, does not represent some happy synthesis or facile convergence of two terms, but "entertains difference without an assumed or imposed hierarchy" (Bhabha 2004, 5). In the migrations of "rubber" detailed above, it is not the rapture of union itself that generates Jason, but the rupture caused by the generative friction of two rubbers rubbing against each other that abrades and thus erases the barrier. The necessity of difference is elaborated in Moon Shadow's description of the stereopticon:

> Later it was explained to me that each eye sees the same object from a slightly different angle, so that each eye has a slightly different picture. It's the brain that combines the two pictures together into one image and creates the stereoptical effect: the depth that the world seems to have for us. (Yep 2000, 135)

While easily interpreted as an image of convergence, it is more properly read as one emphasising the need for different views without which no depth of vision is possible. Without difference, the idea of "dialogue" is drained of meaning, in the same way that Brian Caraher observes metaphors to "lose force or brisk instructive power when they begin to move toward analogy, comparison, and approximation" (Caraher 1981, 82) rather than maintaining a healthy independence of terms. The duality of the Asian-American, while sometimes experienced as a stressful competing of claims, may thus be understood as a combination of different perspectives whose yoking together provides fresh understanding. Third space, then, in its production of hybridity, does not erase the hyphen that ambiguously attests to the connection/disconnection of Asian to American, nor, for that matter, the solidus which Sharmani Patricia Gabriel, drawing on Palumbo-Liu, prefers to the hyphen as installing the ambiguity of the "and/or", as a "line that divides but is also permeable" (Gabriel 2018, 4). Rather, it nurtures the hyphen/solidus, the fragile boundary/bridge.

Despite what must be the pressure or temptation to offer bright messages about integration, blending, and to emphasise "what people share – the 'similarity in differences' – rather than what separates" as Rocio Davis, agreeing with Ivy Chan, suggests (Davis 2004, 391), Asian-American literature for children has for the most part respected the boundary and the need to make and remake, cross and recross those bridges. The hyphen, as Geoffrey Hartman has pointed out, can connect or disconnect or "generally do both at once" (Hartman 2004, 135), and that which is set into "Asian-American" stages and signals the ongoing ambivalence, the two-ness-in-oneness, the ontological duality, that is the condition out of which the Asian-American author writes, and whereof he writes. What is mapped in the Asian-American *Bildungsroman* is not necessarily or simply the contours of an "adolescent outsider experience" in which marginalisation ultimately enables the integration of the individual and the redemption of the community[8] (Helbig 2001, 25). While it might be tempting to write, or read these *Bildungsromane* as narratives of convergence and integration, as fictions charting the young protagonists' paths from outside to inside, from "apart" to "a part", or from hyphenated to whole, the real "end-point" of the Asian-American narrative is seldom so tidy or so clear. The "arrival" of the Asian-American protagonist is less marked by the erasure of the hyphen than an accommodation with it, and an understanding that such accommodations may have to be continually renegotiated and remade, each covenant individually forged. Lensey Namioka's quartet of chapter books about the four children of the immigrant Yang family, traces the various experiences of Yang the Eldest, Second, Third and Youngest in America through the macro-metaphor of the musical form of the string quartet in which as their father, a music teacher, notes, "you have to cooperate with the others, and at the same time you speak out for yourself" (Namioka 1992, 46), each voice having a separate line of development while yet making common cause with the others. Each chapter book is dedicated to a separate Yang child, each of whose experiences, attitudes and strategies of accommodation with the Other that is America is different. The same general understanding informs Kadohata's

Outside Beauty whose protagonist family, like Namioka's, serves both as metonymy and symbol of the Asian-American experience, the four sisters, daughters of Japanese-American Helen Kimura, each having a different father (one generic white American, one Italian, one Japanese and one Chinese) and a different set of complexities to work through. And the same important understanding: that within the common—as it were generalisable—Asian-American experience lie individual and separate stories, that the experience is an evolving rather than static one, and that accommodations must be individually and continually renewed, is what is written into the rubrics of Laurence Yep's *Golden Mountain Chronicles* which collectively trace the contours of the Asian-American experience across 10 volumes and seven generations. The general preface to the *Chronicles* attests to a consciousness that attitudes and strategies for living as an Asian-American do, and must, evolve, given that identity—individual and national—is a thing in flux, a work in progress:

> More than anything else, the Youngs and their friends were adaptable... However some went too far and became so American that they lost track of the Chinese part of their identity and had to discover it again [...] And they changed once more when they discovered that the attitudes that had enabled them to survive over a hundred years of hardships and dangers no longer worked.[9]

This essay, in navigating its way through the intricacies of how Third space serves to facilitate the emergence of that individual/national identity, has emphasised its connections to dialogicity, openness and movement, to passages and crossings, returning, repeatedly, to the figure of the bridge, a final consideration of whose properties brings this essay to a close. Bridges are crossings, leaps of faith into and over open water, open space. They are both connectors and conduits, the means whereby the openness of dialogue is enabled through which the hybridising self is shaped. Yet the *telos* of the bridge is not only to connect but also, as Heidegger phrases it and Bhabha quotes, "to escort men to and fro, so that they may get to other banks [...] The bridge gathers as a passage that crosses" (quoted in Bhabha 2004, 5). The bridge, then, is an intentional path towards a "beyond". The traversal back and forth of bow across the bridge of the violin constructs music, and the baseball is thrown to and fro in order that a player may reach home.

Having escorted two individuals, or communities into the dialogic space of Third space, the bridge then ushers them onward, for Third space is only a waystation, not an end point. The same red thread bridge in Grace Lin's novel, which takes Min Li to "where the mountain meets the moon", returns her to her home. Cowherd and Weaving Maid, "balancing on the shifting uncertain path of warm ticklish bodies" (Yep 2011, 2) come together once a year on the bridge of birds, but then depart separately, onwards. The journey that brings together hybridises, while the journey that leads outwards, again, disseminates, and as Bhabha punningly suggests through his chapter title, it is that dissemination, facilitated by the hybridgings of migration, that eventually shapes and inseminates the culture of the nation. The material effects of that dissemination may be seen in the coexistence of Japanese washi paper and Afghani *doday* (bread) in Wong Plaza, San Francisco, in N.H. Senzai's *Saving Kabul Corner* (2015), or in the sericulture whose migrations from China and Korea to America form the narrative bases of Yep's *Dragons of Silk* (2011) and Linda Sue Park's *Project Mulberry* (2017).

But dissemination has other, more important forms than the material, especially with regard to the formation of culture which in its turn (re)generates nation. The cross-fertilisations of culture which are the result of cultural dissemination enrich and invigorate, making available new ways of seeing, new narratives and with them, new insights. As Yep notes, "It is because America has been able to draw from many cultures that it has been able to revitalise itself for decade after decade. *Multiculturalism* is more than a buzz-word; it is the dynamo that drives America forward" (Yep 2005, 52, italics in original). To revisit an earlier example in this essay: the Chinese papercuts of flowers pasted onto American walls and symbolically revitalising the wasteland is an instance of the dynamising power of cultural dissemination.

Languages inseminate other languages and spawn new words and interfaces, and sometimes even new languages in the formation of pidgins and creoles; the richness of a language is largely the effect of its dalliance with other languages, as the etymological considerations of this chapter have already demonstrated. An example of linguistic dissemination may be found in Asian-American interactions in the way Chinese immigrants in Yep's novels are frequently asked by their white American employers, "You *sabe?*": a complexly inflected sociohistorical-linguistic formulation, which, while not inherently pejorative, carries a whiff of condescension in its assumption that the Chinese worker cannot be interfaced with in proper English. The point of interest, however, lies in the fact that "*Sabe*"—which the *O.E.D.* notes as "*slang* (orig. U.S.)", and which has its roots in the Spanish (an alternative source suggestion being the Portuguese), being a "re-formation after, or a re-borrowing of, Spanish, *sabe*" (*OED Online*, s.v. "sabe, v.") meaning "to know" which migrated into English use via CPE (Chinese Pidgin English) by way of trade connections between the Portuguese and Chinese in eighteenth-century Macau (Benson 2005, 75). ("Savvy", which also derives from "*sabe*", also enters English by means of a pidgin—the *O.E.D.* says "probably originally via early W. African pidgin" (*OED Online*, s.v. "savvy, v.")). In all likelihood then, what is noted as "orig. U.S." enters America by way of Chinese traders and migrant workers who imported the formulation ("You *sabe*? Me *sabe*") from their earlier interactions with the Portuguese and English.[10] Not only is linguistic interaction thus already-informed, already-inflected by the history of its interactions but also by earlier disseminations transplanted and grafted into the linguistic nation.

These cultural disseminations in their many forms—linguistic, artistic, literary—shape ways of seeing and thinking, but also shape the stories that we tell and thus may be said to form and inform the nations that take shape from those stories. This last point has a particular pertinence to Asian-American children's literature, in which is often encountered the inset or worked-in myth or "traditional" tale (in both genuine and faux, *Volks* as well as *Kunst* forms) among whose functions is the dissemination of Asian culture, a sharing or pooling of tales, the skillful deployment of which may serve to demonstrate the continued pertinence of one's Asian past in one's Asian-American present and the continued applicability of its epistemes. This has been the pattern pursued in a number of Asian-American works, such as Yep's *Chronicles* or Gene Luen Yang's graphic novel *American Born Chinese* (2006) in each of which the inset or interwoven tale functions as a way of understanding one's own place in the world and relation to it. The myth of Cowherd and Weaving Maid, for instance, links the five parts of *Dragons of Silk*, which are set in 1835, 1881, 1935, 1962 and 2011, tracking the history of a family from 1835 in China to 2011 in America through its relations with silk. The myth functions as a bridge between generations, joining them, its significance evolving as it is reinterpreted and reinflected in different ways in different times and places. Its interpretation by a minor character as more a tale of loss than love, more partings than meetings, for instance, gives it particular resonance with the migrant experience of loss of home and traversal across distances.

These disseminations have a peculiar force within children's literature, whose affinity with matters of identity formation in individual, communal and national forms has earlier been commented on. The child, as Wordsworth famously observed in the "Immortality Ode", is the father of the man, and the man the atom of the nation. What the child reads forms the child and thus by extension, the nation. Children's literature is in many ways, thus the real Third space, for it is where the child, of whatever ethnicity, nationality or culture, encounters the disseminated Otherness of other cultures and experiences, whose difference, and not just sameness, makes the spaces returned to more inhabitable, more richly strange and more commodious.

NOTES

1. Lefebvre's conception of *thirdspace* comprises "*espace perçu*" (objective space, perceived space), "*espace conçu*" (conceived space—that which is in the mind and which the mind can imagine), and "*espace vécu*" (lived space), the last taking shape out of the interactions of the first two, involving the interactions of real bodies with real places.
2. The first is from Yep's *The Traitor*, the second from Lensey Namioka's "Yang" quartet.
3. The refinement above by my student Justin Goh, was offered in conversation on imessage and thus cannot be more formally referenced. Personal Communication, 1 June 2019.
4. Bhabha represents "Third space" as two words while Soja joins them as one both when referencing and translating Lefebvre, and in his own work. I have followed the respective terminology of each author when referencing their work.
5. According to Edith Wyschogrod the latter derives from the former (57); see also Adrian Poruciuc and Nobert Poruciuc who note: "The root under discussion is presented as base of Indo-European words such as Old Norse *gestr* ('guest') and Latin *hostis* ('enemy (<stranger)')" (8).
6. While Zhang, Meng and Mo's 2005 reading of *Dragonwings* in *Canadian Social Science* does not use Third space and its associated ideas, the broad conclusions drawn there are not dissimilar to some of those drawn here.
7. This is marketed as literary fiction, but is frequently found on YA booklists.

8. Helbig offers the observation with regard to Laurence Yep's novels, but what she describes could just as easily refer (with the qualifications I append above) to the category of children's fiction itself.
9. This preface is printed in front of most of the Chronicles in the Harper-Collins edition and has no page numbers.
10. While Benson claims it evolved in interactions between Portuguese merchants and their Chinese counterparts, other scholarship, e.g. Shi's 1991 article on Chinese Pidgin English in the *Journal of Chinese Linguistics* suggests it did so via the interactions between Portuguese supercargoes and their Chinese house servants. Li's 2016 article on "Trade Pidgins in China" suggests that MPP (Macau Pidgin Portuguese) had an impact on CPE (299) and cites earlier studies to this effect.

REFERENCES

Benson, Phil. 2005. "The Origins of Chinese Pidgin English: Evidence from Colin Campbell's Diary." *Hong Kong Journal of Applied Linguistics* 10, no. 1: 59–78.

Bhabha, Homi K. 2009. "In the Cave of Making: Thoughts on Third Space." In *Communicating in the Third Space*, edited by Karin Ikas and Gerhard Wagner, ix–xiv. London: Routledge.

———. 2018. "Introduction: On Disciplines and Destinations." In *Territories & Trajectories: Cultures in Circulation*, edited by Diana Sorensen, 1–12. Durham: Duke University Press.

———. 2004. *The Location of Culture*. London and New York: Routledge.

Caraher, Brian G. 1981. "Metaphor as Contradiction: A Grammar and Epistemology of Poetic Metaphor." *Philosophy and Rhetoric* 14, no. 2: 69–88.

Davis, Rocio G. 2004. "Reinscribing (Asian) American History in Laurence Yep's Dragonwings." *The Lion and the Unicorn* 28, no. 3: 390–407. https://doi.org/10.1353/uni.2004.0029.

Foucault, Michel. 2010. "Of Other Spaces." In *The Visual Culture Reader*, edited by Nicholas Mirzoeff, 229–236. London and New York: Routledge.

Gabriel, Sharmani Patricia. 2018. "Introduction: East/West—What's at Stake?" In *Literature, Memory, Hegemony: East/West Crossings*, edited by Sharmani Patricia Gabriel and Nicholas O. Pagan, 1–19. London and New York: Palgrave Macmillan.

Hartman, Geoffrey H. 2004. "Purification and Danger in American Poetry." In *The Geoffrey Hartman Reader*, edited by Daniel T. O'Hara, 128–141. Edinburgh: Edinburgh University Press.

Helbig, Alethea. 2001. "The Outsider in Laurence Yep's Serpent Trilogy." In *The Phoenix Award of the Children's Literature Association, 1995–1999*, edited by Alethea Helbig and Agnes Perkins, 25–32. Maryland: Scarecrow Press.

Hillis Miller, J. 1977. "The Critic as Host." *Critical Inquiry* 3, no. 3: 439–447.
Ikas, Karin, and Gerhard Wagner. 2009. Introduction to *Communicating in the Third Space*, 1–7. Edited by Karin Ikas and Gerhard Wagner London: Routledge.
Kwok, Jean. 2011. *Girl in Translation*. New York: Riverhead Books.
Li, Michelle. 2016. "Trade Pidgins in China: Historical and Grammatical Relations." *Transactions of the Philological Society* 114, no. 3: 298–314. https://doi.org/10.1111/1467-968x.12066.
Liberman, Anatoly. 2013. "'Guests' and 'Hosts'." *OUPblog*. Accessed 30 June 2019, https://blog.oup.com/2013/02/guest-host-word-origin-etymology/.
Lim, Shirley Geok-Lin. 1986. "Twelve Asian American Writers: In Search of Self-Definition." *MELUS* 13, no. 1/2: 57–77. https://doi.org/10.2307/467225.
Lin, Grace. 2019. *Dumpling Days*. New York: Little, Brown & Company.
Namioka, Lensey. 1980. *Who's Hu?* New York: Vanguard Press.
———. 1992. *Yang the Youngest and His Terrible Ear*. Boston: Joy Street Books.
Paglia, Camille. 1990. *Sexual Personae: Art and Decadence from Nefertiti to Emily Dickinson*. New Haven: Yale University Press.
Poruciuc, Adrian, and Norbert Poruciuc. 2015. "An Etymological Proposition: Old Germanic Gōd-Spōd 'Good Fortune' As Source of Old Church Slavonic Gospodъ 'Lord, Master'." *Messages, Sages and Ages* 2, no. 2: 7–12. https://doi.org/10.1515/msas-2015-0006.
Soja, Edward W. 2009. "Thirdspace: Towards a New Consciousness of Space and Spatiality." In *Communicating in the Third Space*, edited by Karin Ikas and Gerhard Wagner, 49–61. New York: Routledge.
Wyschogrod, Edith. 2005. "Autochthony and Welcome: Discourses of Exile in Levinas and Derrida." In *Derrida and Religion: Other Testaments*, edited by Yvonne Sherwood and Kevin Hart, 53–62. New York: Routledge.
Yep, Laurence. 2001a. *Child of the Owl: Golden Mountain Chronicles, 1965*. New York: HarperCollins.
———. 2001b. *Dragon's Gate: Golden Mountain Chronicles, 1867*. New York: HarperCollins.
———. 2011. *Dragons of Silk: Golden Mountain Chronicles, 1835–2011*. New York: Harper.
———. 2000. *Dragonwings: Golden Mountain Chronicles, 1903*. New York: HarperTrophy.
———. 2005. "The Outsider in Fiction and Fantasy." *English Journal* 94, no. 3: 52–54. https://doi.org/10.2307/30046419.
———. 2004. *The Traitor: Golden Mountain Chronicles, 1885*. New York: HarperCollins.

INDEX

© The Editor(s) (if applicable) and The Author(s) 2020
B. Wilson and S. P. Gabriel (eds.), *Asian Children's Literature and Film in a Global Age*, Asia-Pacific and Literature in English,
https://doi.org/10.1007/978-981-15-2631-2

389